COMBATING THE BUREAUCRACY

U.S. NUCLEAR DEFENSE POLICY DEVELOPMENT
AND IMPLEMENTATION FOLLOWING
THE COLD WAR

COMBATING THE BUREAUCRACY

U.S. NUCLEAR DEFENSE POLICY DEVELOPMENT AND IMPLEMENTATION FOLLOWING THE COLD WAR

TOBIAS O. VOGT

Aventine Press

Published by Aventine Press
55 E Emerson Street
Chula Vista, CA 91911

ISBN: 978-1-59330-819-3

Library of Congress Control Number: 2013907452

Printed in the United States of America

To my family, friends, colleagues, and students

TABLE OF CONTENTS

TABLES AND FIGURES

TABLES

FIGURES

Acronyms

ANL- Argonne National Laboratory

ABM- Anti-Ballistic Missile Treaty

BMDO- Ballistic Missile Defense Organization

CRS- Congressional Research Service

CTBT- Comprehensive Test Ban Treaty

CTR- Cooperative Threat Reduction

DHS- Department of Homeland Security

DNDO- Domestic Nuclear Defense Office

DNI- Director of National Intelligence

DOD- Department of Defense

DOE- Department of Energy

DOS- Department of State

DTRA- Defense Threat Reduction Agency

FEMA- Federal Emergency Management Agency

FSU- Former Soviet Union

GAO- Government Accountability Office

GPALS- Global Protection Against Limited Strikes

GNDA- Global Nuclear Detection Architecture

HEU- Highly Enriched Uranium

HSPD- Homeland Security Presidential Directive

IAEA- International Atomic Energy Agency

INL- Idaho National Laboratory

LANL- Los Alamos National Laboratory

LLNL- Lawrence Livermore National Laboratory

MPCA- Materials, Protection, Controls, and
  Accounting

NATO- North Atlantic Treaty Organization

NMD- National Missile Defense

NMIP- Nuclear Materials Information Program

NBL- New Brunswick Laboratory

NIS- Newly Independent States (of the former
  Soviet Union)

NNSA- National Nuclear Security Administration

NNWS- Non-Nuclear Weapons State(s)

NMOC- Nuclear Materials of Concern

NPT- Nuclear Nonproliferation Treaty

NRF- National Response Framework

NSC- National Security Council

NSD- National Security Directive

NSPD- National Security Presidential Directive

NTNFC- National Technical Nuclear Forensics
  Center

NWS- Nuclear Weapons State(s)

ORNL- Oak Ridge National Laboratory

PCC- Policy Coordination Committee

PNI- Presidential Nuclear Initiatives

PNNL- Pacific Northwest National Laboratory

R&D- Research and Development

SALT- Strategic Arms Limitation Treaty

SDI- Strategic Defense Initiative

SDIO- Strategic Defense Initiative Organization

SLD- Second Line of Defense

SNL- Sandia National Laboratories

SNM- Special Nuclear Materials

SRNL- Savannah River National Laboratory

SRS- Savannah River Site

SSP- Stockpile Stewardship Program

START- Strategic Arms Reduction Treaty (I, II, and
  III)

THAAD- Theater High Altitude Area Defense

UN- United Nations

UNSC- United Nations Security Council

WGPu- Weapons Grade Plutonium

WMD- Weapons of Mass Destruction

INTRODUCTION

This book examines the United States government's approach to nuclear defense policy development and implementation between 1989 and 2009, spanning the administrations of Presidents George H. W. Bush, William J. Clinton and George W. Bush. During the administration of George H. W. Bush, the United States experienced a paradigm change in its security outlook following the end of the Cold War and collapse of the Soviet Union. While it was no longer the target of tens of thousands of Soviet nuclear weapons, the post-Cold War world was characterized in part by the emergence of four post-Soviet nuclear powers -- Russia, Belarus, Kazakhstan, and Ukraine -- and questionable security for the largest stock of legacy weapons, materials, and expertise in nuclear weapons history. Initial estimates accounted for 10,280 operational strategic warheads, 2,509 operational delivery vehicles, and 650 tons of aggregate fissile material located across the former Soviet republics. Soviet tactical nuclear weapons were also an immediate concern, with estimates ranging from 15,000-21,700 tactical warheads scattered across the former Soviet Union in 1991.[1]

---

1   Russia accounted for 7,327 warheads, 2,074 delivery vehicles and 99% of the fissile material, Kazakhstan 1,360 warheads and 144 delivery vehicles, Ukraine 1,512 warheads and 210 delivery vehicles, and Belarus was a distant fourth at 81 of each. Tactical nuclear weapon estimates vary greatly because of a lack of Russian Federation information. Alexander, Brian, and Alistair Millar, "Uncovered Nukes: An Introduction to Tactical Nuclear Weapons," and Joshua Handler, "The 1991-1992 PNIs and the Elimination, Storage, and Security of Tactical Nuclear Weapons," in Brian Alexander,

Stockpile security anxieties related to the potential for "loose nukes" fed fears of nuclear proliferation to both state and non-state actors. What if Iran, Iraq, North Korea, al-Qaeda, or Chechen separatists obtained an intact nuclear weapon, or acquired materials and know how from the former Soviet Union? Concerns that proliferating states and non-state actors would harness special nuclear materials also raised anxieties associated with the 439 power reactors and 164 highly enriched uranium research reactors operating in 40 countries.[2] The research reactors alone accounted for approximately 30 metric tons of highly enriched uranium located outside the United States and former Soviet Union.[3] Assessments such as these often characterized nuclear worries in the 1990s, but the resulting shift in the strategic landscape had broader implications for nuclear defense.

The end of the global bi-polar order left former Warsaw Pact members, and other Soviet protectorates, without security alliances and associated Cold War constraints. The resulting security environment was characterized by regional concerns, which

and Alistair Millar, eds., *Tactical Nuclear Weapons: Emerging Threats in an Evolving Security Environment*, 2003, pp. 4, 27-28, and 31; (Warheads and Delivery Vehicles) Federation of American Scientists, "The Former Soviet Union: Russia, Ukraine, Kazakhstan, and Belarus," retrieved April 15, 2010; (Fissile material) Daughtry, Emily Ewell, and Fred L. Wehling, "Cooperative Efforts to Secure Fissile Material in the newly independent state," *Nonproliferation Review*, Spring 2000, p. 97.

2   For more on Cold War era special nuclear material concerns, see John McPhee, *The Curve of Binding Energy: A Journey into the Awesome and Alarming World of Theodore B Taylor,* 1974.

3   The Department of Energy has targeted 105 reactors, 20 of which are weapons-usable uranium research reactors, for conversion to low enriched fuel, but to exacerbate matters, much of the highly enriched uranium fuel is of U.S. or former Soviet Union origin. As of 2010, 29 countries had operational energy reactors with another 17 countries in the proposal or construction phase. Government Accountability Office, *Nuclear Nonproliferation: Department of Energy Needs to Take Action to Further Reduce the Use of Weapons-Usable Uranium in Civilian Research Reactors,* July 2004, pp. 7-16; Bunn, Matthew and Anthony Weir, *Securing the Bomb 2006,* May 2006, p. 19; World Nuclear Association, "World Nuclear Power Reactors and Uranium Requirements," retrieved June 15, 2010.

encompassed new and existing nuclear defense considerations. India and Pakistan openly challenged the nonproliferation regime with nuclear tests in 1998.[4] Concerns over nuclear proliferation in Iran, Iraq, and North Korea also came to dominate the U.S. security agenda of the post-Cold War era. North Korea, for example, proved to be a recurring proliferation worry in the context of strategic delivery vehicles, special nuclear materials, and nuclear weapons as of 2006.

In 1998, the timing of North Korea's satellite launch and suspected Taepodong-1 missile test, combined with the Indian and Pakistani nuclear tests, helped to validate worst-case U.S. proliferation threat assessments.[5] These emerging challenges came on top of concerns about Chinese and Russian nuclear modernization. By 1999, there had been several reports that Chinese nuclear espionage had resulted in the theft of data on every type of American warhead from a "dysfunctional [Department of Energy] bureaucracy."[6] As the world progressed into the 21st century, Chinese and Russian positions on nuclear weapons became more assertive in response to United States national missile defense efforts and changing economic conditions. The

---

4   Statements by senior leaders from both countries demonstrated the perceived utility of nuclear weapons for emerging states in the post-Cold War era. The first, by Indian General Krishnaswamy Sundarji, declared that "the lesson of the 1991 war between the United States and Iraq was not to get into a conflict with the United States unless you already had nuclear weapons." This sentiment was later reinforced by Pakistani Brigadier General Atta M. Iqhman when he offered that in addition to deterring Indian aggression the Pakistani nuclear stockpile was "also an insurance policy against the United States." Gusterson, Hugh, "U.S. Nuclear Double Standards," *Bulletin of the Atomic Scientists*, February 20, 2008, retrieved November 15, 2009.

5   Cirincione, Joseph, "Assessing the Ballistic Missile Threat," testimony before the Senate Committee on Governmental Affairs, February 9, 2000.

6   Cox, Christopher, "U.S. National Security and Military/Commercial Concerns with the People's Republic of China," May 1999, p. 68; Bliley, Tom, "Rudman Report: Science at its Best, Security at its Worst," Hearing, June 22, 1999, p. 18; Diamond, Howard, "Cox Panel Charges China with Extensive Nuclear Espionage," *Arms Control Today*, April/May 1999.

Chinese minimum deterrence posture rested on early technologies, but modernization efforts over the past two decades were fuelled by concerns over American missile defense systems.[7] Russia was also opposed to proposed U.S. missile defenses in Europe and declared in their national strategy that the use of nuclear weapons had expanded beyond deterrence.[8] For example, in January 2008, General Yury Baluyevsky stated that Russia would use force to protect itself and its allies, "on a preventative basis, including the use of nuclear weapons."[9]

Non-state actors were associated with weapons of mass destruction concerns in the 1990s, but terrorists were not considered a primary threat in this field until the al-Qaeda attacks of September 11, 2001. The lower security priority continued throughout the Clinton administration despite multiple weapons of mass destruction incidents by Aum Shinrikyo and Chechen separatists, and escalating conventional attacks by al-Qaeda.[10] But, by the George W. Bush administration non-state actors had begun to eclipse traditional nuclear concerns. Non-state actors were touted as the principal adversary in the administration's Global War on Terror while top officials such as U.S. Deputy Defense Secretary Paul Wolfowitz continued to emphasize, "Al

7   Godwin, Paul H. B., and Evan S. Medeiros, "China, America, and Missile Defense: Conflicting National Interests." *Current History: A Journal of Contemporary World Affairs*, September 2000, pp. 285-289; Nuclear Threat Initiative.org, "China's Attitude Toward Nuclear Deterrence," retrieved April 8, 2009.

8   Gard, Robert G., Jr., "National Missile Defense in Europe: Premature and Unwise," Center for Arms Control and Nonproliferation, July 2007, retrieved November 15, 2010.

9   Ibid.

10   For more on Aum Shinrikyo's attempted acquisition of nuclear weapons and materials or their multiple biological and chemical attacks from 1994 and 1995 see David E. Kaplan, and Andrew Marshall, *The Cult at the End of the World*, 1996; for more on the 1995 Chechen separatists dirty bomb incident see Brian M. Jenkins, *Will Terrorists Go Nuclear?*, 2008; for more on the 1998 al-Qaeda embassy bombings and 2000 USS Cole attack see Philippe Migaux, "Al Qaeda," in Gerard Chaliand and Arnaud Blin, eds., *The History of Terrorism: From Antiquity to Al Qaeda*, 2007.

Qaeda leader Osama bin Laden said in the past that the acquisition of weapons of mass destruction by his terrorist gang is a religious duty."[11] While this broad spectrum of nuclear challenges slowly replaced fears of total nuclear war, the organizations and defense mechanisms that developed during the Cold War to address nuclear defense issues remained in place as the emphasis shifted away from deterrence to "the proliferation of nuclear capability and the risk of the theft or accidental detonation of Russia's thousands of nuclear warheads."[12]

It is against this strategic backdrop that the book examines the U.S. government's approach to nuclear defense policy formulation and implementation after the Cold War. The concept of "nuclear defense" equates to efforts to prevent, protect, or respond to a nuclear incident in the United States or against U.S. interests or allies. The approach combines an examination of national policy development and execution to examine how the United States developed and implemented nuclear defense policy. The central research question asks, "How have United States nuclear defense efforts evolved following the Cold War?" While other works have focused on limited aspects of the topic such as nuclear strategy, proliferation, or generalized weapons of mass destruction issues, this book offers a comprehensive empirical study of U.S. government nuclear defense efforts during the time period in question.

The book is guided by two supporting research questions which are designed to address policy development and implementation: 1) "How and why has U.S. nuclear defense policy evolved since the end of the Cold War"; and 2) "How did the U.S. government implement post-Cold War nuclear defense policy, and to what extent were corresponding objectives realized?" By addressing these questions the book seeks to test two

---

11   Garamone, Jim, "Wolfowitz Says Dirty Bomb Plot Highlights WMD Dangers," *American Forces Press Service*, June 11, 2002.
12   Ikle, Fred Charles, "The Second Coming of the Nuclear Age," *Foreign Affairs,* Jan/Feb 1996, "Undeterred by Deterrence."

hypotheses. The first hypothesis states, "U.S. nuclear defense policy formulation during the George H. W. Bush and William J. Clinton administrations was anchored in bureaucratic politics, not collective defense." The research demonstrates that the national policy development process was characterized by a constitutional and statutory framework within which competing stakeholders maneuvered to advance individual positions. The second hypothesis states, "The U.S. government was not organized to address nuclear defense and as a result has not collaboratively implemented evolving national policies." The research demonstrates that policy implementation was directly influenced by segregated department and agency organization, and the lack of a standing national level implementation body to plan and direct federal nuclear defense efforts, with the result being an environment characterized by competing organizations and unsynchronized activities.

The book examines the period beginning with the inauguration of President George H. W. Bush and ending on January 20, 2009, with the departure of President George W. Bush. The start date is selected to include the presidency of George H. W. Bush rather than to coincide exactly with the end of the Cold War. The research involved a qualitative approach based on the participant observation method and archival research. This involved interviews with subject matter experts and desk-based research of primary and secondary open source information pertaining to U.S. government nuclear defense efforts. The book unfolds in two parts. The first part focuses on establishing the progression of post-Cold War nuclear defense policy. The second part examines observations drawn from unscripted interviews from government and non-government experts in various organizations and fields. The resulting policy implementation studies provide an empirical element of the book that is not available in existing academic literature.

U.S. NUCLEAR DEFENSE POLICY

According to Robert Joseph, Senior Director for Proliferation Strategy, Counterproliferation, and Homeland Defense from 2001-2005, President George W. Bush's first term National Security Council staff set out to strengthen prevention, expand protection, and elevate response in an effort to "add more tools to the tool chest" while improving existing nuclear defense efforts from previous administrations.[13] In 2002, the National Security Council staff produced the *National Security Strategy of the United States of America* which outlined a "comprehensive strategy to combat weapons of mass destruction" that consisted of nonproliferation, counterproliferation, and consequence management pillars. This broad document was followed by the 2002 *National Strategy to Combat Weapons of Mass Destruction,* which stated that these pillars seek to prevent, protect, and prepare America to respond to weapons of mass destruction attacks.

Experts in nuclear defense such as Charles Ferguson have emphasized that the comprehensive approach to combating weapons of mass destruction codified by George W. Bush did not represent entirely new thinking on the part of the U.S. government.[14] The George W. Bush administration was instead building on existing policies and capabilities that had been incrementally developed and adjusted during the first two post-Cold War administrations. George H. W. Bush continued to engage the international community as his administration sought to implement unprecedented arms reductions and to shift nuclear defense strategy from Soviet-oriented total nuclear war to smaller regional scenarios. While best remembered for the attempt to move to a counterproliferation emphasis, the William J. Clinton administration implemented many nuclear defense measures

---

13   Interview with National Security Council Staff Senior Director for Proliferation Strategy, Counterproliferation and Homeland Defense, Robert Joseph, June 14, 2010.
14   Interview with Council on Foreign Relations, Fellow for Science and Technology, Charles Ferguson, February 15, 2008.

approved under the first President Bush, and articulated a framework of prevention, protection, and later response, to address developing post-Cold War period concerns.[15]

Administration frameworks and strategies such as these were often cited, but supporting policies frequently differed from presidential intent. For example, this book identifies difficulties associated with domestic nuclear defense policy development and prioritization stemming from broader national security, economic, diplomatic, political, and bureaucratic agendas. Given the complexities of the threat, nuclear defense policy development would be complicated enough in a vacuum, let alone in a democratic society with competing interests. Indeed, social scientists have long attempted to describe the U.S. national security policy formulation process. As the post-World War II bureaucracy evolved, early theorists looked to explain the policy development process as a rational choice represented by a unitary government decision or policy.[16] Other researchers such as Graham Allison and Morton Halperin examined internal government organization and bargaining, and introduced theories based on organizational process and bureaucratic politics.[17] These latter concepts emphasized the role of domestic actors and organizations within a complex policy formulation process based on an aggregation of multiple stakeholder positions.

---

15   Clinton, William J., "Presidential Decision Directive/National Security Council-39: U.S. Policy on Counterterrorism," June 21, 1995; Interview with Department of Defense, Under Secretary of Defense (Policy) Walter Slocombe, November 18, 2010.

16   For more information on the rational policy model see Graham T. Allison and Philip Zelikow, *Essence of Decision: Explaining the Cuban Missile Crises,* 2nd edition 1999, pp. 13-75.

17   Clifford, J. Garry, "Bureaucratic Politics," *The Journal of American History*, Vol. 77, No. 1, June 1990, pp. 161-168; Rosati, Jerel A., "Developing a Systematic Decision-Making Framework: Bureaucratic Politics in Perspective," *World Politics*, Vol. 1, No. 2, January 1981, pp. 234-252; Allison, Graham T., and Morton H. Halperin, "Bureaucratic Politics: A Paradigm and Some Policy Implications," *World Politics,* Vol. 24, Spring 1972, pp. 40-80.

Policy development analysis accounts for a large portion of academic literature, but writing policy and gaining approval is only the initial part of the process. Designing, resourcing, and implementing programs to support policy decisions is a separate problem set. This portion of the process involves the transfer of policy from major formulation stakeholders -- the president and Congress -- to independent bureaucratic organizations. The assumption is often made that implementing organizations work together to execute national policy decisions. However, bureaucratic politics theory calls into question the degree to which actors place organizational interests over collaborative policy execution.[18] This book assumes that bureaucratic organizations have traditionally sought independent implementation arrangements that were deconflicted in a senior level interagency environment.

Thus, this book demonstrates that independent execution allowed each organization to address limited portions of policy decisions that were in line with established departmental missions, capabilities, and preferences. This individual approach to policy execution provided implementing organizations sufficient autonomy, independent resourcing, and influence in their specialty areas. When organizations are required to participate in collaborative implementation, the federal government has relied primarily on two designs: lead agency and national integrator.[19] The most prevalent arrangement originated from the establishment of a lead department or agency, but national integrators have also been used in an effort to shift toward centralized federal policy execution. Examination of these approaches demonstrated limitations to integrated policy implementation within a structure where resources were allocated to individual

---

18   Allison, Graham T., and Morton H. Halperin, "Bureaucratic Politics: A Paradigm and Some Policy Implications," *World Politics,* Vol. 24, Spring 1972, pp. 40-56.
19   National coordinators (commonly referred to as "Czars") are also utilized, but these positions only provide presidential situational awareness, not collective management.

department budget lines with program-specific authorizations and restrictions. The outcome was a highly complex policy implementation landscape without central leadership or oversight.[20]

Examining how and why nuclear defense policy decisions were made enabled the assessment to transition to policy implementation. Did unitary national policy decisions represent coordinated, specific guidance for follow-on implementation efforts, or did the practice of incremental development with compromised and vague policy decisions feed an environment of competing organizations? Initial policy formulation findings highlighted many of the bureaucratic politics phenomena described by authors such as Graham Allison and Morton Halperin.[21] Competing actors influenced stakeholder positions and eventual policy decisions represented further stakeholder compromise. Policy decisions were often quite different to any single stakeholder position at the start of the policy formulation process. Moreover, policy development findings extended into the examination of policy implementation where Allison and Halperin have emphasized the relationship between aggregated decisions and segregated action.[22] Thus, this book provides a greater understanding of U.S. government post-Cold War nuclear defense efforts spanning the national policy formulation and implementation processes. This was accomplished through systematic analyses of labors to prevent proliferation and to protect against a nuclear "incident on U.S. soil or against U.S. interests, or failing that," to ensure "capabilities exist to manage the consequences and attribute the source."[23]

---

20   Murdock, Clark A., and Michele A. Flournoy, "Beyond Goldwater-Nichols: U.S. Government and Defense Reform for a New Strategic Era (Phase II)," Center for Strategic and International Studies Report, July 28, 2005, pp. 26-54.
21   Allison, Graham T., and Morton H. Halperin, "Bureaucratic Politics: A Paradigm and Some Policy Implications," *World Politics,* Vol. 24, Spring 1972, pp. 40-80.
22   Ibid. pp. 50-54.
23   Department of Defense, "U.S. Nuclear Defense," Office of the Deputy Assistant to the Secretary of Defense for Nuclear Matters, retrieved

CHAPTER 1

STRATEGIC ARMS REDUCTION DEVELOPMENT STUDY

Scholars have offered various theories and models to explain the process through which public policy is formulated and implemented.[24] Of the existing theories, rational choice and bureaucratic politics have been two of the most subscribed to approaches for national security and foreign policy analysis.[25] The corresponding rational policy model presents policy formulation as a coherent act executed by cohesive governments. In contrast, the bureaucratic politics model views policy development as an incremental affair involving self-interested actors located throughout government. The bureaucratic politics paradigm built on earlier internal bargaining arguments related to foreign

---

November 5, 2009.

24   Numerous public policy models were related but not limited to: institutions, process, groups, elite actors, incremental response, rational choice, game theory, public choice, and systems. For more on each model, see Thomas R. Dye, *Understanding Public Policy*, 9th edition 1998, pp. 13-38.

25   The bureaucratic politics model was popularized in the 1960's and 1970's, by Graham Allison and Morton Halperin. Allison, Graham T. and Philip Zelikow, *Essence of Decision: Explaining the Cuban Missile Crises*, 2nd edition 1999; Allison, Graham T., "Conceptual Models and the Cuban Missile Crises," *The American Political Science Review*, Vol. 63, No. 3, September 1969, pp. 689-718; Allison, Graham T., and Morton H. Halperin, "Bureaucratic Politics: A Paradigm and Some Policy Implications," *World Politics*, Vol. 24, Spring 1972, pp. 43-56; Halperin, Morton H., and Priscilla A. Clapp, *Bureaucratic Politics and Foreign Policy*, 2nd edition 2006.

policy and offered a model that emphasizes the role of stakeholders and organizations in the policy development process.[26]
This chapter tests the hypothesis that, "U.S. nuclear defense
policy formulation during the post-Cold War administrations of
George H. W. Bush and William J. Clinton was anchored in bureaucratic politics, not collective defense." To test the hypothesis the chapter addresses whether strategic arms reduction policy
evolved as collective U.S. government actions meant to "maximize strategic goals and objectives," or whether policy formulation was the incremental result of intra-governmental conflict
and compromise?[27] Research for the book suggests that strategic arms reduction policy formulation represented the limited
aggregation of actor and stakeholder positions. This process,
which was characterized by actor and stakeholder compromise,
left dissatisfied participants to persist with positional arguments
after strategic arms reduction policy decisions had been taken.

The case study is divided into several sections related to
stakeholders, policy development, and barriers. The first section establishes the rules and actors associated with the key
stakeholders. Each U.S. government stakeholder – the president, Congress, and the bureaucracy -- brought a different
perspective, and different interests, to the policy process. An
introduction to Cold War strategic arms reduction efforts establishes the presence of norms that carried forward into the post-
Cold War era. The strategic arms reduction policy development
process was characterized by debate and compromise amongst
relevant stakeholders in the context of a system with multiple
points of policy origination. The research identified that policy

---

26   Clifford, Garry J., "Bureaucratic Politics," *The Journal of American
History*, Vol. 77, No. 1, June 1990, pp. 161-168; Allison, Graham T. and
Philip Zelikow, *Essence of Decision: Explaining the Cuban Missile Crises*,
2nd edition 1999; Halperin, Morton H., "The Decision to Deploy the ABM:
Bureaucratic and Domestic Politics in the Johnson Administration," *World
Politics*, Vol. 25, October 1972, pp. 62-96.
27   Allison, Graham T. and Philip Zelikow, *Essence of Decision:
Explaining the Cuban Missile Crises*, 2nd edition 1999, pp. 23-26 and 294-313.

development was anchored in stakeholder positions, rules, and norms. In the case of the Strategic Arms Reduction Treaty (START), policy formulation proved to be influenced primarily by the continuation of previous experience, and not a unified response to contemporary circumstances.

STAKEHOLDERS

Key stakeholders included the president, the legislature (two chambers of Congress), and the bureaucracy (implementing government departments and agencies of the executive branch). Stakeholders follow established rules derived from "assorted customs, statutes, and constitutional requirements," and use standardized procedures, referred to as action channels, to produce policy decisions.[28] These stakeholders argue for or against national level policies that support their specific interests. In the case of the president or legislature, interests may include personal or party politics, while the bureaucracy may maneuver with the aim of maximizing budgets, autonomy, and influence.[29]

While the president and Congress derive their authority from the Constitution, the bureaucracy incrementally receives non-statutory and statutory authorities from the president and Congress. General authorities were stated in founding documents, and additional department and agency authorities are outlined in subsequent national policies. Although rules and action channels are subject to change, this occurs slowly and incrementally. For example, the 22nd Amendment, which limited

---

28   Keagle, James M., "Introduction and Framework," in David C. Kozak, and James M. Keagle, eds., *Bureaucratic Politics and National Security: Theory and Practice*, 1988, p.21; Halperin, Morton H. and Priscilla A. Clapp, *Bureaucratic Politics and Foreign Policy*, 2nd edition 2006, pp. 338-344; Allison, Graham T., and Morton H. Halperin, "Bureaucratic Politics: A Paradigm and Some Policy Implications," *World Politics*, Vol. 24, Spring 1972, p. 45.

29   Keagle, James M., "Introduction and Framework," in David C. Kozak, and James M. Keagle, eds., *Bureaucratic Politics and National Security: Theory and Practice*, 1988, pp. 21-22.

the president to two terms in office, was not ratified until 1951.[30] Prior to this, all elected national officials were permitted to serve indefinitely. The president and Congress represent political actors that are more sensitive than the bureaucracy to external factors such as the media, lobbyists, and constituents. The departments and agencies that comprise the bureaucracy are more sensitive to perceived relevance and political actor support.

Each of the major implementing organizations described in chapters 1 and 2 displayed distinct positions prior to 1989. For example, the Department of Defense's position was based on nuclear war-fighting while the Department of State displayed a diplomatic culture focused on arms control. Cold war positional differences such as these were deeply imbedded in the psyche of each organization. The same phenomenon was true of Cold War nuclear defense norms where nonproliferation, non-use, deterrence, and parity existed in a heavily debated national security policy area. These existing rules, actor positions, and norms transitioned from one era to the next and, together with physical infrastructure and long-term investment, had the potential to highlight path dependent arguments in nuclear defense.

THE PRESIDENT

The first major stakeholder in policy development related to strategic arms reduction was the president. There has been a great deal written on the role of the office of the president in policy development.[31] The office comes with authorities and limitations that make it different from other stakeholders. Related constitutional authorities gave the president the ability to make treaties and to appoint designated officials with the advice and

30   The Constitution of the United States and The Declaration of Independence, 22nd printing 2006, p. 31.
31   For more on the presidency, see George C. Edwards III, Steven A. Shull, and Norman C. Thomas, eds., *The Presidency and Public Policy Making*, 1985; and George E. Shambaugh IV and Paul J. Weinstein Jr., *The Art of Policy Making: Tools, Techniques, and Processes in the Modern Executive Branch*, 2003.

consent of the Senate, or in the case of "inferior officers," without congressional approval. The president, as the executive power, is responsible for approving or vetoing statutory policy and ensuring laws are executed. Constitutional constraints prevented the executive branch from resourcing policies without Congress' approval, and limited the president to two terms. Should the Electoral College decide not to re-elect a president this period could be reduced to a single four-year term.[32] These points resonate throughout chapters 1 and 2, highlighting the importance of rules during the policy development process.

The normal nuclear defense policy development process within the White House resided within the National Security Council structure.[33] The National Security Council was traditionally outlined in the first presidential directive from each incoming administration. These documents described similar structures, but did not adequately reflect the personal styles of the presidents that they supported.[34] As a result, modifications, use, and levels of access were unique to each administration. The assistant to the president for national security affairs, also known as the national security advisor, directed the National Security Council staff. This was an appointed position not confirmed by the Senate. Since "very few governmental activities could be performed by one department or agency alone," it was the responsibility of the National Security Council staff to guide

---

32   The Constitution of the United States and The Declaration of Independence, 22nd printing 2006.

33   Shambaugh, George E., IV, and Paul J. Weinstein Jr., *The Art of Policy Making: Tools, Techniques, and Processes in the Modern Executive Branch*, 2003, pp. 26-29.

34   For more on the National Security Council process and the impact of presidential leadership styles, see William W. Newmann, *Managing National Security Policy: The President and the Process*, 2003; Interviews described a level of informal coordination mechanisms in use at the White House that allow staffers to interact well-beyond formal procedures normally depicted in open literature. Interview with National Security Council Staff, Director Office of Iraq and Afghanistan Affairs John Gallagher, August 6, 2009.

the interagency process.[35] The national policy level is a complex environment with powerful actors representing diverse authorities and positions. These actors participate in an interagency process that reflected high-ranking coordination at the principal, deputy, and senior executive levels, but not operational level planning or execution.

President George H. W. Bush was a long-serving public official. After World War II service as a Navy pilot and a brief private sector career, George H. W. Bush went on to serve in the House of Representatives, as ambassador to the United Nations, envoy to China, Director of Central Intelligence, and Vice-President. His key advisors came from the National Security Council, the Department of Defense, and the Department of State. National security advisor Brent Scowcroft had a similar career to President Bush, which included service as the national security advisor during the same time the president was the Director of Central Intelligence.[36] Secretary of Defense Richard Cheney previously served in the Nixon and Ford administrations, and the House of Representatives, while General Colin Powell held the position of Chairman of the Joint Chiefs of Staff, along with other influential postings in the White House that included national security advisor to President Reagan. Secretary of State James Baker was a personal friend of the president and a seasoned appointee, having served previously as President Reagan's Chief of Staff and Secretary of the Treasury.

Party politics during the Bush administration portrayed the Democrats as liberal and the Republicans as conservative on issues such as nuclear weapons and missile defense. Barry Blechman noted that it was the Democratic Congress that forced President Reagan to abide by the second Strategic Arms Limitation Treaty and restricted Strategic Defense Initiative

---

35   Newmann, William, "Change in National Security Processes," *Presidential Studies Quarterly*, Vol. 31. No. 1, March 2001, p. 77.
36   Scowcroft was also a retired Air Force Lieutenant General with a doctorate in international relations from Columbia University.

technologies to conform to Anti-Ballistic Missile Treaty (ABM) restrictions.[37] This increased congressional role in nuclear defense carried forward to the Bush administration as the Democratic Party controlled both houses of Congress during President Bush's tenure. The relationship between the executive and legislative branches during this period could be described as professional, but following concessions to Democratic lawmakers over tax increases in 1990, the president lost support from his own party. This loss of support slowed his agenda, and contributed to the emergence of a third party candidate in the 1992 election, and his eventual defeat after a single term.

The Clinton administration had different agendas and relationships with the legislative branch. President Clinton came into office focused on the economy and domestic programs. His party affiliation, age, and background as a lawyer, state politician, and former governor of Arkansas, meant that he had different priorities from his predecessor. Unlike the previous administration, the most influential advisors for nuclear defense policy were not in the National Security Council staff then led by Samuel "Sandy" Berger. Instead, President Clinton's key nuclear defense advisors gravitated to the Defense Department from Congress and academia.[38] Representative Les Aspin served as the initial secretary followed by a former undersecretary during the Carter administration, William Perry. Within the Defense Department, John Deutch served initially as a deputy secretary and Ashton Carter served as an assistant secretary. Deutch had been a Department of Energy official under President Carter, but

---

37   Blechman, Barry M., *The Politics of National Security: Congress and Defense Policy*, 1990, p. 64.

38   This does not mean to imply that the National Security Council staff did not participate in nuclear defense matters. Interviews with former Clinton administration officials highlighted that the White House was engaged, but not to the extent of the previous administration because many decisions on new policy direction had already been made and the departments were in the process of designing and initiating supporting programs. For a full list of interviews, see the bibliography.

although Ashton Carter served in many legislative and executive branch advisory roles prior, this was his first assistant secretary level position.[39] In the State Department, President Clinton had his former college roommate and nuclear arms control authority Strobe Talbott as the Deputy Secretary of State.[40]

The Democratic Party initially controlled Congress, but in 1995, the composition of Congress changed with Republicans gaining and holding the majority in both houses for the remainder of President Clinton's time in office. Beginning with the 104th Congress the relationship between the executive and legislative branches could be described as adversarial at best. Fierce political partisanship characterized by legislative gridlock that extended into nuclear defense depicted the national policy development environment between 1995 and January 2001. Externally, conditions in Russia also began to stabilize, eventually replacing the period of intense need with a renewed adversarial relationship. This developing situation frustrated nuclear defense efforts as the Russian Federation experienced domestic political disagreement and a return to nationalism. In this regard, President Clinton remarked that it was ironic that democracy played a role in the Russian refusal to ratify the second Strategic Arms Reduction Treaty (START II).[41]

---

39   Graham Allison was also selected by President Clinton to serve as the Assistant Secretary of Defense for Policy and Plans, but controversy over improper actions prior to confirmation and a limited tenure of seven months meant he did not have a significant internal role in the administration's nuclear defense policy. Axelrod, Jonathan N., "Allison Abandons Government Post," *The Harvard Crimson*, February 18, 1994; Department of Defense, *Department of Defense Key Officials 1947-2004*, Historical Office of the Secretary of Defense, 2004, p. 41.

40   In the latter part of the second term Morton Halperin served as the director of the Department of State Policy Planning Staff.

41   Talbott, Strobe, *The Russia Hand: A Memoir of Presidential Diplomacy*, 2003, pp. 372-397.

CONGRESS

Congress was another major stakeholder when it came to U.S. nuclear policy. The legislature is separated into two distinct bodies, the Senate and the House of Representatives, with 535 individual actors representing diverse interests.[42] Each chamber was designated constitutional authorities to ensure no single branch can dominate government. The Senate is responsible for treaty ratification and appointee review while the House originates bills related to revenue.[43] Either chamber can initiate policy development and prevent executive branch policies from passing if there is sufficient opposition. Electoral dynamics mean senators are elected in state-wide contests every six years while members of the House are designated by smaller constituencies every two years. Neither chamber is restricted by term limits.[44] Party majority status has position and procedural advantages in both chambers that can impact legislation beyond simple vote counts.[45] An often cited example is agenda setting by the majority party. This rule allows each chamber's leadership to dictate whether a bill will be debated and the order in which it will be addressed if slated.[46]

Collective congressional norms and action channels related to national security policy have changed over the years. Evidence of increasing congressional activity was presented by Barry Blechman in *The Politics of National Security: Congress*

---

42   Wilson, James Q., *Bureaucracy: What Government Agencies Do and Why They Do It*, 2nd edition 2000, p. 238.

43   The Constitution of the United States and The Declaration of Independence, 22nd printing 2006, pp. 5 and 11.

44   For more on political science literature and arguments pertaining to term limits, see Edward J. Lopez, "Term Limits: Causes and consequences," *Public Choice*, Vol. 114, 2003, pp. 1-56.

45   Cox, Gary W., "On the Effects of Legislative Rules," *Legislative Studies Quarterly*, Vol. 25, No. 2, May 2000, pp. 169-192.

46   Cox, Gary W., "Agenda Setting in the U.S. House: A Majority-Party Monopoly?," *Legislative Studies Quarterly*, Vol. 26, No. 2, May 2001, pp. 185-210.

and U.S. Defense Policy. Changes in the amount of involvement at every point of policy development and implementation are highlighted in the arms control chapter.[47] Blechman demonstrated the use of constitutional instruments and identified reorganization within the legislature intended to maximize leverage on treaty and other nuclear defense topics. He concluded that, "Congress's new role in arms control has some serious problems" since "few House members and Senators are knowledgeable enough to speak authoritatively on the complexities of the issues."[48] This competitive landscape between the executive and legislative branches added to the complexities of negotiations with foreign governments.

The diverse composition of Congress is unified by a two party system. Broad generalizations on national security characterize the Republican Party as conservative and the Democratic Party as liberal, but long-standing policy issues and individual interests often depict a more complex political landscape within the legislature. Each actor within the legislature displays a different starting position related to an extreme end of party positions through to centrist beliefs. For these actors, personal considerations relating, but not limited to, re-election, ideology, and state or district interests, impact individual policy positions and votes. These differences are present to different degrees depending on the profile of the policy and political vulnerabilities of the member. For example, the policy development cases in this book represent high-profile policies while subsequent implementation study chapters depict lower-profile policies that may or may not elicit strong individual or group positions.

THE BUREAUCRACY

The departments and agencies of the executive branch constitute the final stakeholder set. These autonomous and

---

47   Blechman, Barry M., *The Politics of National Security: Congress and Defense Policy*, 1990, pp. 63-111.
48   Ibid., p. 107.

semi-autonomous organizations derive their authorities from customs and statutes, not the Constitution. Different authorities and purposes mean each implementing organization often represents unique expertise and resources. While political appointees head the departments and agencies, career civil servants, military, and contractors comprise the workforce.[49] Career officials may obtain senior positions but remain accountable to rotating presidential appointees and Congress. Relationships with appointees, the White House, congressional committees, and champions are complex.[50] Thomas Hammond and Jack Knott argued that these relationships have been complicated since the founding of the Republic. They related the difficulties experienced by early cabinet secretaries under Jefferson, Madison, and Monroe, as they were forced to answer to the executive and legislative branches while simultaneously attempting to carve out bureaucratic authorities and autonomy.[51]

Scholars have debated not only how government agencies do business, but also the role of the bureaucracy in the policy process.[52] Anthony Downs offered that "bureaucratic officials, like all other agents in society, are significantly – though not solely – motivated by their own self-interests."[53] He went on to say that these officials looked to achieve their goals rationally, and that

49   Wilson, James Q., *Bureaucracy: What Government Agencies Do and Why They Do It*, 2nd edition 2000, pp. 197-200 and 137-153.

50   Champions are senior actors that back an effort or program. R. Douglas Arnold described these actors as coalition leaders and offered explanations for why senior actors would support an effort to this degree and how these actors build coalitions. Arnold, R. Douglas, *Congress and the Bureaucracy: A Theory of Influence*, 1979, pp. 37-54.

51   Hammond, Thomas H., and Jack H. Knott, "Who Controls the Bureaucracy?: Presidential Power, Congressional Dominance, Legal Constraints, and Bureaucratic Autonomy in a Model of Multi-Institutional Policy-Making," *The Journal of Law, Economics, and Organization*, Vol. 12, No. 1, 1996, pp. 119-121.

52   For more on the topic, see James Q. Wilson, *Bureaucracy: What Government Agencies Do and Why They Do It*, 2nd edition 2000, and Anthony Downs, *Inside Bureaucracy*, 1967.

53   Downs, Anthony, *Inside Bureaucracy*, 1967, pp. 1-2.

these goals often related to "power, income, prestige, security, convenience, loyalty (to an idea, institution, or the nation), pride in excellent work, and desire to serve the public interest." In this study, these assertions were applied to several organizations that each had different leadership, goals, and authorities.

Key U.S. government nuclear defense implementing organizations consist of the majority of the executive branch departments, but for the purpose of examination, the development case study chapters concentrate on the U.S. Departments of State and Defense.[54] Each department had participated as a nuclear defense stakeholder since 1946, and represented separate organizational cultures, authorities, and resources. While these departments have undergone significant reorganization over the years their traditional roles have remained constant with the addition of post-Cold War tasks. The Department of State's positions on minimizing the perceived utility of nuclear weapons generally contrasted with those of the nuclear weapons community, which emphasized the need for a robust nuclear stockpile.[55]

---

54   The Department of Energy remained in a supporting weapons development and sustainment role, but was not a significant stakeholder for strategic arms reduction or national missile defense. Department programs such as the Materials Protection, Controls, and Accounting program, the Second Line of Defense program, national laboratory nuclear weapons and materials expertise in support of detection and technical nuclear forensics, and greater infrastructure responsibilities were discussed in the implementation studies. The studies also added the Department of Homeland Security, which was the primary domestic department for nuclear defense with a broad structure that also facilitated participation in each area. The department's forward immigration and customs efforts, border and coastline security, and Federal Emergency Management Agency divisions meant the Department of Homeland Security was a primary actor in international and domestic nuclear defense efforts.

55   For shared positions the Departments of Defense and Energy were referred to as the nuclear weapons community. This reference indicated the separation of responsibility for Defense Department employment and routine maintenance, and Department of Energy requirements for design, manufacture, sustainment, and retirement of nuclear weapons. The Department of Defense was the community advocate for strategic arms reduction and national missile defense positions.

The Department of State was the lead agency for prevention, but had responsibilities in each nuclear defense area. Diplomatic coordination of arms control agreements, reduction activities, partner facilitated interdiction, or the organization of foreign assistance in the event of response operations were all State Department tasks.[56] The Department of Defense was instrumental in protection efforts but it had responsibilities in each nuclear defense area. From threat reduction, nuclear weapons employment, missile defense, elimination operations, foreign consequence management, post-detonation technical nuclear forensics, or retaliation, the largest of the executive departments possesses the resources to participate in a broad range of nuclear defense missions.

The Departments of State and Defense had different mandates, organizational cultures, and capabilities that often resulted in diverging positions on nuclear defense matters. For example, departmental positions on the Africa Nuclear-Weapon-Free Zone Treaty highlighted general differences between prevention and protection oriented organizations. The effort to declare Africa a nuclear-weapon-free zone dated back to the 1960s, but following extension of the Nonproliferation Treaty in 1995, a formal treaty became a possibility.[57] In this instance the Department of State saw the treaty, like the other nuclear-weapons-free-zone treaties, as a nonproliferation success. From a diplomatic standpoint the United States would benefit by repaying Nonproliferation Treaty capital and establish itself as a strong supporter of progressive nuclear weapons policies while President Clinton worked toward a comprehensive test ban agreement.

---

56   The fact that Department of State was a key stakeholder in all international policies required emphasis. If a nuclear defense policy affected international partners, the Department of State had, at a minimum, a representative for the policy and if it was a major issue such as a treaty, the department served in a lead role.

57   The Africa Nuclear-Weapons-Free Zone Treaty was also known as the Treaty of Pelindaba. See Nolan, Janne E., *An Elusive Consensus: Nuclear Weapons and American Security After the Cold War*, 1999, pp. 77-84.

The nuclear weapons community held a different position on the nuclear-weapons-free zone treaty. In this case, the Department of Defense was apprehensive about limits on the use, or threatened use, of nuclear weapons. Department of Defense officials successfully argued against signature until a bureaucratic compromise was reached. In this regard, National Security Council staff Senior Director for Defense Policy and Arms Control Robert Bell offered, although the United States signed the treaty Protocol, it "will not limit options available to the United States in response to an attack by an African nuclear-weapon-free zone party using weapons of mass destruction."[58] However, this compromise did not carry forward to ratification. While President Clinton signed the African Nuclear-Weapon-Free Zone Treaty in 1996, the Senate refused to ratify it. Differences in organizational policy positions were not unique to the Clinton administration, but access and influence depending on positions and relationships were key factors in the direction and outcomes of nuclear defense policy debates.

In regard to policy development several questions arise. Did stakeholders use the catalyst of the altered post-Cold War strategic landscape to develop rational policies designed to respond collectively to contemporary events? Or, did self-interest, tradition, and other systemic constraints dictate adherence to pre-existing positions? Additionally, did stakeholders reach an agreed consensus or did a dominant stakeholder consistently steer policy development? The case studies on strategic arms reduction and national missile defense suggest that organizational positions dictated continued adherence to existing approaches despite the presence of radically different strategic circumstances.

---

58   Protocol I of the treaty invites the Nonproliferation Treaty nuclear weapon states to affirm that they will not threaten use of a nuclear weapon against treaty signatories. White House, "Press Briefing by Mike McCurry and Robert Bell, Special Assistant to the President and Senior Director for Defense Policy and Arms Control, National Security Council," Office of the White House Press Secretary, April 11, 1996.

COLD WAR STRATEGIC ARMS CONTROL EFFORTS

International discussions on limiting nuclear weapons began under President Eisenhower, but it was not until later administrations that agreements materialized to address nuclear testing, proliferation, and use. Bilateral efforts to restrict nuclear stockpile limits began with the 1972 Strategic Arms Limitation Treaty. The treaty, which consisted of the Anti-Ballistic Missile Treaty and an interim agreement on strategic offensive arms, represented the outcome of two years of negotiations between the United States and the Soviet Union.[59] Unfortunately, differences over emerging technologies and verification meant that numerous actors were not satisfied with initial outcomes.[60] This discontent facilitated continued arms limitation talks that led to a second Strategic Arms Limitation Treaty in June 1979. The first part of the second agreement limited each nation to 2,400 launchers with a separate stipulation for 1,320 multiple independently-targetable re-entry vehicle equipped missiles.[61]

---

59   The Anti-Ballistic Missile Treaty was covered in the following section on missile defense. The interim agreement, which dealt with limiting strategic ballistic missile launchers, was an example of nuclear arms control efforts targeting delivery vehicles, not warheads. "Interim Agreement on Certain Measures with Respect to the Limitation of Strategic Offensive Arms," Federation of American Scientists, retrieved April 10, 2009.

60   Multiple independently-targetable re-entry vehicles systems introduced in the late 1960's and early 1970's, meant that a single ballistic missile could be equipped with generally up to ten warheads and countermeasures. This new technology had the ability to increase arsenal lethality since single ballistic missile launchers were reduced and capped under the interim agreement, not warheads or multiple independently-targetable re-entry vehicles. Verification of treaty compliance was also an issue since both parties only agreed to limited monitoring from outside territorial borders. Baker, David, *The Rocket: The History and Development of Rocket and Missile Technology*, 1978, p. 196.

61   "Limitation of Strategic Offensive Arms, 1979," U.S. Department of State, retrieved April 10, 2009.

President Carter signed the treaty in 1979, but it was never ratified by the U.S. Congress. Both parties generally observed the agreement until President Reagan's formal withdrawal in 1986. President Reagan was not opposed to arms control; instead, his administration was intent on establishing a mechanism for nuclear reductions, not just limitations.[62] Although President Reagan announced this change in negotiation strategy from strategic arms limitation to strategic arms reduction in 1982, the final days of the Cold War and the launch of the Strategic Defense Initiative prevented the completion of a new treaty during his presidency. The Soviet Union was worried that a successful missile defense program would nullify their nuclear capabilities. Thus, linkage of the ABM Treaty to arms reduction talks directly contributed to the stagnation of negotiations. Garry Clifford offered insights from senior officials such as Strobe Talbott, that "accounts of arms control policy during the Carter and Reagan years confirm the truism that arriving at a consensus among the various players and agencies within the government is more complicated, if not more difficult, than negotiating with the Soviets."[63] Pre-existing rules, positions, norms, and stakeholder relationships carried forward from the Cold War era. In the case of the Strategic Arms Reduction Treaty, there was even a draft document in place which the George H. W. Bush administration inherited from the Reagan period.

---

62   Paul Lettow argued that President Reagan was actually a nuclear abolitionist that loathed nuclear weapons and the thought of nuclear war. Offering it was this deep seated belief that led to confusing nuclear defense policies of a reignited arms race and a strategic defense initiative concept that was well-beyond immediate technical capabilities. Lettow, Paul, *Ronald Reagan and His Quest to Abolish Nuclear Weapons*, 2006, pp. 70-71.

63   Clifford, J. Garry, "Bureaucratic Politics," *The Journal of American History*, Vol. 77, No. 1, June 1990, p. 163.

POLICY DECISIONS

Several years of additional negotiations and the incremental end of the Cold War facilitated the signing and eventual ratification of the first Strategic Arms Reduction Treaty in 1991. This outcome was preceded by several major compromises, one of which was the Soviet offer to decouple Anti-Ballistic Missile Treaty requirements from arms reductions, and the second concerning the American concession to define treaty levels based on warheads, instead of delivery vehicles.[64] The detailed treaty had a lifespan of 15 years with clauses for extensions if necessary, and permitted on-site inspections, notifications, data exchanges, and national technical means of verification. The Strategic Arms Reduction Treaty outlined reductions in launching platforms, missiles, and warheads, limiting each side to no more than 6,000 deployed warheads on no more than 1,600 ballistic missiles or bombers.[65]

The treaty was the beginning of a contemporary nuclear defense strategy that emphasized threat reduction. However, START had several significant flaws. Detailed inspection protocols were reminiscent of the Cold War with prescribed procedures for every aspect of on-site inspection. Operational limits remained fairly high at 6,000, providing sufficient warheads on multiple independently-targetable re-entry vehicle equipped delivery systems to conduct a robust nuclear campaign. Operational stockpile numbers were reinforced by non-operational reserves, which START did not restrict. This meant that for both the United States and the Soviet Union, treaty compliance could be as simple as shifting an accounting classification from operational to reserve status. The treaty also lacked any mention of tactical nuclear weapons or fissile materials. While START was

---

64   Beschloss, Michael R., and Strobe Talbott, *At the Highest Levels: The Inside Story of the End of the Cold War*, 1993, pp. 117-188, and 405.

65   "Treaty Between The United States of America and The Union of Socialist Republics on the Reduction and Limitations of Strategic Offensive Arms," July 31, 1991.

not perfect, and left the ultimate decision of warhead and fissile material disposition to the respective governments, it was the first of what arms controllers hoped would be a series of agreements that would progressively achieve deeper reductions.[66]

Implementation of START was representative of the time period. After nine years of negotiations the treaty was signed in Moscow on July 31, 1991, but the collapse of the Soviet Union suddenly created three new nuclear weapons-capable states that fell outside both START and the Nonproliferation Treaty. The George H. W. Bush and Yeltsin administrations negotiated with Belarus, Kazakhstan, and Ukraine to rectify the situation. The negotiations resulted in the Lisbon protocol to START on May 23, 1992. This protocol facilitated bringing in the newly independent states to START, with Belarus, Kazakhstan, and Ukraine returning the nuclear weapons they had inherited from the Soviet Union to Russia and their signing of the Nonproliferation Treaty as non-nuclear weapons states.[67]

The United States and the Russian Federation began the reduction of their strategic forces and the newly independent state target groups started the process of denuclearization as they individually negotiated foreign assistance with the United States before the treaty entered into force on December 5, 1994.[68]

---

66   The Cooperative Threat Reduction program covered in chapter 3 proved vital in the transportation, consolidation, security, and elimination of former Soviet Union nuclear weapons, delivery systems, and materials. Secure, environmentally focused nuclear weapon and infrastructure remediation in the former Soviet Union was in many cases primarily funded and completed under the threat reduction programs of the next two administrations.
67   "Treaty Between The United States of America and The Union of Socialist Republics on the Reduction and Limitations of Strategic Offensive Arms," July 31, 1991, Protocol May 23, 1992.
68   While Cooperative Threat Reduction played a vital role in negotiation incentives and later for Strategic Arms Reduction Treaty compliance, each country was in a different state of domestic political and bureaucratic development, approached the varying nuclear weapons program items differently, and displayed unique cultural considerations for access and implementation. For more on the individual accounts of Belarus, Kazakhstan, and Ukraine, see chapters 8-10 of John M. Shields, and William C. Potter, eds.,

President George H. W. Bush was criticized from both sides of the arms control debate with strategic nuclear cuts painted as either too drastic or not going far enough. As a result, negotiations continued and the next segment of reduction talks resulted in START II, which President George H. W. Bush signed during his final days in office. Although drafted and signed in a short amount of time, the U.S. Senate did not ratify the treaty until January 1996, and the Russian Duma refused to ratify the original treaty that called for an operational strategic warhead window of 3,000-3,500.[69]

In 1997, the Helsinki summit produced several nuclear defense related agreements, but by this time Presidents Clinton and Yeltsin both had to deal with confrontational legislative bodies that threatened continued cooperation on arms reduction matters.[70] Both presidents agreed at Helsinki -- under the START II protocol -- to begin negotiations for a third treaty as soon as START II entered into force. They also reaffirmed their dedication to threat reduction and the ABM Treaty, including agreement that limited theater ABM systems were permissible under the existing treaty.[71] The United States, Russia, and newly independent states later signed ABM Treaty related agreements relating to the summit accords, and President Clinton issued new nuclear weapons guidance stating that the U.S. stockpile could be reduced to the 2,000-2,500 strategic nuclear warhead levels envisioned at Helsinki.[72]

Dismantling the Cold War: U.S. and newly independent state Perspectives on the Nunn-Lugar Cooperative Threat Reduction Program, 1997, pp. 151-207.
69   Larsen, Jeffery A., "National Security and Neo-Arms Control in the Bush Administration." *Disarmament Diplomacy,* Issue No. 80, Autumn 2005.
70   Lippman, Thomas W., "Clinton, Yeltsin Agree on Arms Cuts and North Atlantic Treaty Organization," *The Washington Post,* Saturday, March 22, 1997.
71   *National Security Strategy for a New Century,* 1998, pp. 9-10.
72   Landay, Jonathan S., "U.S. Downsizes Its Nuclear-Weapon Ambitions," *The Christian Science Monitor,* December 24, 1997.

Despite presidential goodwill the strategic arms reduction process did not make any further progress at this time because of stakeholder tensions. The administration of President Clinton and Congress were divided on many issues, as were President Yeltsin and the Duma. Relations between the former superpower adversaries shifted from one of intense need in the early 1990s, to one of suspicion and re-emerging rivalry as the Russian economy and government began to stabilize. After the collapse of the Soviet Union, Russia and the newly independent states depended heavily on U.S. aid programs, but as the decade drew to a close, it was the United States that required Russian assistance for shared strategic problems such as proliferation and missile defense. Despite U.S. efforts, the Russian Duma refused to ratify START II, citing the expansion of the North Atlantic Treaty Organization (NATO) and concerns over the ABM Treaty.

Opposition legislators in the Duma used the treaty as leverage in protests against American actions, such as those in Kosovo, and continued to argue against the potential strategic superiority the United States would enjoy under the treaty.[73] The treaty remained dormant in the Duma until Vladimir Putin became the second president of Russia. Due largely to his efforts, and despite continued resistance from the military and opposition legislators, President Putin convinced the Duma to ratify START II on April 14, 2000. Russian ratification was contingent on an additional protocol that required the United States to ratify an earlier ballistic missile agreement and remain compliant with the ABM Treaty.[74] In the United States, the Republican-controlled Congress was dominated by conservative views on national security. As a result, the Senate initially ratified START II but later refused to ratify the additional protocol added by the Russians.[75]

---

73   News Review, "Duma seemingly unswayed by Perry Strategic Arms Reduction Treaty II appeal," *Disarmament Diplomacy*, Issue No. 10, November 1996.
74   Mankoff, Jeffrey, *Russian Foreign Policy: The Return of Great Power Politics*, 2009, pp. 100-101.
75   "Treaty Between The United States of America and The Russian

With both legislative bodies in opposition, the treaties remained in limbo until Russia officially withdrew from START II in response to the American withdrawal from the ABM Treaty in June 2002.[76] The re-emergence of the link between the ABM Treaty and strategic arms reduction, combined with the introduction of Russian democracy, contributed directly to the end of the second strategic arms reduction treaty.[77]

POLICY DEVELOPMENT

Despite the fate of the second treaty the first two administrations of the post-Cold War period had established a policy to reduce the strategic nuclear weapons stockpile in accordance with negotiated bilateral agreements. This policy was the result of internal and external compromise over the course of multiple administrations. In the United States, the primary stakeholders -- the president, Congress, and the bureaucracy -- all had vested interests in strategic arms reductions. Each stakeholder position was based on individual, group, or organizational interests. The president and members of Congress had different security priorities and constituencies to address, while the arms control and nuclear war-fighting organizations also had diverging concerns.

Federation on Further Reduction and Limitation of Strategic Offensive Arms," January 3, 1993, Protocol September 26, 1997.

76   The next administration sought to streamline procedures for an updated arms reduction agreement with the Russian Federation. Efforts resulted in the 2002 Moscow Treaty, also known as the Strategic Offensive Reductions Treaty. The Strategic Offensive Reductions Treaty timeline of signature in May 2002, to entry into force in June 2003, highlighted the laborious process associated with treaties. In this case, the Strategic Offensive Reductions Treaty was a short, follow-on treaty that was to run in conjunction with Strategic Arms Reduction Treaty until December 2009. Even with the unified security climate following 9/11 and the brevity of the treaty, the ratification process still took a year to complete. White House, "Text of the Strategic Offensive Reductions Treaty," Office of the White House Press Secretary, May 24, 2002, Article I.

77   Talbott, Strobe, *The Russia Hand: A Memoir of Presidential Diplomacy*, 2003, pp. 372-397.

THE PRESIDENT

In the spring of 1989, President George H. W. Bush used an Associated Press business luncheon to describe his philosophy on working with Congress and the bureaucracy:

> My starting point has been a respect for American institutions -- for Congress, for the dedicated civil servants in the executive branch, for State and local governments, for the concept of public service -- and a firm belief in the constitutional powers of the Presidency. Each has its role; each can be enlisted in the work at hand. The emphasis is on cooperation, not confrontation, as the surest route to progress.

> ...when I took office, I told the Congress that the American people hadn't sent us to Washington to bicker. They sent us to govern, to work together to solve the urgent problems that confront us, and to shape the long-term strategies to ensure peace and prosperity in the future. I think the work we've done these past three months demonstrates the value of tough, principled negotiations between this administration and the Congress.[78]

This speech was representative of a president with longstanding government service who approached the office from a chief executive officer perspective. Although President Bush served as the vice-president for the previous eight years, he brought with him a different leadership style than his predecessor. While President Reagan was well known for decentralized leadership and decision-making, President Bush returned the National Security Council system to a centralized format and empowered his national security advisor.[79]

The Bush administration intended to apply new ideas concerning arms control as it entered office. Brent Scowcroft and other advisors called for the development of "a coherent approach to arms control policy, nuclear strategy, and Pentagon

---

78   Bush, George H. W., "Remarks at the Associate Press Business Luncheon in Chicago, Illinois," April 24, 1989.
79   Newmann, William, "Change in National Security Processes," *Presidential Studies Quarterly*, Vol. 31. No. 1, March 2001, p. 80.

weapons system purchases, such as mobile intercontinental missiles, before completing the strategic arms reduction treaty." With this in mind, the Bush campaign made statements that there would be a delay in strategic arms negotiations.[80] This delay was formalized after President Bush assumed office, with the caveat that the new administration would honor the basic provisions of existing strategic arms reduction talks.[81]

In addition to statements from his staff, the president offered that although he was "no expert on the technicalities of arms control," he "wanted to reduce nuclear weapons in a way that would not diminish our deterrent capability."[82] Building on these declarations, the administration initiated a comprehensive arms control review that lasted until June 1989. The review represented a broad approach that analyzed arms control positions not included in existing strategic arms reduction documents. It was completed by an interagency group comprised of applicable organizations and chaired by the National Security Council staff. The review was debated in a series of National Security Council meetings, but ultimately, the interagency group settled on a strategy similar to the previous administration.[83] This inclusive interagency process continued for the remainder of strategic arms reduction negotiations, with the president engaged in senior level discussions and the bureaucracy calculating and negotiating the details of the eventual treaty.[84] The president

---

80   Toth, Robert C., "Bush May Delay Resumption of Strategic Arms Talks," *Los Angeles Times*, December 15, 1988.
81   Moseley, Ray, "Bush Will Honor Arms Treaty Provisions," *Chicago Tribune*, March 28, 1989.
82   Bush, George H. W., and Brent Scowcroft, *A World Transformed*, 1998, p. 17.
83   The results were published as National Security Review-14, "Review of United States Arms Control Policies." Newmann, William, "Change in National Security Processes," *Presidential Studies Quarterly*, Vol. 31. No. 1, March 2001, p. 88; Bush, George H. W., "National Security Review-14: Review of United States Arms Control Policies," April 3, 1989.
84   Bush, George H. W., "National Security Directive-40: Decisions on START Issues," May 14, 1990.

was not satisfied with this process and the eventual outcome of the first treaty, but, given the standard interagency process and the requirement for Senate ratification, he settled for this initial reduction in strategic arms.

On September 27, 1991, President George H. W. Bush identified what became known as his presidential nuclear initiatives. During this speech, which would serve as the basis for a second strategic arms treaty, he announced:

- The removal of forward deployed theater nuclear weapons
- The elimination of the majority of said weapons with the limited remaining stock centrally stored
- Preservation of air-delivered nuclear capabilities in Europe for NATO security
- The end of heightened nuclear alert posture
- Accelerated deactivation of Strategic Arms Reduction Treaty designated intercontinental ballistic missiles
- Termination of the Peacekeeper intercontinental ballistic missiles
- Retention of only small single warhead intercontinental ballistic missiles
- Cancellation of nuclear short-range attack missiles
- Establishment of strategic command for consolidated nuclear command and control
- Full funding for the strategic defense initiative and strategic modernization[85]

The president called on the Soviets to match these gestures, to eliminate multiple independently-targetable re-entry vehicle equipped intercontinental ballistic missiles, to engage in further strategic talks, and to discuss possible threat reduction efforts. President Bush stated that he sought a peace dividend that was, "not measured in dollars but in greater security."[86] Soviet President Mikhail Gorbachev responded a few days later on October 5, 1991, affirming the U.S.S.R.'s reciprocal

85   Bush, George H. W., "Address to the Nation on Reducing United States and Soviet Nuclear Weapons," September 27, 1991.
86   Ibid.

commitment. Gorbachev's response proposed further nuclear weapon reductions, fissionable material reductions, and a one-year moratorium on nuclear testing.[87] In January 1992, the new Russian President Boris Yeltsin reaffirmed Gorbachev's commitment and announced even further cuts with a request for U.S. reciprocation in the second round of presidential nuclear initiatives.[88]

The development processes for the first and second strategic arms reduction treaties were different. The first treaty followed normal interagency action channels with discussions in National Security Council forums and negotiations conducted by the State Department over the span of two administrations. The second treaty veered from this process as the president used a close-knit team of advisors to design the general ideas of the follow-on effort and then unilaterally announced his intentions to the American people and Soviet leadership.[89] Standard negotiations between U.S. and Russian delegations solidified presidential efforts, but these were abbreviated by the end of the Soviet Union and President Bush's re-election loss.[90] U.S. presidential

87   Bush, George H. W., and Brent Scowcroft, *A World Transformed*, 1998, p. 547.

88   Keefe, Courtney, "The Presidential Nuclear Initiatives (PNI) on Tactical Nuclear Weapons at a Glance," Arms Control Association, retrieved October 12, 2009.

89   President Bush sent President Gorbachev a letter detailing his announcement and followed it with a phone conversation before his speech. During the initial exchange the only area of concern for the Soviet president was that the initiatives did not include a nuclear testing moratorium. Bush, George H. W., and Brent Scowcroft, *A World Transformed*, 1998, p. 546.

90   Despite President Mikhail Gorbachev's response to the presidential nuclear initiatives, the end of the Soviet Union saw the ascension of Boris Yeltsin to the new Russian Federation presidency. Because of the governmental transition in Russia, negotiations did not begin until June 1992. By that time, the Bush administration had begun to concentrate on the November 1992 presidential elections. Preparation included the transition of Secretary of State Baker in August 1992, to work on the campaign from the White House. The secretary, who had acted as the primary arms control advisor to the president, was replaced by his former deputy, Lawrence Eagleburger. Bush, George H. W., Boris Yeltsin, "Joint Understanding," June 17, 1992.

campaign requirements and differences in U.S. and Russian negotiating positions over downloading timelines for multiple independently-targetable vehicle warheads, nearly combined to prevent the signing of the second treaty before President Bush left office. Nevertheless, last minute negotiations with the backing of the incoming administration facilitated signature of the treaty on January 3, 1993.[91]

President Bush introduced his presidential nuclear initiatives in spite of resistance from implementing organizations and legislative opposition. In the United States, all four military chiefs resisted further reductions, but the president's compartmentalized development and direct involvement overrode the early recommendations of his Department of Defense advisors.[92] Congress held varying positions on further reductions and was yet to debate or ratify the first treaty that had just been signed on July 31, 1991. President Bush's actions demonstrated the effectiveness of the office when directly involved in championing policy, but also highlighted the potential repercussions of circumventing prescribed procedures. For example, the Joint Chiefs of Staff retarded negotiations during the election cycle when they refused to concede additional time and flexibility for the conversion of Russian land-based missiles.[93] Arguments carried forward into the new administration, where the contentious Nuclear Posture Review process in 1994, demonstrated continued advancement of Defense Department positions beyond START policy decisions.[94]

---

91   Talbott, Strobe, *The Russia Hand: A Memoir of Presidential Diplomacy*, 2003, p. 34.
92   The Army had already begun to look at the possible elimination of tactical nuclear weapons, but at this point none of the service chiefs were ready to recommend a new direction for nuclear weapons. Powell, Colin L., *My American Journey*, 1995, pp. 540-541; Interview with Department of Homeland Security, Domestic Nuclear Detection Office Joint Analysis Center official, October 26, 2010.
93   Talbott, Strobe, *The Russia Hand: A Memoir of Presidential Diplomacy*, 2003, p. 34.
94   Nolan, Janne E., *An Elusive Consensus: Nuclear Weapons and*

During the presidential campaign in 1992, candidate Clinton outlined his preference for further reductions in nuclear weapons and a comprehensive test ban agreement. At the time, he suggested that nuclear targets should be reduced to facilitate a "move to substantially lower numbers of weapons," and that "a comprehensive test ban would strengthen our vital efforts to stop the spread of nuclear weapons to other countries."[95] Immediately following the election, president-elect Clinton made it clear that he supported completion of START II before his inauguration.[96] Once in office, ratification of START II was delayed by the developing situation in the newly independent states and entry into force requirements of the first treaty. President Clinton continued to use existing processes, which included normal dialogue with President Yeltsin, however, because of the delays associated with the first treaty, formal Senate hearings for the second treaty did not begin until January 1995. The president and his senior advisors continued negotiations on ratification and the potential for a third agreement, but these efforts were ultimately unsuccessful.[97]

Although the two administrations shared positions on the first and second strategic arms reduction treaties, they differed on other nuclear weapons issues. For example, President Clinton supported a comprehensive test ban treaty during his campaign. Once in office his administration moved quickly to prevent the 15 tests authorized at the end of the existing moratorium.[98] On

---

American Security After the Cold War, 1999, pp. 35-62.

95   Arms Control Association, "Arms Control and the 1992 Election," *Arms Control Today,* 1992, retrieved November 15, 2011.

96   McManus, Doyle, "Arms Reduction Treaty Unlikely to Be Finished by End of Bush's Term: Defense: Nuclear weapons agreement is slowed by Russian requests for changes," *Los Angeles Times*, November 27, 1992.

97   Talbott, Strobe, *The Russia Hand: A Memoir of Presidential Diplomacy*, 2003, pp. 377-378.

98   In September 1992 President George H. W. Bush reluctantly signed a congressionally sponsored unilateral nuclear testing moratorium. The 10-month moratorium was an amendment to the fiscal year 1993 Energy and Water Appropriations Bill that prescribed a self-imposed halt and then

July 3, 1993, President Clinton signed Presidential Decision Directive-11, "Moratorium on Nuclear Testing" and announced to the American public that he had extended the freeze through September 1994.[99] The president went on to extend the moratorium again in March 1994, and announced his intention to negotiate a comprehensive test ban treaty in August 1995. Although the president signed the resulting Comprehensive Test Ban Treaty -- that prohibited parties from conducting any nuclear weapons test explosions -- in September 1996, the Republican controlled Senate refused to ratify it.[100] Divisive arguments concerning testing, stockpile levels, and the return of linking national missile defense to arms reduction represented differences in arms control positions. These differences became more pronounced as the post-Cold War era progressed; ultimately ending further strategic arms reduction efforts for the remainder of the Clinton administration.

CONGRESS

Within both chambers of Congress the roles of seniority and committee assignments could not be understated. The president submitted treaties to the Senate Foreign Relations Committee where they were placed on the agenda and debated before being forwarded to the full Senate. Once debate was complete, treaties must receive a two-thirds majority to pass. While the Foreign Relations Committee was in charge of treaties, the Senate Armed Services Committee was responsible for national

---

slowing of U.S. nuclear testing between the end of the moratorium on July 1, 1993 and 1996. Medalia, Jonathan, "Nuclear Weapons: Comprehensive Test Ban Treaty," *Congressional Research Service Report for Congress*, updated October 11, 2006, p. 1; White House, "Background Information: U.S. Policy on Nuclear Testing and a Comprehensive Test Ban," Office of the White House Press Secretary, July 3, 1993.

99   Clinton, William J., "The President's Radio Address," July 3, 1993.
100   Department of Energy, *United States Nuclear Tests July 1945 through September 1992,* December 2000, pp. viii-ix.

defense.[101] Senators that did not have a direct role in foreign affairs or defense looked to these committee members for expert opinion, and to their party leadership for direction. The role of seniority within Congress ensured senior officials served as committee chairs, ranking members, and chamber leadership. The absence of term limits meant senior members served over the span of multiple presidential administrations, alternating leadership roles based on party majority status.

Barry Blechman explained that Congress was involved in arms control treaties even though it did not have a direct role in the negotiation process.[102] Although divided on the second Strategic Arms Limitation Treaty, congressional leaders began to move closer in centralized support of arms reduction throughout the 1980s. As strategic arms reduction negotiations transitioned into a second administration, key political actors in the Senate from both parties were keen on completion of a new bilateral agreement with the Soviet Union. To demonstrate a collective position, the Senate submitted a resolution of support for resumption of strategic arms reduction talks. This resolution included senior members of both parties in influential party and committee positions.[103] While the resolution supported resumption of the talks, it also stated that the Senate held reservations concerning former Soviet treaty violations and reminded the president that the legislature wanted to be kept abreast of developments during the formulation process.[104] The Bush

---

101   Note the Senate Select Committee on Intelligence also had a major role in arms control verification. For more on the role of the U.S. Senate in treaties, see Congressional Research Service, *Treaties and Other International Agreements: The Role of the United States Senate*, January 2001.

102   Blechman, Barry M., *The Politics of National Security: Congress and Defense Policy*, 1990, pp. 73-77.

103   The resolution was submitted by Senator Mitchell on behalf of himself and Senators Dole, Byrd, Pell, Lugar, Nunn, Stevens, and Chafee.

104   *Congressional Record* 101st Congress (1989-1990), "Senate Resolution 149 – Relating to the Resumption of START Talks," Senate, June 21, 1989, p. S7112.

administration worked with Congress to maintain their support for the remainder of the negotiation period.

Ratification of the first Strategic Arms Reduction Treaty took place nine months after submission on October 1, 1992. Senate debates leading up to ratification centered on concerns over the newly independent states, verification, costs, previous Soviet non-compliance, and the ability for parties to expand stockpiles quickly because reserve weapons were not counted in the treaty. To address these concerns, the Senate Foreign Relations Committee added several conditions related to newly independent state observance of previous agreements, and reporting requirements for the president once the treaty entered into force. Committee debate included testimony from the Joint Chiefs of Staff, a point that Senator Claiborne Pell, Chairman of the Senate Foreign Relations Committee, emphasized during his remarks concerning committee approval of the treaty. Senator Pell noted that, "The Chiefs were unanimous and unreserved in their support for the treaty. They argued forcefully that ratification of START would enhance U.S. national security." To support his statement the Senator referenced remarks by Chairman Colin Powell describing the development process in the executive branch. General Powell shared, "that we [the Joint Chiefs of Staff] have truly been included in the negotiations, totally by Secretary Baker, by Ambassador Brooks, by Secretary Cheney and his staff, and so we have been part of the process, and I think I can speak for all my colleagues when I say we are enormously proud that we are serving at this time, when we [are] able to reduce nuclear weaponry from 11,000 roughly strategic weapons heading down toward 3,500. That is wonderful for the world, it is wonderful for this country."[105]

The general consensus in the Senate supported swift passage and implementation, which resulted in a committee vote

---

105   *Congressional Record* 102nd Congress (1991-1992), "Committee Approval of the START Treaty," Senate, July 2, 1992, pp. S9751-S9753.

of 17-0, and a final Senate vote of 93-6.[106] Quick passage and overwhelming support can be attributed to the lengthy and thorough policy development process, and the rapidly changing strategic landscape. Many Congressional stakeholders that insisted the previous administration adhered to the Strategic Arms Limitation Treaty were still in office when START was submitted to the Senate.[107] Following ratification of the initial treaty Senator Mark Warner stated, "One of the most important reasons for the Senate's overwhelming support of the START Treaty was the fact that, throughout the negotiating process, our negotiators set their standards high and negotiated with tenacity. The vital contributions to these negotiations of one true statesman, a former colleague, must never be forgotten. I am speaking of my good friend, the late Senator John Tower."[108]

Congressional stakeholders were also developing their own policies to target security concerns in the Soviet Union and its successor states. One policy used to assist with immediate concerns and START commitments was the Cooperative Threat Reduction program. In the fall of 1991, Democratic Senator Sam Nunn, Chairman of the Senate Armed Services Committee, and Democratic Congressman Les Aspin, Chairman of the House Committee on Armed Services, introduced legislation to provide emergency supplies and technical assistance to secure Soviet weapons of mass destruction. The Nunn-Aspin legislation was included with the fiscal year 1992 Defense Authorization bill,

---

106   Woolf, Amy F., "Strategic Arms Reduction Treaties (START I&II): Verification and Compliance Issues," *CRS Issue Brief*, November 22, 1996.

107   This included members of the Senate Arms Control Observers Group that had been involved with strategic arms reduction negotiations since 1985. The observer group remained in existence until its mandate was extended in 1999 to include broader national security issues. Blechman, Barry M., *The Politics of National Security: Congress and Defense Policy*, 1990, pp. 76-77; Cochran, Thad, "Lott, Daschle Announce Bipartisan National Security Working Group," Press Release, April 29, 1999.

108   *Congressional Record* 102nd Congress (1991-1992), "The START Treaty," Senate, October 5, 1992, p. S16841.

but because of stiff opposition in the Senate the attachment was removed.[109]

Shortly thereafter, Senator Nunn and Republican Senator Dick Lugar, former Chairman of the Senate Foreign Relations Committee, were briefed by Ashton Carter on the security of Soviet nuclear weapons.[110] The two senators again took up the matter but this time from a bi-partisan perspective that sought, albeit unenthusiastically, White House support. Their initial efforts resulted in an amendment to an unrelated bill that President George H. W. Bush signed on December 12, 1991. This authorization asked for $500 million to address the transportation, security, destruction, and nonproliferation of Soviet weapons of mass destruction, but when the measure left the appropriations committee it amounted to Department of Defense reprogramming authorization for up to $400 million.[111]

In early 1992, the Nunn-Lugar Program (originally the Safe, Secure Dismantlement Program that eventually became Cooperative Threat Reduction) was underway with several conditions. Legislators stipulated criteria for potential former Soviet Union countries to meet before receiving Cooperative Threat Reduction funds, retained reprogramming oversight, and required a "buy American" clause before passage. The program

---

109   Republicans were opposed to specific aspects of the initiative related to officer housing and training. Initial committee votes passed along party lines until Democratic Senator Harrison Wofford energized a general anti-foreign aid sentiment among both parties and chambers. Without congressional or presidential support, the initiative was withdrawn. Combs, Richard, "U.S. Domestic Politics and the Nunn-Lugar Program," in John M. Shields, and William C. Potter, eds., *Dismantling the Cold War: U.S. and newly independent state Perspectives on the Nunn-Lugar Cooperative Threat Reduction Program*, 1997, pp. 42-45.

110   Ashton Carter and his colleagues had recently completed a detailed study of the issue presented in *Soviet Fission: Control of the Nuclear Arsenal in a Disintegrating Soviet Union.*

111   Combs, Richard, "U.S. Domestic Politics and the Nunn-Lugar Program," in John M. Shields, and William C. Potter, eds., *Dismantling the Cold War: U.S. and newly independent state Perspectives on the Nunn-Lugar Cooperative Threat Reduction Program*, 1997, pp. 42-45.

was financed and executed by the Department of Defense but because there was not an existing organization to begin implementation immediately, it took until March 1992, before the Assistant to the Secretary of Defense for Atomic Energy was assigned responsibility for its execution. In January 1993, the assistant secretary delegated execution and management of Cooperative Threat Reduction to the Defense Nuclear Agency. The agency completed its first Cooperative Threat Reduction project later that year, but the initial slow start and congressional restrictions prevented officials from obligating authorized reprogramming funds by the end of the fiscal year. This failure exposed Cooperative Threat Reduction to early opponents such as champion of the America first platform Democratic Senator Harris Wofford, and almost led to discontinuation of the fledgling program after the Republicans returned to the majority in 1995.[112]

Arms control proponents within Congress advocated further strategic nuclear reductions as soon as possible, while more cautious political actors supported finalizing the first treaty

---

112   Early Cooperative Threat Reduction efforts were "criticized from all sides" according to Gloria Duffy. For example, Congress argued that the program did not produce solid dismantlement and denuclearization results and that Cooperative Threat Reduction funding allowed Russia to invest limited defense funds on other programs. U.S. partner corporations and former Soviet Union participants complained the program was too slow and that funding was inadequate. When the Republicans assumed the majority in the House and Senate they attached funding releases contingent on biological and chemical weapons certifications, and reduced overall funding for the program. Anti-Cooperative Threat Reduction efforts in Congress were long party lines, and represented the adversarial relationship of the period. Duffy, Gloria, "Cooperative Threat Reduction in Perspective," and Richard Combs, "U.S. Domestic Politics and the Nunn-Lugar Program," in John M. Shields, and William C. Potter, eds., *Dismantling the Cold War: U.S. and NIS Perspectives on the Nunn-Lugar Cooperative Threat Reduction Program*, 1997, pp. 31-36 and 43-51; Defense Threat Reduction Agency, *Defense's Nuclear Agency 1947-1997: Defense Threat Reduction Agency History Series*, 2002, p. 300.

before moving on.[113] Uncertainty following the failed coup in the Soviet Union and the transition to the Yeltsin regime provided a unifying catalyst for these diverging opinions. Although Congress was opposed to the tactics employed by the Bush administration concerning his presidential nuclear initiatives, it was prepared to support continued arms reduction negotiations. Loss of the 1992 elections confined President Bush to four years in office and re-introduced worries that a change in administrations would cause negotiation delays similar to the first treaty. In the final months of the George H. W. Bush presidency, lawmakers such as Republican Senator Richard Lugar stressed the importance of finishing START II before the administration left office.[114] Congressional and incoming administration support, combined with a sense of urgency within the Yeltsin administration, facilitated signature of the treaty on January 3, 1993.

Hearings in the Senate Foreign Relations Committee initially began in 1992, but were postponed until the second treaty was finalized and entry into force requirements were met on the first treaty.[115] Hearings resumed in 1995, but by this time the second Strategic Arms Reduction Treaty faced two major problems: 1) the deteriorating executive and legislative branch relationship, and 2) the association of the treaty with other items such as missile defense. Senator Strom Thurmond described this changing domestic and international climate in the following way:

---

113   *Congressional Record* 102nd Congress (1991-1992), "START Is No Place to Stop," Senate, September 10, 1991, p. S12680, and "The START Treaty Must Be Postponed," Senate, October 25, 1991, p. S15248.
114   McManus, Doyle, "Arms Reduction Treaty Unlikely to Be Finished by End of Bush's Term: Defense: Nuclear weapons agreement is slowed by Russian requests for changes," *Los Angeles Times*, November 27, 1992.
115   Senator Pell and other committee members were concerned about the impact of the newly independent states on the Strategic Arms Reduction Treaty process, choosing to wait until issues with the four new nuclear weapons states were resolved before progressing with discussions related to the second treaty. *Congressional Record* 103rd Congress (1993-1994), "START II Treaty," Senate, May 12, 1993, p. S5803.

Let us be clear about what does and does not threaten START II. START II will be ratified by the United States. The treaty enjoys overwhelming support in the Senate; there is no threat to it here. In Russia, however, there are many groups opposed to START II, including factions in the military and many hard-line nationalists. These Russians who oppose START II do so for reasons having nothing to do with anything in our conference report [1996 Defense Authorization Conference Report].

But these same Russian opponents of START II have found all kinds of convenient excuses to justify their real objections, including opposition to the expansion of NATO and United States policy in Bosnia. What the administration has done by arguing that the ballistic missile defense provisions in this conference report threaten START II is to create yet another excuse for Russian opponents of START II. Those who have already decided to oppose START II will simply repeat the administration's rhetoric.[116]

Despite escalating statements linking START II to missile defense and other divisive issues, the Senate Foreign Relations Committee voted 18-0 in December 1995, to forward the treaty to the full Senate for consideration. The Senate voted 87-4 to ratify the treaty one month later with similar conditions and declarations as the first treaty.[117] This abbreviated timeline between committee hearings and Senate ratification highlighted the support that existed for START II in early 1996. When the treaty stalled in the Duma, Congress attempted to encourage Russian ratification by restricting the United States from going below the levels prescribed in the first treaty until Russia had done so.[118] The maneuver failed to have the desired effect and later restricted President Clinton from making unilateral reductions.[119]

---

116   *Congressional Record* 104th Congress (1995-1996), "Treaty with the Russian Federation on Further Reduction and Limitation of Strategic Offensive Arms (The START II Treaty)," Senate, December 22, 1995, p. S19206-S19209.
117   Ibid.
118   *National Defense Authorization Act for Fiscal Year 1998* (P.L. 105-85), Sec. 1302.
119   Talbott, Strobe, *The Russia Hand: A Memoir of Presidential*

Congressional support enabled the Strategic Arms Reduction Treaties to follow incremental development according to established rules and channels, but disagreements over issues such as nuclear testing, weapons, and missile defense threatened to derail further reductions. Concerns over stockpile reliability in the absence of nuclear testing arose under President Clinton, prompting his announcement of the stockpile stewardship program. Early requirements simply directed the program "to ensure the preservation of the core intellectual and technical competence of the U.S. in nuclear weapons."[120] Subsequent stockpile stewardship program development by the Department of Energy led to a more detailed department report in 1995, and further revisions described in a 1999 review report.[121] According to these reports, the Department of Energy would use previous data, new non-nuclear data, and computer and advanced technologies to verify the reliability of the stockpile without testing, while weapons experts used modifications and refurbishments to extend the life of stockpile warheads without developing new weapons. The complex retained the mission to return quickly to testing if directed and took on the task of tritium production for stockpile maintenance. The stockpile stewardship program provided funding for consolidation, maintenance and updates while defining a primary post-Cold War nuclear weapons mission for the complex.

Many Republican congressional leaders like House National Security Committee Chairman Floyd Spence did not agree with the administration's position on nuclear weapons. In an October 1996 report, *The Clinton Administration and Nuclear Stockpile Stewardship: Erosion by Design*, Representative Spence's committee declared that the Clinton administration had left the country vulnerable in a risky and uncertain international

---

Diplomacy, 2003, p. 376.
120   *National Defense Authorization Act for Fiscal Year 1994* (P.L. 103-160), Sec. 3138.
121   Ritchie, Nick, *U.S. Nuclear Weapons Policy after the Cold War: Russians, "rogues," and domestic division*, 2009, pp. 49-51.

security environment because of its systematic neglect of the nuclear weapons complex.[122] Disagreements in Congress and between the legislative and executive branches persisted into the next administration, solidifying nuclear weapons as a recurring hot-button issue in post-Cold War nuclear defense politics.

Policy development related to the strategic arms reduction treaties in Congress followed existing channels in accordance with established rules. The treaties were received by the Senate Foreign Relations Committee and debated in the three applicable committees responsible for foreign relations, defense, and intelligence. These committees received expert testimony that included Department of State and Defense witnesses. Internal committee debates focused on treaty specifics, and on whether the agreements should be rejected. In response to committee concerns, the Senate Foreign Relations Committee placed several conditions and declarations on each treaty that did not require re-negotiation. In the case of threat reduction, Congress also used existing authorities to originate complimentary legislation concerning acute security concerns within the former Soviet Union. Initial threat reduction efforts, along with several other nuclear weapons issues, highlighted the growing rift between the Democratic and Republican parties over nuclear defense matters.

THE BUREAUCRACY

The Secretary of State served as the principal advisor to the president for arms control and was responsible for senior treaty negotiations at the ministerial level.[123] Secretary Baker preferred to receive information through his principal deputies and was only accompanied by State Department advisors at his meetings. This was a departure from previous secretaries such as George Shultz who assembled interagency groups for this type of senior

---

122   Spence, Floyd D., *The Clinton Administration and Nuclear Stockpile Stewardship: Erosion by Design*, October 30, 1996.
123   Rowny, Edward L., *It Takes One to Tango*, 1992, pp. 214-217.

negotiation.[124] Interagency delegations comprising representatives from applicable organizations were responsible for daily arms control negotiations.[125] These routine arms control talks took place in Geneva under the direction of an appointed chief negotiator.[126] The State Department's organizational stake in senior and routine arms control negotiations revolved around perceived relevance by the president and Congress.[127] State's resource concerns were related to its individual budget and structure. The department did not have an organizational interest in the preservation of defense infrastructure or systems. Responsibility for these tangible United States concessions was a function of the Department of Defense.[128]

Political appointees and career civil servants served in the delegations. These human resources represented multiple interests. Morton Halperin and Priscilla Clapp examined the personal interests of senior political appointees with pre-existing partisan views and connections, and career civil servants with single organization outlooks. In arms control, senior political appointees have a history of expertise and opinions that may

---

124   Ibid., p. 237.
125   Leitner, Peter M., *Decontrolling Strategic Technology, 1990-1992: Creating the Military Threats of the 21ˢᵗ Century*, 1995, pp. 104-118.
126   The president may also appoint additional advisors, such as the "Special Advisor to the President and Secretary of State for Arms Control Matters," a post that Ambassador Edward Rowny held under Presidents Reagan and Bush. For more on strategic arms reduction negotiations, to include Soviet positions, see Kerry M. Kartchner, *Negotiating START: Strategic Arms Reduction Talks and the Quest for Stability*, 1992.
127   During the Cold War negotiations continued regardless of delayed outcomes, but different expectations during the post-Cold War period resulted in department reorganization and changes in discussion and agreement formats. Between 1961 and 1999 the Arms Control and Disarmament Agency was a semi-autonomous organization under the State Department. Boese, Wade, "State Department Reorganization Advances," *Arms Control Today*, September 2005; Rust, Dean, "Reorganization Run Amok: State Department's WMD Effort Weakened," *Arms Control Today*, June 2006.
128   Halperin, Morton H., and Priscilla A. Clapp, *Bureaucratic Politics and Foreign Policy*, 2ⁿᵈ edition 2006, p. 56.

not always have coincided with administration policy. For these actors, loyalty to outside groups such as policy institutes may have been stronger than loyalty to the administration, and in other cases loyalty to a political party or the administration may have been stronger than loyalty to the organization, namely the Department of State.[129]

Career civil servants, on the other hand, were motivated by the potential for promotion. Halperin and Clapp argued that, "the desire for promotion leads career officials to support the interests of the organization of which they are a member, since they recognize that in large measure, promotion depends on being seen as advancing the interests of the organization." Each department had a distinct culture that attracted different personalities and backgrounds. Once members bought into the group, or a sub-group such as arms control, and developed technical and bureaucratic expertise, they were likely to support their organization's position. This train of thought often extended into the existence of low opinions of other organizations that displayed different cultures, missions, approaches and positions. While officials may have perceived their organization and mission as vital, they may have seen other organizations as having a negative impact on national security. This tension was present between the arms control and nuclear war-fighting communities.[130]

The Department of Defense held strong actor positions concerning nuclear weapons because they represented the organizational essence for some parts of the department.[131] During the Reagan and Bush administrations it was not clear that the Soviet Union would completely dissolve. Because the threat remained intact, the nuclear weapons community fought to retain a large stockpile and modernization programs to service existing targeting requirements. When this traditional threat began to fade, the nuclear weapons community continued to advocate large

---

129   Ibid., pp. 85-89.
130   Ibid.
131   Ibid., p. 27.

numbers of warheads and delivery vehicles and designed new requirements for nuclear technologies.

From an individual service perspective the U.S. Air Force and the Navy had the most to lose from nuclear reductions. The modern Air Force was formed in the nuclear age. Strategic bombers and land-based ballistic missiles defined two specific missions that facilitated the growth and sustainment of the Air Force. Without these missions the Air Force would have to rely on strategic conventional bombing and fighter support to justify manning, infrastructure and budget requirements. The Navy also had a significant stake in strategic nuclear weapons. The submarine launched ballistic missile capability was the cornerstone of the modern submarine force.[132] While these vessels could be retrofitted, the prestige and resource justification associated with nuclear weapon delivery far exceeded other possible supporting missions.

The Army had a stake concerning sub-strategic nuclear weapons, but these tactical munitions and other supporting security roles were not the primary justification for annual resources and did not define the organization's essence. Internally, the Joint Staff had already studied tactical nuclear weapons and, according to Colin Powell, concluded that the United States should "get rid of the small, artillery-fired nukes because they were trouble-prone, expensive to modernize, and irrelevant in the present world of highly accurate conventional munitions."[133] But the Joint Chiefs and Defense Department leadership were not prepared to unilaterally forfeit sub-strategic capabilities while the Soviet Union was still a threat. The Defense Department had also examined the long-standing single integrated operational

---

132   The Trident submarine and missile program is an example of the long-term weapons procurement process. Lauren Holland notes that this controversial replacement for earlier designs spanned every presidential administration since Kennedy. Holland, Lauren, *Weapons Under Fire*, 1997, pp. 60-61.

133   Powell, Colin L., *My American Journey*, 1995, pp. 540.

plan for nuclear targeting.[134] This work would eventually lead to a complete redirection of nuclear targeting, but in the period between 1989 and 1991, planners were not confident enough in the course of the evolving strategic landscape to drastically change existing requirements.[135]

Negotiating delegations executed the interagency position approved by the president and solidified high-level agreements resulting from secretary and presidential commitments. Strategic arms reduction negotiations focused on issues ranging from systems and downloaded warhead limits to inspection, elimination and conversion procedures. The final seven hundred page document resulting from the first strategic arms reduction talks attested to the level of detail comprising the bureaucratic portion of negotiations.[136] The level of detail in the treaty represented the Cold War relationship between the superpowers. This continuity in early post-Cold War negotiation strategies was a by-product of the fact that political appointees and career officials from the previous period continued to hold office across the bureaucracy. For example, chief negotiators during the strategic arms reduction talks were high-profile Cold War officials such as former Lieutenant General Edward Rowny and former Senator John Tower.[137] Both served under Reagan, but Tower was instrumental in establishing Senate buy-in and Rowny remained on as a special advisor to the president and

---

134   Cheney, Dick, with Liz Cheney, *In My Time: A Personal and Political Memoir*, 2011, pp. 232-233.

135   Powell, Colin L., *My American Journey*, 1995, pp. 540-541.

136   Although highly scripted and restrictive, each side followed the letter of the treaty until it expired in 2009. Interview with Defense Threat Reduction Agency, Strategic Arms Reduction Treaty Mission Commander Keith Sloan, January 29, 2010.

137   Richard Burt and Linton Brooks served as chief strategic arms reduction negotiators under President Bush. Edward Rowny, conservative arms control advisor to Nixon and Reagan resigned in 1990, much like he had done in protest to the second Strategic Arms Limitation Treaty in 1979. McCartney, James, "Bush Arms-control Advisor Resigns," *The Philadelphia Inquirer*, April 27, 1990.

Secretary of State during the Bush administration. The level of influence from chief negotiators and special advisors such as Rowny was restricted under President Bush as Secretary of State James Baker assumed the role of lead arms control advisor to the president.[138]

Strategic arms reduction talks followed a sporadic schedule based on several external factors related to differences in country positions, internal Soviet politics, and other more pressing foreign policy matters for the United States, such as the first Gulf War. Arms control talks gradually shifted from the centerpiece of foreign policy to a required task while both countries remained committed to earlier negotiating positions.[139] This inability to modify positions with the developing strategic landscape was based largely on key advisor views and military reluctance to forfeit capabilities. As a result, Secretary Baker functioned as lead negotiator for the most contentious issues, with assistance from President Bush when required.

Although senior-level negotiations were required to complete the treaty, the overall process followed standard interagency development with lengthy analysis and the aggregation of stakeholder positions. The resulting positions formed the bottom-line for U.S. negotiators with contentious points elevated to senior officials and discussed within the National Security Council interagency structure. For time sensitive issues the process was abbreviated with separate meetings and conference calls between the president, the national security advisor, the Secretary of Defense, the Chairman of the Joint Chiefs, and the Secretary of State.

The long, inclusive interagency process helped mute opposition from the Joint Chiefs of Staff to forfeit new and existing weapon systems. National Security Directive-40, "Decisions on START issues," depicted the level of input down to specific

---

138   Rowny, Edward L., *It Takes One to Tango*, 1992, pp. 214-218.
139   Beschloss, Michael R., and Strobe Talbott, *At the Highest Levels: The Inside Story of the End of the Cold War*, 1993, pp. 181 and 115-123.

systems, armaments, and ranges.[140] The nuclear weapons community provided analysis and positions concerning U.S. weapons. In the case of START, the United States and the Soviet Union preferred to retain large numbers of operational systems and exclude reserve and sub-strategic nuclear weapons from the scope of the treaty. By assuming this final position the support of both militaries was possible because each would retain 6,000 operational strategic weapons and the funding to maintain large active and inactive stockpiles.

The lengthy process of the first treaty gave way to the abbreviated development of the second. Three major factors influencing the formulation of START II included: 1) the dissolution of the Soviet Union, 2) a significant American military drawdown following the first Gulf War, and 3) the pending transition in U.S. administrations. Instead of normal interagency procedures, the second treaty originated from a closed discussion of senior advisors to the president without in-depth analysis to support recommendations. The National Security Council staff, the Department of State, and the Department of Defense were included, but in light of the developing situation in Russia following the unsuccessful coup against Mikhail Gorbachev, the president chose to manage the new direction in arms reductions himself. Secretary of Defense Cheney argued against further reductions during initial meetings, but was overridden by the president. As a result, the Department of Defense was given several days, not months or years, to draft reduction recommendations that the president intended to announce by the end of September 1991.[141]

Following President Bush's nuclear initiative speech and discussions with Soviet and Russian leaders, it was the responsibility of the State Department to negotiate and draft supporting

---

140   Bush, George H. W., "National Security Directive-40: Decisions on START Issues," May 14, 1990.
141   Beschloss, Michael R., and Strobe Talbott, *At the Highest Levels: The Inside Story of the End of the Cold War*, 1993, pp. 442-446.

documents. By June 1992, the negotiators had drafted a joint statement on further reductions for Presidents Bush and Yeltsin to sign. The U.S delegation produced a draft treaty a month later, but the Russians did not offer their version until November. In August, James Baker shifted to become the White House Chief of Staff and assist with the presidential re-election campaign while his former deputy, Lawrence Eagleburger, assumed responsibilities as Secretary of State. The shift in focus to the election and differences in position over downloading timelines for multiple independently-targetable vehicle warheads between the Russians and the U.S. Defense Department threatened completion of START II.[142] Several high-level meetings and statements of support from the new administration facilitated completion of the second treaty despite Department of Defense reservations.[143]

Although President George H. W. Bush initiated unprecedented reductions in strategic and sub-strategic arms, the nuclear weapons community fought to continue their life's work in the post-Cold War period. Department of Defense experts turned to regional actors, weapons of mass destruction, and hardened, deeply-buried targets to justify research and development on specialized nuclear weapons. These new nuclear requirements spawned a serious of studies and ultimately general endorsement from outgoing Secretary of Defense Dick Cheney for theater nuclear strategies.[144] During the change in administrations, the nuclear weapons community requested and received funding in the fiscal year 1993 budget for research and development of low-yield (5 Kiloton or less) nuclear programs.[145] In response

142   Talbott, Strobe, *The Russia Hand: A Memoir of Presidential Diplomacy*, 2003, p. 34.
143   Department of State, "Strategic Arms Reduction II Chronology," U.S. Arms Control and Disarmament Agency, December 13, 1995, Retrieved November 13, 2011.
144   Department of Defense, *Defense Strategy for the 1990s: The Regional Defense Strategy*, January 1993, p. 11.
145   Arkin, William M., "Those Loveable Little Bombs," *Bulletin of the*

to this executive endorsement, Congress passed the Spratt-Furse amendment to prevent research and development of new low-yield weapons.[146]

The nuclear weapons community continued existing policies of flexible response and extended deterrence into the Clinton administration while multiple studies were conducted to establish the direction of nuclear weapons strategy in the post-Cold War era.[147] In 1994, the Nuclear Posture Review was one of the national security reviews that sought to define emerging threats and design an updated strategic force structure and strategy to address them.[148] The review acknowledged that nuclear weapons were "playing a smaller role in U.S. security than at any other time in the nuclear age," but it fell short of anticipated conclusions based on former Secretary of Defense Aspin's nuclear positions.[149] The 1994 Nuclear Posture Review process highlighted internal Department of Defense differences. Aggregate

---

Atomic Scientists, July/August 1993, pp. 23-24.

146 Spratt-Furse remained the subject of debate a decade later during the George W. Bush administration's efforts to develop robust nuclear earth penetrator weapons for the previously stated hardened, deeply-buried target requirement. Medalia, Jonathan, "Nuclear Earth Penetrator Weapons," *Congressional Research Service Report for Congress*, January 27, 2003, p. 3.

147 In the years since Clinton left office the lack of emphasis on nuclear deterrence from the president himself has been portrayed as questionable at best. These claims reinforce the Deutch commission finding that, "Presidential leadership is essential in combating proliferation" and that "No organizational structure can overcome a lack of commitment at the top." Nuclear Threat Initiative, "Clinton Lost Nuclear Launch Codes, Retired General Says," *Global Security Newswire*, October 21, 2010; Ambinder, Marc, "Why Clinton's Losing the Nuclear Biscuit Was Really, Really Bad," *The Atlantic*, October 22, 2010; Deutch, John M., "Combating Proliferation of Weapons of Mass Destruction," Commission Report, July 14, 1999, p. 5.

148 In the end the Nuclear Posture Review still identified Russia and the newly independent state as the requirement for the hedge force. Deutch, John M., "Briefing on Results of the Nuclear Posture Review," Hearing September 22, 1994, p. 11-15.

149 Department of Defense, *Annual Report to the President and the Congress*, February 1995, Part IV: Defense Initiatives, Nuclear Posture Review.

assumptions were often made about nuclear weapons topics, but generalizations overlooked differences in arms control, threat reduction, and nuclear war-fighting circles. The approach to each were distinct with arms control locked into formal agreements that attempted to minimize perceived utility, while threat reduction stressed the importance of cooperation and tangible reductions in threat technologies and expertise. Nuclear war-fighters on the other hand espoused the necessity of a viable nuclear stockpile and continued to advocate for integrated conventional and nuclear contingency plans based on uncertainty in Russia.

The Clinton-era Nuclear Posture Review process reflected the distinct separation of intra-departmental actor priorities between political appointees aligned with progressive reduction mindsets and career departmental actors dedicated to the retention of a robust nuclear stockpile.[150] The administration looked at the review as an internal Department of Defense "exercise in political-military analysis, an effort to match the design of forces with the political objectives that nuclear deterrence was meant to uphold."[151] But the process that actually transpired was characterized by internal department politics and bureaucratic maneuvering, which enlisted the assistance of congressional actors.[152]

After continued frustration with the official Pentagon working groups, Assistant Secretary of Defense for International Security Policy Ashton Carter appointed Lieutenant Commander Leo Mackay, his military assistant, and Steve Fetter, a University of Maryland professor active in arms control discussions, to conduct the alternative analysis.[153] This, and other incidents,

---

150   Nolan, Janne E., *An Elusive Consensus: Nuclear Weapons and American Security After the Cold War*, 1999, pp. 35-62.
151   Les Aspin Nuclear Posture Review description as presented by Janne Nolan. Ibid, p.39
152   Deutch, John M., "Briefing on Results of the Nuclear Posture Review," Hearing September 22, 1994, pp. 26-60.
153   Mackay completed his doctoral dissertation on nuclear strategy under Ashton Carter at Harvard University, and Fetter had a background

resulted in senior generals from the combatant commands and joint staff formally opposing Carter's actions. The unified opposition was extended to key congressional actors such as Senator Strom Thurmond, and other Republican senators such as Conrad Burns, Malcolm Wallop, Alan Simpson, and Dirk Kempthorne who eventually engaged the president directly to lobby for the retention of a robust nuclear stockpile.[154]

The fissure between political appointees and career officials contributed to the review's results being driven by a professional bureaucracy comprising military officers and career civil servants representing historic programs located across multiple congressional districts. Ultimately, examinations of alternative targeting strategies and force postures conducted by Assistant Secretary Carter's unofficial appointees were discarded as the professional bureaucracy asserted itself. In the end, unified resistance from career actors backed by congressional support was not matched by senior Defense Department officials.[155]

This section outlined a policy environment within which major stakeholders -- the President and Congress -- shared preferences related to reducing strategic nuclear weapons holdings. The processes associated with the formulation of START and START II generally followed traditional approaches to the development of arms control treaties. The incoming George H.

---

in physics. Nolan, Janne E., *An Elusive Consensus: Nuclear Weapons and American Security After the Cold War*, 1999, p. 52.

154   Ibid., p. 122.

155   The position of maintaining a large nuclear hedge stockpile characterized differences between arms control and nuclear war-fighting proponents. The Clinton era hedge policy equated to the U.S. reserve force which was not accounted for under the provisions of START. For example, while START defined operational limits at 6,000, the United States and Russia were permitted to retain as many non-operational and tactical warheads as they wished. This additional U.S. strategic force allowed the nuclear weapons community to justify resources based a much larger number of nuclear weapons than those accounted for under START. Deutch, John M., "Briefing on Results of the Nuclear Posture Review," Hearing September 22, 1994, pp. 52-56.

W. Bush administration conducted a systematic review that led to little change in approach. Members of the bureaucracy calculated and negotiated reductions with periodic presidential involvement. Negotiators kept Congress informed to a reasonable degree. Communication and shared goals facilitated signature and ratification, but a rapidly changing environment in the former Soviet Union introduced several new considerations to the customary process. But even with the shift to multilateral agreements that accounted for newly independent states and internal maneuverings by President Bush concerning unilateral reductions, the process through to ratification for both treaties remained collegial. At face value this description might imply adherence to the rational policy model, but closer examination demonstrated that differences existed in strategic nuclear weapons positions and these remained beyond initial policy decisions.

BARRIERS TO CHANGE

Several questions concerning the impact of shared attitudes, framework, and organizational constraints arose from the foregoing section.

- What impact did shared attitudes play in policy decisions?
- To what extent were stakeholders free to transform arms control direction in the absence of the Soviet Union?
- What organizational constraints impeded collective action options in the face of a changing strategic landscape?

Graham Allison and Morton Halperin provided several examples of shared Cold War attitudes such as "the United States should act to halt the spread of Communism" or that "only force will deter the Chinese from aggression."[156] Allison and Halperin

156   Allison, Graham T., and Morton H. Halperin, "Bureaucratic Politics: A Paradigm and Some Policy Implications," *World Politics,* Vol. 24, Spring

argued that most stakeholders of the period accepted these attitudes, and that these common images provided the basis for corresponding views of the national interest. Morton Halperin and Priscilla Clapp added that an additional view shared during the Cold War was "nuclear war would be a great disaster and must be avoided," but that there was a period following the Cold War "in which there was not a single set of images held by most participants."[157] They offer that this changed perspective after September 11, 2001 when the shared image that "the post-Cold War liberalization of trade in advanced technologies has facilitated access of poor nations and forces of evil to some of the most destructive military power available, including nuclear, chemical and biological materials" emerged.[158] In post-Cold War nuclear defense, did the major stakeholders share the attitude that strategic nuclear weapons must be reduced? While this attitude could certainly be argued to have been the case for the presidential administrations, many congressional members, and most State Department officials, applying this image to the Defense Department, despite formal testimony by the Joint Chiefs of Staff, would be erroneous.

FRAMEWORK

Established interagency policy formulation was a deliberate process designed to allow all stakeholders adequate opportunities to establish researched and coordinated positions. This process facilitated the aggregation of individual, organization, and issue coalition positions that would ideally lead to unitary policy outcomes. In crisis situations this process was abbreviated, but in steady state policy development for issues such as

1972, p. 56.
157   Halperin, Morton H., and Priscilla A. Clapp, *Bureaucratic Politics and Foreign Policy*, 2nd edition 2006, pp. 9-11.
158   Ibid.

arms control there was much less latitude for policymakers to act. In the case of strategic arms reduction, each administration was highly restricted. Even with the example of President Bush's nuclear initiatives, opponents used time, alternate action channels, and group coalitions to reduce the impact on nuclear weapon stakeholders.

The Constitution prescribed rules for treaties. President Bush followed constitutional requirements for both strategic arms reduction treaties while the administration used established interagency procedures to formulate the first treaty and abbreviated measures to negotiate and finalize signature of the second treaty. The same rules and action channels applied to the Cold War and post-Cold War periods. While the Bush administration attempted to review and reorient arms control, existing rules and action channels produced similar proposals to existing efforts. Process continuation that leveraged Reagan era efforts facilitated support from stakeholders but limited progress. Instead of a new approach to arms reduction that accounted for a rapidly evolving security environment, the Bush administration was initially content to finalize multiyear negotiations. It was Congress that initiated a departure from traditional bilateral arms control, when several influential members used rules that permit policy origination within the legislature to authorize the Cooperative Threat Reduction program. As a result, threat reduction policy was a congressional response to former Soviet Union security and arms reduction treaty adherence concerns voiced during ratification.

President Bush was less transparent with the announcement of the initiatives that would lead to the second Strategic Arms Reduction Treaty. This approach was not in the inclusive spirit of the process but it did not violate established rules. While the U.S. Senate eventually ratified the second treaty, several actions indicated the lack of a unified national position on arms reduction. The shift to regional justification and new low-yield designs by the bureaucracy prompted the Spratt-Furse amendment to the 1994 Defense Authorization bill. This amendment prohibited the research and development of low-yield nuclear weapons. But, in the same year, the bureaucracy validated the existing nuclear posture through adept maneuverings between career Defense Department officials and congressional champions. The final example related to language in the 1998 Defense Authorization bill that prohibited the president from unilaterally reducing U.S. strategic forces. This procedure forced President Clinton to follow prescribed rules concerning treaties once START II had stalled in the Russian Duma.

The continuance of rules and action channels limited the incorporation of new approaches to arms reduction. The rules concerning treaties prevented a single branch from advancing uncoordinated policy. Long serving stakeholders provided continuity and were able to use expanded rules and alternate action channels to continue debates beyond policy decisions. Although statements regarding the ratification of both treaties implied a unified position, the Clinton era nuclear posture review and restrictive nuclear weapon legislation suggested that not all stakeholders shared the view that strategic nuclear weapons must be reduced.

CONSTRAINTS

It is clear that norms influenced the lack of a shared U.S. government attitude concerning arms reduction. Eric Mlyn argued that, "U.S. policymakers widely perceived that nuclear weapons helped deter the Soviets in Europe and other areas of U.S. interests."[159] He maintained that this conviction has continued to drive U.S. nuclear weapons policy following the Cold War. Policy was developed by the same stakeholders during both periods that followed earlier nuclear weapon norms despite

---

159   Mlyn, Eric, "U.S. Nuclear Policy and the End of the Cold War," in T.V. Paul, Richard J. Harknett, and James J. Wirtz, eds., *The Absolute Weapon Revisited: Nuclear Arms and the Emerging International Order*, 2000, pp. 206-207.

a radically transformed strategic landscape. Indeed, debates over missile defense, accounting practices, and mutual reductions carried forward into the post-Cold War era.

Arguments concerning the coupling of arms reductions to the ABM Treaty threatened to end talks under President Bush, and returned again to prevent Russian ratification during the Clinton administration. A more technical norm that related to accounting for delivery systems instead of warheads also proved to be an entrenched principle for senior actors such as national security advisor Brent Scowcroft, but in hindsight the question arose whether this detail should have been pivotal to treaty completion?[160] An emphasis on bilateral reductions also remained during the post-Cold War administrations. President Bush's unilateral nuclear initiatives challenged this norm but the bureaucracy hardened post-Cold War nuclear positions, and Congress ensured his successor was not at liberty to replicate these actions by shifting bilateral reductions from a norm to a rule.

Given the pervasiveness of norms and the longevity of stakeholders, the amount of policy flexibility afforded a president is limited. While the president is restricted to a maximum of two, four-year terms, there is no comparable limit on the other stakeholders. Congressmen may remain in office for an indefinite period provided they continue to win re-election; career civil servants and military officers serve in the bureaucracy for decades; and political appointees routinely rotate in and out of office with their party.[161] As a result deep seated nuclear norms within the

---

160   For more on the nuances of scientists serving in diplomatic roles, see Robert Gilpin, "Scientists as Diplomats," in U.S. Senate Committee on Government Operations, *Negotiation and Statecraft: A Selection of Readings*, 1970; and Harold Karan Jacobson, and Eric Stein, *Diplomats, Scientists, and Politicians: The United States and the Nuclear Test Ban Negotiations*, 1966.
161   Non-governmental and academic experts are important actors not addressed in this chapter. These external actors represented by Bernard Brodie or Albert Wohlstetter often influence nuclear defense arguments beyond a single lifetime. James Wilson offered that the average time in office for political appointees was two years. Wilson, James Q., *Bureaucracy: What Government Agencies Do and Why They Do It*, 2nd edition 2000, pp.

government, according to Eric Mlyn, can only be changed in two ways. Either those that have been around nuclear issues for decades can "change the way they think," or eventually they will be replaced by "new faces."[162] In regard to the second option, the introduction of new actors was influenced by prior education in existing norms and organizational affiliation, so even then, norms and positions continued on with the next generation.

Paul Pierson offered that the broadest version of the path dependent concept "refers to the causal relevance of preceding stages in a temporal sequence," but a universally accepted social science definition has remained elusive.[163] Authors such as Pierson and Scott Page argued for refinement of the idea, but it is often referenced simply as "history matters."[164] Or, to be slightly more precise, history continued to influence contemporary decisions, even if past circumstances were no longer applicable.[165] This last definition offered potential insight into post-Cold War nuclear defense policy development. Organizational constraints in the form of inventories, existing programs, expertise, and doctrine were other areas that Allison and Halperin emphasized in bureaucratic politics.[166] These areas restricted bureaucratic recommendations and actions to current capabilities and proven approaches that benefited the organization. Restrictions, as

---

197-200.

162   Mlyn, Eric, "U.S. Nuclear Policy and the End of the Cold War," in T.V. Paul, Richard J. Harknett, and James J. Wirtz, eds., *The Absolute Weapon Revisited: Nuclear Arms and the Emerging International Order*, 2000, pp. 206-207.

163   Pierson, Paul, "Increasing Returns, Path Dependence, and the Study of Politics," *The American Political Science Review*, Vol. 94, No. 2, June 2000, p. 252.

164   For more information on emerging types of path dependence see Scott E. Page, "Path Dependence," *Quarterly Journal of Political Science*, Vol. 1, 2006, pp. 87-115.

165   Mahoney, James, "Path dependence in historical sociology," *Theory and Society*, Vol. 28, 2000, pp. 508-548.

166   Allison, Graham T., and Morton H. Halperin, "Bureaucratic Politics: A Paradigm and Some Policy Implications," *World Politics*, Vol. 24, Spring 1972, p. 55.

suggested by path dependence theory, may have remained even when previous circumstances were no longer relevant to contemporary concerns.

While norms highlighted the impact of precedence and paradigms in policy development, actor positions were often driven by more tangible considerations. The most notable example in this study came from the Department of Defense. In this case, the Defense Department continued to push for retention of large numbers of operational and reserve nuclear weapons after the transition to the George H. W. Bush administration and later during the shift to the post-Cold War era. During initial strategic arms reduction negotiations the department sought to separate cruise missiles and new weapons systems while they continued to temper reductions by excluding references to sub-strategic and reserve weapons. These omissions allowed the department to maintain a minimum extended deterrence posture in Europe, and to justify large maintenance requirements for the total stockpile in excess of 10,000 weapons despite targeted reductions to 3,000-3,500 strategic warheads under the second treaty.[167]

The actor position espoused by the Department of Defense brought security based arguments into question, while sustained efforts demonstrate the various action channels available for the bureaucracy to develop favorable policy outcomes. If the first and second strategic arms treaties represented unitary policy decisions, why did Congress and the bureaucracy continue to offer conflicting policy options through various action channels? In the case of congressional limitations on unilaterally lowering U.S. strategic nuclear weapons below Strategic Arms Reduction Treaty levels, why did the Congress use the levels of the first treaty instead of the much lower levels of the second? The overall formulation process associated with arms reduction presented in this first case study reflected bureaucratic politics theory before, during, and after policy development.

---

167   U.S. Department of Energy, "Size of the U.S. Nuclear Stockpile and Annual Dismantlements," Office of Classification, May 6, 2010.

CONCLUSION

This chapter set out to examine how and why U.S. nuclear defense policy evolved following the Cold War. The strategic arms reduction study depicted a continuance of Cold War efforts. During the transition between periods, stakeholders adhered to existing rules and norms focused on negotiation of a bilateral agreement anchored in equivalence. Initial policy decisions produced an incremental reduction of strategic weapons that was obsolete before the treaty was ratified. Despite this obsolescence, follow-on efforts during the Bush and Clinton administrations did not reach final ratification. Totals prescribed in the first Strategic Arms Reduction Treaty represented a shift away from nuclear war-fighting stockpiles, but they did not explain why the United States chose to retain large numbers of operational and reserve nuclear weapons.

Examination of the START policy development process suggested that strategic arms reduction was not unified by collective defense considerations. Each stakeholder displayed distinct positions that impacted policy decisions. Both presidents sought further reductions, while the Congress and the bureaucracy were divided on areas such as foreign policy and the contemporary role of nuclear weapons. For example, divergent actor positions accounted for congressional inflexibility during delayed ratification by the Russian Duma, and the bureaucratic insistence on the omission of reserve and tactical nuclear weapons from treaty text. These path dependence related points were exacerbated by a lack of shared images concerning nuclear weapons in a post-Cold War strategic environment. In the post-Cold War timeframe preceding September 11, 2011, stakeholders simply did not agree on a direction for strategic arms control or nuclear weapons policy.

The START case study suggested that U.S. nuclear defense policy formulation during the George H. W. Bush and William J. Clinton administrations did not result in unitary policy decisions.

Instead, research identified a policy development process anchored in bureaucratic politics. The next case study on national missile defense assesses whether this is a unique occurrence, or if the findings from this chapter are applicable to other areas of national nuclear defense policy.

CHAPTER 2
NATIONAL MISSILE DEFENSE DEVELOPMENT STUDY

The previous chapter argued that bureaucratic politics dominated U.S. policy development in the field of strategic arms reductions during the administrations of George H. W. Bush and William J. Clinton. Was this an isolated case, or did the findings related to strategic arms reduction policy represent the general state of post-Cold War nuclear defense policy development in the United States? This chapter continues the examination of post-Cold War nuclear defense policy formulation by exploring a second major policy from the period -- national missile defense.

The first section of this case study identifies rule and actor differences from the situation described in the previous chapter. While the stakeholders remained the same, rule variation related to domestic versus international policy formulation proved essential to the examination of national missile defense policy development. The second section focuses on Cold War missile defense efforts and establishes that this topic was deeply rooted in Cold War developments. The section on policy decisions describes how post-Cold War missile defense policy evolved, while the following two sections analyze why the U.S. government decided to enact the eventual policy of national missile defense. An analysis of policy development in this area depicts a landscape of differing actor and stakeholder positions. The research findings were consistent with the previous case study and suggest the dominance of bureaucratic politics theory in the policy formulation process. Further analysis of barriers to change was also consistent with the strategic arms reduction study. The lack of a shared national image for missile defense, the separation of powers ensured by constitutional and statuary rules, and path dependence, which resulted from the transition of norms from one era to the next, all contributed to inflexibility in the domestic policy development process.

This chapter continues to test the hypothesis that, "U.S. nuclear defense policy formulation during the post-Cold War administrations of George H. W. Bush and William J. Clinton was anchored in bureaucratic politics, not collective defense." National missile defense displayed the same patterns as strategic arms reduction and was characterized by the impact of the separation of power within the American political system. Compromised policies again left dissatisfied actors and stakeholders to continue arguments along alternate channels. Additional action channels were available to the actors examined in this study because the policy development process was not constrained by specified constitutional treaty procedures. This domestic policy formulation setting facilitated multiple attempts to advance actor positions related to the establishment of national missile defense. However, despite incremental policy decisions that required the fielding of missile defense, technological barriers proved to be insurmountable in this respect during the period under consideration.[168]

STAKEHOLDERS

The three national stakeholders – the president, Congress, and the bureaucracy – are all represented in this second policy development case study. The two major differences related to

168   Kimball, Daryl G., and Stephen W. Young, "National Missile Defenses and Arms Control after Clinton's NMD decision," *Disarmament Forum*, Vol. 1, 2001, pp. 13-15.

stakeholders in this chapter stem from the absence of treaty rules and the degree of internal debate within the Defense Department. Unlike the Strategic Arms Reduction Treaty (START) case study, national missile defense was not constrained by constitutional rules governing the formulation of treaties. This difference in rules characterizes a significant portion of the general nuclear defense policy development process where the prescribed treaty flow from negotiation to signature by the executive branch, and ratification by Congress, is not present.

THE PRESIDENT AND CONGRESS

The Constitution of the United States does not specify where national polices must originate. The Constitution vests executive powers in the president and legislative powers in the Congress.[169] The president can make but not resource national policy since only Congress has the authority to lay and collect funds, and borrow on behalf of the United States.[170] Congress can recommend but not fully approve statutory policy unless there is a two thirds vote by the House in response to a returned bill, or if the president fails to act within ten days of receiving a bill.[171] This separation of powers, and the lack of rules concerning policy origination, has facilitated an environment of competing policies within the United States.

The separation of authorities extends into the defense area where the president is designated the Commander in Chief of the Army and Navy of the United States, but Congress is responsible for raising and maintaining military forces.[172] While the president can direct the military to implement an executive policy short of declared war, Congress reserves the ability to refuse funding. Another constitutional rule that impacted

---

169   The Constitution of the United States and The Declaration of Independence, 22nd printing 2006, pp. 9 and 1.
170   Ibid., p. 6.
171   Ibid., pp. 5-6.
172   Ibid., pp. 11 and 6-7.

national missile defense during the Clinton administration was the Senate's "sole power to try all impeachments."[173] Although President Clinton's impeachment proceedings resulted in acquittal by the Senate, the proceedings related to the Lewinsky scandal weakened the Democratic Party during a period of heated national missile defense debate.[174]

THE BUREAUCRACY

The previous chapter demonstrated inter- and intra-departmental differences over policy. While differences were also present in the second case study, national missile defense really highlighted the different actor positions within the Department of Defense. Key actors within the Defense Department were the individual services and the separate agency dedicated to missile defense. Each military service fought to preserve and advance individual designs while the agency representing missile defense provided a consolidated voice for contractors to recommend design and program changes through department channels. Actors remained in conflict over the priority of missile defense and which programs to advance. Defense budget reductions influenced the degree of support for missile defense from the service chiefs, and department reorganizations impacted agency access.

The level of influence afforded to the semi-autonomous agency within the Defense Department responsible for missile defense fluctuated with the political situation and departmental organization. For example, the Strategic Defense Initiative Organization lost major political support when the Reagan administration departed office, but maintained Republican patronage in an executive branch where it had continued direct access to the Secretary of Defense under President Bush. During the Clinton administration, the Strategic Defense Initiative Organization was reorganized and given a new reporting chain

173   Ibid., pp. 3 and 12.
174   Fitzgerald, Frances, *Way Out There in the Blue: Reagan, Star Wars and the End of the Cold War*, 2000, p. 496.

through an undersecretary, but found new political patronage from a Republican Congress.[175]

COLD WAR MISSILE DEFENSE EFFORTS

In 1972, Morton Halperin's article in *World Politics* on the Johnson administration's decision to deploy an anti-ballistic missile system demonstrated that missile defense has been a controversial issue for many years.[176] Early efforts to construct an anti-ballistic missile system under President Johnson set the stage for the 1972 Anti-Ballistic Missile (ABM) Treaty between the United States and the Soviet Union. This treaty limited the signatories to two missile defense deployment zones, one for each capital and another for an intercontinental ballistic missile launch site at a specified distance from the capital zone. A subsequent 1974 protocol reduced the number of sites to one. The intent of the ABM Treaty was to allow both sides to maintain effective second-strike capabilities to deter the other from launching a first-strike. For this reason, development of an effective national missile defense system threatened the primacy of offensive strategic nuclear capabilities, and undermined strategic stability. Opponents of anti-ballistic missile defenses have long used this line of reasoning to argue that without an effective nuclear deterrent nothing prevents the superior nuclear power from conducting a first-strike.

On March 23, 1983, President Reagan gave his famous Strategic Defense Initiative speech from the Oval Office.[177] Referred to as the "Star Wars" speech after Senator Ted Kennedy's comments the following day, the goal of strategic

---

175   Aspin, Les, "The End of the Star Wars Era," Department of Defense News Briefing, May 13, 1993.
176   Halperin, Morton H., "The Decision to Deploy the ABM: Bureaucratic and Domestic Politics in the Johnson Administration," *World Politics*, Vol. 25, October 1972, pp. 62-96.
177   Reagan, Ronald W., "Address to the Nation on Defense and National Security," March 23, 1983.

missile defense described by the president toward the end of the address was as old as missiles themselves.[178] While the security benefit of an effective anti-ballistic missile system was simple to comprehend, enormous costs and inadequate technology had derailed previous missile defense efforts. For example, the United States deployed the one system allowed under the 1974 ABM Treaty protocol at the Grand Forks intercontinental ballistic missile site. The resulting "safeguard" system was only operational for five months between October 1975 and February 1976, before Congress eliminated the program based on cost and inefficiency concerns.[179] Despite earlier setbacks and agreements, President Reagan's intent was to move away from the vulnerabilities inherent with deterrence by establishing an active anti-ballistic missile security system, but in March 1983, the president acknowledged that, at best, it would be the end of the century before such a defense could be fielded.[180]

POLICY DECISIONS

Initially the George H. W. Bush administration continued the Strategic Defense Initiative but with a shift in the design from a large space-based interceptor system to one founded on

---

178   Senator Kennedy was an opponent of the nuclear arms race emerging under President Reagan. He advocated for arms control and disarmament instead of strategic arms modernization and missile defense. The concept of missile defense dated back to initial science and technology intelligence of German V-2 missiles. Once this emerging disruptive threat was identified, British and American planners, scientists, and engineers began researching possible defenses. Theatre and strategic anti-ballistic missile system research advanced through the 1950s and 1960s, until it was curtailed by the 1972 ABM Treaty and the subsequent 1974 protocol mentioned previously. Kennedy, Edward M., "EMK Address at the Brown University Commencement Forum," June 4, 1983.
179   Kaplan, Lawrence M. "Missile Defense: The First Sixty Years," Missile Defense Agency, pp. 3-10, retrieved April 10, 2009.
180   For more on strategic missile defense during the Reagan administration, see Frances Fitzgerald, *Way Out There in the Blue: Reagan, Star Wars and the End of the Cold War*, 2000.

multiple small space and ground-based interceptors. Congress challenged this decision but the perceived success of the Patriot anti-tactical ballistic missile system in the first Gulf War, and a change in threat justification due to concerns over missile pro-liferation, facilitated the introduction of the Global Protection Against Limited Strikes system in 1991. This system focused on smaller scale regional missile threats comprising a few mis-siles, or an accidental launch scenario, instead of the thousands of Soviet missiles envisioned under previous systems.[181] The 1991 National Security Strategy claimed, "With adequate fund-ing, it will be possible to begin to deploy systems that will bet-ter protect our troops in the field from ballistic-missile attack by the mid-1990s and that will protect the United States itself from such attacks by the turn of the century."[182] Missile defense was already a highly political topic in America with general-ly pro-missile defense Republicans arguing for programs and generally anti-missile defense Democrats, unless representing a related constituency or interest, arguing against. For the Bush administration, this disagreement meant reduced budgets and congressional attempts to dictate how missile defense budgets were executed.

Missile defense under President Clinton varied during his first and second terms. Initially, the administration attempt-ed to focus on a ground-based theater missile defense sys-tem headed by the newly renamed Ballistic Missile Defense Organization. President Clinton was determined to ensure that the United States remain compliant with the ABM Treaty but the Republican-controlled Congress that emerged after the mid-term elections during his first term had very different plans for missile defense.[183] As part of their "Contract with America,"

181   Burns, Robert, "GPALS: Bush's Missile Defense Proposal," *The Associated Press*, April 29, 1991; Frederick, Lorinda A., "Deterrence and Space-Based Missile Defense," *Air and Space Power Journal,* Fall 2009.
182   *National Security Strategy of the United States of America,* 1991.
183   During the Reagan administration the ABM Treaty remained in effect under the auspice that the strategic defense initiative was a research

Republican lawmakers repeatedly introduced national missile defense legislation and used parliamentary procedure to shape national policy. This resulted in a plethora of congressional missile defense activities over the course of President Clinton's first and second terms. Republican Senators and Congressmen formed congressional panels, increased budgets, and submitted pro-missile defense resolutions, amendments, and bills. These efforts included the *Ballistic Missile Defense Act of 1995*, *Defend America Act of 1996*, the *National Missile Defense Act of 1997*, and the *American Missile Protection Act of 1998*. During the presidential elections in 1996, the Dole campaign attempted to make missile defense a major issue, but quickly changed tactics after research found that the voting public did not care about this "abstract" topic.[184]

In his second term, President Clinton shifted focus from theater missile defense to national missile defense in a counter proposal called the "three-plus-three" program. This new approach called for three years of research and development with a decision to potentially deploy a system in the second three-year period based on the threat and technical capabilities. Republican lawmakers challenged this plan as not being aggressive enough and used party loyalists such as Donald Rumsfeld to provide alternative threat assessments to counter intelligence community estimates of the emerging missile threat. Republicans also continued to propose withdrawing from the ABM Treaty to expedite fielding a missile defense system that the Chairman of the Joint Chiefs of Staff said could not be rushed into service any faster.[185]

---

program, not a deployable anti-ballistic missile system. "Limitation of Anti-Ballistic Missile Systems, 1972," U.S. Department of State, retrieved April 10, 2009; Nitze, Paul A., "SDI and the ABM treaty - Strategic Defense Initiative; Anti-Ballistic Missile – transcript," Department of State Bulletin, August 1985, retrieved April 10, 2009.

184   Fitzgerald, Frances, *Way Out There in the Blue: Reagan, Star Wars and the End of the Cold War*, 2000, pp. 493-494.
185   Shelton, Hugh, with Ronald Levinson and Malcolm McConnell, *Without Hesitation: The Odyssey of an American Warrior*, 2010, p. 405.

Conservative Republican efforts culminated in the *National Missile Defense Act of 1999*, which made it the policy of the United States to deploy a national missile defense system as soon as technologically possible. While Congress succeeded in redefining national policy on missile defense, President Clinton ultimately deferred the deployment decision to the next administration based on technological and political considerations.[186]

POLICY DEVELOPMENT

The previous sections identified the lack of agreement regarding missile defense policy in the United States. Similar to the strategic arms reduction process, national missile defense policy was the result of internal and external compromise over the course of multiple administrations. This section examines in detail the positions of the primary stakeholders -- the president, Congress, and the bureaucracy. Each stakeholder had substantial interests in missile defense. These interests were articulated as stakeholder positions comprising actor and organizational concerns. The president and members of Congress again had different priorities and constituencies to address, while the

---

186   Unlike his predecessor, President George W. Bush was determined to incrementally field a national missile defense system during his time in office. Efforts at preceding summits and the goodwill following 9/11 reduced early Russian and Chinese opposition when the United States announced it was withdrawing from the ABM Treaty in December 2001. The withdrawal ended legal discussions about the validity of the treaty following the end of the Soviet Union and the decision of President Clinton not to seek congressional advice and consent for efforts to continue the ABM Treaty with the U.S.S.R.'s successor countries. Ibid., pp. 173-194; Bolt, Paul J., Damon V. Coletta, and Collins G. Shackelford, Jr., *American Defense Policy*, 8th edition 2005, pp. 409-414; Hildreth, Steven A., "Ballistic Missile Defense: Historical Overview," *Congressional Research Service Report for Congress*, July 9, 2007; Frederick, Lorinda A., "Deterrence and Space-Based Missile Defense," *Air and Space Power Journal*, **Fall 2009;** "Memorandum of Understanding Relating to the Treaty between the United States of America and the Union of Soviet Socialist Republics on the Limitation of Anti-Ballistic Missile Systems on May 26, 1972," September 26, 1997.

military services, supporting agencies, and civilian leadership within the Department of Defense also had diverging interests.

THE PRESIDENT

President Bush was not an advocate of missile defense during his vice-presidency or during his candidacy for president.[187] His senior advisors, including Brent Scowcroft and Richard Cheney, were also opposed to continuing the Strategic Defense Initiative unless realistic changes were made to the program.[188] However, despite early administration positions, missile defense was already deeply rooted in the conservative Republican psyche. Because of this support the George H. W. Bush administration approached missile defense slowly, using normal review processes associated with presidential transitions before deciding to continue Reagan-era Strategic Defense Initiative policies.[189]

The first major program change was recommended by the Strategic Defense Initiative Organization and approved by the Secretary of Defense. This initial recommendation involved a modification to "phase one" architecture centered on a new space and ground-based interceptor design. Congress resisted the initial change by limiting Strategic Defense Initiative funding. This disagreement set the political stage for the next decision on missile defense; the transition to a reduced scope system designed to address limited missile threats. The new program, Global Protection Against Limited Strikes, was approved by the

187   Beschloss, Michael R., and Strobe Talbott, *At the Highest Levels: The Inside Story of the End of the Cold War*, 1993, p. 114.
188   Fitzgerald, Frances, *Way Out There in the Blue: Reagan, Star Wars and the End of the Cold War*, 2000, p. 480.
189   As denoted in the previous study, President Gorbachev removed the divisive ABM Treaty link to arms reduction negotiations in 1989. This freed President Bush of the arguments that would return during the Clinton administration. President Yeltsin followed this goodwill in 1992 by recommending discussions on a cooperative missile defense plan for regional threats and non-state actors. Beschloss, Michael R., and Strobe Talbott, *At the Highest Levels: The Inside Story of the End of the Cold War*, 1993, p. 118; Talbott, Strobe, *The Russia Hand: A Memoir of Presidential Diplomacy*, 2003, p. 375.

administration in early 1991, but faced an increasingly combative legislature intent on further reducing missile defense funding. Had it not been for early, exaggerated reporting on Patriot anti-tactical ballistic missile system accomplishments in the first Gulf War, the global protection program may not have received funding. Despite the fact that Patriot was not part of the Strategic Defense Initiative, the perceived utility of a larger defense system was not lost on proponents and opponents alike.[190] President Bush capitalized on the positive media coverage of the Patriot missile to announce the redirection the Strategic Defense Initiative in his 1991 State of the Union address. While the Global Protection Against Limited Strikes reorientation was focused on limited attacks, the funding request was for almost twice the amount of the existing Strategic Defense Initiative budget.[191]

President Bush followed normal policy development processes for missile defense. He received recommendations from the Strategic Defense Initiative Organization and the Secretary of Defense and these were staffed through the interagency process prior to any decisions being made. Once approved, the president and senior administration officials championed the new designs and directions despite cost overruns and a lack of progress, that left missile defense open to much criticism. Given

190 Although Patriot missiles were hailed early as a resounding success during the war, the technical infancy of U.S. interception capabilities was later revealed during numerous investigations. Early statements depicted 51 out of 52 kills of Scud missiles, but when these claims were challenged, the U.S. Army contracted Raytheon to provide documented analysis of the Patriot's performance. Initial and other revised reports of a 52% accuracy rate were countered by several opposing studies which refuted excessively high intercept rates. Among the opposition studies was a Government Accountability Office report that only found an accuracy rate of 9%. Despite the erroneous nature of early figures, initial claims tended to outlast the detailed counter-arguments outside the defense community. Eisendrath, Craig, Melvin A. Goodman, and Gerald E. Marsh, *The Phantom Defense: America's Pursuit of the Star Wars Illusion,* 2001, pp. 19-20.

191 Fitzgerald, Frances, *Way Out There in the Blue: Reagan, Star Wars and the End of the Cold War,* 2000, p. 485.

earlier positions this was interesting, but not unique to the Bush administration, as candidate positions often change upon assumption of office. This phenomenon was consistent with policies adopted by his successor. Where President Bush changed missile defense positions based on internal recommendations, President Clinton was forced to accept alternate national missile defense policy by the active Republican majority in Congress.[192]

During his candidacy, William Clinton described his position on the strategic defense initiative as:

> We need to bring a healthy dose of reality to the SDI [Strategic Defense Initiative] program, a quality that it sorely lacks today. Our SDI program should be geared to the real threats we face today and are likely to face in the future, not the fevered rationalizations of a weapons program in search of a mission. I fully support the development of a defense against tactical ballistic missiles to provide protection for limited areas abroad, such as selected U.S. troop deployments as in Desert Shield and Desert Storm, or key areas of tactical or strategic military significance, as Israel was during the war. I would keep open the option of deploying a limited single-site, ground-based defense in the United States. This would not require the wasteful levels of SDI spending that the administration is requesting.[193]

Once in office, President Clinton approved a transition to theater missile defense against shorter-range missiles. The administration chose to remain compliant with the ABM Treaty during testing and approved a major shift in funding allocation from strategic to theater systems. Missile defense remained a politically contentious issue but it did not return to the national policy agenda until after the 1994 Republican Revolution in Congress.

---

192   Fitzgerald, Frances, *Way Out There in the Blue: Reagan, Star Wars and the End of the Cold War*, 2000, pp. 480-481; Talbott, Strobe, *The Russia Hand: A Memoir of Presidential Diplomacy*, 2003, pp. 379-382.
193   Arms Control Association, "Arms Control and the 1992 Election," *Arms Control Today*, 1992, retrieved November 15, 2011.

Prompted by this political change in the legislative branch, the Clinton administration explored new policy options as it battled congressional legislation concerning national missile defense. President Clinton continued theater missile defense efforts while administration officials designed a policy that would enable simultaneous development of a national missile defense system. Even with the transition to national missile defense, the president was still determined to remain compliant with the ABM Treaty, and went to great lengths in discussions with the Russians on treaty reaffirmation and clarification, and later requested changes to facilitate national missile defense deployment. In 1995, these efforts included a joint statement by Presidents Clinton and Yeltsin affirming adherence to the ABM Treaty and the right to defense for both parties provided the systems were not targeted against one another.[194]

Talks between the United States and Russia continued concerning a demarcation line between national and theater systems, and later on the deployment of a national missile defense system, with President Putin. The discussions included standard engagements between negotiators, senior officials, and the American and Russian presidents through to the end of the Clinton administration.[195] While several agreements were reached over the course of the administration, Russia refused to modify the ABM Treaty based on security concerns. Strobe Talbott explained that:

> The Russians based their position on a worst-case scenario that cast the U.S. in the role of nuclear aggressor or at least nuclear blackmailer. By their calculations, the U.S. would have the offensive capability to knock out 90 percent of Russia's strategic arsenal using our nuclear forces and conventional weapons... The surviving 10 percent of their force – say, a hundred warheads – might be within

194   Clinton, William J., and Boris Yeltsin, "Joint Statement Concerning the Anti-Ballistic Missile Treaty," March 21, 1997.
195   Talbott, Strobe, *The Russia Hand: A Memoir of Presidential Diplomacy*, 2003, pp. 383-389.

the capacity of NMD [National Missile Defense] to shoot down before they reached their targets.[196]

President Clinton approved the Democratic response to Republican calls for national missile defense in 1996.[197] The three-plus-three program upgraded national missile defense from a research to a deployment readiness program. The first three years were for technology development, with the second three years reserved for deployment if warranted. Development of the program was based on a hasty response to Republican congressional challenges. Leading Republican legislators such as Senate Majority Leader Trent Lott had offered competing policies calling for the deployment of national missile defense, while Senator Richard Lugar proposed alternate legislation on the very same day that endorsed the three-plus-three program, but attempted to shift the deployment decision to Congress.[198]

Continued congressional pressure on the issue of missile defense reached the level of nearly unanimous consensus with the 97-3 Senate passage of the *National Missile Defense Act of 1999*.[199] This growing consensus, that included a similar House vote of 317-105, forced the administration to act quickly to

---

196   Ibid., 384.
197   1996 was a presidential election year where the Republican challenger, Bob Dole, initially highlighted national missile defense as a key issue. Fitzgerald, Frances, *Way Out There in the Blue: Reagan, Star Wars and the End of the Cold War*, 2000, pp. 493-494.
198   When the three-plus-three program was approved in February 1996, Senator Richard Lugar was also vying for the Republican presidential nomination. Cerniello, Craig, "NMD Debate in Congress Heats Up As Lott, Lugar Introduce New Bills," *Arms Control Today*, Vol. 26, January/February 1997.
199   Strobe Talbott offered that the Clinton "administration was more in danger than ever of losing control of" missile defense in the spring of 1999, when both houses of Congress overwhelmingly approved bills mandating the employment of a national missile defense system "as soon as technologically possible." Talbott, Strobe, *The Russia Hand: A Memoir of Presidential Diplomacy*, 2003, pp. 379-383.

retain control of missile defense.[200] Congressional leaders were still divided on missile defense, but Francis Fitzgerald offered that immediately following the impeachment proceedings, Senate Democrats could only muster the political capital for amendments related to funding and continued Russian strategic arms reduction when the Senator Thad Cochran introduced the *National Missile Defense Act of 1999*.[201]

National security advisor Samuel "Sandy" Berger argued that the language of the legislation allowed room for compromise and devised a strategy to diffuse the act prior to signing. The resulting administration position, announced by President Clinton, focused on the availability of adequate technologies and whether national missile defense would enhance American security.[202] Berger went on to coordinate quickly with the Defense Department for an implementation plan that included defense of all fifty U.S. states, and with the State Department for minimum amendments to the ABM Treaty that would permit an initial national missile defense site in Alaska.[203] He also led the effort to enlist Democratic support for the plan in a "lame duck" environment that was focused on the 2000 presidential elections.[204]

---

200   Moore, Thomas, "White House Steps Back from National Missile Defense – Again," Heritage Foundation Executive Memorandum, April 8, 1999.

201   Fitzgerald, Frances, *Way Out There in the Blue: Reagan, Star Wars and the End of the Cold War*, 2000, p. 496.

202   Clinton, William J., "Statement on Signing the National Missile Defense Act of 1999," July 22, 1999.

203   The plan presented by Sandy Berger called for two anti-missile sites, one in Alaska and one in North Dakota, 250 interceptors, advanced radars, and space-based sensors that wouldn't be available until 2005 or 2010. Talbott, Strobe, *The Russia Hand: A Memoir of Presidential Diplomacy*, 2003, pp. 379-383.

204   David Dunn has offered a model for analysis of the "lame duck" phenomena. He cites limited tenure, preparation for succession, divided government, personnel depletion, agenda exhaustion, scandal, hubris, and policy legacy as contributing factors for inaction in the second term of multiple American presidential administrations. Dunn, David H., "Quacking Like a

Both presidents presided over normal policy development processes at the national level for missile defense, but President Clinton was forced into a reactionary role that occasionally required political maneuvering with abbreviated interagency policy formulation. Despite not being enthusiastic about the topic prior to office, each president championed administration decisions once they were made. They used national forums such as the State of the Union address and personally negotiated ABM Treaty positions with Presidents Gorbachev, Yeltsin, and Putin. Neither demonstrated the Reagan-era commitment to missile defense, nor veered significantly from the recommended positions of technical advisors in the Defense Department.[205]

CONGRESS

Within Congress the generally conservative Republican and liberal Democrat positions on defense applied to the debate over the Strategic Defense Initiative. Conservative Republicans in both houses were intent on supporting the Strategic Defense Initiative when President Reagan left office, but the Republican Party was in the minority and differing internal positions existed between conservatives and centrists. The Democrats controlled both houses of Congress and were generally agreeable to a change in direction for the Strategic Defense Initiative when President Bush assumed office, but the two chambers were not united on missile defense.

When the administration redirected efforts and requested additional funding, opponents of missile defense resisted. The House refused to resource the Global Protection Against Limited Strikes' space-based Brilliant Pebbles program, forcing

Duck? Bush II and Presidential Power in the Second Term," *International Affairs*, Vol. 82, No. 1, January 2006, pp. 95-104.

205   In addition to internal and contractor technical assets, the Defense Department also used independent scientific experts such as the JASON advisory group, to study hard problems. For more on JASON and their role in the Strategic Defense Initiative see Ann Finkbeiner, *The Jasons: The Secret History of Science's Postwar Elite*, 2006.

the Senate to submit the *Missile Defense Act of 1991*. Congress used this act to direct "the Secretary [of Defense] to develop for deployment by fiscal year 1996 a cost-effective and operationally-effective and ABM Treaty-compliant anti-ballistic missile system at a single site as the initial step toward deployment of the anti-ballistic missile system."[206] This act was sponsored by Senators Sam Nunn and John Warner but opposed by Democratic Senators Al Gore, Carl Levin, and Joe Biden, of which the latter two were able to secure an amendment to limit the bill to activities that would not violate the ABM Treaty.[207] Democratic Senator Nunn, a champion of the ABM Treaty, aligned with Republican Senator Warner, a champion of missile defense, to secure funding for controversial Strategic Defense Initiative components that would integrate into the new Global Protection Against Limited Strikes concept. Congress continued to fund strategic and theater missile defense under George H. W. Bush, but demonstrated internal and external disagreement by significantly reducing related appropriations for the remainder of his presidency.

In 1994, the composition of Congress changed. The Republican Party, led by conservatives, took control of both houses and set out to push congressional agendas in numerous areas, including national security.[208] During the first session of the 104th Congress, Representative Robert Livingston introduced the Republican National Security bill that included a new policy to "deploy at the earliest possible moment an antiballistic missile system that is capable of providing a highly effective defense of the United States against ballistic missile attacks."[209]

---

206   The act also directed the secretary to "aggressively pursue" theater missile defense efforts. *National Defense Authorization Act for Fiscal Years 1992 and 1993* (H.R. 2100), SEC. 211, "Missile Defense Act of 1991."
207   Powaski, Ronald E., *Return to Armageddon: The United States and the Nuclear Arms Race, 1981-1999*, 2000, pp. 125-127.
208   "Republican Contract with America," United States House of Representatives, retrieved November 15, 2011.
209   *National Security Restoration Act,* United States House of

This marked the beginning of Republican legislative efforts to force the deployment of national missile defense. For the rest of the Clinton presidency, Congress served as an alternate policymaking body, challenging executive branch authorities and policies concerning missile defense and other national security issues.[210] Robert Hahn emphasized that this alternate policymaking route had evolved over the previous two decades. He argued that the gradual development of institutional structures and processes, such as the reorganization of the Armed Services Committees and reform of the executive branch process through the *Goldwater-Nichols Department of Defense Reorganization Act of 1986*, facilitated legislative policymaking in the post-Cold War era.[211]

As Senator Joe Biden noted, missile defense had, and continued to consume, a large portion of already busy congressional schedules for the next several years.[212] Republicans such as Representative Curt Weldon and Senator Jon Kyl insisted that missile proliferation was "one of the greatest threats to America in the 21st century," while Democrats such as Senators Paul Simon and Carl Levin argued against, citing the cost and the potential negative security impact from proposed missile defense legislation.[213] The Republican-controlled Congress consistently

Representatives, retrieved November 15, 2011.

210   Wilson, James Q., *Bureaucracy: What Government Agencies Do and Why They Do It*, 2nd edition 2000, pp. 240-244.

211   Hahn, Robert F. III, "The Congressional Defense Department: Competitive Strategy Making in the Post-Cold-War Era," *Airpower Journal*, Special Edition, Vol. VIV, 1995, retrieved November 15, 2011; *Goldwater-Nichols Department of Defense Reorganization Act of 1986* (P.L. 99-433).

212   *Congressional Record* 106th Congress (1999-2000), "National Missile Defense," Senate, May 25, 2000, S4399-S4402.

213   *Congressional Record* 104th Congress (1995-1996), "Missile proliferation: one of the greatest threats to America in the 21st- Century," House of Representatives, April 3, 1995, p. H4074; *Congressional Record* 104th Congress (1995-1996), "Threat of Missile attack on the United States and our Allies," Senate, March 15, 1996, pp.S2189-S2191; *Congressional Record* 104th Congress (1995-1996), "Star Wars or Maginot Line? Contract to Bankrupt America," Senate, January 6, 1995, p. S572; *Congressional*

increased funding above annual requests and sought to redefine missile defense policy for the United States.[214] Republican efforts to require the deployment of a national missile defense system that could cover all 50 States from a long-range missile threat were included in the *National Defense Authorization Act for Fiscal Year 1996*. The original wording in the act, also known as the *Ballistic Missile Defense Act of 1995*, required deployment of a national system. This attempt to force the executive branch to field a national missile defense system prompted a presidential veto, forcing a compromise that repealed the earlier requirement to field a system by 1996, and eliminated the requirement to deploy national missile defenses by 2003.[215]

The downgrade in deployment language spurred several additional attempts from conservative Republicans, such as House Speaker Newt Gingrich, to introduce legislation intended to compel national missile defense deployment. His 1996 *Defend America Act* again called for a national missile defense against limited attacks by 2003, but the act was withdrawn after budget estimates were conducted.[216] Senate Majority Leader Trent Lott sponsored the next attempt. The *National Missile Defense Act of 1997* reintroduced the 2003 deployment deadline, and encouraged withdrawal from the ABM Treaty if the Russians would not immediately agree to deployment amendments. This

Record 104th Congress (1995-1996), "Defend America Act increases nuclear threat," Senate, May 23, 1996, pp. S5628-S5631.

214   For more on this type of procedure, see Morton H. Halperin and Kristen Lomasney, "Playing the Add-on Game in Congress: The Increasing Importance of Constituent Interests and Budget Constraints in Determining Defense Policy," in Leon V. Sigal, ed., *The Changing Dynamics of U.S. Defense Spending*, 1999, pp. 88-96.

215   *Congressional Record* 104th Congress (1995-1996), "National Defense Authorization Act for Fiscal Year 1996-Veto message from the President of the United States (H. Doc. No. 104-155)," House of Representatives, January 3, 1996, pp. H12-H14; National Defense Authorization Act of 1996, Subtitle C- "Ballistic Missile Defense Act of 1995."

216   Fitzgerald, Frances, *Way Out There in the Blue: Reagan, Star Wars and the End of the Cold War*, 2000, p. 493.

attempt was again downgraded to specification of a 1999 test, to support a "national missile defense system architecture that could achieve initial operational deployment capability in fiscal year 2003," and mention of treaty withdrawal was replaced by identification of activities that might conflict with the ABM Treaty.[217] Repeated failures prompted authors such as John Isaacs to conclude that although "Senate Republicans declared that they were making national missile defense a top legislative priority in 1997," they "failed to follow through."[218]

In the spring of 1998, Republican Senator Thad Cochran introduced the *American Missile Protection Act*. This separate legislation called for the deployment of national missile defense "as soon as technologically possible," but failed to progress beyond the Senate floor. While Senator Cochran's legislation failed, 1998 proved to be an important year for national missile defense. In May, India and Pakistan for the first time overtly tested nuclear weapons. These tests preceded the release of the Rumsfeld Commission Report, which reassessed the ballistic missile threat to the United States. The commission was established to challenge the intelligence community position "that no country other than the declared nuclear powers will develop or otherwise acquire ballistic missiles capable of reaching the contiguous forty-eight states within the next fifteen years," and "that the likelihood of an accidental or unauthorized missile launch is very low."[219]

An earlier congressionally-directed review led by former Director of Central Intelligence Robert Gates found fault with the intelligence community's level of analysis, but not their assessment of the ballistic missile threat presented in the 1995 National Intelligence Estimate. Contrary to the first review, the

217   *National Defense Authorization Act for Fiscal Year 1998* (P.L. 105-85), Sec. 231.
218   Isaacs, John, "Aiming at ABM," *Bulletin of the Atomic Scientists,* Mar 1998, pp. 14-15.
219   Daggett, Stephen, and Robert D. Shuey, "National Missile Defense: Status of the Debate," *CRS Report for Congress,* May 29, 1998, pp. 3-4.

Rumsfeld Commission found that "the intelligence community's ability to provide timely and accurate estimates of ballistic missile threats to the U.S. is eroding." The commission offered that in addition to the existing threats posed by Russia and China, North Korea, Iran, and Iraq were intent on acquiring missiles that could deliver weapons of mass destruction. Timelines according to the Rumsfeld commission would be much shorter, estimated at five years or less in worst-case scenarios.[220] The month following the report's publication, North Korea used a Taepodong-1 missile to launch a satellite. Analysts debated the success of the launch, and pointed to the incident as a cover for work toward an intercontinental ballistic missile capability. Despite continued differences, legislators were more amenable to national missile defense following the actions of North Korea, India and Pakistan.

In early 1999, Republican Senator Thad Cochran and Representative Curt Weldon introduced new legislation on national missile defense in the Senate and the House. The *National Missile Defense Act of 1999* was a short piece of legislation that stated:

> It is the policy of the United States to deploy as soon as is technologically possible an effective national missile defense system capable of defending the territory of the United States against limited ballistic missile attack (whether accidental, unauthorized, or deliberate) with funding subject to the annual authorization of appropriations and the annual appropriation of funds for national missile defense.[221]

Congressional Democrats added the amendment related to funding authorization but, as a result of the presidential impeachment process, they were not in a position to generate enough votes to sustain another veto.[222] This led President Clinton to

---

220 Rumsfeld, Donald, "Report of the Commission to Assess the Ballistic Missile Threat to the United States," July 15, 1998, Sec. II (A).
221 *National Missile Defense Act of 1999* (P.L. 106-38), July 22, 1999, Sec. 2.
222 The Senate vote was 97-3 in favor of the act. Fitzgerald, Frances,

approve the act in July with specific criteria designed by Sandy Berger to preserve the president's constitutional authorities. Senator Cochran was not pleased with the president's signing remarks, which ultimately blocked the deployment of national missile defense for the remainder of the administration.[223] Debate in Congress continued but the decision to deploy a national missile defense system was deferred by President Clinton prior to the 2000 presidential elections.

Congressional positions carried forward from the Cold War as part of each party's platform. Conservative Republicans, with support from the wider party, consistently pushed for national missile defense, while the Democratic Party worked to block the shift of national missile defense beyond research and development. The opposing groups used parliamentary procedures to establish alternative national missile defense policies. Because there were no congressional term limits, many of the leading legislative actors that participated in the post-Vietnam alternate policymaking reorientation carried polarizing Cold War missile defense arguments into the policy debate of the succeeding era.[224] This longevity and partisan political approach led to a national missile defense environment that former Senator Sam Nunn described as, "a theology in the United States, not a technology."[225]

Way Out There in the Blue: Reagan, Star Wars and the End of the Cold War, 2000, p. 496; CNN, "Senate backs missile defense system: 97-3 vote marks big shift for Democrats," March 17, 1999, retrieved November 15, 2011.

223   *Congressional Record* 106th Congress (1999-2000), "The National Missile Defense Act," Senate, July, 26, 1999, pp. S9174-S9176.

224   Hahn, Robert F. III, "The Congressional Defense Department: Competitive Strategy Making in the Post-Cold-War Era," *Airpower Journal*, Special Edition, Vol. VIV, 1995, retrieved November 15, 2011.

225   Coyle, Philip E. III., "Oversight of Ballistic Missile Defense (Part 3): Questions for the Missile Defense Agency," testimony before the House Committee on Oversight and Government Reform, Subcommittee on National Security and Foreign Affairs, April 30, 2008.

THE BUREAUCRACY

National missile defense was largely a Department of Defense undertaking. The State Department was responsible for negotiations concerning applicable treaties such as the ABM Treaty and the Comprehensive Test Ban Treaty, but did not have a tangible stake in the issue beyond the personal and organizational considerations already described. The primary concern for the State Department was a United States withdrawal or potential withdrawal from the ABM Treaty. Political rhetoric, notably from Republicans in Congress in this regard, impacted other negotiations related but not limited to strategic arms reductions, nuclear testing, and North Atlantic Treaty Organization expansion. Statements that advocated ABM Treaty withdrawal, and the advancement of national missile defense, forced diplomats to use personal and organizational capital to assuage the fears of the Russians and other concerned actors such as China.[226] They also affected schedules and agendas when clarification and re-negotiation of the ABM Treaty was raised to the top of the administration's foreign policy priorities. From a State Department and arms control position, national missile defense became a major distraction with the potential for unintended negative consequences.

Several internal positions on national missile defense existed within the Department of Defense based on service and agency affiliations. The services initially exercised responsibility for theater missile defense systems while a separate agency

---

226 Like Russia, Chinese officials accessed that they could be subject to nuclear coercion or blackmail if a U.S. national missile defense system negated their limited nuclear capabilities. Chinese opposition also extended into advanced theater missile defenses that had the potential to increase United States-Taiwan military ties, and ultimately upset the global strategic balance. China felt that continuation of the ABM Treaty prevented national missile defense implementation and thus, preserved the status quo. Godwin, Paul H. B., and Evan S. Medeiros, "China, America, and Missile Defense: Conflicting National Interests." *Current History: A Journal of Contemporary World Affairs*, September 2000, pp. 285-289.

was responsible for national missile defense. This latter agency retained the Strategic Defense Initiative Office label under President Bush and was re-designated the Ballistic Missile Defense Organization under President Clinton.[227] This separation of responsibilities helped to account for the lack of enthusiasm for national missile defense from the Joint Chiefs of Staff.[228]

Colin Powell, who once argued that "the science of SDI... was mind boggling, but the strategy was fairly elementary," and the service chiefs supported the Bush administration's transition to a regional system against limited threats.[229] The career military officers judged this to be a more technically realistic approach and their services stood to benefit from funding reallocations to traditionally service executed programs, such as the Army's Patriot system. By the time President Clinton assumed office, the Joint Chiefs urged a realistic approach to national and theater missile defense. The lack of threat, poor technological performances, and the large Strategic Defense Initiative Organization budget during a drawdown period motivated the Joint Chiefs to argue for a slower, cost effective strategy that would realign the funding priority in favor of theater missile defense.[230] Once the decision to shift to the three-plus-three program was made, the Joint Chiefs defended the administration's position.[231]

The services followed the same line of reasoning as the Joint Chiefs. Since the Army, Navy, and Air Force each had

---

227   President George W. Bush presided over a third name change to the Missile Defense Agency once he assumed office.
228   Fitzgerald, Frances, *Way Out There in the Blue: Reagan, Star Wars and the End of the Cold War*, 2000, pp. 481; Cirincione, Joseph, "Rush to Failure," *Bulletin of the Atomic Scientists*, May 1998, p. 24.
229   Powell, Colin L., *My American Journey*, 1995, p. 359.
230   Cirincione, Joseph, "Rush to Failure," *Bulletin of the Atomic Scientists*, May 1998, pp. 23-25.
231   August 24, 1998 letter from the Joint Chiefs to Representative James Inhofe reaffirmed their support of the program, their confidence in the intelligence community, and remaining compliant with the ABM Treaty. Shelton, Hugh, with Ronald Levinson and Malcolm McConnell, *Without Hesitation: The Odyssey of an American Warrior*, 2010, p. 405.

theater defense systems prior to the introduction of the Strategic Defense Initiative, their positions were based on individual program interests.[232] The Army's Patriot anti-tactical ballistic missile system became the face of missile defense following the Gulf War, despite subsequent revelations that the initial reports of interception success had not been accurate.[233] When the Clinton administration assumed office the services lobbied for a change in focus to theater defenses. Secretary Aspin approved this course of action that ultimately benefited the Army and Navy.

After a review of the existing systems, the Army Patriot and Theater High Altitude Area Defense programs, and the Navy Aegis program, were selected for acceleration. It was the Army's high altitude system that required a clarification of the demarcation between theater and strategic defenses under the ABM Treaty.[234] These systems were more technologically feasible than national missile defense designs, but still proved frustrating for program scientists and engineers laboring against artificially condensed timelines. In one example presented by Joseph Cirincione, Ballistic Missile Defense Organization

---

232   Rival service missile programs had a long history in the Defense Department. Lauren Holland cited the questionable rationale for the 1950s Thor and Jupiter programs. She offered that the Army saw Jupiter as a way to regain lost defense budget shares, while the Air Force sought to monopolize strategic missions with Thor. In either case, she described both programs as a "Technical Rush to Obsolescence." Holland, Lauren, *Weapons Under Fire,* 1997, pp. 140-141.

233   The degree of Patriot success was heavily debated following initial claims that depicted 51 kills out of 52 Scuds engaged. This, and other revised claims of a 52% accuracy rate, was countered by several opposing studies which refuted excessively high intercept rates. Among the opposition studies was a Government Accountability Office report that only found an accuracy rate of 9%, but the initial claims tended to outlast the detailed counter-arguments outside the defense community. Eisendrath, Craig, Melvin A. Goodman, and Gerald E. Marsh, *The Phantom Defense: America's Pursuit of the Star Wars Illusion,* 2001, pp. 19-20.

234   Fitzgerald, Frances, *Way Out There in the Blue: Reagan, Star Wars and the End of the Cold War,* 2000, pp. 491-495.

Director General Lester Lyles noted that the Army's high altitude system "had been very successful in every aspect" apart
from hitting the test targets.[235] Despite difficulties, the services
repeatedly asserted their ability to overcome technological hur-
dles and to meet timelines with their programs if Congress was
willing to continue annual funding authorizations.

The Strategic Defense Initiative Organization enjoyed $3-4
billion annual budgets prior to the Bush administration.[236] High
funding levels and national prioritization meant that it was in the
best interest of the organization to continue Strategic Defense
Initiative research and development, regardless of performance.[237] The organization was assisted by a large contingent
of support and development contractors with varying amounts
of federal oversight, and reported directly to the Secretary of
Defense. This arrangement of managers, contracting officers,
and contractors was standard practice for major acquisition
systems built by the military-industrial complex.[238] Because
of large research and development efforts maintained by contracting firms and the integrated operating arrangement, data
and technical solutions -- such as Brilliant Pebbles or Global

---

235   As of May 1998, the Theater High Altitude Area Defense system
failed to hit pre-calculated, short-range targets on all four intercept tests.
Cirincione, Joseph, "Rush to Failure," *Bulletin of the Atomic Scientists*, May
1998, p. 24.
236   Between 1985 and 2008 missile defense received $115.8 billion in
funding. Department of Defense, "Historical Funding for milestone decision authority fiscal year 85-10," Missile Defense Agency, retrieved May 15,
2010.
237   William Gregory argued that at worst, the cost-sharing independent
research and development system where the Defense Department leverages
civilian capabilities, generated "technology in search of a mission" and "an
illusion that all the country's military problems can be solved with money and
equipment." Gregory, William H., *The Defense Procurement Mess*, 1989, pp.
29-30.
238   Wilson, James Q., *Bureaucracy: What Government Agencies Do
and Why They Do It*, 2nd edition 2000, pp. 317-325; for more on defense
acquisition structure and management see J. Ronald Fox with James L. Field,
The Defense Management Challenge: Weapons Acquisition, 1988.

Protection Against Limited Strikes -- were routinely suggested by contractors and ultimately recommended by appointed administration officials.[239]

Contracting firms also lobbied for administration and congressional approval, in what William Hartung and Michelle Carrocca depicted as an environment of conflicted interests.[240] These authors cited political action committee contributions of $2 million to pro-missile defense candidates during the 1996 presidential election cycle, and the same figure donated between 1989 and 1999, to the Center for Security Policy -- a missile defense think tank founded by Frank Gaffney. These figures quantified the political influence of missile defense contractors such as Boeing, Lockheed Martin, Raytheon, and TRW incorporated.[241] This influence was not unique to missile defense and was representative of major military acquisition politics in the United States.[242]

In her book, *Weapons Under Fire*, Lauren Holland offered several theories to explain the functioning of the United States" weapons procurement decision process.[243] She began by asking, "If not rational, then what?" In answer to this question, Holland offered pragmatic, technical, and political arguments. The pragmatic argument stated that: 1) strategic forecasting and intelligence estimation was extremely difficult; 2) decision makers could not ignore non-military concerns such as organizational survival; and 3) people disagreed about the need and

239   Hampson, Fen, *Unguided Missiles: How America Buys Its Weapons,* 1989, pp. 6-9.
240   Hartung, William D., and Michelle Carrocca, "Star Wars II: Here We Go Again," *The Nation*, June 19, 2000.
241   TRW originally stood for "Thompson Ramo Wooldridge." Ibid.
242   Accusations that the Department of Defense purchased overpriced items such as $435 hammers in the 1980s, led to multiple acquisition reforms. These measures included the *Goldwater-Nichols Department of Defense Reorganization Act of 1986* and *Federal Acquisition Reform Act of 1995*. Fairhall, James, "The case for the $435 hammer – investigation of the Pentagon's procurement," *Washington Monthly*, January 1987.
243   Holland, Lauren, *Weapons Under Fire,* 1997, pp. 3-19.

use of military hardware. The technical argument stated that technology could substitute for military need to justify initial approval, and that advanced technology was alluring. The final political argument offered that, "behind each weapon there is a group of legislators responding to constituent demands, bureaucrats seeking to perpetuate their organization, executive officers reacting to governmental pressures, and defense contractors struggling for economic survival."[244] These arguments are all directly applicable to understanding the dynamics underlying national missile defense.

Each Secretary of Defense from the Bush and Clinton administrations followed standard procedures for balancing the president's vision and recommendations from intra-departmental stakeholders. The technical foundation for each of the national missile defense plans offered during the period of study originated in the Strategic Defense Initiative Organization or the Ballistic Missile Defense Organization. Secretary Richard Cheney initially reduced the Strategic Defense Initiative budget but accepted the recommendation of the outgoing Strategic Defense Initiative Organization's director to shift the phase one space-based implementation system to a new design comprising thousands of tiny space and ground-based interceptors. This decision reversed initial funding cuts. Secretary Cheney again followed the recommendation of the Strategic Defense Initiative Organization's director to reorient missile defense to Global Protection Against Limited Strikes in 1991.[245] While this limited system accounted for the emerging threat assessment and benefited from positive perceptions of service missile defenses in the first Gulf War, it was ultimately a means for missile defense proponents to continue their efforts.[246]

---

244   Ibid.
245   Fitzgerald, Frances, *Way Out There in the Blue: Reagan, Star Wars and the End of the Cold War*, 2000, pp. 484-490.
246   Clausen, Peter, "Star warriors try again," *Bulletin of the Atomic Scientists,* June 1981, pp. 9-10 and 42.

Limited programs did not fair any better technologically than their Strategic Defense Initiative predecessors.[247] In this regard, Frances Fitzgerald described the state of missile defense testing as:

> After studying the seven major flight tests of SDI interceptors conducted between January 1990 and March 1992, GAO [Government Accountability Office] investigators found that SDIO [Strategic Defense Initiative Organization] officials had at least exaggerated the success of four of them. The other three tests were correctly depicted by the SDIO as either complete failures or only partially successful. According to the GAO, no Brilliant Pebbles test had succeeded, in spite of SDIO claims...[248]

Global Protection Against Limited Strikes and other missile defense programs continued despite numerous technological setbacks, but repeated testing failures and concerns over intentional misinformation negatively impacted executive and legislative branch relations by the end of the George H. W. Bush administration.[249]

Poor performance, deteriorating relations, and a new administration meant a redirection for missile defense following the Defense Department's 1993 Bottom-Up Review. Secretary Aspin reversed priorities by emphasizing theater over of national missile defense. He maintained the same level of funding requests but downgraded the newly labeled Ballistic Missile Defense Organization. Instead of reporting directly to the Secretary of Defense, the organization's director would report to the Under Secretary of Defense for Acquisitions and Technology. In a news briefing to announce these decisions, Secretary Aspin declared "the end of the Star Wars era."[250] These changes represented the

---

247   Finkbeiner, Ann, *The Jasons: The Secret History of Science's Postwar Elite*, 2006, pp. 167-169.
248   Fitzgerald, Frances, *Way Out There in the Blue: Reagan, Star Wars and the End of the Cold War*, 2000, pp. 488-490.
249   Ibid.
250   Aspin, Les, "The End of the Star Wars Era," Department of Defense

positions of the administration, the Defense Secretary, and the military leadership, but ultimately proved to be unsustainable in the highly politicized national missile defense environment that followed the 1994 Republican Revolution.

By 1996, sustained congressional pressure prompted the administration to formulate a new missile defense policy, with Secretary of Defense William Perry overseeing the work of Ballistic Missile Defense Organization in this respect. Working with the Army and the Air Force, the Ballistic Missile Defense Organization designed a treaty compliant national missile defense option with a limited capability and an incremental development and fielding timeline. The administration's alternative to Republican pressure for immediate deployment of national missile defense centered on establishing baseline technology for a single site, improving that technology, and then progressing to national coverage at two or more sites.[251] Thus, the three-plus-three program hinged on a successful test and verification of need prior to a deployment decision in 2000.

In January 1999, Secretary of Defense William Cohen attempted to placate Congress on missile defense. The secretary requested increased funding for missile defense, cited North Korean threat concerns consistent with the Rumsfeld Report, and assured members that the administration was prepared to negotiate with the Russians or leave the ABM Treaty if multiple interceptor sites were deemed necessary to protect the entire United States.[252] These attempts failed and, as a result of the *National Missile Defense Act of 1999*, the department was forced to hastily redesign a national missile defense system that could cover all 50 States. According to Ballistic Missile Defense Organization experts, the system would need at least two interceptor sites and take five to ten years to construct. Secretary

News Briefing, May 13, 1993.
251   Mowthorpe, Matthew, *The Militarization and Weaponization of Space*, 2003, pp. 187-190.
252   Fitzgerald, Frances, *Way Out There in the Blue: Reagan, Star Wars and the End of the Cold War*, 2000, pp. 495-496.

Cohen recommended these changes to the White House and worked with other interagency officials to assist the president in persuading the Russians to amend the ABM Treaty.[253]

Even with increased budgets, testing exceptions, and priority deadlines, poor performance continued to hamper missile defense in the post-Cold War era. By the end of the Clinton administration the technical difficulties associated with "hitting a bullet with a bullet" were well known.[254] Despite setbacks the bureaucracy continued to support missile defense. The Joint Chiefs and the services lobbied for theater missile defense that benefited their organizations while the Ballistic Missile Defense Organization continued to recommend multiple approaches to missile defense that required sustained and additional funding. Each Secretary of Defense aggregated administration intent with technical recommendations to continue missile defense, in spite of earlier positions.

BARRIERS TO CHANGE

The foregoing examination of strategic missile defense again highlights the importance of understanding shared attitudes, framework, and organizational constraints in the policy development process. During the early post-Cold War period, characterized by the lack of "a single set of images held by most participants," many of the earlier shared attitudes such as "nuclear war would be a great disaster and must be avoided" carried forward.[255] However, these inherited shared images did not

---

253   Talbott, Strobe, *The Russia Hand: A Memoir of Presidential Diplomacy*, 2003, pp. 380-386.

254   Welch, Larry, Chair, "Report of the Panel on Reducing Risk In Ballistic Missile Defense Flight Test Programs," Department of Defense, February 27, 1998; Government Accountability Office, *National Missile Defense: Even With Increased Funding Technical and Schedule Risks Are High*, June 1998; Cirincione, Joseph, "Rush to Failure," *Bulletin of the Atomic Scientists*, May 1998, pp. 23-25.

255   Halperin, Morton H., and Priscilla A. Clapp, *Bureaucratic Politics*

contribute to a consensus on relevant threat actors in the developing strategic environment. While the image that nuclear war or attacks must be avoided, the methods by which the United States should defend against emerging nuclear threats were highly debated. This lack of consensus perpetuated historical arguments and policy solutions despite the absence of the Cold War's circumstances.

FRAMEWORK

The question of how much flexibility policymakers had concerning missile defense is answered by an examination of the administrations of Presidents Bush and Clinton. Prior to assuming office neither president was an ardent supporter of missile defense, but their positions shifted toward capability development once they were confronted with domestic political and military-industrial pressures. In the case of Congress, rival policymaking practices after the 1994 elections severely limited presidential flexibility. When Congress disagreed with administration policy it refused to fund programs, added additional funds above presidential requests, or attempted to legislate alternative policies.[256] This combative environment, characterized by multiple stakeholder positions, meant that each administration had limited room to maneuver on missile defense.

Contractor commitment to the program under President Reagan also proved resilient, offering new approaches to replace technological and political impediments to program continuation. Theoretically, private industry is said to be more responsive and flexible, but Eugene Gholz and Harvey Sapolsky argued that the Reagan build-up imbedded a "production-capacity overhang" in the structure of the defense industry that distorts

---

and Foreign Policy, 2nd edition 2006, pp. 9-11.
256   Hahn, Robert F. III, "The Congressional Defense Department: Competitive Strategy Making in the Post-Cold-War Era," *Airpower Journal*, Special Edition 1995.

defense policy in the United States.[257] This Cold War defense contracting infrastructure served as an organizational constraint for the Department of Defense. For example, because missile defense was a highly technical undertaking, existing contractors were in the best position to develop, and then internally and externally lobby for new designs. This meant that the Global Protection Against Limited Strikes and three-plus-three concepts emanated from the same source: defense contractors and the Strategic Defense Initiative Organization. Despite being from different political parties, the Republican Bush administration and the Democratic Clinton administration received reports and policy recommendations from the same bureaucratic actors. These actors relayed technical recommendations from contractors that had vested interests in program continuation, regardless of results or costs.[258]

Rules prescribed by the Constitution and statutory policies framed national missile defense efforts. Again, these were the same rules and action channels as those present during the Cold War period. Craig Eisendrath, Melvin Goodman, and Gerald Marsh cited this phenomenon to argue that "many problems encountered in handling missile defense are endemic to the system of government in the United States."[259] Key aspects of policy development within the United States represented in this study are the ability of each stakeholder to establish policy, the enduring composition of the Congress and the bureaucracy, and the existence of channels for unsatisfied stakeholders to continue policy debates. The impact of shared government was a recurring theme of the analysis. In the U.S. system there was no a single stakeholder empowered to set and execute policy.

---

257   Sigal, Leon V., ed., *The Changing Dynamics of U.S. Defense Spending*, 1999, pp. 153-154.
258   Hartung, William D., and Michelle Carrocca, "Star Wars II: Here We Go Again," *The Nation*, June 19, 2000.
259   Eisendrath, Craig, Melvin A. Goodman, and Gerald E. Marsh, *The Phantom Defense: America's Pursuit of the Star Wars Illusion*, 2001, pp. 29-41.

Compromise was required in policy development which, as was the case with national missile defense, routinely led dissatisfied stakeholders to continue the debate along different action channels over the span of multiple administrations.

CONSTRAINTS

President Reagan was responsible for redefining the national missile defense norm. While proponents still existed in the period between the signing of the ABM Treaty and the announcement of Strategic Defense Initiative, the prominent belief was that missile defense was a costly endeavor that was not technologically feasible at the time. This norm was replaced with partisan positions that facilitated the expansion of supporting missile defense infrastructure. Frances Fitzgerald remarked that national missile defense "survived declining defense budgets. It survived the fall-off of public interest so complete that many consistent newspaper readers thought the program had died. It survived the collapse of the Soviet Union. It survived despite the fact that there was no technological breakthrough, and that by 1999 the prospects for deploying an effective interceptor remained not very much brighter than they had been in 1983."[260] Regardless of these barriers, and numerous expert predictions to the contrary, Reagan's national missile defense norm endured well into the 21st century.

An explanation for the continuation of the national missile defense norm can be found in path dependence and procurement politics theory.[261] In the case of the military-industrial complex, the large infusion of funding during the Reagan administration expanded supporting infrastructure and political influence. The importance of contract firm influence and strategic dispersion cannot be underestimated. For example, Peter Leitner, Senior

---

260   Fitzgerald, Frances, *Way Out There in the Blue: Reagan, Star Wars and the End of the Cold War*, 2000, pp. 479-480.
261   For more on U.S. military procurement, see Thomas L. McNaugher, *New weapons, old politics: America's military procurement muddle*, 1989.

Strategic Trade Advisor for the Defense Technology Security
Administration from 1986-2007, recalled:

> In 1990, during a visit to McDonnell Douglas's headquarters in St.
> Louis I was invited into their "war room." This room was a large
> planning/conference room that had a large map of the United States
> on the wall. This map was divided into congressional districts and
> each was color-coded to indicate the dollar amount, number of jobs,
> and the specific product line some entity in that district was subcon-
> tracted to build or supply for McDonnell Douglas. I was told the
> purpose was to quickly generate a great deal of political pressure
> on Congress if a program needed to be funded or a cut in funding
> was threatened. The only district in the U.S. that had no McDonnell
> Douglas activity was the Wisconsin district of Congressman Les
> Aspin, who was seen as an enemy of defense spending in general,
> and McDonnell Douglas specifically.[262]

This type of strategic dispersion of infrastructure to important political constituencies in conjunction with significant
campaign and political action committee contributions ensured
maximum representation.

Even during the period directly following the dissolution
of the Soviet Union, existing missile defense efforts were sufficient to sustain programs in the absence of a defined threat.
This line of reasoning extended to President Clinton's initial
term where reduced national missile defense efforts continued
until the Republican ascendancy in Congress after the 1994
elections. Opponents were not in a position to completely end
national missile defense even at its lowest points during the two
transitions in administrations, and efforts to redefine the priority
to limited or regional missile defense were unable to replace the
national emphasis of conservative Republicans.

An examination of actor positions assists with understanding
why national missile defense remained the norm following the

---

262   Interview with Department of Defense, Defense Technology
Security Administration, Senior Strategic Trade Advisor, Peter Leitner,
January 22, 2011.

Cold War. In reference to general military procurement, James Wilson offered that, a "sinister military-industrial complex" is not "conspiring to keep new weapons flowing."[263] On the contrary, "the armed services want them because they believe, rightly, that their task is to defend the nation against real though hard to define threats; the contractors want them because they believe, rightly, that the nation cannot afford to dismantle its productive capacity; Congress wants them because its members believe, rightly, that they are elected to maintain the prosperity of their states and districts."[264] In this explanation, two of the three key stakeholders, Congress and the bureaucracy, had a vested interest in the continuation of missile defense. The third stakeholder, the president, had a limited, transitory stake in missile defense.

Neither administration examined in this case study was a proponent of national missile defense prior to assuming office. Nevertheless, once in office, national missile defense programs retained funding despite initial efforts by both administrations to alter existing missile defense efforts. Neither administration had the political capital to end national missile defense or to realign national objectives to limit missile defense. Despite repeated failures, it remained in the best interest of the Defense Department to offer new design recommendations for program continuation, instead of recommending a return to pre-Reagan norms. If this were the case, the department would have forfeited high-profile policy influence, billions in annual funding, and inferred its increasing irrelevance in the post-Cold War era.

The issue of missile defense was demonstrative of the highly politicized nature of nuclear defense where multiple actors influenced the policy development process. Competing stakeholder agendas and unrealistic policy, facilitated by the lack of an immediate threat and public disinterest, allowed missile defense

---

263   Wilson, James Q., *Bureaucracy: What Government Agencies Do and Why They Do It*, 2nd edition 2000, p. 325.
264   Ibid.

programs to benefit for many years. Domestic politics affected international relations to the point of negatively impacting other nuclear defense efforts such as START II. Missile defense highlighted the inability of the system to change rapidly and the long-term effects of enduring congressional actors, bureaucracies, and contractors that transcend presidential administrations.[265] As a result of this stagnation, many recurring nuclear defense arguments such as those associated with missile defense were based largely on elite opinion, group interests, and historic norms, and not on collective security solutions developed to reflect the existing and emerging strategic environment.

CONCLUSION

This chapter continued the examination of how and why U.S. nuclear defense policy evolved following the Cold War. National missile defense policy formulation illustrated that there are multiple sources of national policy origination, that personal and organizational interests are of primary importance, and that participants adhere to norms despite altered circumstances. The executive and legislative branches, as well as the political parties, held different positions on missile defense. Conservative Republicans were determined to establish a national missile defense system despite changes to the strategic landscape, technological barriers, or potentially negative impacts on the global strategic balance. Democrats were generally not in favor of national missile defense but did not present a consistent, unified

---

265 Non-elected political appointees rotated in and out of government with their party of choice. These career political staffers continued to influence nuclear defense policy in various governmental and non-governmental positions while their party was out of the executive branch or in the minority. But authors such as David Dunn have noted that there was a difference in appointees between first and second terms due to availability and burnout. Dunn, David H., "Quacking Like a Duck? Bush II and Presidential Power in the Second Term," *International Affairs*, Vol. 82, No. 1, January 2006, pp. 95-120.

opposition. Compromised policy decisions continued to enable multiple arguments for the duration of the George H. W. Bush and William J. Clinton administrations as stakeholders repeatedly sought to impose their agendas through different channels in the national policy process.

The research for this case study identified that post-Cold War U.S. missile defense policy was anchored in bureaucratic politics, not collective defense. As suggested in the START case study, actors and stakeholders displayed distinct positions that influenced policy decisions. These positions were tied to personal and organizational interests, not national nuclear defense. The national missile defense study revealed the influence of contracting firms on the policy development process. The president, Congress, and the bureaucracy relied on contractor expertise for technical solutions. The same contracting firms used political contributions and strategic factory locations to place coordinated pressure on actors involved in policy development. Despite a drastically altered threat, this support enabled national missile defense proponents to continue Cold War policy arguments in the period of transition under President Bush, and to aggressively seek national missile defense legislation during the Clinton administration.

The next chapter moves beyond policy development to examine policy execution and the questions of how and to what extent implementation reflected national policy objectives. Given that national policies were the result of aggregating multiple positions -- and are often written in vague, general language if internal to the United States -- this was not a straightforward task. Unlike treaties, domestic nuclear defense policies were generally little more than an idea when adopted. The result of the policy development process as described in this chapter is an ambiguous policy foundation that facilitated a new action channel for bureaucratic actors. While the president and Congress exert superior influence under the policy development rules, the bureaucracy benefits from career service, subject matter expertise, infrastructure, coalition participation, and a lack of oversight from political actors during the execution of national nuclear defense policies.[266]

---

266   Kozak, David C., and James M. Keagle, eds., *Bureaucratic Politics and National Security: Theory and Practice*, 1988, p. 22.

CHAPTER 3

THREAT REDUCTION
IMPLEMENTATION STUDY

The previous case study chapters dealt with United States national nuclear defense policy development following the Cold War. Once approving authorities finalize national policy, implementing organizations then establish programs to achieve the stated objectives. The assumption has been made that these organizations loyally implement policymaker intent, but many authors have questioned the extent to which government bureaucracies faithfully execute national policy decisions.[267] To understand this part of the process better, the second supporting research question asks, "How has the U.S. government implemented post-Cold War nuclear defense policy, and to what extent have corresponding objectives been realized?"

The main thrust of the policy implementation chapters is to examine the extent to which corresponding implementation programs reflected the visions and decisions of policymakers. They consider the extent to which implementing organizations collectively executed policy decisions to maximize federal efforts, and whether dissatisfied actors used their operational role

---

267 Allison, Graham T., and Morton H. Halperin, "Bureaucratic Politics: A Paradigm and Some Policy Implications," *World Politics,* Vol. 24, Spring 1972, pp. 54-56; Keagle, James M., "Introduction and Framework," in David C. Kozak, and James M. Keagle, eds., *Bureaucratic Politics and National Security: Theory and Practice,* 1988, p. 22.

as an action channel to continue positional arguments. In short, does the bureaucracy place organizational interests above idealized national policy execution? Bureaucratic politics theory emphasizes that policy decisions "leave considerable leeway" for interpretation and implementation, and "are rarely tailored to facilitate monitoring."[268] This suggests that implementing organizations have the flexibility to execute policy in the manner which they see fit. In this respect, then, the hypothesis for the policy implementation studies states, "The U.S. government was not organized to address nuclear defense, and as a result did not collaboratively implement evolving national policies." The chapters also examine the association between segmented policy development and implementation, and the relationship of the identified programs within the layered nuclear defense structure.

This chapter and the next two examine the intricacies of policy implementation by focusing on three different nuclear defense areas and federal approaches. The current chapter investigates the nuclear defense area of "prevention," which comprises efforts to prevent the spread of nuclear weapons, materials, delivery systems, sensitive information, or expertise to state and non-state actors. As the Cold War ended, congressional leaders quickly identified that the collapse of the Soviet Union posed a threat in the context of the tons of unsecured legacy fissile materials and tens of thousands of nuclear weapons, some of which could not be accounted for because of inaccuracies in record keeping and political instability. The resulting congressional efforts to prevent the proliferation of former Soviet weapons of mass destruction, materials, and expertise through controlled reduction, enhanced security, and re-employment became known as the Cooperative Threat Reduction (CTR) program.

Initial efforts were placed in the Department of Defense, but once operations were underway, it was apparent that expertise

---

268   Allison, Graham T., and Morton H. Halperin, "Bureaucratic Politics: A Paradigm and Some Policy Implications," *World Politics,* Vol. 24, Spring 1972, p. 53.

and capabilities related to all aspects of threat reduction resided throughout the federal government.[269] In 1995, the Clinton administration shifted CTR to an interagency implementation approach, where departments conducted independent execution with minimal White House-led coordination. The Department of Defense retained responsibility for weapons and delivery vehicles, the Department of Energy continued to focus on fissile material and expertise, the Department of State remained oriented on expertise and interagency reporting, and other departments and agencies assisted as required.[270]

This case study examines national threat reduction actors before conducting a detailed analysis of the Department of Defense CTR program from 2001 to 2009. The study uses a single program branch within CTR, related to Strategic Offensive Arms Elimination. The chapter begins by examining relevant policy decisions before proceeding to consider national threat reduction actors, CTR organization and workflow, and program evaluation. The section on policy decisions identifies that CTR legislation established department specific objectives. The actor section continues the representation of separate national threat reduction efforts. It further identifies segregated federal design where each department derived policy objectives, specified instructions, and funding from multiple sources within a national threat reduction landscape lacking a unified federal strategy or operational plan.

The organization and workflow section describes the Defense Threat Reduction Agency and CTR Directorate. While other organizations within the Office of the Secretary of Defense

---

269   Interview with Department of Defense, Defense Threat Reduction Agency, Cooperative Threat Reduction Strategic Offensive Arms Elimination Program Official, February 19, 2010.

270   The Department of Defense retained the Cooperative Threat Reduction title, while other departments used different names to refer to related threat reduction programs. Woolf, Amy F., "Nunn-Lugar Cooperative Threat Reduction Programs: Issues for Congress," *CRS Report for Congress*, March 6, 2002, pp. 2-6.

were involved in policy implementation, the CTR Directorate was responsible for the execution of all Defense Department CTR projects. The section on workflow introduces the Strategic Offensive Arms Elimination program branch. This portion of the chapter uses the individual program branch to identify organizational limitations that prohibited integrated policy execution. For example, each Strategic Offensive Arms Elimination project was executed as a Department of Defense contract and not as a collective interagency endeavor. These individual efforts followed federal contracting procedures, but were solely executed and managed by mechanisms internal to the Defense Department.

The chapter finishes with a program evaluation section drawing on criteria related to pace, accountability, defined host nation responsibilities, interagency integration, the extent to which policy objectives were realized, counterarguments, and theoretical applicability. These criteria were derived from previous reports, investigations, and the second supporting research question. This section focuses on the Strategic Offensive Arms Elimination program branch to examine issues of pace, accountability, and defined Russian Federation responsibilities before evaluating the extent to which the Defense Department CTR program realized specified policy objectives. The final three criteria -- interagency integration, counterarguments, and theoretical applicability -- encompass national threat reduction efforts. The evaluation reveals that separate departmental projects and programs were designed to comply with standard operating procedures, federal regulations, and internal policy objectives, rather than national threat reduction policy implementation.

POLICY DECISIONS

Congressional champions, such as Senators Sam Nunn and Richard Lugar, defined initial threat reduction policy objectives as efforts to prevent the unauthorized transfer of nuclear weapons, material, or expertise from the former Soviet Union.[271] In fiscal year 1992, Congress directed the Department of Defense to reprogram $400 million of their current year budget to implement new threat reduction programs.[272] Although authorization and initial funding reprogramming had been approved by Congress and the White House, there initially existed no standing organization to execute the new tasks.[273] Moreover, host nation governments were in-flux because of the dissolution of the Soviet Union, and it was readily apparent that the specialized expertise required for many technical and diplomatic tasks was dispersed across the Departments of Defense, Energy, and State. The identification of required interagency functions meant that threat reduction represented what Anthony Downs describes as shared policy space – that is, areas where organizations have "overlapping and intertwining relations."[274] In Downs' theory of bureaucratic decision-making, organizations that operate in shared policy space strive to distinguish their programs to ensure survival.[275] In this regard, agencies are highly defensive of interior territory related to traditional tasks, and attempt to minimize conflict in exterior zones where the organization has little or no influence. Thus, according to Downs, organizations

---

271   *Soviet Nuclear Threat Reduction Act of 1991* (H.R 3807, P.L. 102-228, Title II).

272   In the case of the initial CTR authorization, there was no incentive for the Defense Department to redistribute reallocated funds to other departments. Combs, Richard, "U.S. Domestic Politics and the Nunn-Lugar Program," in John M. Shields, and William C. Potter, eds., *Dismantling the Cold War: U.S. and NIS Perspectives on the Nunn-Lugar Cooperative Threat Reduction Program*, 1997, p. 44.

273   Morton Halperin and Priscilla Clapp offered that when new functions come with new funds they are desirable to an organization, but when they are a reallocation of old funds they may need to be resisted, especially if the new tasks are not closely related to existing functions. Halperin, Morton H., and Priscilla A. Clapp, *Bureaucratic Politics and Foreign Policy*, 2nd edition 2006, p. 57.

274   Downs used the term "policy space." Downs, Anthony, *Inside Bureaucracy*, 1967, p. 212.

275   Ibid., pp. 212-218.

"consume a great deal of time and energy in territorial struggles that create no socially useful products."[276]

At first, the Department of State used diplomatic channels to begin negotiations with the newly independent states of the former Soviet Union. When the Department of Defense began to assign threat reduction tasks it became clear that, although it had responsibility for nuclear weapons employment, weapons designers and manufacturing-related professionals resided within the Department of Energy's nuclear weapons complex. Initially, the Department of Defense contracted civilian firms and other government departments and agencies to conduct, or to subcontract, projects related to their areas of expertise. However, this early lead agency process proved slow and presented an easy target for opposition congressional actors such as America first platform Democratic Senator Harris Wofford, and conservative Republicans that saw the program simply as foreign aid.[277]

In terms of funding, threat reduction projects experienced delays until the program matured. For example, the initial funding authorization was passed late in the first quarter of fiscal year 1992, which left only eight months for policy execution and one month for budget close-out procedures in that fiscal year.[278]

---

276   This dynamic is portrayed as "interagency coordination." Ibid., p. 216.

277   Duffy, Gloria, "Cooperative Threat Reduction in Perspective," and Richard Combs, "U.S. Domestic Politics and the Nunn-Lugar Program," in John M. Shields, and William C. Potter, eds., *Dismantling the Cold War: U.S. and NIS Perspectives on the Nunn-Lugar Cooperative Threat Reduction Program*, 1997, pp. 31-36 and 43-51.

278   The federal budget process required organizations to obligate or reprogram and execute funds that were set to expire at the end of the fiscal year during the month of September. Funding that was not spent in or obligated against the prior fiscal year could not be used in subsequent fiscal years without congressional approval. Because of the length of many CTR projects, Congress realized that annual funds were not ideal and extended transfer authorizations in the first two years. Initial appropriations were categorized as no-year funds, before shifting to the current three year funding. These no-year and multiple-year classifications minimized annual close out constraints and routine delays associated with new fiscal year funding.

This meant the Defense Department only had limited time to assign program responsibility, to coordinate projects, to request reprogramming, to initiate contracting procedures, to supervise work, to issue payment, to rectify accounts, and to report back to Congress before the funds expired at the end of the fiscal year.[279] This process was further complicated and constrained by initial legislative direction to "buy American," fluctuation in host nation currencies and differing contracting and accounting practices within the former Soviet Union.[280] Indeed, funding and contracting complexities were exacerbated by dissatisfaction on the part of interested political actors and target groups. These early troubles nearly converged to end threat reduction efforts before they began.[281]

---

279   The Department of Defense used the program objective memorandum as part of the planning, programming, budgeting, and execution process to forecast funding requirements five years beyond the current fiscal year (six years total). This standardized process was not possible in the beginning because CTR was not a funded program, and cumulative data to forecast projections did not exist. Instead, funding for fiscal year 1992 and 1993 was discretionary transfer authority for $400 million each year in funds from other Department of Defense accounts. In this case, the funds going to Department of Energy for example were transferred within Department of Defense, then to Department of Energy, and finally dispersed per contract terms. As a result of tensions, compromise, and inefficiencies associated with a new program, CTR forfeited $330 million in unused funds at the end of fiscal year 1993. Combs, Richard, "U.S. Domestic Politics and the Nunn-Lugar Program," in John M. Shields, and William C. Potter, eds., *Dismantling the Cold War: U.S. and NIS Perspectives on the Nunn-Lugar Cooperative Threat Reduction Program*, 1997, pp. 47-49; Army Force Management School, *An Executive Primer: Department of Defense Planning, Programming, Budgeting, and Execution (PPBE) Process/Army Planning, Programming, Budgeting, and Execution (PPBE) Process*, May 2006.
280   The buy American and differences in contracting practices between the United States and Russia are examples of what James Wilson described as political rules. Although these impediments are often associated with bureaucratic "red tape," they are actually the result of political, not bureaucratic constraints. Wilson, James Q., *Bureaucracy: What Government Agencies Do and Why They Do It*, 2nd edition 2000, p. 121.
281   Downs, Anthony, *Inside Bureaucracy*, 1967, p. 7-8.

In fiscal year 1994, CTR was included as a funded program in the annual National Defense Authorization Act, but shortly thereafter it underwent a highly-political continuation process following mid-term elections.[282] Threat reduction shifted from a Defense Department program to interagency implementation in fiscal year 1995.[283] Despite this change in federal approach, political objectives continued to adhere to the *Cooperative Threat Reduction Act of 1993*.[284] The redesign decentralized funding oversight to separate congressional committees, thus complicating Republican efforts led by Congressman Floyd Spence and Senator Strom Thurmond to eliminate threat reduction programs.[285]

National policy objectives were largely unchanged throughout the transition to interagency implementation. By fiscal year 1996, the specific CTR objectives of the Department of Defense were to establish:

---

282   *National Defense Authorization Act for Fiscal Year 1994*, Title XII, Sec. 1205.

283   Combs, Richard, "U.S. Domestic Politics and the Nunn-Lugar Program," in John M. Shields, and William C. Potter, eds., *Dismantling the Cold War: U.S. and NIS Perspectives on the Nunn-Lugar Cooperative Threat Reduction Program*, 1997, pp. 49-50.

284   *National Defense Authorization Act for Fiscal Year 1994*, Title XII, Sec. 1203(b).

285   The Department of Defense and Department of Energy nonproliferation authorizations continued to emanate from the annual defense authorizations acts, but appropriations for each department came from different congressional committees. The Department of Defense fell under the Defense Subcommittees, Department of Energy the Energy and Water Subcommittees, and Department of State the Foreign Relations Committees for authorization and Foreign Operations Committees for appropriations. Each of these committees used different funding requirements and restrictions. Combs, Richard, "U.S. Domestic Politics and the Nunn-Lugar Program," in John M. Shields, and William C. Potter, eds., *Dismantling the Cold War: U.S. and NIS Perspectives on the Nunn-Lugar Cooperative Threat Reduction Program*, 1997, pp. 50-56.

(1) Programs to facilitate the elimination, and the safe and secure transportation and storage, of nuclear, chemical, and other weapons and their delivery vehicles.

(2) Programs to facilitate the safe and secure storage of fissile materials derived from the elimination of nuclear weapons.

(3) Programs to prevent the proliferation of weapons, weapons components, and weapons-related technology and expertise.

(4) Programs to expand military-to-military and defense contacts.[286]

The conversion to interagency implementation reduced national coordination requirements, and allowed the individual departments to work with their designated congressional committees related to defense, energy and water, and foreign affairs. While this approach represented a move away from "national implementation" under a lead federal agency, it did eliminate formal and cumbersome interagency requirements related to planning and execution, and reduced the active role of the National Security Council (NSC) staff.[287] From a resource standpoint, CTR also became a decentralized and therefore more difficult target for its political opponents to attack. Ultimately, the decision by Deputy Secretary of Defense John Deutch to reduce the visibility of CTR by shifting funding directly to departmental budgets -- especially with deteriorating American relations with

---

286   This definition was carried forward to fiscal year 1997, and then simply referenced as the programs specified in section 1501(b) of the fiscal year 1997 act, until the fiscal year 2008 National Defense Authorization Act, when Congress began to look beyond the former Soviet Union in sections 1303 and 1305. *National Defense Authorization Act for Fiscal Year 1996*, Title XII, Sec. 1201.

287   Prior to separation the NSC staff deconflicted departmental differences and led hasty efforts such as Project Sapphire, a United States (Departments of Defense, Energy, State, and the Central Intelligence Agency), Russia, and Kazakhstan covert operation to remove 600 kilograms of highly enriched uranium from Ust-Kamenogorsk, Kazakhstan. These intensive requirements were reduced with the transfer to interagency execution. Interviews with Department of Defense, Defense Threat Reduction Agency Historian Joseph Harahan, April 26, 2010; Carter, Ashton B., and William J. Perry, *Preventive Defense: A New Security Strategy for America*, 1999, pp. 65-69.

the former Soviet Republics during the Clinton administration -- helped to continue threat reduction efforts.[288]

New post-9/11 requirements to expand CTR work outside of the former Soviet Union emerged in conjunction with the war on terror. Policy decisions in this respect were the result of early Iraq debates that included the potential for elimination of weapons of mass destruction following an invasion. Although Congress funded threat reduction programs individually in annual legislation, it routinely provided reprogramming latitude within the former Soviet Union based on needs and specified procedures. Initial authorization to reprogram funds for use outside the former Soviet Union came in fiscal year 2004, with procedures simplified in fiscal year 2008.[289] The 2008 change, coincided with the recommendations of a National Academy of Sciences study which evaluated the prospects of threat reduction expansion beyond the former Soviet Union, and the reorientation from weapons and delivery vehicle programs to special nuclear materials.[290]

288   Combs, Richard, "U.S. Domestic Politics and the Nunn-Lugar Program," in John M. Shields, and William C. Potter, eds., *Dismantling the Cold War: U.S. and NIS Perspectives on the Nunn-Lugar Cooperative Threat Reduction Program*, 1997, pp. 49-50.

289   CTR conducted successful operations in Albania to destroy a Soviet era chemical weapons cache, but similar efforts did not materialize during the George W. Bush administration. National Academy of Sciences, *Global Security Engagement: A New Model for Cooperative Threat Reduction,* Committee Report, 2009, p. 34; Interviews with Department of Defense, Under Secretary of Defense for Policy, Cooperative Threat Reduction Policy Office Director James Reid, and NSC Staff, Director of Proliferation Strategy Susan Koch, April 29, and May 10, 2010.

290   Completion of the National Academy of Sciences report, and subsequent changes extended into the Obama administration. Special nuclear materials referred to fissile materials, for a complete definition and disposition of special nuclear materials, see the *Atomic Energy Act of 1954, as Amended,* and Government Accountability Office, *Securing U.S. Nuclear Material: Department of Energy Has Made Little Progress Consolidating and Disposing of Special Nuclear Material,* October 2007.

Just as Allison and Halperin suggested, there was considerable leeway in terms of interpreting and implementing CTR policy objectives.[291] Initial, and revised, political objectives specified program types with legislative constraints added based on political actor positions rather than implementation considerations. On this last point, James Wilson emphasizes the changing nature of Congressional influence over the bureaucracy. Where Congress once directed implementation, it now uses constraints to guide bureaucratic actions.[292] Constraints can be specific to a single policy, such as "buy American" for CTR, or generally extend into multiple areas such as the "goal of fairness" in federal contracting regulations.[293] The bureaucratic politics approach also suggests that major change was associated with senior actor deadlines and junior actor interests in search of a problem, but threat reduction formulation did not demonstrate this aspect of the theory.[294] Rather, change occurred in response to a catalyst event, the dissolution of the Soviet Union.

NATIONAL THREAT REDUCTION ACTORS

Because of the diverse nature of threat reduction which encompassed legacy weapons, materials, and expertise, the realization of single program achievements such as the elimination of weapons and delivery systems did not equate to the successful completion of all national CTR objectives. From a federal threat reduction perspective, interagency programs and

---

291   Allison, Graham T., and Morton H. Halperin, "Bureaucratic Politics: A Paradigm and Some Policy Implications," *World Politics,* Vol. 24, Spring 1972, p. 53.

292   Wilson, James Q., *Bureaucracy: What Government Agencies Do and Why They Do It,* 2nd edition 2000, pp. 237-241.

293   Ibid., pp. 126-129.

294   Allison, Graham T., and Morton H. Halperin, "Bureaucratic Politics: A Paradigm and Some Policy Implications," *World Politics,* Vol. 24, Spring 1972, pp. 53-54.

implementation were vital to completing broader U.S. government policy objectives. However, despite the requirement for
interagency implementation, a national director for threat reduction with the power to direct collaborative planning and execution, or to approve individual department budgets, did not exist.

CONGRESS

The primary congressional committees charged with
CTR oversight were the House and Senate Armed Services
Committees.[295] The *National Defense Authorization Act for
Fiscal Year 2001* added the requirement of an annual CTR
report to Congress.[296] The act dictated that the report must be
delivered no later than the first Monday in February of each year
and include a five-year plan, cost estimates, program descriptions and program examinations.[297] The act also called for a
Russian non-strategic nuclear arms assessment within 30 days
of enactment, and a yearly classified intelligence annex and
comptroller general assessment of the CTR five-year plan and
accountability reporting 60 days after submission of the annual
report.[298] This new constraint was a reactionary requirement in

---

295   The Appropriations Committee allocated funds in the annual defense appropriations acts based on the authorization acts and input of the
Appropriations Subcommittee. The CTR portion of the annual act was a single paragraph that stated the purpose, aggregate funding amount, expiration,
and any specific program amounts. *Department of Defense Appropriations
Act, 2006* (H.R. 2863, P.L. 109-148), Title II, Former Soviet Union Threat
Reduction Account.
296   The legislation did not stipulate distribution, but these reports
were routed through the Armed Services Committees and other interested
committees. *National Defense Authorization Act for Fiscal Year 2001*, Title
XIII, Sec. 1308; U.S. Government Accountability Office, *Cooperative Threat
Reduction Program Annual Report,* December 2, 2002; Anthony, *Inside
Bureaucracy*, 1967, pp. 145-146.
297   The first report was submitted by the Defense Department on
September 3, 2002, nearly 19 months late. U.S. Government Accountability
Office, *Cooperative Threat Reduction Program Annual Report,* December 2,
2002.
298   *National Defense Authorization Act for Fiscal Year 2001*, Title

response to two significant Department of Defense management failures covered later in the chapter, rather than an attempt to improve active national oversight.[299] As a result, it only accounted for the threat reduction efforts of a single department, not the entire federal government. This point was explained by the 2008 Project on National Security Reform study, *Forging a New Shield.* The study concluded that Congress provided resources and oversight in ways that reinforced systemic limitations and precluded collaborative interagency operations.[300] Findings indicated that Congress focused "almost exclusively on department and agency capabilities," and that current congressional organization meant that no committee was "devoted to overseeing interagency mechanisms or multi-agency operations."[301] In this regard, the Armed Services Committees were only concerned with Defense Department programs, and limited Department of Energy initiatives that fell under the purview of defense authorization.

Beyond the formal legislative structures several congressional champions actively supported threat reduction.[302] The two most notable champions were Senators Sam Nunn and Richard Lugar whose names were synonymous with threat reduction and whose efforts continued beyond the initial legislation.[303] Senator Nunn left the Senate in 1997, but Senator Lugar remained as a

---

XIII, Sec. 1308(e).
299   Wilson, James Q., *Bureaucracy: What Government Agencies Do and Why They Do It*, 2nd edition 2000, pp. 126-129.
300   Locher, James R. III, Executive Director, *Forging a New Shield,* Project on National Security Reform, 2008, p. 594.
301   Ibid.
302   In addition to committee staffs, member staffs such as Senator Lugar's, played an active role in formal and informal communications and legislation preparation.   Interviews with Department of Defense, Under Secretary of Defense for Policy, Cooperative Threat Reduction Policy Office Director James Reid, and Senior Legislative Assistant for Foreign Policy to Senator Lugar, Andrew Semmel, April 29, and November 17, 2010.
303   Lugar, Richard G., "The Nunn-Lugar Threat Reduction Program," retrieved June 10, 2010.

recognized subject matter expert and active champion of the program.[304] Senator Lugar had an enlarged Nunn-Lugar Scorecard displayed in his office area, routinely spoke on and provided press releases about the program, and educated interested members of Congress on the merits of CTR.[305] This example demonstrated the importance of a knowledgeable political actor championing policy formulation and implementation, especially in regard to topics that divide politicians along party or ideological lines.[306]

WHITE HOUSE

Similar to other administrations, the NSC staff under George W. Bush comprised less than 200 members, with many career civil servants and military personnel leveraged from the departments and agencies.[307] This small, highly-diverse staff was organized by geographic, functional, and support directorates of five to ten members, with responsibilities for policy advice and development, implementation dissemination, and situational awareness at the federal level.[308] During the Bush administration

---

304   Former Senator Sam Nunn continued his support through non-governmental organization forums. He remained an active representative of the program through speeches, appearances, lobbying, and formation of the Nuclear Threat Initiative.

305   Senator Lugar's outreach efforts included partnering with then Democratic Senator Barrack Obama when he entered the Senate in 2005. Lugar, Richard G., "The Nunn-Lugar Threat Reduction Program," retrieved June 10, 2010; Biegun, Stephen E., Presider, and Richard G. Lugar, and Barrack Obama, Speakers, "Challenges Ahead for Cooperative Threat Reduction," transcript, Council on Foreign Relations, Washington, D.C., November 1, 2005.

306   Arnold, R. Douglas, *Congress and the Bureaucracy: A Theory of Influence*, 1979, pp. 41-54.

307   For more on the general structure of the NSC staff, see White House, "William J. Clinton Administration: NSC Staff," Office of the White House Press Secretary, retrieved November 5, 2008.

308   During the George W. Bush presidency, there was also a Homeland Security Council staff that coordinated with the NSC staff and departments on a range of nuclear defense issues related to homeland security. This new staff did not play a significant role in established threat reduction implementation.

the Proliferation Strategy Policy Coordinating Committee was responsible for threat reduction. This committee was chaired by the Special Assistant to the President and Senior Director for Proliferation Strategy, Counterproliferation, and Homeland Defense.[309]

The senior director led the Office of Proliferation Strategy. This NSC staff directorate consisted of a director and four personnel responsible for broad portfolios in all weapons of mass destruction areas, supporting programs, treaties and regimes, and related national strategies. The directorate set general policy for U.S. nonproliferation programs, but did not have control of implementation operations or departmental budgets.[310] By 2001, the NSC staff was not engaged in routine operating functions related to threat reduction.[311] Joseph Harahan referenced a discussion with Clinton NSC staff member Steven Pifer, where the latter related that threat reduction disappeared from the routine portfolio once it was separated into an interagency program.[312] Susan Koch, who served on the George H. W. and George W. Bush NSC staffs and in the Office of the Secretary of Defense during the Clinton administration, also emphasized that threat reduction required much more direct involvement from senior leaders and staffs during the early years, but had been institutionalized by 2001.[313]

Interviews with Homeland Security Council Staff, Office of Nuclear Defense Policy Director Timothy Nank, and NSC Staff, Director of Proliferation Strategy Susan Koch, April 24, and May 10, 2010.
309   Government Accountability Office, *Weapons of Mass Destruction: Nonproliferation Programs Need Better Integration*, January 2005, p. 7.
310   Ibid.
311   Interviews with Department of Defense, Defense Threat Reduction Agency Historian Joseph Harahan, and NSC Staff, Director of Proliferation Strategy Susan Koch, April 26, and May 10, 2010.
312   Interview with Department of Defense, Defense Threat Reduction Agency Historian Joseph Harahan, April 26, 2010.
313   Interview with NSC Staff, Director of Proliferation Strategy Susan Koch, May 10, 2010.

During this period the policy implementing departments had leeway for operations and routine actions, such as data submission or clarification, with congressional staff members. The NSC staff was involved when policy areas included multiple departments, in the case of priority international actors, or during the development of prominent documents such as the CTR annual report to Congress. The George W. Bush White House played several critical roles concerning validation, funding oversight, interagency coordination, and the expansion of threat reduction programs outside of the former Soviet Union.

Initially George W. Bush's NSC staff conducted a review of U.S. threat reduction programs across the federal government.[314] The results of this study were released in December 2001, and reaffirmed the president's previous commitments to "strong, effective cooperation with Russia and the other states of the former Soviet Union to reduce weapons of mass destruction and prevent their proliferation."[315] This reaffirmation subsequently translated into the G8 Global Partnership "10 plus 10 over 10" program. This G8 initiative established a minimum threat reduction annual funding level of $1 billion per year from the United States to be matched by G8 partners for a period of ten years. The NSC staff monitored federal threat reduction funding through the Office of Management and Budget for the remainder of the administration to ensure the total amount of funding for interagency programs met the president's pledge.[316]

In accordance with the review, the NSC staff also sought to improve interagency execution of U.S. government

---

314   White House, "Fact Sheet: Administration Review of Nonproliferation and Threat Reduction Assistance to the Russian Federation," Office of the White House Press Secretary, December 27, 2001.

315   Ibid.

316   The Department of Defense was identified as the only department that President George W. Bush had to remind about the minimum threat reduction funding commitment. Interview with NSC Staff, Director of Proliferation Strategy Susan Koch, May 10, 2010.

nonproliferation efforts.[317] Through the use of sub-policy coordination committee meetings at the assistant and deputy assistant secretary levels, the NSC staff established interagency guidelines for nonproliferation programs.[318] These guidelines were coordinated at sub-policy coordination committee meetings, and issued by the director of proliferation strategy in classified memoranda format to establish clear lines of responsibility and procedures for interagency coordination.[319] Prompted by the potential weapons of mass destruction elimination requirements in Iraq, the staff also played a critical role in gaining congressional approval for threat reduction expansion outside the former Soviet Union. Following the failure to discover major Iraqi weapons of mass destruction stockpiles, the NSC staff continued to champion the geographical expansion of threat reduction to countries such as Libya.[320]

INTERAGENCY

Although multiple departments and agencies fulfilled threat reduction roles, the three primary departments were the Departments of Defense, Energy, and State. The Department of State was responsible for redirecting scientific expertise and diplomatic efforts, the Department of Energy focused on fissile materials, and the Department of Defense concentrated on weapons and delivery vehicles. Each department had dedicated

---

317   Anthony, *Inside Bureaucracy*, 1967, pp. 54-58.
318   Anthony Downs offered that in the case of overlapping jurisdictions, when lower-level officials cannot agree on how to carry out joint functions, "they must refer the matter to their superior, thus in effect shifting power" to the senior office or official. If subordinate agencies wish to avoid this power shift, they can divide responsibilities along traditional functional lines to maximize independent execution, and minimize potential compromises and the requirement for senior-level intervention. Ibid., pp. 147-148.
319   Interview with NSC Staff, Director of Proliferation Strategy Susan Koch, May 10, 2010.
320   Bowen, Wyn Q., "Libya and Nuclear Proliferation: Stepping back from the brink," The International Institute for Strategic Studies, Adelphi Paper 380, May 2006, pp. 71-79.

threat reduction directorates with program areas bounded by clearly delineated lines of responsibility. Where program areas overlapped between departments, a lead federal agency format was utilized in all but a few cases.[321] In instances where this was not the case, interagency guidance from the NSC staff was used to address questions of responsibility.[322] The majority of threat reduction communication during the period was by e-mail and telephone, or via the Washington Area Secure Facsimile System. Interagency meetings were held as required at the departmental policy level with key actors invited as required. Normally the initiating department hosted interagency meetings with sub-policy coordination committee meetings held at the Old Executive Building.[323] Interagency attendees primarily included policy actors with only an infrequent requirement for the attendance of implementation experts beyond the provision of information papers or pre-briefs.[324]

DEPARTMENT OF STATE

The State Department fulfilled its traditional diplomatic role for new and existing negotiations, and provided international legal expertise as well as limited coordination for and between departments. State obviously played a significant part in communicating with other governments, for example, it cleared every Department of Defense Cooperative Threat Reduction Policy Office cable before it was sent to a host nation government.[325] Beyond general functions, the Department of State

---

321   Government Accountability Office, *Weapons of Mass Destruction: Nonproliferation Programs Need Better Integration,* January 2005, pp. 17-19.
322   Ibid., p. 17.
323   Interview with Department of Defense, Defense Threat Reduction Agency, Cooperative Threat Reduction Director, June 18, 2010.
324   Interview with Department of Defense, Under Secretary of Defense for Policy, Cooperative Threat Reduction Policy Office Director James Reid, April 29, 2010.
325   Ibid.

was responsible for two threat reduction programs – the Global Threat Reduction program and the Export Control and Related Border Security Assistance program.[326]

The Global Threat Reduction program focused on human capital employment. By 2008, the State Department program had 39 countries participating in two international science center's located in Moscow, Russia, and Kiev, Ukraine. This program sought full and partial employment for nuclear scientists through the centers, grants, and partnerships with universities, industry, and other government organizations. The Export Control and Related Border Security Assistance program concentrated on the prevention of smuggling and illegal exports from countries in and around the former Soviet Union. This program included Department of Defense and Energy programs, but the extent and effectiveness of coordination has been questioned by "analysts inside and outside of the government."[327] Despite questions of effectiveness, State's programs demonstrated the greatest extent of interagency integration of the three departments.

DEPARTMENT OF ENERGY

The Department of Energy consolidated several existing threat reduction activities into the Material Protection, Control, and Accounting program.[328] The program's objectives were to

---

326   Woolf, Amy F., "Nonproliferation and Threat Reduction Assistance: U.S. Programs in the Former Soviet Union," *CRS Report for Congress,* February 4, 2010, pp. 24-28.
327   Ibid., pp. 27-28.
328   Existing efforts included the Department of Defense government-to-government program, the Department of Energy laboratory-to-laboratory program, and expansion programs included the Department of Energy Second Line of Defense, and material conversion and consolidation programs. Augustson, Ronald H., and John R. Phillips, as told to Debra A. Daugherty, "Russian-American MPC&A: Nuclear Materials Protection, Control, and Accounting in the Russian Federation," *Los Alamos Science,* Number 24, 1996, pp. 72-83; Department of Energy, "Beyond Guns, Gates and Guards: An Integrated Approach to Nuclear Material Security," National Nuclear Security Administration Briefing, 2008.

secure and reduce fissile materials in the former Soviet Union. The program worked to accomplish these objectives by securing, controlling, and accounting for fissile materials at the sites of origin, and then down-blending the materials. In addition to Material Protection, Control, and Accounting, the Department of Energy had three other material related programs: the Global Initiatives for Proliferation Prevention, the Elimination of Weapons-Grade Plutonium Production program, and the Fissile Materials Disposition program.[329]

The Global Initiatives for Proliferation Prevention incorporated two legacy initiatives designed to employ former Soviet nuclear weapons scientists and to convert select nuclear cities to commercial enterprises. The Elimination of Weapons-Grade Plutonium Production program supported bilateral United States-Russian Federation agreements to replace nuclear reactors with proliferation resistant energy sources. The Fissile Materials Disposition program supported a separate bilateral agreement regarding the conversion of weapons-grade plutonium. This accord called for the United States and Russia to convert surplus plutonium to mixed oxide fuel or another form that could not be used in a nuclear weapon. While the first initiative overlapped with the Departments of State and Defense, the second and third programs were unique to the Department of Energy.

DEPARTMENT OF DEFENSE

The Defense Department is the largest single agency in the U.S. government, and CTR is the oldest program represented in the implementation studies. As such, departmental actors represented a complex management arrangement to ensure compliance with contextual goals and constraints.[330] Departmental

---

329   Woolf, Amy F., "Nonproliferation and Threat Reduction Assistance: U.S. Programs in the Former Soviet Union," *CRS Report for Congress*, February 4, 2010, pp. 28-44.

330   James Wilson defined "contextual goals" as "descriptions of desired states of affairs other than the one the agency was brought into being

responsibility for the Cooperative Threat Reduction program was split between the Assistant Secretary of Defense for International Security Policy, and the Assistant to the Secretary of Defense (Nuclear and Chemical and Biological Defense Programs).[331] The Assistant Secretary of Defense for International Security Policy reported to the Under Secretary of Defense for Policy, while the Assistant to the Secretary of Defense (Nuclear and Chemical and Biological Defense Programs) reported to the Under Secretary of Defense for Acquisition, Technology, and Logistics. The Under Secretary of Defense for Policy, through the Assistant Secretary of Defense for International Security Policy, and the Director, Cooperative Threat Reduction Policy Office, were responsible for policy guidance and oversight, implementation policy, and international agreements.[332] The Under Secretary of Defense for Policy was responsible for external communication with the NSC staff, Congress and relevant interagency partners. In the fiscal year 2008 annual report, the Under Secretary of Defense for Policy defined supporting Cooperative Threat Reduction program objectives as:

---

to create." Wilson, James Q., *Bureaucracy: What Government Agencies Do and Why They Do It*, 2nd edition 2000, pp. 129-134.

331   The Assistant Secretary of Defense for International Security Policy and the Assistant to the Secretary of Defense (Nuclear and Chemical and Biological Defense Programs) were senior executive positions. Department of Defense Directive 5111.14, "Assistant to the Secretary of Defense for International Security Policy," March 22, 2005, sections, 3.1.7 and 3.1.7.1.

332   The assistant secretary position shifted several times during the lifespan of CTR, but the Under Secretary of Defense for Policy and Cooperative Threat Reduction Policy Offices remained the same through multiple reorganizations. For the majority of the George W. Bush administration the Assistant Secretary of Defense for International Security Policy oversaw the Cooperative Threat Reduction Policy Office. Department of Defense, *Management Structure of the Cooperative Threat Reduction Program*, Inspector General Report, February 4, 2004, pp. 2-3; Interview with Department of Defense, Under Secretary of Defense for Policy, Cooperative Threat Reduction Policy Office Director James Reid, April 29, 2010.

[Objective 1] Dismantle former Soviet Union weapons of mass destruction and associated infrastructure,

[Objective 2] consolidate and secure former Soviet Union weapons of mass destruction and related technology and materials,

[Objective 3] increase transparency and encourage higher standards of conduct, and

[Objective 4] support defense and military cooperation with the objective of preventing proliferation.[333]

The Under Secretary of Defense for Acquisition, Technology, and Logistics, through the Assistant to the Secretary of Defense (Nuclear and Chemical and Biological Defense Programs), the Deputy Assistant to the Secretary of Defense (Chemical Demilitarization and Threat Reduction), and the Cooperative Threat Reduction Oversight Office, were responsible for acquisition related guidance, risk reduction, and implementation oversight. The Defense Threat Reduction Agency director reported to the Assistant to the Secretary of Defense (Nuclear and Chemical and Biological Defense Programs) for agency-wide operations, relying on the Under Secretary of Defense for Acquisition, Technology, and Logistics for resources and senior departmental representation.[334]

Within the Assistant to the Secretary of Defense (Nuclear and Chemical and Biological Defense Programs) structure, the Cooperative Threat Reduction Oversight Office was directly responsible for threat reduction implementation guidance and

---

333   Department of Defense, *Cooperative Threat Reduction Annual Report to Congress,* Defense Threat Reduction Agency, Fiscal Year 2008, p. i.

334   The assistant secretary also sponsored the Threat Reduction Advisory Committee. This senior committee was a special advisory panel that was formed in 1998 by Secretary of Defense Cohen to assist with national weapons of mass destruction issues. Ibid, pp. 1-4; Department of Defense, "Department of Defense Launches Threat Reduction Advisory Committee," Office of the Assistant Secretary of Defense (Public Affairs), July 15, 1998; Interview with Department of Defense, Defense Threat Reduction Agency, Deputy Cooperative Threat Reduction Director Mark Foster, April, 16 2010.

oversight.[335] The Under Secretary of Defense for Acquisition, Technology, and Logistics was the formal information conduit between the Under Secretary of Defense for Policy and the Defense Threat Reduction Agency, and served as a milestone decision authority for designated projects.[336]

The workflow of the Office of the Secretary of Defense changed with different administrations.[337] Throughout the

---

335   This position was created in response to the heptyl incident. Between the formation of Defense Threat Reduction Agency, and the introduction of Deputy Assistant to the Secretary of Defense (Chemical Demilitarization and Threat Reduction), there was no active oversight of the Cooperative Threat Reduction program by the Under Secretary of Defense for Acquisition, Technology, and Logistics. By 2007, the Deputy Assistant to the Secretary of Defense (Chemical Demilitarization and Threat Reduction) was no longer a part of the Assistant to the Secretary of Defense (Nuclear and Chemical and Biological Defense Programs) organization, but the Cooperative Threat Reduction Oversight Office was still staffed with the Assistant to the Secretary of Defense (Nuclear and Chemical and Biological Defense Programs), serving as the Under Secretary of Defense for Acquisition, Technology, and Logistics milestone decision authority. Department of Defense, *Management Structure of the Cooperative Threat Reduction Program*, Inspector General Report, February 4, 2004, pp. 5-6; Interview with Department of Defense, Under Secretary of Defense for Acquisition, Technology, and Logistics, Cooperative Threat Reduction Oversight Director Mark West, May 20, 2010.
336   Department of Defense Directive 5000.1, stated that the milestone decision authority "is the designated individual with overall responsibility for a program. The milestone decision authority shall have the authority to approve entry of an acquisition program into the next phase of the acquisition process and shall be accountable for cost, schedule, and performance reporting to higher authority, including congressional reporting." The milestone system established review gates for each project, to reduce risk associated with issues that may be identified periodically in the acquisition cycle. Department of Defense Directive 5000.1, "Defense Acquisition System," November 20, 2007, p. 4.
337   Since the names of the subordinate directorates within Under Secretary of Defense for Policy and Under Secretary of Defense for Acquisition, Technology, and Logistics changed several times during the evolution of Cooperative Threat Reduction, the major offices were used throughout the chapter for continuity unless greater specificity was required. When referring collectively to both offices, the term Office of the Secretary of Defense was used.

history of CTR the role of the Under Secretary of Defense for Acquisition, Technology, and Logistics was both emphasized and deemphasized. By design, the Under Secretary of Defense for Policy maintained responsibility for policy oversight while the Under Secretary of Defense for Acquisition, Technology, and Logistics maintained responsibility for implementation oversight.[338] Unlike the majority of the Defense Department that subscribed to a rigid reporting hierarchy, the CTR program followed a "horizontal" communication model where information and requests originated from multiple levels.[339] For example, daily e-mail correspondence from a project manager routinely accounted for courtesy copies to applicable junior and senior interagency actors. The reverse was also true with the Office of the Secretary of Defense which routinely broadcasted to all applicable recipients within the CTR structure. Despite this communication arrangement, reports and decisions followed standard hierarchical procedures within the department.

Examination of the various actors involved in the implementation of CTR policy demonstrates that, while there was communication and senior coordination during the period, there was a lack of integrated planning and national threat reduction leadership.[340] In 2002, a joint working group from the

---

338   Between 1998 and 2003 these Cooperative Threat Reduction-related Under Secretary of Defense for Acquisition, Technology, and Logistics positions were not filled. During other periods, the Under Secretary of Defense for Acquisition, Technology, and Logistics stressed a hierarchical flow, emphasizing formal communications be routed between the Defense Threat Reduction Agency and the Under Secretary of Defense for Policy, through the Under Secretary of Defense for Acquisition, Technology, and Logistics. Department of Defense, *Management Structure of the Cooperative Threat Reduction Program*, Inspector General Report, February 4, 2004, p. 7-9.

339   CTR followed this pattern for information dissemination because the program was reliant on junior subject matter experts. Interview with Department of Defense, Defense Threat Reduction Agency, Cooperative Threat Reduction Project Manager Dale Taylor, February 21, 2010; Downs, Anthony, *Inside Bureaucracy*, 1967, pp. 112-115.

340   In 1999, an interagency coordinator was instituted to address management criticisms, but budgets remained within individual departments

Carnegie Endowment for International Peace and the Russian-American Nuclear Security Advisory Council found that threat reduction lacked a coordinated strategy.[341] Three years later the Government Accountability Office concluded that there was "no overall strategy" integrating the threat reduction and nonproliferation programs in the Departments of Defense and Energy or elsewhere.[342] The Government Accountability Office further concluded that the Departments of Defense and Energy developed "their own strategic plans," prioritized "their own program activities," and measured "their own program performance." Moreover, the Government Accountability Office observed that, while this helped to "keep the departments on track" in terms of meeting their own objectives, government-wide guidance for CTR and nonproliferation programs was absent.[343] In this regard, the Project on National Security Reform offered because "the U.S. national security apparatus is inconsistent and too rarely achieves integrated policy and unity of purpose. Analysis, planning, and implementation are driven by organizational equities, paradigms, and incentive structures that decrease interagency cooperation."[344]

ORGANIZATION AND WORKFLOW

This section demonstrates that the Department of Defense was organized to execute single agency threat reduction

---

and the position did not carry forward beyond the Clinton administration. Nuclear Threat Initiative, "The Nunn-Lugar Cooperative Threat Reduction (CTR) Program," retrieved April 15, 2010.

341   Carnegie Endowment for International Peace and the Russian-American Nuclear Security Advisory Council, *Reshaping U.S.-Russian Threat Reduction: New Approaches for the Second Decade,* 2002, pp. 2-3.

342   Government Accountability Office, *Weapons of Mass Destruction: Nonproliferation Programs Need Better Integration,* January 2005, pp. Highlights, 22.

343   Ibid.

344   Locher, James R. III, Executive Director, *Forging a New Shield,* Project on National Security Reform, 2008, p. 95.

contracts with senior official participation in interagency and host nation coordination fora. This individual department, acquisition-based approach to nuclear defense is a consistent theme across the implementation case studies in this book.[345] Within the Department of Defense, the Strategic Offensive Arms Elimination program was one of the oldest CTR efforts. The branch supported early security measures in the former Soviet Union and Strategic Arms Reduction Treaty levels envisioned by Congress.[346] This individual program represented how the U.S. government implemented evolving nuclear defense policies in the post-Cold War era. It was characterized by departmental project management with actual policy implementation outsourced to contracting firms.[347]

DEFENSE THREAT REDUCTION AGENCY

The Secretary of Defense originally assigned threat reduction responsibilities to the Assistant to the Secretary of Defense (Nuclear and Chemical and Biological Defense Programs). The

---

345 Wilson, James Q., *Bureaucracy: What Government Agencies Do and Why They Do It*, 2nd edition 2000, pp. 126-129.

346 Each country was distinctly different. For example, in Kiev the smaller government structure facilitated closer relationships, whereas the Russian Federation government was much larger and added degrees of separation between Russian Federation and U.S. CTR actors. Interview with Department of Defense, Defense Threat Reduction Office, Moscow Division Chief Luke Kluchko, May 21, 2010.

347 Contractors were responsible for implementation, including those awarded prime contracts (a large contractor awarded an entire project) and sub-contracts (normally smaller firms contracted by a prime contractor for a portion of a project). Since threat reduction programs were international in scope, the term CTR integrating contractor was used for U.S. firms that sub-contracted and monitored host nation contractors. Threat reduction contracts awarded to host nation contractors were made either on an integrating or direct basis depending on the project and/or firm involved. Contract support also extended to the provision of daily advice and assistance activities for the CTR Directorate. Interview with Department of Defense, Defense Threat Reduction Agency, Cooperative Threat Reduction Project Manager Dale Taylor, February 21, 2010.

assistant secretary used a CTR program office to administer threat reduction activities until the formation of the Defense Threat Reduction Agency on October 1, 1998. The Defense Threat Reduction Agency represented the consolidation of the program office, the Defense Special Weapons Agency, the On-Site Inspection Agency, and the Defense Technology Security Administration.[348] The new agency initially had a fiscal year 1999, operating budget of $1.9 billion with 2,110 personnel dispersed across multiple locations in and around Washington, D.C., New Mexico, Utah, California, and several overseas sites.[349]

The Defense Threat Reduction Agency's director was a politically appointed senior executive who did not serve in a direct CTR implementation role beyond general leadership and decision making authority over program milestones. Daily interaction, a weekly staff meeting, monthly reports, and horizontal information sharing kept the director abreast of projects and issues affecting the Cooperative Threat Reduction Directorate. While this was the norm, Deputy CTR Director Mark Foster offered that the Defense Threat Reduction Agency's leadership was more involved in operational direction, coordination with the Office of the Secretary of Defense, and consultation with the Threat Reduction Advisory Committee, immediately following the heptyl and solid rocket motor incidents.[350]

---

348   Downs, Anthony, *Inside Bureaucracy*, 1967, pp. 5-8.
349   In late 2005, the majority of the Washington, D.C. personnel were relocated to the Defense Threat Reduction Center on Fort Belvoir, Virginia. Adams, Bianka J., and Joseph P. Harahan, *Responding to War, Terrorism, and weapons of mass destruction Proliferation: History of Defense Threat Reduction Agency, 1998-2008*, 2008, pp. 18 and 104.
350   The heptyl and solid rocket motor incidents are covered later in the chapter. Interview with Department of Defense, Defense Threat Reduction Agency, Deputy Cooperative Threat Reduction Director Mark Foster, April, 16 2010.

CTR DIRECTORATE

Within the Defense Threat Reduction Agency, the Cooperative Threat Reduction Directorate, comprising approximately 200 personnel, was responsible for CTR implementation. The directorate was led by a career senior executive who was assisted by a deputy in the grade of Colonel or civilian General Schedule-15, and an immediate staff. The directorate contracted threat reduction missions to civilian contractors and supervised program completion. It was divided into five program branches with additional forward support stationed at American embassies in recipient countries and the United Kingdom.[351] The program branches consisted of: 1) Strategic Offensive Arms Elimination; 2) Nuclear Weapons Safety and Security; 3) Biological Weapons Proliferation Prevention; 4) Chemical Weapons Elimination; and 5) Weapons of Mass Destruction Proliferation Prevention.[352] Each branch was staffed by military, civil service, and contract personnel with broad ranging skills that included administration, government contracting, translation, weapons of mass destruction, and program management expertise. Strategic Offensive Arms Elimination projects focused on the conversion or elimination of Russian strategic weapons, delivery systems, and related infrastructure.[353] The branch operated under the main United States-Russian Federation umbrella agreement, a

---

351   Countries included Russia, Ukraine, Kazakhstan, Uzbekistan, Azerbaijan, and Georgia. Adams, Bianka J., and Joseph P. Harahan, *Responding to War, Terrorism, and weapons of mass destruction Proliferation: History of Defense Threat Reduction Agency, 1998-2008,* 2008, p. 125.
352   For a brief description of each program branch, see Government Accountability Office, *Cooperative Threat Reduction: Department of Defense Has Improved Its Management and Internal Controls, but Challenges Remain,* June 2005, pp. 9-15.
353   This included submarine nuclear fuel, launchers, submarine launched ballistic missiles, and liquid and solid fuel intercontinental ballistic missiles, to include rail, road mobile, and supporting infrastructure. See Department of Defense, *Cooperative Threat Reduction Budget Estimates,* Defense Threat Reduction Agency, Fiscal Year 2009, pp. 847-848.

separate Strategic Offensive Arms Elimination implementing agreement, and in support of treaties and agreements such as the Strategic Arms Reduction Treaty.[354] In fiscal year 2008, the program objectives for the Strategic Offensive Arms Elimination branch were:

Eliminate 13 SS-18 intercontinental ballistic missiles and 22 SS-19 intercontinental ballistic missiles	Decommission 10 SS-18 intercontinental ballistic missile silo launchers
Decommission 1 SS-18 launch control centers	Decommission 30 SS-19 intercontinental ballistic missile silo launchers
Eliminate 20 SS-19 intercontinental ballistic missile silo launchers	Decommission 1 SS-19 launch control center
Eliminate 2 SS-19 launch control centers	Eliminate 10 SS-N-18 and 7 SS-N-20 submarine launched ballistic missiles
Disassemble and eliminate 40 SS-25 intercontinental ballistic missiles	Eliminate 30 SS-25 road-mobile launchers and demilitarize 122 support vehicles
Continue lease activity to repair, maintain, and convert railcars to support the SS-25 intercontinental ballistic missiles project	Initiate work to dismantle 2 Delta III class SSBNs [ballistic missile submarines]
Complete Typhoon 724 dismantlement, including elimination of 20 submarine launched ballistic missile launchers, sectioning the reactor unit, scrapping salvageable material from the launcher section, handling radioactive hazardous materials, and transporting the six-compartment reactor unit to Murmansk	Provide logistical support for Cooperative Threat Reduction program-provided equipment; and Provide for contractor administrative and advisory support

FIGURE 3.1. STRATEGIC OFFENSIVE ARMS
ELIMINATION PROGRAM OBJECTIVES[355]

STRATEGIC OFFENSIVE ARMS ELIMINATION BRANCH

Key positions within the branch revolved around the program and project managers. Program managers oversaw up to

354   Strategic Offensive Reductions Treaty verification was completed under Strategic Arms Reduction Treaty procedures through December 2009. For more information on the umbrella and Strategic Offensive Arms Elimination implementing agreements, see Department of Defense, *Cooperative Threat Reduction Annual Report to Congress,* Defense Threat Reduction Agency, Fiscal Year 2008, pp. 35-36.

355   Program objectives for fiscal year 2008. CTR received three-year funds; therefore projects funded in fiscal year 2008 may have extended into fiscal year 2010. Projects of longer duration received new funding if justification remained valid. Department of Defense, *Cooperative Threat Reduction Budget Estimates,* Defense Threat Reduction Agency, Fiscal Year 2009, pp. 863-864.

10 project managers and their corresponding projects.[356]   The
Strategic Offensive Arms Elimination program manager provided immediate oversight, guidance to advice and assistance
to contractor task leads, and participated in weekly teleconferences with executive agent counterparts in Russia.[357]   Program
managers oversaw new project acquisition planning, reports,
reviews and milestone schedules, and spot checked routine projects. They also engaged more heavily with sensitive projects or
negotiations, and traveled to Russia for executive reviews twice
a year.[358]

Project managers were the federal officials that interacted directly with their Russian Federation counterparts and contractors
on a daily basis. Each project manager was responsible for four
to eight projects with up to six project managers serving in the
Strategic Offensive Arms Elimination branch.[359] Assigned projects were in various stages that accounted for ongoing efforts and

---

356   Program managers were military colonels or civil service General
Schedule-15s. In some instances where branches merged, program managers utilized deputies as branch chiefs. This was the case with the Strategic
Offensive Arms Elimination and Nuclear Weapons Site Security branches
during the period of research, where a single program manager used deputies
to manage nine project managers, six in Strategic Offensive Arms Elimination
and three in Nuclear Weapons Site Security. Interview with Department of
Defense, Defense Threat Reduction Agency, Cooperative Threat Reduction
Strategic Offensive Arms Elimination Program Official, February 19, 2010.
357   An executive agent is the organization that has been assigned specific responsibilities and authorities for an area by their government. For
threat reduction, multiple executive agents were assigned by the U.S. and
Russian Federation governments. Interview with Department of Defense,
Defense Threat Reduction Agency, Cooperative Threat Reduction Director,
June 18, 2010.
358   By 2004, Strategic Offensive Arms Elimination branch related CTR
matters centered primarily on projects in the Russian Federation. Interview
with Department of Defense, Defense Threat Reduction Agency, Cooperative
Threat Reduction Strategic Offensive Arms Elimination Program Official,
February 19, 2010.
359   Interviews with Department of Defense, Defense Threat Reduction
Agency, Cooperative Threat Reduction Project Managers January 29, and
February 21, 2010.

requirement development. Project managers were military majors or lieutenant colonels and their civil service equivalents.[360] Project managers supervised contracts from the Defense Threat Reduction Agency at Fort Belvoir, Virginia. This process included monitoring, verification of work completion, authorization of payment, and contract closeout. Project managers conversed with their counterparts and contractors through routine phone and e-mail traffic, and held regularly scheduled teleconferences while at the Defense Threat Reduction Center.[361] They provided input for weekly staff updates, reviewed contractor progress reports, and supplied detailed project information for monthly directorate reports that were disseminated to all departmental actors. The duty position was travel intensive requiring project managers to visit projects in the former Soviet Union roughly every six weeks. The travel schedule meant that project managers were generally on-site at ongoing projects between quarterly program management and semi-annual executive reviews.

ON-SITE VERIFICATION

Threat reduction management operations were conducted by ad hoc integrated process teams consisting of a project manager, a translator, and advice and assistance contractors.[362] Support personnel rotated between project managers depending on need with contractors receiving work priority guidance from their task lead and not individual project managers. For example,

---

360   Note, the author chose to use Army, Marine, and Air Force rank terminology, but naval officers also served in authorized billets. Civil service General Schedule grades are normally 14.
361   Wilson, James Q., *Bureaucracy: What Government Agencies Do and Why They Do It*, 2nd edition 2000, pp. 320-321.
362   Advice and assistance contract support for operations, logistics, program management, financial, and engineering was provided by Science Applications International Corporation, Threat Reduction Support Center, and other sub-contractors at the time of this writing. Interview with Department of Defense, Defense Threat Reduction Agency, Cooperative Threat Reduction Advice and Assistance Contractor, January 29, 2010.

translators supported multiple project managers, and advice and assistance personnel served in varied capacities for travel or new project teams based on prioritized requirements. During periods of direct support, contractors and specialists functioned as team members for the specific project at hand until they returned to a general supporting role for multiple project managers at the Defense Threat Reduction Center.[363]

The frequency and length of each site visit depended on the characteristics of the contract. During travel the project manager formed a travel team that flew to Moscow using commercial airlines. A routine travel team consisted of the project manager, a primary project support contractor, and an interpreter.[364] In Moscow, the team linked up with and was accompanied by a Strategic Offensive Arms Elimination forward officer that traveled with them to the project site. An example of a routine travel schedule involved the team departing Washington, D.C. on a Wednesday, arriving in Moscow on the Thursday and then boarding a train (or other mode of transportation based on site distance and access) before arriving at the project site that evening. On the Friday the team would be on-site all day for technical discussions and work verification. On the Saturday morning the team departed the project site for Moscow. Team members would depart Moscow on Sunday morning arriving the next day in Washington, D.C.

---

363   All personnel attended initial project management and business practice training sponsored by the Defense Threat Reduction Agency. The directorate conducted annual refresher training twice a year. Interview with Department of Defense, Defense Threat Reduction Agency, Cooperative Threat Reduction Project Manager Dale Taylor, February 21, 2010.

364   Team composition was mission dependent. For example, inventories may have required an additional logistics specialist, contract extension discussions may have required a cost estimator, new contracts may have required a contracting officer, senior site interaction may have included a Defense Threat Reduction Office representative, etc. Standard Strategic Offensive Arms Elimination procedures limited travel teams to no more than 10 personnel. Ibid.

Verification of work was conducted according to the contract scope of work and applicable treaty protocols. While contracts may have supported Strategic Arms Reduction Treaty requirements, work verification by the CTR project manager and on-site verification by the Strategic Arms Reduction Treaty inspection teams took place separately. Strategic Offensive Arms Elimination projects were large industrial undertakings that required years to complete and were thus verified in phased increments. An example scope of work from a fixed-price, direct contract awarded to Rosobschemash -- a Russian Federation contractor -- for the elimination of SS-18 and SS-19 silos was divided into four phases:

1. Site mobilization and limited infrastructure repair.
2. Decommissioning- the defueling and removal of the intercontinental ballistic missile from a silo, and transport of the missiles and liquid rocket fuel to storage and elimination facilities.
3. Dismantlement- the removal of security infrastructure, dismantlement of the launch silo and launch control center operational equipment.
4. Elimination- the explosive elimination of the silo, including all surrounding support buildings.[365]

This project took place at four separate missile regiment sites: Dombarovskiy and Uzhur for the SS-18s, and Kozel'sk and Tatishchevo for the SS-19s. A regiment generally comprised ten missile silos, a training silo, and a launch control center silo, with other supporting buildings and infrastructure. A single SS-18 was 36.5 meters in length x 3.0 meters in diameter, and weighed

---

365   This was an example of the phased contract approach that allowed project managers "to make the appropriate changes, delay, or stop a project if a problem occurs," which reduced acquisition risk. Liquid Propellant Intercontinental Ballistic Missile Silo Elimination Project Executive Summary provided during interview with Department of Defense, Defense Threat Reduction Agency, Cooperative Threat Reduction Project Manager, January 29, 2010; Government Accountability Office, *Cooperative Threat Reduction: Department of Defense Has Improved Its Management and Internal Controls, but Challenges Remain*, June 2005, p. 12.

211,100 kilograms, while the newer SS-19 was smaller, at 27.0 meters x 2.5 meters, weighing 105,600 kilograms.[366] Both missiles were liquid fuelled which meant defueling was required -- and shipping the hazardous fuel to storage sites -- before being transported by rail to the Surovatikha destruction facility. Destruction in the scope of work for delivery vehicles meant preventing any chance of future use and included accounting for the potential posed by dual-use components.[367]

For silos, destruction primarily meant explosive procedures, while missiles were separated into smaller elements and destroyed through cutting and other measures. Not all silos were required to be destroyed according to the example scope of work; they could also be dismantled or decommissioned. Dismantlement meant the silo was not converted or re-loaded with another intercontinental ballistic missile for a period of ten years. Decommissioning required the Russian Federation to either backfill the silo with a single-warhead intercontinental ballistic missile, or to leave it empty for a period of ten years.[368] A point missed in many CTR assessments was that host nation

---

366   Warfare.RU, "SS-18 Satan," and "SS-19 Stiletto," retrieved April 15, 2010.

367   An example of failure to account for dual-use items related to submarine launched ballistic missiles comes from Iraq. In 1995, Jordanian intelligence intercepted 240 gyroscopes and accelerometers that were en route to Baghdad. This interdiction led to the discovery of additional components in the Tigris River near the Iraqi capital. The used gyroscopes and accelerometers were exported as scrap metal with an unclear level of Russian government involvement. While the supply line was believed to have been severed, Russian investigations did not produce any significant criminal prosecutions. Since this incident, Russian export control laws have been amended and strengthened, but dual-use items of this type represent a nuclear defense risk from missile component proliferation if not properly accounted for during elimination. Orlov, Vladimir, and William C. Potter, "The Mystery of the Sunken Gyros," *Bulletin of the Atomic Scientists*, November/December 1998, pp. 34-39.

368   This decommissioning-related reduction in warheads and yield also provided greater surety measures, a point that was often overlooked by opponents to Russian Federation strategic nuclear weapons modernization.

executive agents drove project requests. Resulting requirements encompassed elimination and conversion, and often supported other policy goals or international agreements such as the Strategic Arms Reduction Treaty.[369]

IN COUNTRY ASSISTANCE

The Defense Threat Reduction Office-Moscow ensured agreement on licensing, permits, customs issues, and other legal requirements were met, and provided in-country expertise for the U.S. government. Additionally, the Strategic Offensive Arms Elimination forward team, which was located separately in Moscow, interacted with the Defense Threat Reduction Office, executive agents, and in-country contractors for branch specific items.[370] In 2003, the solid rocket motor disposition facility incident (for SS-24, SS-25, and SS-N-20 missiles) highlighted the importance of in-country supervision. In this incident, the Department of Defense invested $99.7 million to design and build a facility at Votkinsk, in the Udmurt Republic, only to be denied land allocation as a result of local opposition.[371]

Thus, projects over $50 million and/or new construction required an on-site manager. Previously, projects did not have

---

369   The example project was originally written to support the second Strategic Arms Reduction Treaty, but complete elimination goals and intercontinental ballistic missiles types were changed to account for other forms of reductions once the treaty stalled. Interview with Department of Defense, Defense Threat Reduction Agency, Cooperative Threat Reduction Advice and Assistance Contractor, January 29, 2010.

370   Interview with Department of Defense, Defense Threat Reduction Agency, Cooperative Threat Reduction Project Manager Dale Taylor, February 21, 2010.

371   Department of Defense, *Cooperative Threat Reduction Solid Rocket Motor Disposition Facility Project,* Inspector General Report, September 11, 2003, p. 4; Interviews with Department of Defense, Under Secretary of Defense for Acquisition, Technology, and Logistics, Cooperative Threat Reduction Oversight Director Mark West, and Department of Defense, Defense Threat Reduction Office, Moscow Division Chief Luke Kluchko, May 20, and May 21, 2010.

this level of on-site management, but this statutory requirement implemented following the heptyl incident in 2002, became the responsibility of the Defense Threat Reduction Office.[372] This second incident centered on the construction of a liquid propellant storage facility in Krasnoyarsk, Russia for heptyl and amyl. The Russian government requested the project in 1994, but when the facility was completed in 2002, the Russian Federation executive agent stated that the liquid propellant had been used to fuel commercial space launches.[373]

Confusion between the different Russian ministries, and a lack of American acquisition risk reduction measures, periodic reviews, inspections, and broader interagency coordination, allowed the CTR program to disperse $95.5 million to design and build the facility.[374] Investigations and corrective measures resulted in tighter oversight through congressionally mandated on-site management requirements, annual reports to Congress, and a Defense Threat Reduction Agency-driven shift to federal acquisition-based procedures.[375]

---

372   While on-site responsibility fell on the Defense Threat Reduction Office, this office was not the contracting officer representative and thus did not have tasking authority. Interview with Department of Defense, Defense Threat Reduction Office, Moscow Division Chief Luke Kluchko, May 21, 2010; *National Defense Authorization Act for Fiscal Year 2004*, Title XIII, Sec. 1305.

373   Interview with Department of Defense, Under Secretary of Defense for Policy, Cooperative Threat Reduction Policy Office Director James Reid, April 29, 2010.

374   This figure did not include additional funds required for operations and maintenance at the time of the Department of Defense Inspector General report. Department of Defense, *Cooperative Threat Reduction Program Liquid Propellant Disposition Project*, Inspector General Report, September 30, 2002, p. 12.

375   The Russian Federation space program was championed by the U.S. National Aeronautics and Space Administration, but the administration did not inform the Department of Defense of the alternate heptyl use. Interview with Department of Defense, Under Secretary of Defense for Policy, Cooperative Threat Reduction Policy Office Director James Reid, April 29, 2010.

IDENTIFICATION OF REQUIREMENTS

One of the corrective measures implemented by the U.S. government following the incident was the implementation of executive review. Russian Federation executive reviews subsequently took place in Moscow twice a year with each executive agent.[376] The Under Secretary of Defense for Policy, Under Secretary of Defense for Acquisition, Technology, and Logistics, and the CTR Directorate all had representatives at the executive reviews. The Cooperative Threat Reduction Policy Office director chaired the American delegation with review agendas revolving around ongoing and new projects. These reviews used the joint requirements implementation plan to identify actor requirements. The joint requirements implementation plan was an unclassified document that defined the budgets, schedules, risks, assumptions, and responsibilities of the United States and corresponding host nation executive agents by project.[377] The Strategic Offensive Arms Elimination joint requirements implementation plan was reviewed and updated twice a year, and signed by the CTR director and his host nation executive agent

---

376   The Russian executive agent charged with maintaining the implementing agreement was the Russian Federal Space Agency (Roscosmos). Although Roscosmos was the signatory to the Strategic Offensive Arms Elimination implementing agreement, two other executive agents -- the Russian Ministry of Defense and the Russian Federal Atomic Energy Ministry -- also played significant roles. The Russian Federation Ministry of Defense accounted for the 12th Main Directorate and the Strategic Rocket Forces. The division of responsibilities in Russia meant that the Federal Space Agency dealt with missiles and delivery vehicles (including submarines), the Atomic Energy Ministry handled nuclear warheads, and the Ministry of Defense was responsible for nuclear warhead storage, site security, and annual defense-related quota allocations. Interview with Department of Defense, Defense Threat Reduction Agency, Cooperative Threat Reduction Project Manager Dale Taylor, February 21, 2010.

377   Cooperative Threat Reduction followed the defense acquisition definition of risk, "a measure of future uncertainties in achieving program performance goals and objectives within defined cost, schedule, and performance constraints." Department of Defense, *Defense Acquisition Guidebook*, Defense Acquisition University, Sec. 4.2.3.1.5., retrieved April 15, 2010.

equivalent. Project managers, with immediate supervision from program managers, were responsible for outlining and updating United States and Russian Federation responsibilities. Points of contention that could not be resolved remotely were addressed at the semi-annual executive reviews.[378]

Host nation executive agents drove CTR project selection. Russian Federation executive agents provided annual letter requests no later than December for their next calendar year needs.[379] Ongoing projects were reassessed and funds were verified after each review. New requests required full planning and contracting procedures following the December review. These recommended projects were assessed, and initial planning was conducted by the applicable CTR Directorate project manager and/or program manager. If a new request was declined, or if a request was under consideration but funding issues caused a delay, they did not need to be staffed beyond the directorate. If a new project proposal was approved by the Cooperative Threat Reduction Directorate, an approval request was then staffed through to Under Secretary of Defense for Policy. The Under Secretary of Defense for Policy verified that the project did not violate existing policies and was within the CTR scope. In the event of disapproval, the decision was communicated to all actors. If approved by the Under Secretary of Defense for Policy, the proposal became a valid requirement that was staffed with accompanying guidance back to the Defense Threat Reduction Agency through the Under Secretary of Defense for Acquisition,

---

378   Executive reviews began in July 2002. Department of Defense, *Cooperative Threat Reduction Program Liquid Propellant Disposition Project,* Inspector General Report, September 30, 2002, p. 12.

379   The Department of Defense budgeting, and the Russian Federation Ministry of Defense weapons decision cycles did not match. The U.S. was already in the first quarter of the current budget fiscal year when they received the annual CTR letter. Interviews with Department of Defense, Defense Threat Reduction Agency, Cooperative Threat Reduction Project Manager Dale Taylor and Department of Defense, Defense Threat Reduction Agency, Cooperative Threat Reduction Deputy Director Mark Foster, February 21, and April 16, 2010.

Technology, and Logistics. This collaborative process sought to capitalize on the expertise of the Cooperative Threat Reduction Directorate, the Under Secretary of Defense for Acquisition, Technology, and Logistics, and Under Secretary of Defense for Policy before a decision was made.

PROJECT APPROVAL

Once the requirement and accompanying guidance was received it was the responsibility of the CTR integrated process team to initiate the acquisition cycle.[380] At this point in the initial planning, the project manager defined the scope of work, decided what type of contractor was best suited for the project, and conducted an initial cost estimate. The scope of work was based on determining items and components for reduction, the best approach for reduction, and the duration of the project. Next, the project manager evaluated what type of contract expertise was required for the project. Direct host nation contracts were potentially negotiated at a lower rate with known contractors, but direct contracts placed a greater management burden on the CTR project manager, who was responsible for multiple projects, and only made on-site visits several times a year. Even with Strategic Offensive Arms Elimination forward and Defense Threat Reduction Office support, difficulties related to workload, lack of clarity, and proximity limited oversight of direct contracts. American contracting firms for project integration were pre-designated, and although the costs may have been higher, project management using this method provided greater

---

380   New project planning teams consisted of the project manager, program manager, advice and assistance contract personnel, contracting representatives, chief financial advisor, CTR program integration manager, and CTR representative for acquisition, to ensure compliance with applicable federal acquisition and Department of Defense regulations. Interview with Department of Defense, Defense Threat Reduction Agency, Cooperative Threat Reduction Strategic Offensive Arms Elimination Program Official, February 19, 2010.

oversight and inclusion of U.S. companies.[381] Use of integrating contractors allowed American companies to sub-contract to host nation firms, and reduced project manager interaction requirements to periodic reviews and performance evaluations, instead of the day-to-day requirements associated with direct contracts.[382] Initial project planning also included cost estimates on a per-unit and complete contract basis.

The statement of work and cost estimate constituted a procurement request package that was forwarded to the applicable milestone decision authority. A milestone decision authority was designated for each project based on the total dollar amount and/or assessed risk of the procurement request.[383] New requests generated a meeting and decision briefing with the designated milestone decision authority. The decision briefing was based on the acquisition plan format that included defined exit criteria for

---

381   CTR integrating contracts had historically been 17% higher than direct contracts. Interview with Department of Defense, Defense Threat Reduction Agency Historian Joseph Harahan, April 26, 2010.

382   There were no pre-existing requirements for integrated versus direct contracts. All contract awards were in accordance with the *Competition in Contracting Act of 1984* (P.L. 98-369). Interview with Department of Defense, Defense Threat Reduction Agency, Cooperative Threat Reduction Project Manager Dale Taylor, February 21, 2010.

383   The CTR director generally acted as the milestone decision authority for low-risk projects under $10 million. For projects ranging between $10 million and $50 million, or with elevated risk, the Defense Threat Reduction Agency director routinely served as the milestone decision authority. The Assistant to the Secretary of Defense (Nuclear and Chemical and Biological Defense Programs) usually served as the milestone decision authority for projects over $50 million or categorized as high-risk. Interviews with Department of Defense, Under Secretary of Defense for Acquisition, Technology, and Logistics, Cooperative Threat Reduction Oversight Director Mark West, Department of Defense, Defense Threat Reduction Agency, Cooperative Threat Reduction Deputy Director Mark Foster, May 20, and April 16, 2010; Government Accountability Office, *Cooperative Threat Reduction: Department of Defense Has Improved Its Management and Internal Controls, but Challenges Remain*, June 2005, p. 11.

each milestone.[384] The decision briefing resulted in one of three outcomes: approval, disapproval, or the requirement for changes to the proposed acquisition strategy. Milestone decision authority approval was granted in acquisition decision memoranda format, and at that point a government contracting specialist packaged and released the procurement request for proposal. If a CTR integrating contractor was chosen, the current integrating firms submitted responses to the request for proposal.[385]

Direct contract solicitation was limited to Russian Federation executive agent recommendations based on the scope of work, security, and previous performance considerations.[386] After the period of solicitation closed, the proposals generated collaborative development that included a technical reduction plan. Upon completion of negotiations and required business processes, the contracting officer and the selected contractor signed a binding contract, and work began. A new project planning factor of 270-days was used to represent the amount of time it would take to conclude a signed contract once approved requirements were

---

384   See Department of Defense, "Sample Acquisition Plan Format," Defense Acquisition University, retrieved April 15, 2010.

385   For example, On September 7, 2001, indefinite delivery/indefinite quantity CTR integrating contracts totaling $5 billion were awarded to five U.S. contractors. Contracting firms awarded CTR integrating contracts included Kellogg Brown and Root, Raytheon, Washington Group International, Bechtel National, and Parsons Delaware. U.S. CTR integrating contractor firms established offices in Moscow, Perm, Votkinsk, Piban'shur, Bryansk, Krasnoarmeysk, and Zlatoust. Adams, Bianka J., and Joseph P. Harahan, *Responding to War, Terrorism, and weapons of mass destruction Proliferation: History of Defense Threat Reduction Agency, 1998-2008,* 2008, p. 132; Department of Defense, "Cooperative Threat Reduction Integrating Contracts (CTRIC)," Defense Threat Reduction Agency, retrieved April 15, 2010; Department of Defense, *Cooperative Threat Reduction Annual Report to Congress,* Defense Threat Reduction Agency, Fiscal Year 2008, p. 12.

386   Russian Federation officials pre-screened host nation contracting firms and designated who was eligible to submit proposals. Interviews with Department of Defense, Defense Threat Reduction Agency, Historian Joseph Harahan and Department of Defense, Defense Threat Reduction Agency, Cooperative Threat Reduction Project Manager Dale Taylor, April 26, and February 21, 2010.

received.[387] The Defense Contract Management Agency and the Defense Contract Audit Agency assisted the directorate for all aspects of resourcing and contract administration to include invoice payment, closeout, accounting oversight, and routine audits and examinations.[388] Once a contract was completed and closed, no additional support was provided by the Cooperative Threat Reduction Directorate.

Important internal program themes that emerged in this section included: the use of contractors to execute CTR policy; federal project management; a complicated process of oversight by, and communication with, the Office of the Secretary of Defense; and reliance on host nation partners. It was shown that American officials were not physically on site in Russia eliminating strategic offensive arms. These implementation tasks were contracted to American and host nation firms that completed mutually established threat reduction requirements with federal oversight. While interagency communication was evident, the emphasis was on deconfliction and situational awareness, and not on collaborative U.S. government implementation. The examination of Strategic Offensive Arms Elimination confirmed a lack of direction for national threat reduction because American officials developed stand-alone requirements based on requests from the Russian Federation. The program also highlighted an absence of national oversight illustrated notably by the heptyl and solid rocket motor incidents, and the related internal corrective measures to the Department of Defense that followed.

Although Congress required a reactive annual CTR report, oversight remained an internal department affair even in the wake of the two incidents. While internal oversight and

---

387   This mark was used for planning purposes, but as CTR matured, the time approached 180-days. Interview with Department of Defense, Defense Threat Reduction Agency, Cooperative Threat Reduction Strategic Offensive Arms Elimination Program Official, February 19, 2010.

388   Department of Defense, *Cooperative Threat Reduction Annual Report to Congress,* Defense Threat Reduction Agency, Fiscal Year 2008, p. 5, and Fiscal Year 2009, p. 26.

participant communication improved following the incidents, difficulties of managing complex multimillion dollar projects from the United States, and reliance on host nation partners, emerged as key internal CTR themes. Externally, the absence of a single national director, and the emphasis placed on segregated department threat reduction efforts -- routinely de-conflicted but separately planned and resourced -- highlighted the realities of U.S. government interagency implementation.

The CTR program described in this section was the result of existing functions and standard operating procedures in the Department of Defense.[389] The interagency approach to federal execution represented thus far, suggested that the large number of actors involved in national threat reduction efforts impeded achievement of policymaker intent and decisions. In this regard, organizations sought to maximize organizational interests by participating in interagency coordination forums, while conducting separate departmental execution.[390] The Strategic Offensive Arms Elimination program exemplified little more than federal contracting efforts. As a result, these operations were constrained by general federal acquisition guidelines and specific program and agency limitations, such as multiple layers of departmental mangers and annual funding authorizations.[391]

PROGRAM EVALUATION

The remainder of this chapter evaluates the Strategic Offensive Arms Elimination branch, the Defense Department's CTR program and broader threat reduction efforts when required, based on the following six criteria: pace, clearly defined Russian Federation responsibilities, interagency integration, realization

---

389   Allison, Graham T., and Morton H. Halperin, "Bureaucratic Politics: A Paradigm and Some Policy Implications," *World Politics,* Vol. 24, Spring 1972, pp. 54-56.
390   Ibid.
391   Wilson, James Q., *Bureaucracy: What Government Agencies Do and Why They Do It,* 2nd edition 2000, pp. 131-134 and 243-244.

of policy objectives, counterarguments, and theoretical applicability. CTR evaluation did not neatly lend itself to quantifiable measurement. Anthony Downs has offered that, as a public sector undertaking, programs such as CTR are divorced from output markets. In this regard, CTR did not provide an "output in a voluntary quid pro quo transaction with a buyer."[392] As such, revenue from the sale of outputs did not fund the program. Instead, these types of governmental efforts received their input funding from a central source -- Congress -- that was unrelated to performance. Other economic tools such as cost-benefit related analysis -- based on monetary inputs and outputs related to weapons systems, materials, and infrastructure reductions -- did not fully explain the contributions of threat reduction to the "collective good" of nuclear defense.[393] The solution to design complexities associated with evaluation in the context of this project, was to derive the previously stated criteria from several external studies of the CTR program, and topics specific to the book.

In 2002, the Congressional Research Service updated an earlier report that covered CTR background and issues for and among Congress, and summarized long-term political objectives. Between 2002 and 2006, several reports by the Department of Defense Inspector General, the Government Accountability Office, and the Office of Management and Budget focused on program structure and implementation. The 2002 Congressional Research Service and Department of Defense Inspector General audit reports of CTR were driven by the heptyl incident.[394] The

392   Downs, Anthony, *Inside Bureaucracy*, 1967, pp. 29-31.
393   Anthony Downs defined "collective good" as an invisible benefit to everyone, regardless of individual contribution. McConnell, Campbell R., and Stanley L. Brue, *Economics: Principles, Problems, and Policies*, 17th edition 2008, pp. 5 and 546-547; Downs, Anthony, *Inside Bureaucracy*, 1967, p. 33.
394   Former CTR Deputy Director Mark Foster noted that the directorate provided internal work space for external evaluators for much of 2002. Interview with Department of Defense, Defense Threat Reduction Agency, Cooperative Threat Reduction Deputy Director Mark Foster, April, 16, 2010.

background of the Congressional Research Service report described the CTR program from initial legislation through to the end of the Clinton administration. This early period, described by CTR professionals as a policy-driven, results-focused program emphasizing a "hands off approach with no control as far as expenditures," subsequently led to the procedural and cultural changes described in this study.[395] Implementation problems highlighted by the Congressional Research Service report focused on pace.[396] The Department of Defense Inspector General reports provided richer findings related to the implementation process, and emphasized the importance of clearly defined Russian Federation responsibilities.[397]

In response to these evaluations, the Defense Threat Reduction Agency mandated CTR to shift to acquisition procedures that resulted in a more positive assessment of the program by the Government Accountability Office in 2005.[398] However, a separate Government Accountability Office report from the same year noted that there was room for improvement in the area of "interagency integration."[399] The final evaluation criteria were derived from the research question, program opponents,

---

395   Interviews with Department of Defense, Defense Threat Reduction Agency, Cooperative Threat Reduction Project Manager and Deputy Director Mark Foster, January 29, and April, 16, 2010; Downs, Anthony, *Inside Bureaucracy*, 1967, pp. 18-20.

396   Woolf, Amy F., "Nunn-Lugar Cooperative Threat Reduction Programs: Issues for Congress," *CRS Report for Congress*, March 6, 2002, pp. 13-14.

397   Department of Defense, *Cooperative Threat Reduction Program Liquid Propellant Disposition Project,* Inspector General Report, September 30, 2002, p. 4.

398   A separate Government Accountability Office report still identified a weakness in continuation practices by not disseminating program lessons learned directorate-wide. Government Accountability Office, *Cooperative Threat Reduction: Department of Defense Has Improved Its Management and Internal Controls, but Challenges Remain,* June 2005, p. 22.

399   Government Accountability Office, *Weapons of Mass Destruction: Nonproliferation Programs Need Better Integration,* January 2005, p. 22-24.

and bureaucratic politics theory. These included: the extent to which CTR realized policy objectives; how previous and current criticisms of the program were accounted for; and linkages to bureaucratic politics theory. The Strategic Offensive Arms Elimination program branch was used to evaluate pace, accountability, and defined Russian Federation responsibilities. The greater Defense Department CTR program was utilized to measure the extent to which policy objectives were realized, and the final three criteria related to interagency integration, counterarguments, and theoretical applicability included national threat reduction efforts.

PACE

From 2002, the pace of new and ongoing CTR projects reflected the realities of the Department of Defense's acquisition requirements, differing bureaucratic cycles in the United States and Russia, and the size and complexity of threat reduction projects. Criticisms in this respect reflected disparities between the relevant actors. While political and external actors cited slow progress, the Defense Department had to use established systems and practices to design and execute projects in accordance with existing laws, regulations, and standard operating procedures in the United States as well as in host nations. Departure from acquisition practices would have left the program open to unnecessary risk and negated potential savings at the beginning of projects.[400] Poor perceived performance and loss of autonomy could follow new incidents should they become recurring in nature.

The impact of partner government participation on CTR projects during the period in question could not be overemphasized. Executive agents in the former Soviet Union drove

---

400   James Wilson argued that one impact of multiple goals and constraints is the strong incentive managers have to focus more on constraints than tasks. Wilson, James Q., *Bureaucracy: What Government Agencies Do and Why They Do It*, 2nd edition 2000, p. 131.

new requirements and, without a letter of request from them, U.S. government officials could not initiate projects. The 270-day planning factor for new projects was from the time of letter receipt. This letter, which arrived in the first quarter of the fiscal year, did not follow the Department of Defense's biennial budgeting cycle, which meant that the time from original project idea to award of the contract often equaled one year or longer. If a project was recommended and initiated in a current fiscal year, funds had to be reprogramd from existing projects to cover unforecasted start-up costs. While planning factors may have seemed excessive to legislators that functioned on an annual national defense authorization cycle, the Government Accountability Office and Office of Management and Budget studies reiterated that CTR was a cooperative effort executed in conjunction with partner governments. This characteristic meant that no matter how institutionalized the procedures became, a significant lead-time was always required for new project implementation.

CLEARLY DEFINED RUSSIAN FEDERATION RESPONSIBILITIES

Following the incident in 2002, the Under Secretary of Defense for Policy placed additional emphasis on the specificity of implementation agreements, while the Cooperative Threat Reduction Directorate incorporated executive reviews, and the joint requirements implementation plan for synchronization with executive agents.[401] The joint requirements implementation plan clearly stated the responsibilities of the United States and host nation partners. The plan was updated as required

---

401   The Office of the Secretary of Defense found the implementation agreement updates to be a bit too restrictive following the incident, and subsequently worked toward a balance between the agreements and joint requirements implementation plan as the executive review process matured. Interview with Department of Defense, Defense Threat Reduction Agency Historian Joseph Harahan, April 26, 2010.

with the intent for host nation partners to assume additional project responsibilities when feasible. In March 2004, Deputy Under Secretary of Defense for Technology Security Policy and Counterproliferation Lisa Bronson stated that, "executive reviews have transformed the way we do business with Russia by putting a premium on regularized transparency, accountability and open dialogue."[402]

Unlike the Strategic Arms Reduction Treaty procedures, CTR emphasized the cooperative goal of personal interaction between former adversaries at every level. Participants had access to documents in their own language, direct communication was leveraged, on-site contractor and U.S. government support was available, and -- after decades of interaction -- joint bureaucratic procedures became familiar to both parties. Host nation actors recognized the benefits of CTR assistance for the safety, security, and well-being of the personnel and communities supported by the projects. While improved coordination existed between executive agents, this emphasis did not incorporate other interagency programs.

INTERAGENCY INTEGRATION

The lack of an integrated interagency threat reduction strategy or plan was a symptom of a larger bureaucratic problem. Simply stated, the U.S. government lacked a federal staff to plan and implement policies at the national level. The applicable threat reduction departments each addressed their individual responsibilities from a single department approach. There was communication at the departmental policy level, liaison, technical exchanges, and the use of interagency expertise, but an organization for integrated federal planning did not exist.[403] In

---

402   Bronson, Lisa, "Cooperative Threat Reduction Program," testimony, March 10, 2004, p.5.
403   The George W. Bush administration sought to improve U.S. government planning by introducing the Integrated Planning System, but this attempt still leveraged a lead federal agency design. Bush, George W.,

January 2005, the Government Accountability Office found that,
"While both Department of Defense and Department of Energy
have individual strategies governing their respective threat reduction and nonproliferation programs, there is no overall strategy that integrates these plans with one another, or with those of
other agencies."[404] The report concluded that, U.S. government
organization and resourcing did not facilitate an integrated approach to threat reduction, and as a result there was not a collaborative federal plan driving implementation.

REALIZATION OF POLICY OBJECTIVES

The following congressionally mandated CTR policy objectives dated back to 1997:

> [Objective 1] Programs to facilitate the elimination, and the safe
> and secure transportation and storage, of nuclear, chemical, and
> other weapons and their delivery vehicles.
> [Objective 2] Programs to facilitate the safe and secure storage
> of fissile materials derived from the elimination of nuclear
> weapons.
> [Objective 3] Programs to prevent the proliferation of weapons,
> weapons components, and weapons-related technology and
> expertise.
> [Objective 4] Programs to expand military-to-military and defense
> contacts.[405]

Other accounts of intent existed but these four objectives
had subsequently been reiterated in annual legislation from the

---

"Homeland Security Presidential Directive-8: National Preparedness,"
December 17, 2003, Annex 1, and Department of Homeland Security, *The
Integrated Planning System*, January 2009.
404   Government Accountability Office, *Weapons of Mass Destruction:
Nonproliferation Programs Need Better Integration,* January 2005, p. 3.
405   These fiscal year 1996 objectives were carried forward to fiscal
year 1997 and then simply referenced as "the programs specified in sec-
tion 1501(b) of the fiscal year 1997 act" until the fiscal year 2008 National
Defense Authorization Act when Congress began to look beyond the former
Soviet Union in section 1303. *National Defense Authorization Act for Fiscal
Year 1996,* Title XII, Sec. 1201.

time of the separation of departmental programs.[406] When as-
sessed individually, the case could be made that the Cooperative
Threat Reduction Directorate had designed and implemented
programs to work toward accomplishment of each departmental
objective. For example, the directorate's five program branches
oversaw projects in specific areas: 1) Strategic Offensive Arms
Elimination (All Objectives); 2) Nuclear Weapons Safety and
Security (All Objectives); 3) Biological Weapons Proliferation
Prevention (Objectives 1, 3, 4); 4) Chemical Weapons
Elimination (Objectives 1, 3, 4); and 5) Weapons of Mass
Destruction Proliferation Prevention (All Objectives).

While the national policy objectives were program-centric,
the broader intent to prevent the unauthorized transfer of nuclear
weapons, material, or expertise from the former Soviet Union,
was reiterated by champions and opponents alike. Congress
specified types of programs and Defense Department policies
and goals drove program implementation.[407] This structure required CTR officials to establish quantifiable measures to justify
program continuation. As CTR organization and management
evolved so did performance criteria and program evaluation
metrics. For example, the following tables represented the cumulative funding inputs and nuclear reduction outputs for the
CTR program:

406   These other accounts referred to what James Wilson described
as contextual goals. Wilson, James Q., *Bureaucracy: What Government
Agencies Do and Why They Do It*, 2nd edition 2000, p. 129.
407   Ibid., pp. 34-36.

CTR	FY 1992	FY 1993	FY 1994	FY 1995	FY 1996	FY 1997	FY 1998	FY 1999	FY 2000
Funding	12.9	246.3	592.7	380	295	363.6	381.5	440.4	458.1
Cumulative	12.90	259.20	851.90	1,231.90	1,526.90	1,890.50	2,272.00	2,712.40	3,170.50

		FY 2001	FY 2002	FY 2003	FY 2004	FY 2005	FY 2006	FY 2007	FY 2008
Funding		442.4	400	416	450.8	409.2	415	372	425.9
Cumulative	3,170.50	3,612.90	4,012.90	4,428.90	4,879.70	5,288.90	5,703.90	6,075.90	6,501.80

TABLE 3.1. COOPERATIVE THREAT
REDUCTION FUNDING[408]
(MILLIONS OF U.S. DOLLARS)

Of this funding, a total of $1,161,770,000 was expended by Strategic Offensive Arms Elimination as of December 31, 2007, with $90,652,000 requested in fiscal year 2008.[409] This input correlated to the reductions listed in Table 3.2.

Declared	Item	Reductions to date	Percent of 2012 Targets	2012 Targets
13,300	Warheads Deactivated	7,298	79%	9,222
1,473	Intercontinental Ballistic Missiles Destroyed	728	67%	1,078
831	Intercontinental Ballistic Missiles Sites Eliminated	496	77%	645
442	Intercontinental Ballistic Missile Mobile Launchers Destroyed	137	51%	257
48	Nuclear Weapons Carrying Submarines Destroyed	31	88%	35
936	Submarine Launched Ballistic Missiles Eliminated	631	91%	691
728	Submarine Launched Ballistic Missiles Launchers Eliminated	456	81%	564
906	Nuclear Air-to-Surface Missiles Destroyed	906	100%	906
233	Bombers Eliminated	155	100%	155
194	Nuclear Test Tunnels/Holes Sealed	194	100%	194
	Nuclear Weapons Transport Train Shipments	411	66%	620
	Nuclear Weapons Storage Site Security Upgrades	18	75%	24

TABLE 3.2. COOPERATIVE THREAT
REDUCTION SCORECARD[410]
(AS OF DECEMBER 17, 2008)

---

408   Lugar, Richard G., "The Nunn-Lugar Threat Reduction Program," retrieved June 10, 2010.
409   Department of Defense, *Cooperative Threat Reduction Annual Report to Congress,* Defense Threat Reduction Agency, Fiscal Year 2009, pp. 32 and 35.
410   Lugar, Richard G., "The Nunn-Lugar Threat Reduction Program," retrieved June 10, 2010.

COUNTERARGUMENTS

Criticisms of CTR peaked following the 1995 Republican revolution in Congress, and were largely absent during the George W. Bush administration. References to opponent positions often used older literature to support arguments pertaining to slow pace, lack of accountability, wasted American resources, and a foreign aid aspect of the program that facilitated military modernization.[411] For example, the most significant threat reduction outcomes repeatedly cited by political and program leaders were the reduction of nuclear weapon states.[412] As a result of diplomatic and CTR implementation efforts, Kazakhstan (1995), Belarus (1996), and Ukraine (1996) were, since the mid-1990s, non-nuclear weapons states.[413] While important, these events were the result of early efforts that looked distinctly different from contemporary programs.

Foreign aid arguments were related to the second major contribution of CTR -- assisting the former Soviet Union to remain compliant with the Strategic Arms Reduction Treaty.[414] When viewed as a parallel program to facilitate treaty agreements, CTR proved successful in assisting the steady reduction of Russian Federation strategic arms and delivery vehicles. Criticism for this portion of CTR from opponents such as Republican Senator Jon Kyl focused on subsidizing new weapons programs in Russia

---

411   Squassoni, Sharon, "Nuclear Threat Reduction Measures for India and Pakistan," *CRS Report for Congress*, February 17, 2005, p. 7; Kelly, Rich, "The Nunn-Lugar Act: A Wasteful and Dangerous Illusion," *Cato Foreign Policy Briefing no. 39*, March 18, 1996; Bukharin, Oleg, "Minatom and Nuclear Threat Reduction Activities," in John M. Shields, and William C. Potter, eds., *Dismantling the Cold War: U.S. and NIS Perspectives on the Nunn-Lugar Cooperative Threat Reduction Program*, 1997, pp. 211-230.
412   Lugar, Richard G., "The Nunn-Lugar Threat Reduction Program," retrieved June 10, 2010.
413   Cirincione, Joseph, Jon B. Wolfsthal, and Miriam Rajkumar, *Deadly Arsenals: Nuclear Biological, and Chemical Threats*, 2nd edition 2005, pp. 365-380.
414   Ibid.

by helping to eliminate older systems.[415] These criticisms often omitted the benefits to nuclear defense of safe, supervised, environmentally-sound elimination, as well as a Russian modernization program that included conversion to single-warhead delivery vehicles with improved security mechanisms.

THEORETICAL APPLICABILITY

The four areas of bureaucratic politics theory highlighted by this case study of threat reduction policy implementation were: 1) policy decisions came from senior actors but junior actors were responsible for implementing them; 2) actions associated with major policy departures were determined by existing programs and standard operating procedures; 3) the larger the number of actors, the less implementation reflected policy decisions; and 4) bureaucracies sought to maximize organizational interests.[416] The first several years of threat reduction work could be characterized by a disconnection between political actor vision and the capabilities of implementing organizations. This disconnect was described by the Congressional Research Service:

> When Congress passed the Nunn-Lugar amendment in 1991, many
> Members and experts outside government expected a relatively
> simple program. They seemed to envision an effort where, using
> funds from the Department of Defense budget, officials from
> the United States would travel to Russia, Ukraine, Belarus, and
> Kazakhstan to quickly safeguard and help dismantle nuclear,
> chemical, and other weapons left vulnerable by the demise of the
> Soviet Union. But the process of program implementation, both
> within the U.S. government and between the United States and

---

415   Combs, Richard, "U.S. Domestic Politics and the Nunn-Lugar Program," in John M. Shields, and William C. Potter, eds., *Dismantling the Cold War: U.S. and NIS Perspectives on the Nunn-Lugar Cooperative Threat Reduction Program,* 1997, pp. 55-56.
416   Allison, Graham T., and Morton H. Halperin, "Bureaucratic Politics: A Paradigm and Some Policy Implications," *World Politics,* Vol. 24, Spring 1972, pp. 54-56.

the newly independent states of the former Soviet Union, was far slower and more complex than many expected.[417]

Early CTR efforts faltered because there was not an existing organization within the U.S. government designed to execute policy in this new domain. As time went on, the applicable departments demonstrated that current programs and standard operating procedures dictated bureaucratic responses. Procedures and inadequate departmental capabilities delayed budgeting and policy execution to the point that senior actors were forced to separate responsibilities along departmental lines. The eventual shift to interagency execution allowed separate departments to divide the execution of threat reduction policy to reflect existing authorities and capabilities. This division maximized organizational interests at the expense of collaborative federal execution, and shifted the emphasis from a limited duration endeavor to a series of long-term programs within the Departments of Defense, Energy, and State.

An evaluation of CTR identified an adaptive program that compartmentalized overall execution and developed procedures to emphasize acquisition-based program management. These procedures had standardized timelines and improved accountability for complex projects executed in the former Soviet Union. The incorporation of lessons learned from previous projects had positive impacts on internal management and communication with host nation partners.[418] Uniform executive management procedures improved the establishment of requirements and streamlined implementation procedures. Although U.S. government partners were not represented in the individual department design, utilization of the interagency coordination systems had, at a minimum, limited overlap. While the separate departmental programs were independently executed, interagency coordination

---

417   Woolf, Amy F., "Nunn-Lugar Cooperative Threat Reduction Programs: Issues for Congress," *CRS Report for Congress*, March 6, 2002, p. 5.

418   Downs, Anthony, *Inside Bureaucracy*, 1967, pp. 18-20.

and situational awareness were evident. Ultimately, one of the unique areas associated with this study was the measurement of outputs. In this regard, the Defense Department program served as an example of what James Wilson referred to as a "production organization" -- when an agency can observe both operators at work and outcomes.[419] This measured, verifiable impact on nuclear defense was not replicated by the other U.S. government efforts covered in this book.

CONCLUSION

The research question driving this chapter asked, "How did the U.S. government implement post-Cold War nuclear defense policy, and to what extent were corresponding objectives realized?" The hypothesis offered was, "The U.S. government was not organized to address nuclear defense, and as a result did not collaboratively implement evolving national policies." The chapter demonstrated that CTR was only one program within a broad array of federal threat reduction labors spread across multiple organizations. Early CTR efforts dealt as much with program survival as they did with threat reduction. The Department of Defense immediately realized that the expertise required for program execution resided in other departments. This dependency, amplified by separate organizational interests and political actor opposition, resulted in a design shift from lead agency to interagency execution.

By spreading threat reduction responsibilities across departments, program proponents were able to reduce exposure and ensure that national oversight would be a difficult process. The heptyl and solid rocket motor disposition facility incidents demonstrated the lack of national oversight in regard to threat reduction. Following these incidents, the majority of implementation changes were internally driven. The new requirement for

---

419   Wilson, James Q., *Bureaucracy: What Government Agencies Do and Why They Do It*, 2nd edition 2000, pp. 159-163.

an annual report to Congress simplified examination of the program, although this report was merely consolidated information
from the Department of Defense submitted to a general popu-
lation. The reports did not account for other threat reduction
programs spread across the U.S. government, and therefore, did
not represent all federal government efforts in this area. Threat
reduction policy was characterized by segregated interagency
implementation in the absence of central leadership or effective
oversight at the national level.

Departmental programs were driven by existing organizational procedures and regulatory requirements. Each effort took
on the organizational aspects of the executing department and
worked toward individually defined objectives. Because objectives were individually assigned and broadly articulated, the
CTR program demonstrated successful realization of policy objectives. While the process examination in this chapter inferred
a complete focus on acquisition procedures, it was this shift to
acquisition-based project management that reduced the potential for political actor interference, and allowed CTR Directorate
managers to focus on long-term reduction goals. Resulting
management improvements established better operating procedures, minimized congressional limitations, and expanded the
scope of, and partner support for, the program. The transition
of the Department of Defense to an acquisition mindset and
approach reduced outside criticisms and distractions, shifted
a greater burden to host nation and international partners, and
provided better nuclear defense results in parallel with project
management procedures.

This initial implementation study examined a single department approach to threat reduction. Each of the primary implementing departments coordinated with one another but did not
collaboratively plan or execute U.S. government threat reduction programs. The foundation of the separate implementation
approaches could be drawn back to ad hoc policy development
that incorporated separate resource allocation measures and

authorities. The resulting programs were designed by implementing organizations and reflected statutory authorities that resided with individual secretaries, differing appropriations sources, and distinct departmental cultures and capabilities.

The phenomenon of decentralized policy development extending into segregated implementation is also evident in the next case study. The three policy implementation case studies in this book were designed to demonstrate the overlapping nature of the nuclear defense areas, and to provide conceptual depth as the book progresses from an examination of international to domestic programs. The next chapter examines the Department of Energy's Second Line of Defense Office, and in doing so continues the examination of organizational procedures utilized to implement a forward focused protection initiative. The second case study reveals similarities in the Department of Energy and Department of Defense's federal acquisition-based project management, resourcing practices, and their independent departmental approaches to nuclear defense.

CHAPTER 4

MARITIME RADIATION DETECTION IMPLEMENTATION STUDY

The first two implementation case studies examine inter-agency and lead agency approaches to policy implementation. In both cases, multiple departments and agencies participated in the implementation process. This chapter examines a support-ing program in a lead agency design. The establishment of lead agencies such as the Department of Homeland Security for the Global Nuclear Detection Architecture is a routine organization-al arrangement for federal policy execution. However, despite the prevalence of use, this designation rarely includes requisite interagency authorities for accomplishing objectives. In this regard, the second implementation case study illustrates the negative security impact of disjointed departmental authorities derived from decentralized policy development.

This chapter represents the nuclear defense area of "pro-tection," which includes efforts to deter, interdict, and de-fend against nuclear attack on the United States or its allies. Protection came to the forefront of the agenda under President Clinton when post-Cold War threat assessment shifted to the new nuclear danger of "perhaps a handful of nuclear devices in the hands of rogue states or even terrorist groups."[420] While the Cold War nuclear defense approach of "deterrence, arms

---

420   Aspin, Les, "Defense Secretary Aspin speech to the National Academy of Sciences," December 7, 1993.

control, and a nonproliferation policy based on prevention" had proven sufficient in the past, the new era brought with it a set of challenges that required a more proactive posture.[421] In response to a changing nuclear landscape, the U.S. government sought to establish multiple barriers to protect against possible prevention failures.[422]

Part of the emerging counterproliferation requirement was to detect and interdict the movement of nuclear weapons and special nuclear materials before they could be used. Officials realized that very little capability existed to detect and interdict such items and materials en route to buyers, or potential targets, if a nuclear weapon or special nuclear materials were stolen from secure sites. One of the programs created by the Department of Energy to address this weakness was the Second Line of Defense. This program was designed to "strengthen the capability of foreign governments to deter, detect, and interdict illicit trafficking in nuclear and other radioactive materials across international borders" and later "through the global maritime shipping system."[423]

In the case of maritime shipping there was a general consensus following 9/11 that an emphasis should be placed on addressing this perceived security vulnerability. But even then the question remained, "did departments and agencies place organizational interests above national policy execution?" The previous chapter highlighted that policy decisions "leave considerable leeway" for interpretation and "are rarely tailored to facilitate monitoring" by Congress or the president.[424] Bureaucratic

---

421   Ibid.
422   See the introduction for a description of the post-Cold War strategic landscape.
423   Department of Energy, "Fact Sheet: National Nuclear Security Administration's Second Line of Defense," National Nuclear Security Administration, December 2008.
424   Allison, Graham T., and Morton H. Halperin, "Bureaucratic Politics: A Paradigm and Some Policy Implications," *World Politics,* Vol. 24, Spring 1972, p. 53.

politics theory also suggested that actions "which require co-operation between two independent organizations are unlikely to be advanced by either of these organizations."[425] These propositions, combined with the findings from chapter 3, would appear to suggest that a supporting program in a lead agency design would lead to the pursuit of organizational interests over national interests.

With responsibility for the primary federal program to scan maritime cargo for special nuclear materials prior to arrival at an American port, an assumption could reasonably be made that the resources of the Department of Energy would be critical to countering global nuclear trafficking. However, like other independent nuclear defense tasks, the limited scope of the department's mission meant the program was only one small part of interagency maritime security efforts. This study illustrates that the lead federal department for global nuclear detection -- the Department of Homeland Security -- lacked operational control of supporting department and agency programs such as the Megaports Initiative.

The chapter continues to test the second hypothesis: "The U.S. government was not organized to address nuclear defense, and as a result did not collaboratively implement evolving national policies." It follows the policy implementation study format by considering in turn the policy decision, the national actors involved, organization and workflow, and program evaluation. The policy decision section presents a reactionary policy formulation landscape with separate task-specific legislation. Maritime radiation detection policy comprised mission areas falling under multiple interagency coordination bodies. This section illustrates the impact of numerous statutory authorities for different departments and the need for the establishment of realistic policy objectives that have the potential for completion. The national actors section again highlights the inability of a

---

425   Ibid., p. 75.

single department to execute all mission area national policy objectives in the present-day operating environment.

The workflow section identifies how the Department of Energy's National Nuclear Security Administration implemented maritime radiation detection policy. It describes the role and organization of the Second Line of Defense and Megaports Initiative offices before entering into a detailed analysis of the latter. It is shown that each Megaports Initiative project was conducted on an individual basis. While the Megaports Initiative maintained communications with interagency coordination groups and partners, individual projects were executed as Department of Energy contracts and not as collaborative national operations.

The chapter ends with a program evaluation section utilizing the criteria identified in the previous chapter: pace, defined host nation responsibilities, interagency integration, the extent to which policy objectives were realized, counterarguments, and theoretical applicability. The evaluation section reveals an approach based on individual implementation in support of departmental standard operating procedures and requirements. Implementation was delayed by haphazard federal maritime security efforts which were offered to potential host nations on an individual basis. Primary policy objectives were defined internally while the single statutory requirement, of which the Department of Energy was a supporting agency, was deemed unachievable by federal officials. These findings, which suggest a lack of collaborative execution and national oversight, are consistent with the Cooperative Threat Reduction study.

POLICY DECISIONS

The Second Line of Defense program was conceived and initiated within the Department of Energy in response to increasing incidents of nuclear trafficking. Previously, the department had focused on security at former Soviet nuclear sites through improvements to control systems and accounting as part of the Material Protection, Control, and Accounting program.[426] The Second Line of Defense program was envisioned as an extension of these early efforts in the event that nuclear weapons or special nuclear materials were illegally removed from secure locations. To protect against illicit trafficking attempts, program officials initially worked with the Russian Federation State Customs committee to place radiological detection equipment at key Russian ports, airports, and border crossings.[427]

Originally, the Second Line of Defense was funded by a combination of Department of Energy nonproliferation funds and the Department of State's Nonproliferation and Disarmament Fund.[428] The program was authorized and eventually funded under the Department of Energy but the only specific mention of the Second Line of Defense in defense authorization acts since 1998, was in 2007, when the program was granted the authority to receive outside funds from foreign governments and non-governmental organizations to offset project costs.[429] As a departmental effort, policy objectives originated internally and were articulated as a mission statement and corresponding program goals:

---

426   Materials Protection, Controls, and Accounting was a 1997 consolidation of the prior government-to-government and laboratory-to-laboratory programs. This program was informally referred to as "guns, gates, and guards," and represented what the Department of Energy referred to as the "first line of defense," securing nuclear weapons and special nuclear materials at source sites.

427   The Russian Federation State Customs Committee was renamed the Russian Federation Federal Customs Service in 2004. Department of Energy, "Richardson, Russian Federation Dedicate 'Second Line of Defense' U.S. Nuclear Detection Technology to Help Secure Russian Borders," Office of the Press Secretary, September 2, 1998.

428   Baker, Howard, and Lloyd Cutler, Chairs, *A Report Card on the Department of Energy's Nonproliferation Programs with Russia,* January 10, 2001, p. 14.

429   *John Warner National Defense Authorization Act for Fiscal Year 2007* (H.R. 5122), Sec. 3114.

> The mission of the National Nuclear Security Administration's Second Line of Defense program is to strengthen the capability of foreign governments to deter, detect, and interdict illicit trafficking in nuclear and other radioactive materials across international borders and through the global maritime shipping system. The goal is to reduce the probability of these materials being fashioned into a weapon of mass destruction or a radiological dispersal device ("dirty bomb") to be used against the United States or its key allies and international partners.[430]

In 2003, the Department of Energy was directed "to install radiation detection equipment at the top 20 major overseas seaports to detect and interdict special nuclear material prior to arrival in the United States."[431] According to congressional documents, "the top 20 foreign seaports identified in the Megaports Initiative as priority upgrades are the source of 70% of the container traffic from all overseas ports destined for U.S. ports."[432] The House Energy and Water Development Appropriations Subcommittee stated that they were "fully supportive of the Megaports concept of interdicting source material for a weapon of mass destruction as far from the U.S. border as feasible," and directed "the department [of Energy] to expand this new program in fiscal year 2004."[433] Although the Megaports Initiative was directed as part of post-9/11 maritime security efforts, subsequent legislation and the *National Strategy for Maritime Security* designated the Department of Energy as a supporting department.[434] The lack of specific statutory requirements and oversight, and the general supporting technical role of international radiation

---

430   Department of Energy, "Fact Sheet: National Nuclear Security Administration's Second Line of Defense," National Nuclear Security Administration, December 2008.
431   Hobson, David, "Committee on Appropriations accompanying report to the fiscal year 2004 Energy and Water Development Appropriations Bill (H.R. 2754, 108-212)," July 16, 2003.
432   Ibid.
433   Congressional members did not define their intent for program expansion. Ibid.
434   *National Strategy for Maritime Security*, September 2005, p. 18.

detection, allowed the Department of Energy to design its own port-related initiative outside of other U.S. government maritime programs.[435]

Indeed, the Department of Energy articulated an independent Megaports Initiative goal: "to scan as much container traffic at a port as possible (including imports, exports, and transshipments) regardless of destination," with a long-term program goal "to install radiation detection equipment at 20 ports by 2010."[436] The "regardless of destination" approach stood in contrast to the Department of Homeland Security's emphasis on containers bound for the United States.[437] James Wilson suggested that autonomy is the primary goal of public sector executives.[438] This argument states that necessary resources follow when an "agency's goals are popular, its tasks simple, its rivals nonexistent, and the constraints minimal."[439] In the case of the Megaports initiative, Department of Energy officials could clearly point to a program that was distinct from other federal efforts and that, on the surface, added to the shared policy space of maritime security.[440] This autonomous approach to the establishment of

---

435   In a 2008 Government Accountability Office report on the status of maritime security national planning and implementation, the only mention of Department of Energy was, "Also, the Departments of Commerce, Energy, and Transportation, among others, have responsibilities for various aspects of maritime security." Government Accountability Office, *Maritime Security: National Strategy and Supporting Plans Were Generally Well-Developed and Are Being Implemented,* June 2008.

436   Huizenga, David, "National Nuclear Security Administration's Megaports Initiative and Its Role in the Secure Freight Initiative (SFI)," testimony, June 12, 2008; Government Accountability Office, *Preventing Nuclear Smuggling: Department of Energy Has Made Limited Progress in Installing Radiation Detection Equipment at Highest Priority Foreign Seaports,* March 2005, p. 18.

437   Huizenga, David, "National Nuclear Security Administration's Megaports Initiative and Its Role in the Secure Freight Initiative (SFI)," testimony, June 12, 2008.

438   Wilson, James Q., *Bureaucracy: What Government Agencies Do and Why They Do It,* 2nd edition 2000, pp. 179-195.

439   Ibid., p. 181.

440   Downs, Anthony, *Inside Bureaucracy,* 1967, p. 212.

global departmental policy objectives ensured distinction during annual funding requests.[441]

By 2006, Congress used the *Security and Accountability for Every (SAFE) Port Act* to explore the feasibility of 100% screening of cargo containers, and 100% scanning of high-risk cargo containers before their arrival in the United States.[442] Initial legislation did not mandate a deadline for completion but, in 2007, the *Implementing Recommendations of the 9/11 Commission Act* went on to require:

> (b) Full-Scale Implementation-
> > (1) IN GENERAL- A container that was loaded on a vessel in a foreign port shall not enter the United States (either directly or via a foreign port) unless the container was scanned by nonintrusive imaging equipment and radiation detection equipment at a foreign port before it was loaded on a vessel.
> > (2) APPLICATION- Paragraph (1) shall apply with respect to containers loaded on a vessel in a foreign country on or after the earlier of--
> > (A) July 1, 2012; or
> > (B) such other date as may be established by the Secretary under paragraph (3).[443]

The secretary charged in both acts with foreign scanning was the Secretary of Homeland Security. As a result, while Congress was focused on cargo bound for the United States and

---

441   Morton Halperin and Priscilla Clapp also emphasized the importance that organizations affix to autonomy. These authors offered that organizations want to spend their budgets, direct their manpower, and implement policy as they choose. As such, bureaucratic organizations resist senior intrusions and are prepared to forfeit resources to maintain autonomy. Halperin, Morton H., and Priscilla A. Clapp, *Bureaucratic Politics and Foreign Policy*, 2nd edition 2006, p. 51.

442   *Security and Accountability for Every (SAFE) Port Act of 2006* (H.R. 4954, P.L. 109-347), Sec. 233.

443   *Implementing Recommendations of the 9/11 Commission Act of 2007* (H.R. 1, P.L. 110-53), Title XVII-Maritime Cargo, Sec. 1701.

the establishment of a firm deadline for comprehensive radiation scanning, the Megaports Initiative goal increased to "over 75 Megaports, scanning over 50% of global shipping traffic by 2013."[444] This meant that, even if met, the Second Line of Defense goal would fall short of the statutory policy objective of 100% radiation scanning at a foreign port before containers entered the United States.

The Megaports Initiative highlighted the importance of passing realistic policy decisions complete with national oversight mechanisms to ensure integrated implementation. For example, legislating all-inclusive requirements for foreign ports under the control of sovereign states immediately came into question because of the scale of the task and the political challenges of doing so. In comparison, complimentary legislation which required 100% scanning prior to departure of an American port was a more realistic policy objective. While it was a daunting task, the United States government had access to domestic ports, whereas the presence and responsibilities of American officials or equipment overseas had to be negotiated with individual foreign governments. The other immediate issue that concerned the policy decisions was the combination of screening and scanning. Foreign screening was a Department of Homeland Security function that did not require radiation detection, whereas scanning for radiation emissions was primarily a Department of Energy-facilitated host nation function.

The Megaports Initiative again established that there was substantial leeway in terms of interpreting and implementing national policy objectives.[445] Congress specified radiation

---

444   By 2010, the Megaports Initiative goal was "Over 100 Megaports, scanning over 50% of global shipping traffic by 2015, and approximately 83% of U.S. bound imports shipped through these ports." Department of Energy, "Megaports Initiative: Morocco Transshipment Conference," National Nuclear Security Administration briefing, May 2008; Department of Energy, "Program Overview: Office of the Second Line of Defense," National Nuclear Security Administration briefing, March 2010.
445   Allison, Graham T., and Morton H. Halperin, "Bureaucratic Politics:

detection equipment for 20 major seaports and initial undefined expansion. The legislative branch later added the requirement of 100% scanning of high-risk cargo containers before they reached the United States, but this was the extent of national policy objectives for the program. Similar to the previous case study, the bureaucratic politics phenomenon, where major change was associated with senior actor deadlines and junior actor interests in search of a problem, was also present in the Megaports Initiative. While change occurred in response to a catalyst event -- the terrorist attacks of 9/11 -- maritime radiation detection was one small part of a much greater set of maritime security tasks approved by a reactionary Congress. Once approved, the Megaports Initiative demonstrated the applicability of junior actor interest in search of a problem through the initiative's global focus and continual expansion.[446]

NATIONAL MARITIME CARGO SECURITY ACTORS

National policy and oversight for the Megaports Initiative emanated from Congress but, unlike Cooperative Threat Reduction, there was no requirement for detailed reporting. Although the Megaports Initiative was a proliferation-oriented program, the responsible officials primarily participated in maritime security fora. The maritime aspect of the Megaports Initiative meant that interagency integration with other proliferation programs was for the most part limited to Second Line of Defense policy coordination. In contrast to the Department of Defense, the Department of Energy had a streamlined organizational structure that facilitated direct intra-departmental communication and decentralized implementation. For example, where the two Defense Department offices for policy and acquisition

A Paradigm and Some Policy Implications," *World Politics,* Vol. 24, Spring 1972, p. 53.
446   Ibid., pp. 53-54.

oversight, and the Cooperative Threat Reduction Directorate leadership, interacted with senior officials in host nations to establish requirements, Megaports Initiative personnel conducted their own host nation negotiations. These international exchanges were limited and took place on a global basis. Consequently, Department of Energy officials relied on the Department of State to facilitate outreach and high-profile agreements. Collectively, each of the actors highlighted below was vital to Megaports Initiative operations, but because it was a small supporting maritime security program, the amount of congressional oversight and the ability of the lead agency to influence Department of Energy actions, were negligible.[447]

CONGRESS

The House and Senate Armed Services committees performed the primary oversight roles for the Department of Energy's Defense Nuclear Nonproliferation programs. Unlike Cooperative Threat Reduction, Defense *Nuclear Nonproliferation* activities fell under the Energy and Water Appropriations Subcommittee and were not identified at the program level. This meant that, while the Armed Services committees authorized National Nuclear Security Administration defense nonproliferation programs, the Energy and Water Appropriations Subcommittee was responsible for allocating funds during the annual appropriations process. The Department of Energy's *Defense Nuclear*

---

447   In the broader area of maritime security, shipping firms, maritime terminal operators, and supporting manufactures and retailers were key actors. But these private sector actors did not play a significant role in Megaports Initiative implementation beyond the consideration for the balance between security and commerce. During the creation of the *National Strategy for Maritime Security,* private sector partners specified that there was a maximum shut-down rate of 4-5 days, before even the largest firms began to lose money. This consideration prompted the U.S. government to declare a position of "resilience" in the strategy, and to clearly articulate to all maritime security actors the importance of the free-flow of global commerce. *National Strategy for Maritime Security*, September 2005, pp. 25-26.

Nonproliferation portion of the annual appropriations act was a single paragraph that stated the purpose and aggregate funding amount, but one significant difference in the appropriation sources was the no-year authorization that allowed funding to "remain available until expended."[448]

Other committees and subcommittees also had routine formal and informal questions that required staff information or testimony from Department of Energy officials because the Megaports Initiative was related to global shipping and nonproliferation. These bodies included committees such as the House Energy and Commerce, Senate Commerce, Science, and Transportation, and the House Oversight and Government Reform subcommittees. The Megaports Initiative did not receive specific legislated intent or limitations which left the appropriations process as the primary congressional oversight tool. While accompanying reports provided an explanation of original congressional intent, and legislators requested Government Accountability Office investigations for information beyond routine testimonies, Congress was generally supportive and content to fund the initiative as it expanded between 2003 and 2009.[449]

WHITE HOUSE

The National Security Council and Homeland Security Council staffs coordinated American counterproliferation policy during the administration of George W. Bush. This meant that, in addition to the segregated departmental implementation

---

448   *Energy and Water Development Appropriations Act, 2006* (H.R. 2419, P.L. 109-103), Title II, Defense Nuclear Nonproliferation.

449   Hobson, David, "Committee on Appropriations accompanying report to the fiscal year 2004 Energy and Water Development Appropriations Bill (H.R. 2754, 108-212)," July 16, 2003; Government Accountability Office, *Preventing Nuclear Smuggling: Department of Energy Has Made Limited Progress in Installing Radiation Detection Equipment at Highest Priority Foreign Seaports,* March 2005; Caldwell, Stephen L. "The SAFE Port Act: Status and Implementation One Year Later," testimony, October 30, 2007.

structure, the White House also had a separate national and homeland security staff structure that conducted joint meetings, working groups, and policy coordination committees.[450] Complex relationships were illustrated, for example, by dual-released national and homeland security presidential directives. Within the White House, the Second Line of Defense programs fell under different offices and committees. The core program aligned with proliferation bodies covered in the Cooperative Threat Reduction chapter, while the primary committee for the Megaports Initiative was the Maritime Security Policy Coordination Committee, and its corresponding Maritime Security Working Group, both of which were formed in 2004.[451] According to National Security Presidential Directive-41/ Homeland Security Presidential Directive-13, "Maritime Security Policy," these forums were co-sponsored by National Security Council and Homeland Security Council staff members with designated executive directors that coordinated and chaired routine meetings.[452] National policy coordination from the National Security Council and Homeland Security Council staffs was ad hoc and informal with limited formal interaction during scheduled maritime working group meetings. According to the Office of Combating Terrorism's Associate Director for Maritime Security, Rick Nelson, the original intent of the

450   Murdock, Clark A., and Michele A. Flournoy, "Beyond Goldwater-Nichols: U.S. Government and Defense Reform for a New Strategic Era (Phase II)," Center for Strategic and International Studies Report, July 28, 2005, p. 26.

451   The Second Line of Defense core program also participated in National Counterterrorism Center coordinating and planning meetings. Interview with Department of Energy, National Nuclear Security Administration, Second Line of Defense Core Program Official, June 25, 2010.

452   Flag and senior officers from the Navy and the Coast Guard represented the respective National Security Council and Homeland Security Council staffs as chairs and executive directors during the George W. Bush administration. Interview with National Security Council Staff, Office of Combating Terrorism Associate Director for Maritime Security Rick Nelson, August 25, 2010.

working group was to develop a national maritime security strategy and to organize the post-9/11 maritime security initiatives that "were being funded and put forward, but that weren't necessarily being coordinated, not only at the policy level, but at the operational level as well."[453]

The efforts of the working group resulted in the September 2005 *National Strategy for Maritime Security,* as well as eight supporting maritime plans prepared by designated lead agencies.[454] From the perspective of the Megaports Initiative, the National Security Council/Homeland Security Council staffs were concerned with how the initiative fitted into the larger strategic structure and not with specific plans and daily operations. As separate executive oversight layers concerned with interjecting national strategic direction and deconflicting maritime security programs, neither staff was required to approve annual department strategic plans or budgets. These White House organizations were not designed as national interagency staffs.[455] As a result, the Project on National Security Reform argued that, "a burdened White House cannot manage the national security system as a whole, so it is not agile, collaborative, or able to perform well."[456] The report went on to offer that because "the

---

453   Initially, the Maritime Security Working Group met weekly, but the frequency decreased significantly once the presidential directive, national strategy, and eight supporting plans were approved and released. The multiple initiatives in this area represented the contextual goal of improving maritime security. Ibid.; Wilson, James Q., *Bureaucracy: What Government Agencies Do and Why They Do It,* 2nd edition 2000, p. 129.

454   For example, the Department of State was the lead agency for the *International Outreach and Coordination Strategy for the National Strategy for Maritime Security,* released in November 2005. For more information on the supporting plans, see Department of Homeland Security, "National Security Presidential Directive 41/Homeland Security Presidential Directive 13 National Strategy for Maritime Security Supporting Plans," March 26, 2008, retrieved July 15, 2010.

455   Wilson, James Q., *Bureaucracy: What Government Agencies Do and Why They Do It,* 2nd edition 2000, pp. 272-274.

456   Locher, James R. III, Executive Director, *Forging a New Shield,* Project on National Security Reform, 2008, p. 96.

system is grossly imbalanced, supporting strong departmental capabilities at the expense of integrating mechanisms" was the norm in interagency operations.[457]

INTERAGENCY

The three key departments highlighted in this chapter are the Departments of Homeland Security, State, and Energy. Separate operational plans were specific to each department and did not account for interagency capabilities. Instead, federal proliferation and maritime security management was a policy coordination function where individual directors and officials attended interagency meetings and corresponded directly between program offices. The Departments of Homeland Security and Energy relied on State Department support, but the various proliferation and maritime security initiatives were not integrated. Thus, an interagency environment characterized by senior coordination and situational awareness, but lacking in operational planning and execution, was again evident in this study. Research findings were consistent with the Project on National Security Reform's argument that, "departments and agencies use their resources to support the capabilities they need to carry out their core mandates rather than national missions."[458]

DEPARTMENT OF HOMELAND SECURITY

The Department of Homeland Security was the lead federal department for the Global Nuclear Detection Architecture. The department's Domestic Nuclear Detection Office was responsible for the architecture although multiple organizations within the department had responsibilities related to nuclear detection and maritime security. For example, Customs and Border Protection was a lead agency for maritime cargo security with

---

457   Ibid.
458   Ibid.

responsibility for the Container Security Initiative.[459] In 2002, this initiative began as a pilot program, and it was later codified in the *Security and Accountability for Every (SAFE) Port Act of 2006*. Under the Container Security Initiative, Customs and Border Protection stationed approximately 150 officers at 58 international ports to screen U.S. bound maritime cargo for weapons of mass destruction.[460] Global shipping information from this initiative was consolidated by the National Targeting Center for cargo to assess maritime targeting information 24-hours a day. Since 2001, the Customs and Border Protection" National Targeting Center grew from a staff of 26 to an interagency operation of over 60 personnel drawn from several departments, including the Federal Bureau of Investigation, the Food and Drug Administration, and the Transportation Security Administration.[461]

The Megaports Initiative agreed to equip the 58 Container Security Initiative ports with radiation detection equipment, and to provide training and data access for Customs and Border Protection concerning containers bound for the United States. Megaports Initiative officials served as conduits into the Department of Energy, but once a port became operational

---

459   Even though these officers were in-country, the host nation retained operational control of Megaports Initiative equipment. Interview with Department of Homeland Security, Customs and Border Protection, Container Security and Secure Freight Initiatives Director, September 15, 2010.

460   Department of Homeland Security, *Customs and Border Protection's Container Security Initiative Has Proactive Management and Oversight but Future Direction Is Uncertain,* Inspector General Report, February 2010, p. 1.

461   The Laboratories and Scientific Services (LSS) reachback section was housed in the Department of Homeland Security, Customs and Border Protection, National Targeting Center (Cargo). Department of Homeland Security, "National Targeting Center keeps terrorism at bay," *U.S. Customs and Border Protection Today*, March 2005; Interviews with Department of Homeland Security, Customs and Border Protection, National Targeting Center Assistant Director for Cargo, and Container Security Initiative Watch Commander, September 1, 2010.

the primary relationship was between Customs and Border Protection officers and the host nation. Formal and informal communications between United States and host nation on-site personnel were critical for Container Security Initiative operations. In addition to host country equipment, Customs and Border Protection in-country personnel had Department of Homeland Security handheld radiation detectors, but these were purely secondary devices available for support if alerted by the host nation.[462]

In response to the *Security and Accountability for Every (SAFE) Port Act* requirement to determine the feasibility of 100% scanning of containers bound for the United States, the Departments of Homeland Security and Energy established the Secure Freight Initiative to integrate the Container Security and Megaports Initiatives.[463] The U.S. government's goal for the Secure Freight Initiative was "to deploy next-generation tools and integrated systems, along with other proven technologies, to scan maritime container cargo."[464] This resulted in a new program office in the Department of Homeland Security, and a new requirement for the National Targeting Center to coordinate Container Security Initiative and Megaports Initiative

462   Interview with Department of Energy, National Nuclear Security Administration, Second Line of Defense Megaports Initiative Official, July 21, 2010.

463   Participation in the Department of Homeland Security and Department of Energy initiatives was voluntary for international partners. Because a country could choose to participate in the Megaports, Container Security, and/or Secure Freight Initiatives, the standard operating procedures varied from country-to-country, and even from port-to-port. Interviews with Department of Energy, National Nuclear Security Administration, Second Line of Defense Megaports Initiative Official, and Department of Homeland Security, Customs and Border Protection, Container Security and Secure Freight Initiatives Director, July 21, and September 15, 2010.

464   Department of Homeland Security, "Secure Freight Initiative: Vision and Operations Overview," Office of the Press Secretary, December 7, 2006.

capabilities at a handful of initial pilot ports. However, the introduction of the Secure Freight Initiative did not alter independent department goals or operating procedures.[465]

DEPARTMENT OF STATE

The State Department provided diplomatic and functional support. The Bureau of International Security and Nonproliferation's Export Control and Related Border Security Assistance program helped governments to develop and implement export control systems. The Bureau of Economic, Energy, and Business Affairs facilitated maritime issues. International Security and Nonproliferation was traditionally the lead agency at State for proliferation, and Export Control and Related Border Security Assistance was an interagency program supported by the Departments of Commerce, Energy, and Homeland Security.[466] Within the Second Line of Defense, the core program interacted with Export Control and Related Border Security Assistance, while the Megaports Initiative coordinated with the Department of State's Bureau of Economic, Energy, and Business Affairs.[467]

The Office of Transportation Policy's Maritime Security Director represented the State Department at the Maritime Security Working Group, and conducted routine coordination with the Megaports Initiative. The office attempted to coordinate

---

465   Interviews with Department of Energy, National Nuclear Security Administration, Second Line of Defense Megaports Initiative Official, and Department of Homeland Security, Customs and Border Protection, Container Security and Secure Freight Initiatives Director, July 21, and September 15, 2010.
466   The Department of Defense's Weapons of Mass Destruction-Proliferation Prevention Initiative, under the Cooperative Threat Reduction Directorate, also targeted former Soviet Union border and customs officials for training and equipment assistance. Department of State, "Export Control and Related Border Security Program: Strategic Plan," Bureau of International Security and Nonproliferation, September 15, 2006.
467   Interviews with Department of Energy, National Nuclear Security Administration, Second Line of Defense Core Program Official, and Second Line of Defense Megaports Initiative Official, June 25, 2010.

and synchronize U.S. government maritime initiative messages with country plans, and consolidated visits and discussions with host nation partners when possible. The office also served as an education conduit for Foreign Service Officers by organizing seminars, training, and information provision such as Megaports Initiative briefing slides made available on the department's intranet.[468]

DEPARTMENT OF ENERGY

In 2000, Congress mandated the formation of the National Nuclear Security Administration to assume responsibility for management of the country's nuclear stockpile, and the Department of Energy's nonproliferation and naval reactor programs.[469] The agency was divided into six primary directorates and headed by an Administrator/Under Secretary of Energy for Nuclear Security.[470] The next level of leadership applicable to the Second Line of Defense Office was the *Principal Assistant Deputy Administrator for Defense Nuclear Nonproliferation. The deputy administrator supervised seven program offices including Global Threat Reduction, Nonproliferation Research and Development, Nuclear Risk Reduction, Nonproliferation and International Security,* International Material Protection and Cooperation, Fissile Materials Disposition, and International

468   Interview with Department of State, Bureau of Economic, Energy, and Business Affairs, Office of Transportation Policy Maritime Security Director, August 25, 2010.
469   The National Nuclear Security Administration reorganized internally in 2002. *National Defense Authorization Act for Fiscal Year 2000,* Title XXXII, National Nuclear Security Administration.
470   The directorates were: Military Application (which oversaw the national laboratories), *Defense Nuclear Nonproliferation,* Naval Reactors, Emergency Operations, Infrastructure and Environment, and Defense Nuclear Security. The management and administration office, and service center supported all directorate offices. Each office had a numeric designation beginning with NA and then the office number. For example, Defense Nuclear Nonproliferation was NA-20. Department of Energy, "Organization Chart," National Nuclear Security Administration, May 2010.

Operations.[471] Beyond support functions, guidance, budget, and routine testimony, the National Nuclear Security Administration and Defense Nuclear Nonproliferation leadership were not actively involved in day-to-day Megaports Initiative activities.[472]

The Office of International Material Protection and Cooperation was the starting point for daily oversight of the Second Line of Defense Office. International Material Protection and Cooperation was led by a career senior executive with the title of assistant deputy administrator. The office comprised the Materials Protection, Controls, and Accounting, and Second Line of Defense programs.[473] In addition to routine guidance and situational awareness, International Material Protection and Cooperation issued an annual strategic plan primarily focused on Materials Protection, Controls, and Accounting.[474] The lack of focus on the Second Line of Defense program allowed the office to develop an independent strategic plan.[475] The deputy administrator participated in international events such as global shipping conferences, and was the first level Department of

---

471   The Office of International Operations had locations in Astana, Kazakhstan, Baghdad, Iraq, Baku, Azerbaijan, Bangkok, Thailand, Beijing, China, Islamabad, Pakistan, Kiev, Ukraine, Russian Federation (Moscow, St. Petersburg, and Yekaterinburg), Paris, France, Sofia, Bulgaria, Tbilisi, Republic of Georgia, Tokyo, Japan, and Vienna, Austria.

472   Department of Energy, National Nuclear Security Administration planning, programming, budgeting, and execution guidance was normally released in March, and included fiscally constraining funding levels for each of the nonproliferation programs. Interview with Department of Energy, National Nuclear Security Administration, International Material Protection and Cooperation Budget Official, October 5, 2010.

473   Materials Protection, Controls, and Accounting was divided into four offices, Nuclear Warhead Protection, Weapons Material Protection, Material Consolidation and Civilian Sites, and National Infrastructure and Sustainability.

474   Department of Energy, "Office of International Material Protection and Cooperation 2006 Strategic Plan," National Nuclear Security Administration.

475   Department of Energy, "Office of the Second Line of Defense 2006 Strategic Plan," National Nuclear Security Administration.

Energy official to testify before Congress or meet with its members concerning Second Line of Defense programs.[476]

Various sources of policy were evident from an examination of relevant national actors. This issue extended into a process of decentralized policy execution where the White House attempted to gain control of a maritime security landscape filled with independently resourced and led initiatives. National Security Council and Homeland Security Council staff efforts resulted in the formulation of a national maritime strategy, but the extent to which autonomous federal actors adhered to this reactionary direction during the execution process is covered in the following sections. The complexities of national management were compounded by proliferation and maritime security responsibilities which fell under several coordinating committees, each with different priorities. This distinction meant additional coordination requirements, and separately administered national strategies for two different mission areas were added to an already complex interagency environment.

The above situation reflected bureaucratic politics theory propositions related to policy decisions rarely facilitating policy monitoring, and the larger the number of actors involved the less that implementation reflects national policy.[477] The absence of coordinated national policy development and oversight followed through into segregated federal government implementation where independent departmental programs, such as the Megaports Initiative, were characterized by separate

---

476   The National Nuclear Security Administration had a congressional liaison office to facilitate communication. Formal testimony and member interaction began with the International Material Protection and Cooperation assistant deputy administrator, but Second Line of Defense and Megaports Initiative directors were frequently called upon to brief congressional staffers on program specifics. Interview with Department of Energy, National Nuclear Security Administration, Second Line of Defense Megaports Initiative Official, July 21, 2010.
477   Allison, Graham T., and Morton H. Halperin, "Bureaucratic Politics: A Paradigm and Some Policy Implications," *World Politics*, Vol. 24, Spring 1972, pp. 53-56.

organization, resourcing, and operating procedures.[478]   This segregated national execution addressed interagency interaction from the basis of coordination and deconfliction, not collaborative federal implementation.[479]   The next section highlights this last point and provides a second example of an independent department approach to collective nuclear defense issues.

ORGANIZATION AND WORKFLOW

This section establishes that the Department of Energy was organized to execute single agency contracts with program leadership participation in interagency coordination fora. The maritime radiation detection study represents a smaller nuclear defense program that benefited from previous U.S. government efforts and a supporting status. As a post-9/11 program, the Megaports Initiative was facilitated by an existing office within the Department of Energy's National Nuclear Security Administration.[480] Initiative personnel used federal acquisition procedures and participated in department planning and budgeting efforts from inception.[481] The single output of radiation detection stations meant that Megaports Initiative personnel, working with the national laboratories and contracting firms, could quickly learn from trial and error.[482] Standardized packages tailored to design and host nation considerations stood in contrast to differing conversion and elimination scenarios experienced by Cooperative Threat Reduction officials. A small supporting National Nuclear Security Administration structure meant that close coordination of routine work phases occurred

---

478   Murdock, Clark A., and Michele A. Flournoy, "Beyond Goldwater-Nichols: U.S. Government and Defense Reform for a New Strategic Era (Phase II)," Center for Strategic and International Studies Report, July 28, 2005, p. 26.
479   Downs, Anthony, *Inside Bureaucracy*, 1967, p. 216.
480   Ibid., pp. 220-221.
481   Wilson, James Q., *Bureaucracy: What Government Agencies Do and Why They Do It*, 2nd edition 2000, pp. 126-129.
482   Downs, Anthony, *Inside Bureaucracy*, 1967, pp. 18-19.

from outreach to sustainability, and that implementers routinely attended senior policy coordination meetings.

SECOND LINE OF DEFENSE

The Second Line of Defense Office comprised approximately 40 personnel with a director, deputy director, and separate program directors for the core, Megaports, and sustainability programs.[483] Within the Second Line of Defense Office there were centralized management, sustainability, and contracting officer representatives. Additional expertise was provided as needed by the national laboratories and contracting firms such as Ahtna Government Services Corporation, Ses-Tech Global Solutions, and Randolph Construction Services. Primary laboratory support for the Megaports Initiative came from Pacific Northwest National Laboratory for project management and training, from Sandia National Laboratories for maritime prioritization, from Los Alamos National Laboratory for technology assistance, and communications expertise came from Oak Ridge National Laboratory.[484] Although Second Line of Defense had two major programs this study focused on the Megaports Initiative between 2003 and 2008.

MEGAPORTS INITIATIVE

The Megaports Initiative is responsible for installing radiation detection equipment at multiple port entry and exit points for land and sea movement in international partner countries. These radiation detection units are linked to a central alarm

483   The Second Line of Defense Office leadership consisted of a career senior executive director, with a General Schedule-15 equivalent deputy.
484   This introduction was meant to highlight laboratory participation. Note that each laboratory provided multiple services in support of Second Line of Defense and Megaports Initiative. Government Accountability Office, *Preventing Nuclear Smuggling: Department of Energy Has Made Limited Progress in Installing Radiation Detection Equipment at Highest Priority Foreign Seaports,* March 2005, pp. 34-35.

station and supported by additional specialty equipment to locate and identify nuclear materials discovered by initial monitors. During the Morocco transhipment conference of May 2008, the Second Line of Defense and Megaports Initiative directors reiterated that the Megaports implementation goal was completion of "over 75 Megaports, scanning over 50% of global shipping traffic by 2013," and that the program status included the ports listed in Figure 4.1.[485]

Implementation Complete (12)	Operational Testing (1)	Implementation Phase (19)	Over 50 other major international seaports with agreements pending (to include)
Belgium (Zeebrugge)	Thailand (Laem Chabang)	Belgium (Antwerp)	Argentina (Buenos Aires)
China (Hong Kong; Shanghai)		Honduras (Cortes)	Djibouti (Djibouti)
Colombia (Cartagena)		Netherlands (Rotterdam)	Portugal (Lisbon)
Dominican Republic (Caucedo)		Singapore (Singapore - Pilot)	Lebanon (Beirut)
Dubai, UAE (Jebel Ali)		Sri Lanka (Colombo)	UAE (Khor Fakkan)
Egypt (Alexandria)		U.K. (Southampton)	
Israel (Ashdod)		Jamaica (Kingston)	
Hong Kong		Mexico (Veracruz)	
Bahamas (Freeport)		Oman (Salalah)	
Greece (Piraeus)		Panama (Balboa. Manzanillo)	
Israel (Haifa – Pilot)		Malaysia (Port Klang)	
Pakistan (Qasim)		Singapore (Singapore - Phase II)	
Philippines (Manila)		South Korea (Busan)	
Spain (Algeciras)		Taiwan (Kaohsiung)	

**FIGURE 4.1. SECOND LINE OF DEFENSE
MEGAPORTS INITIATIVE PROGRESS**[486]
(AS OF MAY 2008)

Key positions within the Megaports Initiative revolved around the program leadership and federal project managers. Program leadership -- a director and deputy director -- were responsible for planning, budgeting, and oversight.[487] Because

---

485   Department of Energy, "Megaports Initiative: Morocco Transshipment Conference," National Nuclear Security Administration briefing, May 2008.
486   Ibid.
487   These positions were normally General Schedule-15 equivalent, with specific duty and responsibility delineation at the discretion of the director. During the period of study the Department of Energy used the pay band system instead of the general schedule system. For continuity, federal pay grades referenced throughout the book were represented as General Schedule

of limited personnel, the director and deputy director served simultaneously as regional and country managers. In addition to regional alignment, the Megaports Office consisted of management and operations, support, service, and budget sections that were augmented by laboratory contractors. These sections dealt with equipment, threat, and administrative services support.

Country and regional managers represented the U.S. government as federal project managers for equipment installation, training, and sustainment.[488] Regional managers, while responsible for all applicable countries in their regions, did not directly supervise country managers.[489] The number of countries in a country manager's portfolio varied based on gaps, experience, port maturity, additional responsibilities, and port complexities. Country managers may simultaneously have served in multiple additional roles spanning regional manger through program director. With a total staff of ten civil servants, most Megaports officials served in more than one position and traveled abroad approximately four months out of every year.[490]

Workflow was broken down into three phases: 1) outreach; 2) implementation; and 3) sustainability. Typically, a program

---

equivalent.

488   Country managers were not always regionally aligned. New country managers were normally assigned three to six ports that represented each phase of the Megaports Initiative, and were paired with office and laboratory project manager mentors. They attended formal training at Pacific Northwest National Laboratory for project manager certification, and either the executive or operator equipment orientation course. Additional training was conducted at Oak Ridge National Laboratory for data analysis.

489   Megaports regions were aligned with the Department of State: Africa, East Asia Pacific, Europe and Eurasia, Near East Asia, South and Central Asia, and the western hemisphere. Interview with Department of Energy, National Nuclear Security Administration, Second Line of Defense Megaports Initiative Official, July 21, 2010.

490   Interview with Department of Energy, National Nuclear Security Administration, Second Line of Defense Megaports Initiative Official, June 25, 2010; Department of Energy, "Megaports Initiative: Morocco Transshipment Conference," National Nuclear Security Administration briefing, May 2008.

country was visited by a federal project manager once for outreach, three to four times annually for implementation, and once a year for the period of sustainability support. Megaports officials had flexible travel schedules that depended on the phases and needs of their countries. The duration of each country manager's trip was generally one business week, with countries at great distances scheduled together to limit travel time and repetitive costs. While schedules were normally planned in advance, unforecasted problems routinely required immediate federal oversight of varying duration.[491]

The Megaports Initiative was a global program that depended on the cooperation of international partners. Typical host nation executive agents came from national finance, customs, or atomic energy type organizations. For example, in the Netherlands the Ministry of Finance signed the initial memorandum of understanding with the Department of Energy. While ministries primarily acted as executive agents, the host nation customs, border, port, fire, or atomic energy services normally functioned as the working level implementers and weapons of mass destruction competent authorities.[492] By design, the program transferred site control to host nation partners after installation. In this capacity host nations operated and maintained the equipment, and were responsible for physically interdicting any special nuclear materials or weapons under their legal framework.[493]

491   Interview with Department of Energy, National Nuclear Security Administration, Second Line of Defense Megaports Initiative Official, June 25, 2010.
492   Interview with Department of Energy, National Nuclear Security Administration, Second Line of Defense Megaports Initiative Official, July 21, 2010.
493   Because the initiative dealt with a wide-range of international ports, one aspect of host nation support that differed from Cooperative Threat Reduction or the Second Line of Defense core programs was the variation in size and capabilities. For example, while some countries were well-versed in English and able to leverage current e-mail and teleconference technologies, others relied on rudimentary technologies, and the use of interpreters as their primary means of communication. Interview with Department of

OUTREACH

The Megaports Initiative used American embassies and other Department of State assets to support outreach operations.[494] Unlike the Cooperative Threat Reduction programs that were focused on the former Soviet Union, the Megaports Initiative was a global endeavor without forward assets. Outreach consisted of the regional manager or program leadership contacting an embassy and arranging a meeting with the appropriate port or ministerial authority. The program representative traveled with a technical expert to the country and provided a standard brief that included program history, framework, benefits, and host nation considerations. Embassy support varied depending on the country and staffing issues, but the Department of State at a minimum provided an official to assist from initial contact through to the signature of an agreement.[495] The agreement was primarily a non-binding memorandum of understanding that pertained specifically to the Megaports project(s) in that country. Although specific to the country, these memoranda of understanding were generally four pages long and broadly covered signatory responsibilities for the three phases of the program, and communication for the duration of the equipment lifespan.

When it became clear that a country was going to sign a Megaports Initiative memorandum of understanding, the country

---

Energy, National Nuclear Security Administration, Second Line of Defense Megaports Initiative Official, June 25, 2010.

494 The Megaports Initiative did not have a staff of interpreters at headquarters. Instead, they relied on embassy-recommended host nation contract interpreters for in-country trips and routine communications. Overall, because of the international nature of the shipping business, there normally was some level of English at each port. Ibid.

495 This was often the ambassador signing on behalf of Department of Energy, but for high-profile counties such as Argentina, the U.S. Secretary of State occasionally signed Megaports Initiative memoranda of understanding. Department of State, "Secretary Clinton and Argentine Foreign Minister Taiana Sign U.S.-Argentina Megaports Agreement to Prevent Nuclear Smuggling," Office of the Spokesman, April 13, 2010.

manager initiated the budget process based on general planning figures. The general estimate per port was $15 million, but initial budget planning was driven by the fiscal year, the availability of funds, and specific laboratory estimates by phase.[496] The focus of this preliminary process was, at a minimum, to assign the new country enough initial funding from unobligated or reprogramd funds to begin the site survey and design processes. Countries that were approved late in the fiscal year, for example, may only have received funding for site survey and design requirements with contract, installation, and sustainment funds dependent on the next fiscal year. Once the agreement and preliminary funds were in place, the country manager assembled and led a technical team to conduct an initial site survey. Teams varied based on port numbers and complexity with smaller ports usually having a single member per activity. General composition included a Pacific Northwest National Laboratory project manager and training lead, a design and communications lead from Sandia National Laboratories, a Los Alamos National Laboratory equipment lead, and a sustainability lead that, depending on the region, came from any of the laboratories.

IMPLEMENTATION

Country managers began their implementation duties by initiating planning and coordinating preliminary site surveys that resulted in a port security report and a cost-benefit analysis. These

496   The cost estimate of $15 million used throughout this chapter is from the 2005 Government Accountability Office report, and interviews with Megaports Initiative personnel. In a separate 2007 Government Accountability Office document, per port cost estimates ranged from $2.6 million to $30.4 million. Government Accountability Office, *Preventing Nuclear Smuggling: Department of Energy Has Made Limited Progress in Installing Radiation Detection Equipment at Highest Priority Foreign Seaports,* March 2005, p. 5; Caldwell, Stephen L. "The SAFE Port Act: Status and Implementation One Year Later," testimony, October 30, 2007, pp. 41-42; Interview with Department of Energy, National Nuclear Security Administration, Second Line of Defense Megaports Initiative Official, June 25, 2010.

federal managers were empowered to make routine decisions and conduct coordination that did not impact multiple countries, the core program, or violate contracting regulations.[497] Country managers were generalists that drew specific expertise from the national laboratories and integrating contractors. Assistance included a project manager from the Pacific Northwest National Laboratory to supervise individual ports. Project managers provided standardized monthly schedule reports, participated in weekly teleconferences with country managers, and communicated as needed.[498]

Site survey products were the responsibility of the Pacific Northwest, Los Alamos and Sandia National Laboratories working in conjunction with the project and country managers. These surveys resulted in design and training requirements. Designs consisted of port layout, proposed equipment needs, installation requirements, and overall site design. One important criteria for each port design was the requirement to install equipment in a manner that did not impede traffic and container flow.[499] Pacific Northwest National Laboratory provided site operations training in the United States, in-country training, and a visit to an operational megaport.[500] Training costs were normally funded by the Megaports Initiative unless it was a high-income country or a cost-sharing agreement was negotiated prior to signature

---

497   For issues beyond the experience of the country manager, or issues that impacted multiple countries, the Megaports Initiative director was the decision authority. Core program impacts were elevated to the Second Line of Defense Office, whereas federal contracting problems were referred to the contracting team. Anthony, *Inside Bureaucracy*, 1967, pp. 133-134 and 53-54.

498   Anthony, *Inside Bureaucracy*, 1967, pp. 145-146.

499   Department of Energy, "National Nuclear Security Administration and the Vietnamese Ministry of Finance Agreement," U.S. Department of State Foreign Press Center Briefing by Director of Megaports Initiative William Kilmartin, July 2, 2010.

500   U.S. training was conducted at the Hazardous Materials Management and Emergency Response facility located in Richland, Washington.

of the memorandum of understanding.[501] The intent was to involve applicable host nation entities, such as an atomic energy commission or customs service, in American-based training so they could lead ensuing in-country training. The planning factor for Hazardous Materials Management and Emergency Response training was 25 host nation personnel with follow-on training varying per country and port requirements.

The approach to system layout and equipment was standardized to support primary, secondary, and tertiary inspection areas. The Megaports radiation detection equipment was installed at port entry and exit points for vehicle, rail, and pedestrian traffic. Fixed radiation portal monitors and newer advanced spectroscopic portals, equipped with additional optical character recognition and license plate recognition systems, were linked to a central alarm station. Sandia approved software was used in the central alarm station to record and evaluate incidents. Handheld equipment that included personal radiation pagers, radioisotope identifiers, and radiation survey meters, was provided for host nation personnel to conduct secondary inspections. Mobile equipment, such as specially designed straddle carriers, or the newer mobile radiation detection and identification system, was furnished to address transhipment containers.[502] The radiation

---

501   The Megaports Initiative used the World Bank index for cost-sharing negotiations. For example, a high-income country such as the U.K. would be asked to share installation and training costs, whereas an upper middle income country may have the initial port funded by the U.S., and be asked to cost-share for additional ports within the country. Interview with Department of Energy, National Nuclear Security Administration, Second Line of Defense Megaports Initiative Official, July 21, 2010.

502   Before secondary inspections were ordered, host nation personnel were trained to examine all container and reading information available in order to prevent false alarms from delaying port operations. The Megaports Initiative used multiple vendors for radiation detection equipment to include, Transportation Security Administration Systems, Hi-Tech Solutions, and Ortec. Department of Energy, "Megaports Initiative: Morocco Transshipment Conference," National Nuclear Security Administration briefing, May 2008; Department of Energy, "National Nuclear Security Administration and the Vietnamese Ministry of Finance Agreement," U.S. Department of State

technology used by the Megaports Initiative was passive in nature. This meant that the equipment received and processed information from scanned items without violating container integrity. In a foreign press briefing for the announcement of the United States-Vietnam program, the Megaports director described the scanning process as:

> So a truck will drive through a portal monitor. The portal monitor is... on. It collects background information, some natural background radiation. And when a truck drives through, it creates an occupancy and if the truck container...has a higher radiation level than the occupancy... then it will alarm. This is basically just a gross detection detector. So there is no harm to public health. And it is not... the x-ray systems... or high energy systems that look inside a container.... Those are active interrogation systems where they actually produce an image and you see the image. That is a different technology than the radiation portal monitors. We are a passive system that just collects energy from the container to ensure that the radiation level -- that there's nothing inside the container that could do harm to the citizens of Vietnam or impact the shipping community.[503]

Final designs required formal approval from the country manager through the contracting process. Designs may have been approved or modifications requested based on team input or prior experience. If there were changes during the life of the project that were outside the original contract, the country manager followed the established federal contracting processes to gain new approval. Once conceptual designs were complete, the contracting officer carried the project through the contracting process.

Foreign Press Center Briefing by Director of Megaports Initiative William Kilmartin, July 2, 2010; Interviews with Department of Energy, National Nuclear Security Administration, Second Line of Defense Megaports Initiative Officials, June 25, and July 21, 2010.
503   Department of Energy, "National Nuclear Security Administration and the Vietnamese Ministry of Finance Agreement," U.S. Department of State Foreign Press Center Briefing by Director of Megaports Initiative William Kilmartin, July 2, 2010.

Much like Cooperative Threat Reduction, the Megaports Initiative used three integrating contractors -- Ahtna Government Services Corporation, Ses-Tech Global Solutions, and Randolph Construction Services -- for competitive procurement.[504] Upon receipt of integrating contractor proposals, the project management team evaluated the bids based on cost and technical solution using set criteria.[505] After award of the project, the integrating contractors became an integral member of the project team. Depending on the size and complexity of the project, contractors may have deployed a site manager or management team to the port for the duration of the installation, testing, and handover. Integrating firms had the option to sub-contract installation requirements to host nation contractors as necessary. The contractor installation and management approach was included during the bidding process and considered by the contracting officer and country manager prior to award.

A detailed design and approval process that included engineering surveys preceded actual construction. Either the country manager or the project manager traveled with specific technical leads during this portion of the project. Once all surveys, contractors, and equipment were in place, construction and equipment installation began. The Megaports Initiative had designed a step-by-step process for implementation that facilitated replication, phased installation, and tracking with only minor layout variations to accommodate port designs. Deliverables specified in each statement of work were the same from one project to the next. The same American radiation detection equipment was

---

504   For cost-sharing ports, there may not have been an integrating contractor on site. Interview with Department of Energy, National Nuclear Security Administration, Second Line of Defense Megaports Initiative Official, June 25, 2010.

505   As with Cooperative Threat Reduction, the Megaports Initiative looked for the best, not necessarily the cheapest solution for port installation. Interview with Department of Energy, National Nuclear Security Administration, Second Line of Defense Megaports Initiative Official, July 21, 2010.

used at all ports, unless a change was specifically requested by the host nation, or a port specific modification was required. Of note in this area was the routine local purchase of equipment, such as computers and other supporting infrastructure, to facilitate familiarity in operations and maintenance.[506] Standardization also included the deliverable review and approval process for which the country manager was responsible. Once work had been verified by the country manager and contracting officer, representative national laboratories and contracting firms received payment. Laboratory payment was internal to the Department of Energy, while payments to contracting firms followed federal contracting guidelines and procedures.[507]

The implementation process was overseen and routine problems were handled by the laboratory project manager who ensured the project schedule and milestones were met and that the project remained within budgeting parameters. Host nation representatives assisted with issues such as licensing, construction permits, or testing permits for radioactive sources that needed to be brought in for final equipment testing. Once all equipment was installed and calibrated, the country manager oversaw final testing and ensured all deliverables were complete. While the Megaports Initiative director offered that a typical port such as Cai Mep in Vietnam would take 12 to 15 months to complete once the agreement was signed, it was important to note that the outreach and implementation processes described here were lengthy.[508] Long lead-times accounted for the completion of

---

506   While communication platforms were not standardized, there were specific software requirements that had to be verified by Sandia before installation. Interview with Department of Energy, National Nuclear Security Administration, Second Line of Defense Core program official, June 25, 2010.

507   Ibid.

508   Department of Energy, "National Nuclear Security Administration and the Vietnamese Ministry of Finance Agreement," U.S. Department of State Foreign Press Center Briefing by Director of Megaports Initiative William Kilmartin, July 2, 2010.

only 12 countries between 2003 and 2008, a rate of 2.4 per year during that period.[509]

SUSTAINABILITY

While implementation was still ongoing, the sustainability lead coordinated transition, maintenance, and sustainability plans with their host nation counterpart. The Megaports Initiative provided three years of funding and support for each project and continued to develop long-term support requirements as the program matured. Equipment transitioned to the host nation once testing was complete and the country manager and the contracting officer representative had determined all contractual requirements had been met. At this point, the project team dispersed to new projects, the contracting officer closed out the contract, and the country manager and sustainability lead became the primary points of contact for the country. The sustainability lead replaced the laboratory project manager for milestone tracking, and day-to-day interaction with the host nation. After transition, the host nation operated the site, with a local firm contracted to conduct routine maintenance.[510] The sustainability lead worked

---

509   Countries may have had multiple ports that participated in the program, further increasing the time to complete a country. Completion rates were calculated based on information provided in the Megaports Initiative brief for the 2008 Morocco Transhipment Conference. Department of Energy, "Megaports Initiative: Morocco Transsshipment Conference," National Nuclear Security Administration briefing, May 2008.

510   Routine maintenance consisted of tasks such as checking camera alignment, checking and replacing batteries, and monitoring equipment readings to ensure they remained within specifications. Megaports Initiative structural engineering was rated at 15 years while equipment such as the radiation portal monitors were rated at seven years before major scheduled overhauls were required. Interview with Department of Energy, National Nuclear Security Administration, Second Line of Defense Megaports Initiative Official, July 21, 2010. For more information on Megaports Initiative equipment and layouts, see Department of Energy, "Office of the Second Line of Defense Megaports Initiative," National Nuclear Security Administration briefing, July 2006; Department of Energy, "National Nuclear Security

with the host nation to ensure that there were systems in place for budgeting, sustainment training, data collection, and other steady state operations and maintenance requirements once the support period ended. Travel during this phase normally included the country manager and sustainability lead with other members added if required. For example, if there was an equipment malfunction that could not be resolved on-site or in consultation with the Second Line of Defense help desk, a technical expert from the appropriate laboratory would provide support.[511]

Beyond routine benign readings there were two types of serious detection incidents of proliferation consequence that generated communication through the embassy. Each embassy was organized differently, but the reading information was standardized and transmitted by cable back to all applicable U.S. government departments and agencies.[512] Early in the installation process, Megaports Initiative managers attempted to identify appropriate host nation elements for operations and response. As a result of these key relationships built from the earliest project stages, informal communications flowed directly to Megaports Initiative personnel before embassy dissemination. In all cases, incident reporting was at the discretion of the host nation and not in real-time.

The detailed workflow description revealed that, as with Cooperative Threat Reduction, Megaports Initiative federal

Administration and the Vietnamese Ministry of Finance Agreement," U.S. Department of State Foreign Press Center Briefing by Director of Megaports Initiative William Kilmartin, July 2, 2010.

511   Interview with Department of Energy, National Nuclear Security Administration, Second Line of Defense Official, June 25, 2010.

512   Megaports Initiative data was not real-time. The program relied on host nation countries to manually notify the embassy, and then for the embassy to disseminate incidents through cables. These incidents were processed by other government agencies such as Customs and Border Protection's National Targeting Center (Cargo), and consolidated and analyzed for the Megaports Initiative by Oak Ridge. Interviews with Department of Energy, National Nuclear Security Administration, Second Line of Defense officials, June 25, and July 21, 2010.

program managers did not physically implement nuclear defense policy. While host nation contracting firms played a vital role, there was not the same degree of habitual employment seen in the previous study. Host nation firms were contracted for multiple ports within a country or for continued sustainability contracts but, unlike Cooperative Threat Reduction, the same firms would not move from one project to another with multiyear timelines. Unlike limited duration host nation contracts, American integrating contractors and participating national laboratories benefited from consistent employment associated with continued Megaports Initiative expansion. The Megaports Initiative exemplified a small effort of limited duration that evolved into an enduring program. Because of decentralized federal organization that lacked national oversight, the original intent of a temporary program for radiation detection equipment installation at the 20 largest ports for shipping bound for the United States turned into a permanent office within the Department of Energy.

This section identified that numerous federal managers designed and implemented an initiative that corresponded to existing programs and standard operating procedures. In fact, nearly every federal official in the Megaports Initiative Office had the title of manager.[513] As James Wilson suggested, these officials approached the task of equipping large foreign ports with radiation detection equipment from a process, not outcome standpoint.[514] Department of Energy officials sought to promote organizational interests and avoided integration with other maritime security programs.[515] Instead, the Megaports Initiative

---

513   James Wilson offered that because of numerous constraints, public bureaucracies require a large number of managers to ensure compliance. Wilson, James Q., *Bureaucracy: What Government Agencies Do and Why They Do It*, 2ⁿᵈ edition 2000, p. 133.
514   Ibid., p. 131.
515   Allison, Graham T., and Morton H. Halperin, "Bureaucratic Politics: A Paradigm and Some Policy Implications," *World Politics*, Vol. 24, Spring 1972, pp. 54-56.

was characterized by a process where Department of Energy contracts were executed under a design that maximized agency autonomy and where progress was measured by how officials went about their jobs, not whether the desired outcomes were being achieved.[516]

PROGRAM EVALUATION

Like other nuclear defense areas, maritime radiation detection programs are difficult to evaluate from a market or cost-benefit standpoint. Attempting to justify annual expenditures based on serious incidents reported from the prior fiscal year could have lead to discontinuation of the Megaports Initiative.[517] The program also presents a barrier to evaluation because, as James Wilson argued, many government agencies cannot be evaluated based on a market test related to revenues in excess to cost.[518] The Megaports Initiative supplies a service for which there are no willing customers. In this regard, the program cannot be evaluated based on demand, for example, the number of countries they attracted. Moreover, because the Megaports Initiative by design gives equipment and data to the host nation, this adds further complication to any assessment.

---

516   Wilson, James Q., *Bureaucracy: What Government Agencies Do and Why They Do It*, 2nd edition 2000, p. 164.

517   Unlike the International Atomic Energy Agency illicit trafficking database, Second Line of Defense did not release consolidated statistics on significant detections or interdictions. Instead, National Nuclear Security Administration officials such as Damien LaVera and Dave Huizenga repeatedly used the same examples cited later in the chapter. Palla, Stephanie, "Review Set for Major U.S. Radiation Detection Program," *Global Security Newswire,* March 31, 2010; Huizenga, David, "Radiation Detection," testimony, September 18, 2007; Huizenga, David, "National Nuclear Security Administration's Megaports Initiative and Its Role in the Secure Freight Initiative (SFI)," testimony, June 12, 2008.

518   Wilson, James Q., *Bureaucracy: What Government Agencies Do and Why They Do It*, 2nd edition 2000, pp. 117-118; Downs, Anthony, *Inside Bureaucracy*, 1967, pp. 29-31.

In order to provide a more useful program evaluation, then, this portion of the chapter employs the standardized evaluation criteria from the initial implementation study related to: pace, host nation partners, interagency efforts, realization of policy objectives, counterarguments, and theoretical applicability. Given the importance of defending against nuclear attack, did the Megaports Initiative represent timely implementation, or was maritime radiation detection approached simply as another federal acquisition program? Did this implementation include host nation and interagency collaboration? Based on stated national and agency policy objectives, to what extent did the Department of Energy programs work toward completion? Was the Megaports Initiative free of criticisms, or did opponents raise legitimate concerns over program design and performance? Lastly, were elements of bureaucratic politics theory applicable to this implementation study?

The Megaports Initiative was much smaller and limited in scope compared to Cooperative Threat Reduction. The approach to installing equipment in each country and ensuring sustainability was standardized.[519] This limited scope and standardization saw capital investment ranges of $2.6 million to $30.4 million per port. As a consequence, the Megaports Initiative and greater Second Line of Defense culture was not dominated by acquisition-based project management. Acquisition-based project management was present from the very beginning of the program and was treated as a routine part of the overall process. The Megaports Initiative also differed from Cooperative Threat Reduction because it was a supporting program that remained on the periphery of both proliferation and maritime security.[520] While Department of Energy officials interacted with interagency partners, and participated in senior policy coordination efforts, the chapter has shown that they did not collectively conduct

---

519   Downs, Anthony, *Inside Bureaucracy*, 1967, pp. 18-20.
520   Ibid., pp. 212-218.

operational interagency planning and execution.[521] This lack of operational integration brought into question the presence of the Megaports Initiative within the Department of Energy when the Secretary of Homeland Security had responsibility for the Global Nuclear Detection Architecture and maritime cargo security.[522]

The remainder of this section evaluates the Megaports Initiative for pace, host nation responsibilities, and counterarguments. The first criterion reveals the slow pace of the program, which left the initiative open to questions of viability if only a few ports could be equipped over a several year period. The host nation examination reinforces doubts related to design and benefit. Based on equipment forfeiture and maintenance, the voluntary non-real time notification of a serious incident is brought into question. While there are numerous arguments against the practicality of the Megaports Initiative, this criterion focuses on arguments related to competing technologies, minimal coverage, and the absence of reporting summaries.

The Second Line of Defense Office and Megaports Initiative are used to evaluate the extent to which Department of Energy policy objectives were realized. The evaluation suggests that the department benefited from an ill-defined supporting status that facilitated the establishment of internal objectives designed

---

521   Neither the Container Security Initiative, nor the Second Line of Defense plans referenced for this study accounted for collaborative planning and execution between the two departments.   Department of Homeland Security, *Container Security Initiative: 2006-2011 Strategic Plan*, U.S. Customs and Border Protection, August 2006; Department of Energy, "Office of the Second Line of Defense 2006 Strategic Plan," National Nuclear Security Administration.

522   Several officials questioned why the Megaports Initiative was still located in Department of Energy, and provided background on discussions concerning requests to transfer the program first to the Department of Homeland Security Office of the Under Secretary for Science and Technology, and then to the Domestic Nuclear Detection Office once it was formed. Other Department of Energy, National Nuclear Security Administration officials questioned why the program had not been shifted to the Deputy Under Secretary for Counterterrorism when that position was created. For a full list of interviewees, see the bibliography.

to aid in program expansion. Department of Homeland Security programs are included in the evaluation of interagency integration, theoretical applicability, and the third statutory policy objective. In these areas, the study reveals a distinct separation in programs between departments that illustrate several bureaucratic politics propositions regarding faithful execution, existing programs and standard operating procedures, organizational interests, and the negative impact of large numbers of actors on envisioned implementation.

PACE

In the first two years the Megaports Initiative completed two ports and three additional agreements. Department of Energy officials noted that it had been difficult to convince host governments to cooperate because some countries had "concerns that screening large volumes of containers will create delays that could inhibit the flow of commerce at their ports," and that some nations were "reluctant to hire the additional customs officials needed to operate the radiation detection equipment."[523] By 2008, the initiative accounted for 12 operational ports, 19 ports at various stages of implementation, one port in final testing, and agreements pending with over 50 other countries.[524] These accomplishments were part of the stated completion goal of 75 high-priority ports that were identified from the 1,200 ports evaluated annually by Sandia National Laboratory's maritime prioritization model.[525] If the program met the internal goal of

---

523   Government Accountability Office, *Preventing Nuclear Smuggling: Department of Energy Has Made Limited Progress in Installing Radiation Detection Equipment at Highest Priority Foreign Seaports,* March 2005, p. 4.
524   Department of Energy, "Megaports Initiative: Morocco Transshipment Conference," National Nuclear Security Administration briefing, May 2008.
525   The original goal was 20 ports by 2010. Government Accountability Office, *Preventing Nuclear Smuggling: Department of Energy Has Made Limited Progress in Installing Radiation Detection Equipment at Highest Priority Foreign Seaports,* March 2005, p. 5; Zenko, Micah and Matthew

75 ports by 2013, the total cost would be an estimated $1.125 billion, with 1,025 ports of various priorities still without American supplied radiation detection capabilities.[526]

The Megaports Initiative used lessons learned from earlier projects to standardize procedures and train incoming personnel. New personnel were brought in as country managers before progressing to become regional managers or program leaders. This emphasis given to on-the-job training and the incorporation of lessons learned resulted in a dramatic increase in productivity with a doubling of the number of operational ports from 2008.[527] This increase in productivity facilitated the expansion of program goals to 100 ports by 2015.[528] However, critics pointed to the slow progress between 2003 and 2008, and the large number of ports that remained unequipped, but at a rate of 2.4 countries per year and a cost of $15 million per port, equipping all analyzed ports was an unrealistic expectation. It was also unrealistic to expect the United States to fund the installation of radiation monitors at ports with little to no national strategic interest to Washington. An examination of the Container Security Initiative ports, which accounted for 86% of container traffic to the United States, called into question the need for the expansion of the Megaports Initiative goal to 100 ports, much less all the ports included on the maritime prioritization model.[529]

Bunn, "Interdicting Nuclear Smuggling: Second Line of Defense Program," Nuclear Threat Initiative, November 20, 2007, retrieved July 15, 2010.

526   Estimate based on the $15 million general planning factor.

527   The number of completed ports between 2008 and 2010 went from 12 to 27. Department of Energy, "Megaports Initiative Homepage," National Nuclear Security Administration, retrieved July 15, 2010.

528   Department of Energy, "Program Overview: Office of the Second Line of Defense," National Nuclear Security Administration briefing, March 2010.

529   Because the Megaports, Container Security, and Secure Freight Initiatives were separate programs that a host nation had to agree to individually, the standing minimum agreement between the Megaports and Container Security Initiatives was a radiation portal monitor stationed with Container Security Initiative personnel if the port was not part of the Megaports Initiative. Interview with Department of Energy, National Nuclear Security

CLEARLY DEFINED HOST NATION
RESPONSIBILITIES

Before a country agreed to participate in the Megaports Initiative it received a briefing and draft memorandum of understanding.[530] There was not an agreed upon suspense for a participation decision, which often meant that it took one to two years from initial outreach through to completion of a memorandum of understanding. The U.S. government led installation, training, and testing efforts, and provided sustainment support for three years. However, according to Megaports officials there had not been a case where the initiative denied support beyond the three year agreement.[531] Clear delineation of partner responsibilities, and the limited scope of each project, allowed the United States and host nations to develop and maintain good working relationships. One area that was different from Cooperative Threat Reduction was U.S. government prioritization. Instead of receiving requests from the host nation, Megaports Initiative personnel annually prioritized ports and engaged in outreach activities. While host nation support was vital, program expansion did not originate with requests from a foreign partner. If a

Administration, Second Line of Defense Megaports Initiative Official, July 21, 2010; Department of Homeland Security, *Customs and Border Protection's Container Security Initiative Has Proactive Management and Oversight but Future Direction Is Uncertain*, Inspector General Report, February 2010, p. 1.

530   This was one of the lessons learned from earlier pilots that accounted for different agreements and in the case of the Port of Southampton, no formal long-term agreement. The Megaports Initiative did not follow standardized procedures for the Port of Southampton based on the U.S.-U.K. special relationship. This resulted in HM Revenue and Customs manning the Megaports Initiative site for six months, before handing control of the site and equipment back to the U.S. due to funding constraints. Interview with Department of Energy, National Nuclear Security Administration, Second Line of Defense Megaports Initiative Official, July 21, 2010.

531   Interviews with Department of Energy, National Nuclear Security Administration, Second Line of Defense Megaports Initiative Officials, June 25, and July 21, 2010.

country decided not to participate, the program simply moved on to other potential countries identified in the annual Megaports Initiative plan.[532]

INTERAGENCY INTEGRATION

The Department of Energy programs were part of the U.S. government's layered defense against trafficking of nuclear weapons and special nuclear materials, but the integration of programs was less evident at the formal working level. For example, in the Container Security Initiative Strategic Plan there was no mention of the Second Line of Defense, or other programs outside of the Department of Homeland Security.[533] The Container Security Initiative goal stated by Customs and Border Protection Commissioner W. Ralph Basham, was to "process 85 percent of all containers headed for the United States through Container Security Initiative ports by 2007."[534] This goal was not linked to the Megaports Initiative's global maritime shipping network orientation, or the *Security and Accountability for Every (SAFE) Port Act*, that was signed into law two months later.[535]

According to the Container Security Initiative strategic plan, "non-intrusive inspection involves the use of X-ray or gamma ray scanners to generate an image of the contents, which Customs and Border Protection officers review for anomalies. Customs and Border Protection officers also scan cargo using radiation detection devices. If an irregularity is identified, officers may

---

532   Interview with Department of Energy, National Nuclear Security Administration, Second Line of Defense Megaports Initiative Official, June 25, 2010.

533   Department of Homeland Security, *Container Security Initiative: 2006-2011 Strategic Plan*, U.S. Customs and Border Protection, August 2006.

534   Ibid., p. ii; Department of Energy, "Office of the Second Line of Defense 2006 Strategic Plan," National Nuclear Security Administration, p. 15.

535   *Security and Accountability for Every (SAFE) Port Act of 2006* (H.R. 4954, P.L. 109-347).

physically examine all or a portion of the container's contents." The plan did not account for host nation radiation detection capabilities and training provided by the Department of Energy.[536] Additionally, the Container Security Initiative's cost estimate to achieve operational status per port in fiscal year 2004 was $395,000 and $227,324 in fiscal year 2005. This was in contrast to the Megaports Initiative general cost estimate of $15 million per port.[537]

According to the Secure Freight Initiative Fact Sheet, "The Secure Freight Initiative, through its International Container Security scanning project, represents the evolution of both programs [Container Security Initiative and Megaports Initiative] by providing the integration of data that makes the combined

---

536   It was the responsibility of the host nation competent authority for chemical, biological, radiological, nuclear, and high-yield explosives to lead subsequent detection and removal efforts once a container registered an alert and was identified as a potential hazard during secondary screening. Customs and Border Protection, Container Security Initiative officers on-site conducted initial four-corner readings to transmit back to the Laboratories and Scientific Services, but they were guests in the host nation. Containers that failed the secondary screening were quarantined until the host nation competent authority assumed responsibility for further analysis. Interview with Department of Energy, National Nuclear Security Administration, Second Line of Defense, Megaports Initiative Official, July 21, 2010.

537   "The average cost per Container Security Initiative port includes: site assessments and certifications, telecom circuit installation, Local Area Network and office equipment, commercial-off-the-shelf software, office furniture, Radiation Isotope Identification Device equipment, purchase of automobiles, initial lease and utilities costs and initial shipping costs." Interviews with Megaports Initiative personnel confirmed the 2009, general cost estimate per port was still $15 million, with a caveat that ports ranged in size and complexity. Department of Homeland Security, *Container Security Initiative: 2006-2011 Strategic Plan,* U.S. Customs and Border Protection, August 2006, p. 34; Government Accountability Office, *Preventing Nuclear Smuggling: Department of Energy Has Made Limited Progress in Installing Radiation Detection Equipment at Highest Priority Foreign Seaports,* March 2005, p. 5; Interview with Department of Energy, National Nuclear Security Administration, Second Line of Defense Megaports Initiative Official, June 25, 2010.

effort greater than the sum of each part."[538] The Secure Freight Initiative vision and overview went on to describe responsibilities of the Departments of Homeland Security, Energy, and State, as well as private sector partners. From a nuclear defense standpoint, the Secure Freight Initiative's focus on maximum integration and utilization of interagency programs was a logical U.S. government goal. However, from the partner capacity mission of the Megaports Initiative, direct U.S. government interaction was limited, especially once the three year sustainability period ended. From its inception the Megaports Initiative attempted to improve procedures to include communications agreements, equipment, and training for host nation partners. These efforts -- highlighted by International Material Protection and Cooperation Assistant Deputy Administrator David Huizenga in 2008 -- benefited the Container Security Initiative and Secure Freight Initiative programs, but were not directly managed by the Department of Energy once a port became operational.[539] In the broadest sense, the Megaports Initiative functioned as a specialized sub-contractor for radiation detection systems, while the Department of Homeland Security served as an ineffective general security contractor for global nuclear detection and maritime cargo flowing into the United States.

REALIZATION OF POLICY OBJECTIVES

James Wilson offered that many public organizations have at best vague goals from which to derive supporting tasks.[540] This was the case with the Department of Energy, which was assigned only minimal national goals for radiation detection.

---

538   Department of Homeland Security, "Fact Sheet: Secure Freight with Container Security Initiative, Megaports," U.S. Customs and Border Protection, October, 2007.
539   Huizenga, David, "National Nuclear Security Administration's Megaports Initiative and Its Role in the Secure Freight Initiative (SFI)," testimony, June 12, 2008.
540   Wilson, James Q., *Bureaucracy: What Government Agencies Do and Why They Do It*, 2nd edition 2000, pp. 32-36.

Consequently, the first two policy objectives were internally driven, while a third, of which the department was a supporting agency, was a statutory requirement:

[Objective 1] To strengthen the capability of foreign governments to deter, detect, and interdict illicit trafficking in nuclear and other radioactive materials across international borders and through the global maritime shipping system.

[Objective 2] To install radiation detection equipment at 20 ports by 2010, which expanded to over 75 Megaports, scanning over 50% of global shipping traffic, by 2013.

[Objective 3] A container that was loaded on a vessel in a foreign port shall not enter the United States (either directly or via a foreign port) unless the container was scanned by nonintrusive imaging equipment and radiation detection equipment at a foreign port before it was loaded on a vessel.[541]

The Department of Energy approached the first objective by establishing the Second Line of Defense Office, which consisted of the core program and later on the Megaports Initiative. While the core program was concerned with land-based detection in the former Soviet Union, the Megaports Initiative embarked on global activities designed to provide radiation monitoring capabilities at high-priority foreign seaports (Objective 1). The mission of building partner radiation detection capacity was addressed by both programs. The Second Line of Defense mission statement, and the supporting goal -- "to reduce the probability

---

541   Department of Energy, "Fact Sheet: National Nuclear Security Administration's Second Line of Defense," National Nuclear Security Administration, December 2008; Huizenga, David, "National Nuclear Security Administration's Megaports Initiative and Its Role in the Secure Freight Initiative (SFI)," testimony, June 12, 2008; Government Accountability Office, *Preventing Nuclear Smuggling: Department of Energy Has Made Limited Progress in Installing Radiation Detection Equipment at Highest Priority Foreign Seaports,* March 2005, p. 18; Department of Energy, "Megaports Initiative: Morocco Transshipment Conference," National Nuclear Security Administration briefing, May 2008; *Security and Accountability for Every (SAFE) Port Act of 2006* (H.R. 4954, P.L. 109-347), Sec. 233; *Implementing Recommendations of the 9/11 Commission Act of 2007* (H.R. 1, P.L. 110-53), Title XVII-Maritime Cargo, Sec. 1701.

of these materials being fashioned into a weapon of mass destruction or a radiological dispersal device ("dirty bomb") to be used against the United States or its key allies and international partners" -- did not include quantifiable measures of success in regard to probability analysis, or program goals beyond outreach, installation, and sustainability.

The absence of quantifiable measures of success is indicative of what James Wilson described as a "procedural organization" -- an agency that can observe operators at work, but not outcomes.[542] Wilson argued that measurement of worker output does not tell senior officials what they need to know, that is, if the program or system actually has the intended effect.[543] Thus, the initiative's lack of demonstrated effect and continued program expansion led Representative Edolphus Towns, chairman of the House Oversight and Government Reform Committee, to request a Government Accountability Office audit to get a "better understanding of how much money is being spent on the Megaports Initiative, where the money is being spent, and whether we are getting what we are paying for."[544]

SLD	1998	1999	2000	2001	2002	2003	2004	2005	2006	2007	2008
Budget	2.915	2.515	1	1.925	46.185	136.95	46.349	75.001	119.954	191.89	257.621
Cumulative	2.915	5.43	6.43	8.355	54.54	191.49	237.839	312.84	432.794	624.684	882.305

**TABLE 4.1. SECOND LINE OF
DEFENSE FUNDING[545]
(MILLIONS OF U.S. DOLLARS, PER FISCAL YEAR)**

542   Wilson, James Q., *Bureaucracy: What Government Agencies Do and Why They Do It*, 2nd edition 2000, pp. 163-164.
543   Ibid.
544   Towns, Edolphus, "Letter to Government Accountability Office requesting a new review of the Megaports Initiative," January 13, 2010; Committee spokeswoman Jenny Rosenberg quote, as referenced in Stephanie Palla's article, "Review Set for Major U.S. Radiation Detection Program," *Global Security Newswire*, March 31, 2010.
545   Nuclear Threat Initiative, "Interactive Threat Reduction Budget Database: Second Line of Defense 1998-2008," July 15, 2010.

Realization of the second objective began with funding inputs (Tables 4.1 and 4.2). Calculating the budget of the Megaports Initiative was difficult because it had multiple funding sources, and was aggregated with National Nuclear Security Administration nonproliferation and Second Line of Defense funding.[546] When the program was authorized in 2003, it was funded under a wartime supplemental appropriation. After the first year, it was included in *Defense Nuclear Nonproliferation* funding for the National Nuclear Security Administration.

Megaports	2003	2004	2005	2006	2007	2008
Budget	84	28	15	74	40	50
Cumulative	84	112	127	201	241	291

TABLE 4.2. MEGAPORTS INITIATIVE FUNDING[547]
(ROUNDED IN MILLIONS OF U.S. DOLLARS,
PER FISCAL YEAR)

By the end of calendar year 2009, the Megaports Initiative had "Installed over 200 radiation portal monitors, straddle carriers, spectroscopic portal monitors, and handheld equipment in 23 countries."[548] These completed installations took place "at 30 Megaports" with "installations ongoing at 16 additional

546   According to Stephanie Palla, "the initiative is expected to require $1.4 billion to meet the goal of within five years equipping 100 ports with radiation portal monitors." Palla, Stephanie, "Review Set for Major U.S. Radiation Detection Program," *Global Security Newswire,* March 31, 2010.

547   Funding data confirmed with the Megaports Initiative and referenced as: [2003] Emergency Wartime Supplemental Act (EWSA), Nuclear Threat Initiative Overview Legislative Summary (OLS), [2004] EWSA, Nuclear Threat Initiative OLS, [2005] Consolidated Appropriations Act, interview, July 21, 2010, [2006] Energy and Water Appropriations Act (EWAA), interview, July 21, 2010,[2007] EWAA, interview, July 21, 2010, [2008] Omnibus Appropriations Bill, Center for Arms Control and Nonproliferation Appropriations fiscal year 2008-Nuclear Nonproliferation Highlights.

548   Department of Energy, "Program Overview: Office of the Second Line of Defense," National Nuclear Security Administration briefing, March 2010.

Megaports" (Objective 2).[549] Successful accomplishment of the initial Megaports Initiative goal, alignment with Container Security and Secure Freight Initiatives, threat analysis, and other Department of Energy factors, led to internal approval of program expansion in 2008.[550]

The third objective focused on mandated performance. Congress specified in 2006, and again in 2007, that 100% of cargo containers entering the United States must be scanned for radiation.[551] However, a pilot program and background information from the Departments of Energy and Homeland Security revealed that this may have been an unrealistic policy objective.[552] The departments referenced the requirement to partner with foreign governments without disrupting trade, and the operational limitations associated with transshipped containers as the major impediments to completing this objective. The issue of transhipment containers, which did not proceed through entry or exit choke points, did not permit 100% scanning until containers were departing American ports, where all transportation entrances and exits could be equipped by Department of

---

549   Ibid.

550   Although outside the time period covered in this chapter, the Megaports Initiative goal shifted again by 2010 to "over 100 Megaports, scanning over 50% of global shipping traffic by 2015 and approximately 83% of U.S. bound imports shipped through these ports." During discussions, officials offered that they did not envision expansion much beyond 100 ports. Ibid; Interviews with Department of Energy, National Nuclear Security Administration, Second Line of Defense and Megaports Initiative Officials, July 21, and October 5, 2010.

551   The Department of Energy was included as a supporting department in this legislation. *Security and Accountability for Every (SAFE) Port Act of 2006* (H.R. 4954, P.L. 109-347), Sec. 233; *Implementing Recommendations of the 9/11 Commission Act of 2007* (H.R. 1, P.L. 110-53), Title XVII-Maritime Cargo, Sec. 1701; Department of Energy, "Program Overview: Office of the Second Line of Defense," National Nuclear Security Administration briefing, March 2010.

552   Huizenga, David, "National Nuclear Security Administration's Megaports Initiative and Its Role in the Secure Freight Initiative (SFI)," testimony, June 12, 2008; Government Accountability Office.

Homeland Security radiation detectors (Objective 3). While the Department of Energy had partnered with Department of Homeland Security on a pilot program, the Megaports Initiative had not fulfilled its commitment to install radiation detection equipment in all Container Security Initiative ports during the period of study.

Interagency implementation was impeded by differing departmental priorities, a Secure Freight Initiative design that allowed countries to choose between programs, and the failure of the Megaports Initiative to establish the installation of radiation detection equipment at the 58 Container Security Initiative ports as the principal requirement for the program. For example, by 2009, the Megaports Initiative accounted for 46 ports completed or in the installation phase.[553] If the Department of Energy would have adopted the same Container Security Initiative ports, they would have approached a 79% completion rate that year. In this case, the 58 ports would have served as a defined end state for the Megaports Initiative.

From its inception the Megaports Initiative developed without specific statutory limitations or oversight. In 2003, the House Energy and Water Development Appropriations Subcommittee stated that the Megaports Initiative was "intended to install radiation detection equipment at the top 20 major overseas seaports to detect and interdict special nuclear material prior to arrival in the U.S.," noting that those ports were "the source of 70% of the container traffic from all overseas ports destined for U.S. ports."[554] Nevertheless, Congress did not include this language in any legislation and did not oversee the initiative. As time went by, Congress continued to authorize funding increases requested

---

553   Department of Energy, "Program Overview: Office of the Second Line of Defense," National Nuclear Security Administration briefing, March 2010.
554   Hobson, David, "Committee on Appropriations accompanying report to the fiscal year 2004 Energy and Water Development Appropriations Bill (H.R. 2754, 108-212)," July 16, 2003.

by the Department of Energy to expand the program.[555] These increases validated internally escalating goals which now accounted for global shipping and not just containers bound for the United States. The lack of an operational interagency planning mechanism, and congressional absence with regard to specific policy objectives and oversight, allowed the Departments of Homeland Security and Energy to take different directions with the Container Security and Megaports Initiatives.

Americas	Europe and Africa	Asia and the Middle East
Montreal, Vancouver, and Halifax, Canada	Rotterdam**, The Netherlands	Singapore***
Santos, Brazil	Bremerhaven and Hamburg, Germany	Yokohama, Tokyo, Nagoya, and Kobe, Japan
Buenos Aires, Argentina	Antwerp** and Zeebrugge**, Belgium	Hong Kong
Puerto Cortes***, Honduras	Le Havre and Marseille, France	Pusan***, South Korea
Caucedo**, Dominican Republic	Gothenburg, Sweden	Klang** and Tanjung Pelepas, Malaysia
Kingston**, Jamaica	La Spezia, Genoa, Naples, Gioia Tauro, and Livorno, Italy	Laem Chabang**, Thailand
Freeport**, The Bahamas	Felixstowe, Liverpool, Thamesport, Tilbury, and Southampton***, United Kingdom	Dubai, United Arab Emirates
Balboa**, Colon**, and Manzanillo**, Panama	Piraeus**, Greece	Shenzhen and Shanghai, China
Cartagena**, Colombia	Algeciras**, Barcelona, and Valencia, Spain	Kaohsiung** and Chi-Lung, Taiwan
	Lisbon**, Portugal	Colombo**, Sri Lanka
	Alexandria, Egypt	Salalah***, Oman
	Durban, South Africa	Qasim***, Pakistan
		Ashdod** and Haifa**, Israel

FIGURE 4.2. CONTAINER SECURITY
INITIATIVE PORTS[556]
(AS OF JUNE 18, 2009)

---

555   Downs, Anthony, *Inside Bureaucracy*, 1967, pp. 16-18.
556   *Also Secure Freight Initiative, **also an operational Megaport, *** also both Secure Freight Initiative and an operational Megaport. As of 2010, the Container Security Initiative and Secure Freight Initiative were consolidated under a single Customs and Border Protection administrator, and only two of the pilot Secure Freight Initiative ports remained. Department of Homeland Security, "Container Security Initiative Ports," U.S. Customs and Border Protection, as of June 18, 2009, retrieved July 15, 2010; Department of Energy, "Program Overview: Office of the Second Line of Defense," National Nuclear Security Administration briefing, March 2010; Interviews with Department of Energy, National Nuclear Security Administration, Second Line of Defense Megaports Initiative Official, and Department of Homeland Security, Customs and Border Protection, Container Security and Secure Freight Initiatives Director, July 21, and September 15, 2010.

COUNTERARGUMENTS

Non-governmental experts and other federal officials leveled basic criticisms concerning equipment and coverage against the Megaports Initiative. Both sets of actors questioned the effectiveness of current radiation detection monitors.[557] Depending on material, shielding, and other variables such as the environment, then current technologies provided mainly benign readings. Numerous false alarms led to delays in commerce and desensitized operators. Equipment criticisms were compounded when questionable technology was paired with a global effort to scan 100% of containerized cargo before it reached the United States. This policy decision limited search strategies and port designs because of the requirement to scan every container bound for the United States.[558] These technical and scope limitations were on top of internal program issues concerning access, installation, operations and maintenance, transhipment, and receipt of delayed data.

In 2005, the Government Accountability Office issued a report that found the Megaports Initiative had made "limited progress," but lacked a "comprehensive long-term plan."[559] While progress and internal planning improved, the lack of detailed funding for performance output metrics left the program open

557   There were numerous debates over favored detection technologies between the different departments and agencies. This topic came up in multiple interviews as officials argued for or against a specific type of technology. For a full list of interviewees, see the bibliography; O'Harrow, Robert Jr., "Radiation Detection Plan Falls Short, Audit Shows: Concerns About Costs and Effectiveness Could Curtail Program," *The Washington Post*, September 4, 2008; Shea, Dana A., John D. Moteff, and Daniel Morgan, "The Advanced Spectroscopic Portal Program: Background and Issues for Congress," *CRS Report for Congress*, December 30, 2010.

558   Palla, Stephanie, "Review Set for Major U.S. Radiation Detection Program," Global Security Newswire, March 31, 2010.

559   Government Accountability Office, *Preventing Nuclear Smuggling: Department of Energy Has Made Limited Progress in Installing Radiation Detection Equipment at Highest Priority Foreign Seaports*, March 2005, pp. 10-13.

to questions related to efficiency and the cost-benefit balance.[560] For example, a quantifiable addition to the standard Megaports briefing could be as simple as adding the previous funding chart, followed by a chart that listed the port name, the year outreach was initiated, the year the site went into operation, total costs of implementation and operation through the three year sustainability period, and the number of significant incidents at that location. While straightforward to put together, this information was not requested and, in the absence of a requirement, was not made readily available by the department. Instead, senior departmental leadership such as National Nuclear Security Administration International Material Protection and Cooperation Assistant Deputy Administrator David Huizenga offered repetitive testimony concerning the performance of the Megaports Initiative:

September 2007
Unfortunately, we have clear evidence that the detection systems are necessary. In 2003, Georgian border guards, using U.S.-provided portal monitoring equipment at the Sadakhlo border crossing with Armenia, detected and seized approximately 173 grams of highly enriched uranium carried by an Armenian national. Also, in late 2005, a Megaports radiation portal monitors picked up a small neutron signal from a scrap metal container leaving Sri Lanka bound for India. The source of the signal turned out to be an extremely small neutron source, which was found by the Indian authorities.

June 2008
For example, in 2003, Georgian border guards, using U.S.-provided portal monitoring equipment at the Sadakhlo border crossing with Armenia, detected and seized approximately 173 grams of highly enriched uranium (HEU) carried by an Armenian national. Also, in late 2005, a Megaports radiation portal monitors (RPM) picked up a neutron signal from a scrap metal container leaving Sri Lanka bound for India. The source of the signal turned out to be an extremely small commercial neutron source, which was found by the Indian authorities. More recently, in November 2007, several

---

560   James Wilson defined efficiency as "obtaining the most output for a given level of resources." Wilson, James Q., *Bureaucracy: What Government Agencies Do and Why They Do It*, 2nd edition 2000, p. 347.

Cesium-137 sources were detected in a container of scrap metal leaving Honduras bound for a smelting facility in the Far East. An NNSA [National Nuclear Security Administration] team assisted the Honduran Government with the recovery of the industrial sources, preventing those sources from reaching, and possibly contaminating, the facility.[561]

THEORETICAL APPLICABILITY

Four areas of bureaucratic politics theory relevant to the maritime radiation detection case study included the following: 1) implementing organizations did not feel obliged to faithfully execute decisions if they were not involved in the development of the policy; 2) actions associated with major policy departures were determined by existing programs and standard operating procedures; 3) the bureaucracy sought to maximize organizational interests; and 4) the larger the number of actors involved in implementation the less it reflected policy decisions.[562] The Department of Energy was not involved in the initial development of national maritime security policy. Immediately following the 9/11 attacks, individual departments and agencies developed independent programs and then sought increased funding and national approval. By the time the White House attempted to coordinate these separate initiatives, they were already underway. Thus, reactionary national strategic planning facilitated program continuation instead of federal integration.

The independent programs reflected the cultures and existing capabilities of their respective departments and agencies. For example, the Megaports Initiative was only concerned with

561   Huizenga, David, "Radiation Detection," testimony, September 18, 2007; Huizenga, David, "National Nuclear Security Administration's Megaports Initiative and Its Role in the Secure Freight Initiative (SFI)," testimony, June 12, 2008.
562   Allison, Graham T., and Morton H. Halperin, "Bureaucratic Politics: A Paradigm and Some Policy Implications," *World Politics,* Vol. 24, Spring 1972, pp. 54-56.

radiation detection and not broader maritime security issues nor the role that these technical capabilities could and should play in national nuclear defense efforts. This single concern facilitated program continuation to the benefit of the Department of Energy. Lead agency concerns for nuclear detection and maritime cargo security were a lesser priority in comparison to organizational interests. This final point was highlighted by the complexities of the two interdependent tasks of nuclear detection and maritime cargo security. While the Department of Homeland Security served in a lead role for both, separate internal organizations -- the Domestic Nuclear Defense Office and Customs and Border Patrol -- had different mandates. These competing tasks added multiple intra-departmental actors to an already complex interagency operating environment. While the first area was not highlighted by the threat reduction case study, the remaining three were evident in both implementation studies.

Program evaluation revealed several important issues relevant to overall nuclear defense policy implementation. While the Department of Energy participated in the interagency coordination system, the research reinforced the point that no single person or office was in charge of U.S. government nuclear defense policy. Different departments and agencies served in varying roles through programs like the Megaports Initiative, and participated in interagency forums, but these separate policies, programs, and plans competed for resources and access. Internally, evaluation of the Megaports Initiative demonstrated a well-managed program that worked to improve outreach, implementation and remain compliant with federal constraints for the benefit of the department.[563] These efforts extended to host nation partners, supporting contracting firms, and the national laboratories that actually installed, trained, and maintained equipment sites.

---

563   Wilson, James Q., *Bureaucracy: What Government Agencies Do and Why They Do It*, 2nd edition 2000, p. 131.

The workflow and evaluation sections of this chapter again reinforce the picture of a segmented approach to U.S. government nuclear defense policy implementation as described in the previous study of Cooperative Threat Reduction. Instead of defining complementary goals to the Container Security Initiative, the Megaports Initiative was adapted to address global shipping. This move was repeatedly cited as the primary rationale for not conducting joint planning and execution with Customs and Border Protection, and instead focusing on traffic bound for the United States and meeting statutory policy objectives.[564] In the absence of direct integration and national oversight, the program expanded on its own without demonstrating performance-related metrics. The absence of verified performance was not unique to the initiative, and as James Wilson identified, in highly constrained areas such as acquisition it is routine for managers "to worry more about process than outputs."[565] The Megaports Initiative study revealed gaps and inefficiencies associated with decentralized policy formulation and execution, where haphazard policy development failed to provide national direction and oversight for independent programs spread across multiple departments and agencies.

CONCLUSION

This policy implementation study posed the question, "How has the U.S. government implemented post-Cold War nuclear defense policy, and to what extent have corresponding objectives been realized?" The hypothesis offered was: "The U.S. government was not organized to address nuclear defense, and as a result did not collaboratively implement evolving national policies." Multiple actors from various departments and agencies

---

564   Interviews with Department of Energy, National Nuclear Security Administration, Second Line of Defense Megaports Initiative Officials, June 25, and July 21, 2010.
565   Wilson, James Q., *Bureaucracy: What Government Agencies Do and Why They Do It*, 2nd edition 2000, p. 131.

participated in maritime radiation detection and security. While the Department of Homeland Security was the federal lead, this designation did not come with the authority to plan, resource, or collaboratively execute global radiation detection and maritime cargo security.

Although Megaports Initiative efforts did not conflict with other programs, questions of collective U.S. government implementation were raised when the initiative was considered as a critical enabler of statutory requirements.[566] As a supporting technical organization in the wider maritime security arena, the Megaports Initiative was able to remain quietly in the background as it worked to support internal policy objectives. A lack of external oversight contributed to periodic expansion of the program based on internal recommendations and approval, and subsequent congressional endorsement through the appropriations process. By remaining a supporting organization without specific statutory limitations or guidance, mission creep related to transhipment challenges, upgrade and replacement issues, and limitless threat scenarios, meant that annual Megaports Initiative budget requests continued to grow without performance justification.[567]

The decentralized policy formulation process described in chapters 1 and 2 facilitated the creation and continuation of numerous uncoordinated nuclear defense programs such as the Megaports Initiative. In combination, the first two

---

566   The disconnect in program goals resulted from the Megaports Initiative global emphasis, as opposed to the 100% scanning requirement for U.S. bound containers established by Congress. Although not specifically aligned with statutory requirements, the global Megaports Initiative emphasis targeted two major areas of vulnerability, 1) detection and interdiction of shipments of special nuclear materials between countries, and 2) detection and interdiction of completed nuclear weapons before they reached American soil. The Department of Homeland Security, Domestic Nuclear Detection Office scanning efforts targeted points of entry/exit at U.S. ports much more effectively than international efforts.

567   Palla, Stephanie, "Review Set for Major U.S. Radiation Detection Program," *Global Security Newswire*, March 31, 2010.

implementation studies represented a nuclear defense-in-depth but highlighted numerous gaps created by segregated programmatic execution. In this case, the lead agency for the Global Nuclear Detection Architecture and maritime cargo security interacted with the Second Line of Defense Office, but was not able to direct Megaports Initiative execution priorities. This is not unique to the case study. In 2007, Kenneth Dahl provided a hypothetical example where the Department of State was the lead agency for an interagency response that included the Departments of Defense and Justice.

> Justice and Defense will send representatives to the interagency meetings, but they don't really work for the State Department. The State Department has no real authority over Justice and Defense. When the interagency effort requires manpower or funding, we can expect that only State will be enthusiastic about committing these resources. Justice and Defense are not inclined and poorly motivated to contribute resources they have secured for their own priorities. Furthermore, the committees in Congress which have provided the authorizations and appropriations to Justice and Defense often prohibit their use for other purposes. So even if the non-lead agencies were inclined to support, in some cases they may be unable to do so.[568]

The first two implementation studies examined comparably managed programs that demonstrated the overlap of prevention and protection efforts. The next chapter shifts focus to attribution as part of "response." During the Cold War, very little emphasis was placed on technical nuclear forensics. In traditional state scenarios, the Soviet Union represented the primary adversary with China a distant second. This was not the case in post-Cold War era where state-sponsored or non-state nuclear attack scenarios could mean single or multiple nuclear devices employed by anonymous actors. The final policy implementation study

---

568   Dahl, Kenneth R., "New Security for New Threats: The Case for Reforming the Interagency Process," Brookings Institution Report, July 2007, pp. 12-13.

looks at the issue of identifying responsible parties through technical nuclear forensic analysis. This is a relatively new topic in nuclear defense that spans pre- and post-detonation incidents. The Department of Homeland Security provides a third individual department example as the technical nuclear forensics mission area reinforces the interagency nature of nuclear defense in the post-Cold War world.

CHAPTER 5

NUCLEAR FORENSICS
IMPLEMENTATION STUDY

The previous policy implementation studies examined independently executed programs with policy level coordination. While these case studies demonstrated a similar acquisition-based programmatic approach, they also established the absence of central U.S. government nuclear defense leadership or direction. Collectively, the Cooperative Threat Reduction and Megaports Initiative programs depicted the foreign portion of a layered defense that originated at nuclear weapon or materials sites, and progressed across maritime routes. This final policy implementation study considers the domestic layer of nuclear defense, and shifts focus from individual department implementation to a national integrator approach specifically for nuclear attribution.

This final study addresses the nuclear defense area of "response," which comprises consequence management, attribution, and retaliation. For decades there have been numerous elements of the response portion of nuclear defense policy. Public information campaigns, fallout shelters, and continuity of government programs, as well as declaratory policy concerning retaliation to nuclear attack, are nearly as old as nuclear weapons themselves. However, one area that was not a concern until more recently involves attribution.[569] Following the Cold War, unease over the

---

569   The Department of Homeland Security indicated that attribution

potential for the proliferation of loose nuclear weapons or fissile materials to various actors added the requirement of attributing the source of such events to policy discussions. These fears increased dramatically after al-Qaeda launched unprecedented terrorist attacks against the United States in 2001. Following the attacks, a key attribution capability to receive senior level attention was national technical nuclear forensics. Based on earlier findings and worries of further terrorist attacks, the George W. Bush administration established the Domestic Nuclear Detection Office within the Department of Homeland Security. Shortly thereafter, the National Technical Nuclear Forensics Center was created within this office to coordinate "the collection, analysis, and evaluation of pre- and post-detonation radiological/nuclear materials, devices, and debris, as well as prompt effects from a nuclear detonation."[570]

In this instance senior political actors identified segregated execution as a problem, but as with the previous studies, the question raised here is whether "departments and agencies placed organizational interests above national interests" in implementing policy? The Cooperative Threat Reduction and Megaports Initiative studies depicted an interagency environment comprised of independent departments. Did this trend continue in the field of nuclear forensics or did supporting departments unify under a designated systems integrator at the national level? Graham Allison and Morton Halperin offered that organizations strive to maintain autonomy in pursuit of what they perceive as the essence of their organization's activities.[571] They argued

entailed "merging the results from the forensic analyses with info from various sources to identify those responsible for the planned or actual attack." Department of Homeland Security, "National technical nuclear forensics: Overview, QA, and Expertise Development," Domestic Nuclear Detection Office briefing, September 14, 2009.

570   Bush, George W., "National Security Presidential Directive-43/ Homeland Security Presidential Directive-14: Domestic Nuclear Detection," April 15, 2005.

571   Allison, Graham T., and Morton H. Halperin, "Bureaucratic Politics: A Paradigm and Some Policy Implications," *World Politics*, Vol. 24, Spring

that organizations compete for roles and missions, and are not inclined to participate in schemes that require elaborate coordination with other organizations. Such bureaucratic maneuverings are seen to be facilitated by the limited amount of time that senior actors have to dedicate to single issues, and in the case of executive branch political appointees, the limited time they serve in government. In contrast, Allison and Halperin noted that career civil servants have much more time to devote to single issues over the span of lengthy careers.[572] Earlier findings and theoretical propositions suggest that the federal bureaucracy would continue to leverage rules and action channels to maximize organizational interests in the field of nuclear forensics.

This final study continues to test the second hypothesis, which states that "the U.S. government was not organized to address nuclear defense, and as a result did not collaboratively implement evolving national policies." The chapter follows the policy implementation study format with sections that examine the policy decision, national actors, organization and workflow, and program evaluation. These sections highlight the multi-departmental approach that characterized America's layered nuclear defenses. In 2007, national nuclear forensics entailed the executive branch creating a Department of Homeland Security office to serve as a national integrator. However, policy decisions remained vague, and this allowed separate departments to retain existing programs despite the introduction of a center charged with national integration. The nuclear forensics actor section continues to illustrate independent actors participating to varying degrees in an emerging federal framework.

The workflow section examines how the Department of Homeland Security approached national integration of technical nuclear forensics through the National Technical Nuclear Forensics Center. This section shows that the center lacked budget and operational authorities for independent departmental

---

1972, pp. 49-50.
572   Ibid.

programs. While interagency planning and research and development efforts for nuclear forensics demonstrated increased integration, limited real-world operations identified adherence to independent execution, not newly drafted plans. The chapter ends with a program evaluation section that utilized the criteria identified in the previous studies: pace, interagency integration, host nation responsibilities, the extent to which policy objectives were realized, counterarguments, and theoretical applicability. This final section reinforces several international and interagency barriers to collaborative national implementation. In regard to the international community, the absence of rewards for participation in a materials database severely restricted rapid attribution. Domestically, segregated U.S. government organization that gives department secretaries separate authorities and budgets meant that nuclear forensics interagency coordination comprised little more than territorial preservation in a shared policy space.[573]

Unlike the other implementation studies, the National Technical Nuclear Forensics Center did not display a primarily federal acquisition-based approach to implementation. While the National Technical Nuclear Forensics Center did have responsibility for a portion of the technical nuclear forensics mission set that required limited acquisition, the center was created primarily for systems integration, and not programmatic implementation. Despite national integration efforts, this final federal implementation design shared systemic limitations related to organizational interests with the previous interagency and lead federal agency studies.

POLICY DECISIONS

References to attribution and technical nuclear forensics existed within scientific and policy circles for several years before the realization by the White House that these efforts needed

---

573   Downs, Anthony, *Inside Bureaucracy*, 1967, pp. 212-218.

to be better integrated and elevated in priority.[574] The creation
of the Department of Homeland Security's Domestic Nuclear
Detection Office was formally approved in April 2005, and later
given statutory authorities under the *Security and Accountability
for Every Port Act of 2006*.[575] The subsequent legislation reiterated the office's responsibilities *"for coordinating federal efforts
to detect and protect against the unauthorized importation, possession, storage, transportation, development, or use of a nuclear explosive device, fissile material, or radiological material
in the United States, and to protect against attack using such
devices or materials against the people, territory, or interests of
the United States."*[576] Formation directives and early legislation
did not include technical nuclear forensics tasks.

*The U.S. government's ability to analyze pre- and post-det-
onation nuclear materials and devices were areas of concern
gaining traction in the White House in conjunction with the
formation of Domestic Nuclear Detection Office, and the creation of a Global Nuclear Detection Architecture. This concern
resulted in an additional* classified presidential directive that,
among other things, established the National Technical Nuclear
Forensics Center within the Domestic Nuclear Detection Office.
Initial policy objectives for the new center included:

> First, the National Technical Nuclear Forensics Center is intended to
> serve as the national "capability provider" to develop and advance
> capabilities to perform nuclear forensics on pre-detonation nuclear
> and radiological materials. The second mission for the National

---

574   According to James Wilson this tendency toward central management has been displayed by numerous presidential administrations over
the previous century. Wilson, James Q., *Bureaucracy: What Government
Agencies Do and Why They Do It*, 2nd edition 2000, p. 272.
575   Interview with Department of Homeland Security, Domestic
Nuclear Detection Office Director Vayl Oxford, September 13, 2010; *Security
and Accountability for Every (SAFE) Port Act of 2006* (H.R. 4954, P.L. 109-
347), Sec. 1802.
576   *Security and Accountability for Every (SAFE) Port Act of 2006*
(H.R. 4954, P.L. 109-347), Sec. 1802.

Technical Nuclear Forensics Center is to implement national level integration, centralized planning, exercising, evaluation, and
stewardship across the full spectrum of U.S. government nuclear
forensics capabilities, from pre- to post-detonation -- in essence to
serve as the "System Integrator" for the end-to-end national capabilities. These missions are specifically directed to be carried out
"in coordination" with our partners in the Department of Defense,
Department of State, Department of Energy, Department of Justice,
and the Office of the Director of National Intelligence.[577]

With this addition, the Domestic Nuclear Detection Office
expanded its global portfolio to include design, implementation, and national systems integration for nuclear/radiological
detection and technical nuclear forensics operations. Congress
did not oppose the addition of the National Technical Nuclear
Forensics Center and, in January 2009, Representative Adam
Schiff reintroduced the *Nuclear Forensics and Attribution Act* to
add statutory authorities and legislative branch support to on-going efforts in this area.[578]

NATIONAL NUCLEAR
FORENSICS ACTORS

The integrator design adopted for nuclear forensics differ-
entiates this study from the earlier implementation examples.
Congress continued to serve in its traditional authorization, resourcing, and oversight roles, but with the national integrator
model the White House delegated the implementation functions
normally associated with the National and Homeland Security
Council staffs to a departmental office.[579] Since the Department

---

577   Oxford, Vayl, "Hearing on H.R. 2631, the Nuclear Forensics and
Attribution Act," statement, October 10, 2007.
578   This legislation was not signed into law until February 2010.
Nuclear Forensics and Attribution Act of 2010 (H.R. 730, P.L. 111-140).
579   In the case of the Office of the Director of National Intelligence, the
office was formed as an autonomous entity outside of existing departments
and agencies.

of Homeland Security was charged with national implementation, the White House staffs could concentrate on policy priorities for technical nuclear forensics and related areas. This
differed from earlier start-up examples, such as Cooperative
Threat Reduction, where the National Security Council staff was
heavily involved with implementation during the first few years,
and with the Megaports initiative where the staffs worked to
integrate existing programs through a centralized maritime security strategy and supporting plans. In each federal implementation design, participation by interagency actors was voluntary.

CONGRESS

Multiple Congressional committees and subcommittees provided oversight of the Department of Homeland Security. Unlike
the annual defense authorization acts, a comparable annual authorization act for homeland security was not passed during the
George W. Bush administration. Upon completion of a decentralized authorization process, the National Technical Nuclear
Forensics Center received aggregate funding under the Domestic
Nuclear Detection Office's budget as part of the annual homeland
security appropriations acts. In the House, the Subcommittee on
Emerging Threats, Cybersecurity, and Science and Technology
was an important actor in terms of the nuclear forensics and
wider attribution agendas.[580] Chaired by Representative James
Langevin and ranking member Representative Michael McCaul,
the subcommittee held hearings on the nuclear forensics bill that
was introduced by Representative Adam Schiff in June 2007.[581]

---

580   This was a subcommittee of the Committee on Homeland Security.
Representative Peter King from the House Committee on Homeland Security
also served as a nuclear forensics champion in Congress. Interview with
Department of Homeland Security, Domestic Nuclear Detection Office
Director Vayl Oxford, September 13, 2010.
581   The original bill did not pass. It was reintroduced during the next
session of Congress before being signed into law by President Obama in
2010. *Nuclear Forensics and Attribution Act of 2010* (H.R. 730, P.L. 111-
140); Langevin, James, "Markup of H.R. 2631, the Nuclear Forensics and

Unlike the House, the Senate Committee on Homeland Security and Governmental Affairs did not demonstrate comparable interest. Despite limited congressional support, the process was not complicated by bureaucratic political issues beyond the standard legislative process because the National Technical Nuclear Forensics Center was not a politically divisive topic, and it only required an insignificant budget.

WHITE HOUSE

Multiple White House offices were involved with the formation and oversight of the Domestic Nuclear Detection Office and the National Technical Nuclear Forensics Center.[582] Although policy coordination committees and routine meetings were co-chaired by the National Security Council and Homeland Security Council offices, the Office of the Vice-President was directly involved in nuclear defense matters. In the case of the National Technical Nuclear Forensics Center, the Office of the Vice-President was fully engaged with ensuring that the new center was included in the president's budget by the Office of Management and Budget. There was little executive branch opposition to creating the National Technical Nuclear Forensics Center because the issue originated in the White House and had a senior champion -- Vice-President Cheney -- that wanted to improve U.S. government technical nuclear forensics collaboration.[583] According to the initial director of the Domestic Nuclear

Attribution Act," statement, October 10, 2007; Schiff, Adam, "Hearing on H.R. 2631, the Nuclear Forensics and Attribution Act," statement, October 10, 2007.

582   In the National Security Council, it was the Office of Proliferation Strategy, the Office of Nuclear Defense within the Homeland Security Council, the Office of the Vice-President Homeland Security Advisor, and for funding, the Office of Management and Budget. Interviews described a level of informal coordination mechanisms in use at the White House, which allowed staffers to interact beyond formal procedures normally depicted in open literature. Interview with National Security Council Staff, Office of Iraq and Afghanistan Affairs Director John Gallagher, August 6, 2009.

583   Interview with Deputy Homeland Security Advisor to the President

Detection Office, there was discussion early on regarding the best location for the center, but once his office was established the supporting presidential directive was completed in "near-record time."[584] After the National Technical Nuclear Forensics Center was formed, and departmental actors agreed on the general national technical nuclear forensics approach, the center took on many of the implementation coordination responsibilities normally associated with the White House staffs.

While the formation of the National Technical Nuclear Forensics Center was implemented swiftly, the accompanying Attribution Assessment Working Group was not approved until the end of the George W. Bush administration, and did not meet prior to January 2009.[585] The intent of the Attribution Assessment Working Group at that time was to have a designated group to convene to handle attribution cases. Within the Executive Office of the President, the Office of Science and Technology Policy was also a well-positioned champion of technical nuclear forensics for research and development prioritization.[586]

INTERAGENCY

One of the first things identified during the initial technical nuclear forensics assessment was the existence of multiple

---

Kenneth Rapuano, November 8, 2010.

584   Within the White House process, the vice-president was given a special review of the budget before it was presented to the president. Interview with Department of Homeland Security, Domestic Nuclear Detection Office Director Vayl Oxford, September 13, 2010.

585   Ibid.

586   This office was established by Congress in 1976 to "(1) advise the president of scientific and technological considerations involved in areas of national concern; (2) evaluate the scale, quality, and effectiveness of the federal effort in science and technology and advise on appropriate actions; (3) advise the president on scientific and technological considerations with regard to federal budgets; and (4) assist the president in providing general leadership and coordination of the research and development programs of the federal government." *National Science and Technology Policy, Organization, and Priorities Act of 1976* (P.L. 94-282).

relevant efforts in this area. While there were numerous programs, the federal government collectively lacked an executable plan for any of the event types. Different departments and agencies had response plans, procedures, and capabilities, but a collaborative strategy to integrate and focus these segregated efforts at the national level did not exist.

FEDERAL BUREAU OF INVESTIGATION

The Federal Bureau of Investigation was the U.S. government lead for nuclear incident investigation and co-chair of the Attribution Assessment Working Group.[587] In 2006, the Bureau established the Weapons of Mass Destruction Directorate in its newly formed National Security Branch. The mission of the directorate was "to bring together the units within the Federal Bureau of Investigation that were addressing the response, investigation, intelligence dissemination and analysis, and countermeasures programs into one unified structure."[588] This restructuring included the existing Laboratory Division, which housed the Bureau's traditional and nuclear forensic assets under the Chemical Biological Science Unit, and the forward deployed teams of the Hazardous Material Response Units.[589] As part of the shift to rapid attribution, the Chemical Biological Science Unit formed multidisciplinary teams designed to move to incident sites instead of automatically transporting evidence back to the appropriate laboratories, while the Hazardous Material Response Units provided crime scene training for interagency partners.

Beyond the Weapons of Mass Destruction Directorate, the Federal Bureau of Investigation maintained its traditional organization based on the Washington D.C. headquarters and

---

587   The Attribution Assessment Working Group was chaired by the intelligence community.
588   Majidi, Vahid, "Hearing on H.R. 2631, the Nuclear Forensics and Attribution Act," statement, October 10, 2007.
589   Ibid.

field offices. After 9/11, the Bureau added additional intelligence positions, participated in newly formed Department of Homeland Security state and regional fusion centers, and elevated terrorism prevention to the highest priority.[590] In partnership with the Departments of Homeland Security and Defense, the Federal Bureau of Investigation trained international partners on how to search, detect, and interdict nuclear materials, border security, undercover investigations, nuclear forensics, and crisis management. It also provided law enforcement assistance and coordination through the Legal Attaché program in participating countries.[591] In the case of the Domestic Nuclear Detection Office, the Bureau provided detailees that worked in various office directorates. Instead of simply performing liaison functions, these personnel served in key positions within the Domestic Nuclear Detection Office such as the director of the Office of Operations Support, and brought a federal law enforcement perspective into the Department of Homeland Security's interagency environment.[592]

---

590   The Assistant Director of the Federal Bureau of Investigation Weapons of Mass Destruction Directorate stated that, "Within that priority [terrorism prevention], the Weapons of Mass Destruction (WMD) terrorist threat is clearly our most pressing concern." Mines, Michael, "The Federal Bureau of Investigation and Fusion Centers," statement, September 27, 2007; Majidi, Vahid, "Hearing on H.R. 2631, the Nuclear Forensics and Attribution Act," statement, October 10, 2007.
591   The Bureau's Legal Attaché program stations agents at American embassies. These officials serve as the director's representative for a specific country or region, and are charged to establish connections with host nation law enforcement and security agencies. Fuentes, Thomas V., "The FBI's Legal Attaché program," statement, October 4, 2007.
592   Mueller, Robert S. III, "Nuclear Terrorism: Prevention is our Endgame," speech, June 11, 2007; Lewis, John, "Detecting and Neutralizing Potential Terrorist Threats Involving Nuclear Weapons," statement, October 27, 2005.

DEPARTMENT OF DEFENSE

The Defense Department was responsible for post-detonation debris collection and analysis, and was represented on the Attribution Assessment Working Group. The Department of Defense's primary combat support organization for post-detonation was the Defense Threat Reduction Agency, but multiple Department assets, such as the 20th Support Group, also participated.[593] As the lead for post-detonation material characterization, the Department of Defense was responsible for sample collection, analysis, and evaluation in support of U.S. government attribution efforts. To facilitate this area of responsibility, the Defense Department resourced dedicated and dual-use infrastructure, research and development, and conducted training exercises.[594]

The department was already working to improve the post-detonation mission area for several years before the National Technical Nuclear Forensics Center was formed. In 2000, following the Defense Science Board report on Unconventional Nuclear Warfare Defense, the Defense Threat Reduction Agency, under the leadership of Jay Davis, formed the Domestic Nuclear Event Attribution program.[595] This program was intended "to improve U.S. government post-detonation nuclear forensics capabilities and develop a focused system for rapid and accurate attribution of a domestic nuclear or radiological event."[596] Pre-existing capabilities and an overall mission set

593   Department of Defense, *Quadrennial Defense Review Report*, February 6, 2006, pp. 51-52.
594   Department of Defense, "Nuclear Forensics and Attribution," Defense Threat Reduction Agency and U.S. Strategic Command Center for Combating Weapons of Mass Destruction, retrieved October 25, 2010.
595   Jay Davis, Defense Threat Reduction Agency Director October 1, 1998-June 24, 2001, came from and returned to Lawrence Livermore National Laboratory, where he had been familiar with discussions related to an unattributed nuclear detonation.
596   Evenson, Michael K., "Hearing on H.R. 2631, the Nuclear Forensics and Attribution Act," statement, October 10, 2007; Davis, Jay, "The

that accounted for operating in hazardous environments meant that the Department of Defense remained the optimum choice for post-detonation operations abroad.[597] After further analysis of other interagency capabilities, it also became clear that the Defense Department was the only federal actor equipped to operate in a post-detonation environment. Based on this assessment, the department was assigned "the responsibility to ensure a worldwide post-detonation national technical nuclear forensics capability, including ground and air sample collection, analysis of post-detonation debris, developing and sustaining a concept of operations, and supporting enhancements to post-detonation scientific and technical capabilities."[598]

DEPARTMENT OF ENERGY

The Department of Energy was responsible for pre- and post-detonation device characterization, laboratory support throughout the spectrum of technical nuclear forensics areas, nuclear emergency response assets, and the Nuclear Materials Information Program database. The department was also represented on the Attribution Assessment Working Group. The primary national laboratories participating in the national technical nuclear forensics mission were Lawrence Livermore National Laboratory, Los Alamos National Laboratory, Sandia National Laboratory, Idaho National Laboratory, National Institute of Standards and Technology, Pacific Northwest National

---

Attribution of Weapons of Mass Destruction Events," *Journal of Homeland Security*, April 2003.

597   Following the formation of the National Technical Nuclear Forensics Center, the Defense Department renamed the Domestic Nuclear Event Attribution program. It was changed to the Defense Threat Reduction Agency-National Technical Nuclear Forensics (D-NTNF) program, under the Washington Technical Support Group. U.S. Department of Defense, "Defense Threat Reduction Agency FY2008 Supplemental Funding Request," retrieved April 15, 2010, pp. 75-76.

598   Evenson, Michael K., "Hearing on H.R. 2631, the Nuclear Forensics and Attribution Act," statement, October 10, 2007.

Laboratory, New Brunswick Laboratory, Argonne National Laboratory, Oak Ridge National Laboratory, and Savannah River National Laboratory.[599]

Each laboratory brought years of expertise and specialized skills and equipment to the broader technical nuclear forensics mission. Of all the laboratories, Lawrence Livermore and Savannah River were the primary ones specializing in initial analysis. Lawrence Livermore National Laboratory stood out for its leading role in the definition of early post-Cold War technical nuclear forensics. This included founding the forensic science center in 1991, co-founding the Nuclear Smuggling International Technical Working Group in 1996, and serving as its co-chair since formation.[600] Moreover, Lawrence Livermore was responsible for contributing to the International Technical Working Group's international nuclear forensics model action plan, which was adopted by the International Atomic Energy Agency in 2006.[601]

In 2000, the creation of the Nuclear Counterterrorism Design Support program marked a new departure for the development of expertise related to potential designs for improvised nuclear devices. According to Deputy Under Secretary for Counterterrorism Steven Aoki, "weapons designers at our national laboratories analyze and model potential improvised

---

599   For more information on the role of each laboratory, see Appendix D of the Joint Working Group of the American Physical Society (APS) and the American Association for the Advancement of Science (AAAS), *Nuclear Forensics: Role, State of the Art, Program Needs*. Department of Homeland Security, "National Technical Nuclear Forensics: Overview, QA, and Expertise Development," Domestic Nuclear Detection Office briefing, September 14, 2009.

600   Heller, Arnie, "Forensics Science Center Maximizes the Tiniest Clue: Livermore chemists are coaxing a wealth of information from increasingly small samples," *Science and Technology Review*, April 2002, pp. 11-18.

601   Heller, Arnie, "Identifying the Source of Stolen Nuclear Materials: Livermore scientists are analyzing interdicted illicit nuclear and radioactive materials for clues to the materials" origins and routes," *Science and Technology Review*, January/February 2007, p. 18.

nuclear device designs, drawing on computational tools, exper-
imental data, and expertise originally developed in the nuclear
weapons program.[602] The knowledge gained was applied to
nuclear search and detection, forensic analysis, nuclear device
render-safe, nuclear facility security, and intelligence assessments."[603] Laboratories also supplied the Department of Energy's
response asset roles such as the radiological assistance program,
and nuclear emergency support teams. These teams provided
capabilities to assist other interagency actors with "search and
recovery operations for nuclear materials, weapons, or devices,"
and to "assist in identifying and deactivating" nuclear devices.[604]

In order to assist with nuclear attribution and exclusion,
President George W. Bush directed that a Nuclear Materials
Information Program be established as "an interagency effort
managed by the Department of Energy's Office of Intelligence
and Counterintelligence."[605] This program was directed "to
consolidate information from all sources pertaining to worldwide nuclear materials holdings and their security status into an
integrated and continuously updated information management
system."[606] Despite authorization, initial efforts to meet the
president's intent did not result in a comprehensive materials
catalogue as of January 2009.[607]

---

602   Aoki, Steven, "Hearing on H.R. 2631, the Nuclear Forensics and
Attribution Act," statement, October 10, 2007.
603   Ibid.
604   The nuclear emergency support team was one of seven Department
of Energy specialized emergency response assets. Department of Energy,
"Fact Sheet: Nuclear Emergency Support Team (NEST)," National Nuclear
Security Administration, 2010.
605   Mowatt-Larsen, Rolf, "The Threat of Nuclear Terrorism," statement, April 2, 2008.
606   Ibid.
607   Interview with Department of Homeland Security, Domestic
Nuclear Detection Office Director Vayl Oxford, September 13, 2010.

DEPARTMENT OF HOMELAND SECURITY

The Department of Homeland Security had multiple organizations with nuclear defense responsibilities, and was represented on the Attribution Assessment Working Group. Within the department, the Domestic Nuclear Detection Office was an interagency office of less than 150 federal and contracted personnel drawn from the Department of Homeland Security, and the greater federal government, to include the Nuclear Regulatory Commission.[608] The office was created in response to the evolving nuclear threat, "specifically the nuclear terrorist threat, and the need to bring an interagency approach to the problem."[609]

The Domestic Nuclear Detection Office's missions and staffing were designed to capitalize on an interagency approach to nuclear defense with the initial task to develop a Global Nuclear Detection Architecture. This architecture was envisioned as the layered U.S. government nuclear detection strategy that would account for all domestic and international programs and capabilities. However, separate statutory authorities that permitted individual department secretaries to retain authority for their programs obstructed implementation. This legislative protection of bureaucratic turf was as an example of organizational impediments to collaborative implementation.[610] Thus, by the time the Domestic Nuclear Detection Office was created there were already:

> 72 programs across the U.S. government focused on radiological and nuclear management. For the most part, the Department of Defense, the Department of Energy, and the Department of State

---

608   Department of Homeland Security, *Homeland Security Budget-in-Brief Fiscal Year 2009*, p. 109; Oxford, Vayl S., "Energy Facility Contractors Group (EFCOG) 2007 Executive Council Meeting," Domestic Nuclear Detection Office briefing, February 21-22, 2007.
609   Interview with Department of Homeland Security, Domestic Nuclear Detection Office Director Vayl Oxford, September 13, 2010.
610   Wilson, James Q., *Bureaucracy: What Government Agencies Do and Why They Do It*, 2nd edition 2000, pp. 179-195.

Tobias O. Vogt

manage these programs... The Domestic Nuclear Detection Office estimates that more than $2.2 billion has been spent on these programs in Fiscal Year 2006. However, this estimate does not reflect all spending on the 72 programs, as some programs had additional elements that did not involve nuclear management, and the amount for nuclear management could not be isolated.[611]

DEPARTMENT OF STATE

The State Department was the lead agency for technical nuclear forensics coordination and outreach abroad, and was represented on the Attribution Assessment Working Group. In this capacity, the department provided in-country and regional support to various technical nuclear forensics actors. Within the Bureau of International Security and Nonproliferation, the Office of Weapons of Mass Destruction Terrorism was responsible for nuclear forensics assistance, and the development of international support policies and procedures. To facilitate and coordinate international technical nuclear forensics efforts, the office created the Forensics Engagement Working Group under the pre-existing Nuclear Trafficking Response Group. The Department of State's international efforts included participation in the International Atomic Energy Agency illicit trafficking database, the International Technical Working Group, and international outreach events such as the Science and Technology Center in Ukraine Nuclear Forensics Experts" Workshop. Should an international nuclear incident have occurred, State's Nuclear Trafficking Response Group was tasked to coordinate U.S. government assistance. The Department of State also provided detailed personnel support to the Domestic Nuclear Detection Office.[612]

The national actors section demonstrated that there were

---

611   Department of Homeland Security, *DHS" Domestic Nuclear Detection Office: Progress in Integrating Detection Capabilities and Response Protocols,* Inspector General Report, December 2007, pp. 5-9.
612   Grant, Andrew, "Hearing on H.R. 2631, the Nuclear Forensics and Attribution Act," statement, October 10, 2007.

already deeply rooted programs throughout the federal government for nuclear forensics when the National Technical Nuclear
Forensics Center was formed in 2007.[613] Because each of the
interagency actors had a stake in the shared policy space of
nuclear forensics, program survival was the driving factor for
voluntary participation.[614] This observation was consistent
with Anthony Downs' argument that organizations "consume a
great deal of time and energy in territorial struggles that create
no socially useful product." Instead of national collaboration,
nuclear forensics interagency coordination represented a territorial struggle, where organizations sought to prevent the loss of
territory, resources, and influence.

ORGANIZATION AND WORKFLOW

This section establishes that the Department of Homeland
Security was not effectively organized to integrate interagency
programs. The absence of senior leadership and operational authorities meant the department could not direct national nuclear
forensic efforts located throughout the federal government.[615]
The integrator model was limited by bureaucratic competition,
and lacked control of budgets and policy execution.[616] If a

---

613   For example, the Air Force Technical Applications Center was
founded in 1947. U.S. Department of Defense, "Fact Sheet: Air Force
Technical Applications Center," November 2008; Allison, Graham T., and
Morton H. Halperin, "Bureaucratic Politics: A Paradigm and Some Policy
Implications," *World Politics,* Vol. 24, Spring 1972, p. 54.
614   Downs, Anthony, *Inside Bureaucracy,* 1967, pp. 212-218.
615   Anthony Downs and James Wilson have both argued that no government agency will willingly allow another agency to direct their operations
or control their resources. In this regard, agencies cooperate to ensure autonomy, not to improve collaborative implementation. Ibid.; Wilson, James
Q., *Bureaucracy: What Government Agencies Do and Why They Do It,* 2nd
edition 2000, pp. 192-194.
616   Murdock, Clark A., and Michele A. Flournoy, "Beyond Goldwater-
Nichols: U.S. Government and Defense Reform for a New Strategic Era
(Phase II)," Center for Strategic and International Studies Report, July 28,
2005, pp. 26-36.

participating department decided not to resource an established technical nuclear forensics requirement, or decided not to follow procedures during an incident response, then the relatively junior National Technical Nuclear Forensics Center leadership were hard-pressed to enforce compliance.[617] Thus, the lack of national integrator command and control authorities resulted in severe limitations in collaborative execution under this design.

The National Technical Nuclear Forensics Center is a modest interagency office of less than 20 personnel. It is a directorate of the Domestic Nuclear Detection Office, and as such "all National Technical Nuclear Forensics Center actions and initiatives were worked through Domestic Nuclear Detection Office leadership mechanisms. Domestic Nuclear Detection Office leadership participated as appropriate in technical nuclear forensics specific activities, to include those with the NSS [National Security Staff]."[618] The National Technical Nuclear Forensics Center encompassed a Domestic Nuclear Detection Office Assistant Director (NTNFC), a Federal Bureau of Investigation deputy director, employees from the Department of Homeland Security, interagency detailees, and contractors.

The center focused on strategic planning, integration, and the advancement of technical nuclear forensics. This approach meant that existing organizations maintained responsibility for their nuclear forensics programs while simultaneously participating in the larger federal effort. Formation of the National Technical Nuclear Forensics Center resulted in increased national priority, and additional funding from the Department of Homeland Security for pre-detonation material research and development, expertise maintenance and replenishment, and operational readiness requirements. As a result, the center enjoyed

---

617   Locher, James R. III, Executive Director, *Forging a New Shield,* Project on National Security Reform, 2008, p. 95.
618   Department of Homeland Security, Domestic Nuclear Detection Office, National Technical Nuclear Forensics Center Official [written response], October 12, 2010.

COMBATING THE BUREAUCRACY   241

a great deal of support from participating organizations during the establishment phase.

The National Technical Nuclear Forensics Center was functionally organized according to operational readiness, expertise development, and technological advancement requirements. There were program managers for each functional area with general service and contractor support. The director and program managers also served as facilitators for the interagency forums by coordinating administrative requirements, and acting as full-time nuclear forensic subject matter experts during meetings comprised of interagency representatives. This internal structure serviced a senior interagency executive committee, a steering committee, and working groups, which were designed to support collaborative national technical nuclear forensics efforts at the implementer level.[619]

Formal congressional testimony on technical nuclear forensics-related issues was delivered by the director of the Domestic Nuclear Detection Office and his equivalents in other applicable departments.[620] If necessary, the national laboratories also provided senior scientists in specific fields of interest.[621] Interaction with congressional staff began with the director of the National Technical Nuclear Forensics Center. The Department of Homeland Security promoted collective representation with interagency partners where appropriate in dealing with Congress. Even if the center was asked for a simple response from an individual staffer, it still attempted to keep relevant interagency

619   The steering committee was at the General Schedule-15/Colonel level. Oxford, Vayl, "Hearing on H.R. 2631, the Nuclear Forensics and Attribution Act," statement, October 10, 2007.
620   This routinely meant directors from the Department of State, Office of Weapons of Mass Destruction Terrorism, Bureau of International Security and Nonproliferation, the Federal Bureau of Investigation, Weapons of Mass Destruction Directorate, Department of Defense, Defense Threat Reduction Agency Associate Director for Operations, and the Department of Energy, Under Secretary of Energy for Counterterrorism.
621   Burns, Carol J., "Hearing on H.R. 2631, the Nuclear Forensics and Attribution Act," statement, October 10, 2007.

partners informed.[622] Beyond the immediate center and the close working relationships created by a common mission focus, the active committee and working group structures meant that department representatives established relationships with their interagency counterparts because of their regular interaction.[623]

OPERATIONAL READINESS

In 2007, work on an integrated strategy began by identifying obstacles to national technical nuclear forensics, and shifting to a reverse planning approach that established the end goal first, so that all supporting efforts could be focused on working toward a single outcome. Before the center was created, nuclear forensics was treated as a separate function in support of U.S. weapons data or foreign weapons assessments. In contrast, the reverse planning approach started with the end goal of supporting timely attribution, and not simply conducting independent scientific analysis. This new emphasis identified the purpose of generating technical nuclear forensics data as supporting rapid attribution. Planning efforts and resulting national procedures were also compartmentalized into pre-detonation materials or devices, and post-detonation responses.

With multiple actors, jurisdictions, and capabilities, one of the first planning tasks was to designate mission area responsibilities (Figure 5.1). This task consumed much of 2007 through 2009, as capability assessments were merged into an integrated strategy. The agreed upon interagency approach limited the opposition from powerful departments such as Defense and State, and confirmed that many of the technical nuclear forensics capabilities were leveraged from other funded areas. Moreover, it acknowledged that a single technical nuclear forensics budget was an unreasonable expectation based on existing

622   Downs, Anthony, *Inside Bureaucracy*, 1967, pp. 54-56.
623   Ibid., pp. 67-73; Interview with Department of Homeland Security, Domestic Nuclear Detection Office Director Vayl Oxford, September 13, 2010.

U.S. government organization and statutory authorities. One drawback realized during the planning phase was that the bulk of national technical nuclear forensics efforts were a small part of other program budgets. The size of the center's budget was also an issue. Because the National Technical Nuclear Forensics Center's budget remained minute, it lacked a surge capacity for unforecasted requirements, unforeseen technological concerns, or actual operational costs associated with a real-world event.[624]

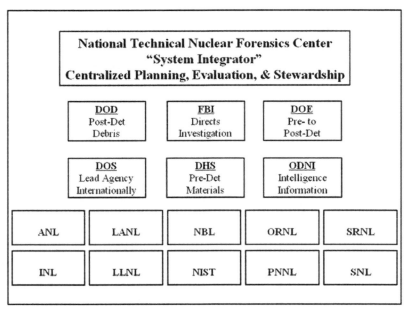

**FIGURE 5.1. TECHNICAL NUCLEAR FORENSICS
INTERAGENCY ORGANIZATION**[625]

624   Interview with Department of Homeland Security, Domestic Nuclear Detection Office Director Vayl Oxford, September 13, 2010.

625   Department of Defense (DOD), Federal Bureau of Investigation (FBI), Department of Energy (DOE), Department of State (DOS), Department of Homeland Security (DHS), Office of the Director of National Intelligence (ODNI), Argonne National Laboratory (ANL), Los Alamos National Laboratory National Laboratory (LANL), New Brunswick Laboratory (NBL), Oak Ridge National Laboratory (ORNL), Savannah River National Laboratory (SRNL), Idaho National Laboratory (INL), Lawrence Livermore National Laboratory (LLNL), National Institute of Standards and Technology

The National Technical Nuclear Forensics Center generated a working plan for national nuclear forensics by 2009. The plan was written by the new interagency working groups and approved at the executive council level but not by the president.[626] It took until April 2010, and a change in administrations, before the president approved the first "Strategic Five-Year Plan for Improving the Nuclear Forensics and Attribution Capabilities of the United States."[627] Even as the U.S. government was working toward collective planning and integration, it was realized that issues such as scientific standardization had a direct impact on the technical ability of different actors to communicate results, both domestically and internationally. Since technical nuclear forensics was a significant part of the nuclear attribution assessment process, it was critical to provide a high-level of confidence using standardized scientific findings.

Much of this confidence is derived from joint analysis and findings that can be replicated during peer review, but to conduct repeatable analysis there had to be universal standards for technical nuclear forensics recognized by the global scientific community. Although the Nuclear Smuggling International Technical Working Group had worked toward the development of international "protocols for collecting evidence, prioritizing techniques for forensic analyses of nuclear and associated non-nuclear samples, conducting inter-laboratory forensic exercises, and developing forensic databanks to assist in interpretation" since 1996, universal scientific standards did not exist prior to 2007.[628]

(NIST), Pacific Northwest National Laboratory (PNNL), Sandia National Laboratories (SNL). Department of Homeland Security, "National Technical Nuclear Forensics: Overview, QA, and Expertise Development," Domestic Nuclear Detection Office briefing, September 14, 2009.

626   Interview with Department of Homeland Security, Domestic Nuclear Detection Office Director Vayl Oxford, September 13, 2010.

627   Lute, Jane Holl, "Nuclear Terrorism: Strengthening Our Domestic Defenses, Part II," testimony, September 15, 2010.

628   The Nuclear Smuggling International Technical Working Group is comprised of scientists from 28 countries. Heller, Arnie, "Identifying the Source of Stolen Nuclear Materials: Livermore scientists are analyzing

In order to improve standardization, the National Technical Nuclear Forensics Center and supporting national laboratories, including Lawrence Livermore and Savannah River, adopted international standards where applicable, and sought International Organization for Standardization laboratory accreditation to advance common global technical nuclear forensics practices.[629]

EXECUTION

All of the nuclear forensics mission areas -- pre-detonation materials or devices, and post-detonation debris -- shared the same approach of collection, analysis, and evaluation. However, existing capabilities and authorities dictated the nature of planning and operational assignments.[630] Many of the same resources, such as scientific expertise at the national laboratories, are used in all types of events but the time-sensitive procedures associated with each mission area differ. For example, if there is an alarm at a U.S. port that cannot be adjudicated on-site, Customs and Border Protection would notify the Federal Bureau of Investigation and the Department of Homeland Security's

interdicted illicit nuclear and radioactive materials for clues to the materials" origins and routes," *Science and Technology Review*, January/February 2007, p. 18; Rennie, Gabriele, "Tracing the Steps in Nuclear Material Trafficking: Forensic scientists are combining an array of technologies to track illicit nuclear materials to their sources," *Science and Technology Review*, March 2005, p. 17.

629   The International Organization for Standardization is a non-governmental organization of 163 countries headquartered in Vienna, Austria. The organization is dedicated to developing and publishing international standards in a variety of fields. International Organization for Standardization, "About International Organization for Standardization," retrieved October 27, 2010.

630   For more information on technical nuclear forensics procedures and techniques, see the International Atomic Energy Agency, "Technical Guidance Reference Manual: Nuclear Forensics Support," *International Atomic Energy Agency Nuclear Security Series No. 2*, 2006; and Kenton J. Moody, Ian D. Hutcheon, and Patrick M. Grant, *Nuclear Forensic Analysis*, 2005.

National Operations Center.[631] The Department of Homeland Security would review the incident and, if deemed suspicious, issue a warning notice to the Department of Energy and the Federal Bureau of Investigation.[632] This initial notice highlights the potential for deployment as preliminary alarm resolution procedures are underway. On-site personnel would work to resolve the alarm with reachback assistance from the Laboratories and Scientific Services located in their National Targeting Center, and, if necessary, the National Nuclear Security Administration's Office of Emergency Response.[633] If internal capacity is

---

631   Shifting outward for responsibility from the port was the Coast Guard, Department of Defense, and Department of State. Each organization used separate procedures from those listed in this example. The general levels of radiation alarm adjudication progressed from immediately resolved, to field adjudication, and then, if necessary, reachback to the applicable federal organization based on the location and jurisdiction of the alarm.

632   Often material incidents were deemed benign due to natural radiation emissions from standard products such as raw materials or scrap metals. If this was the case, Customs and Border Protection resolved the alarm on-site.

633   In the case of state and local incidents, the Department of Homeland Security's Joint Analysis Center serves in a reachback capacity. The Domestic Nuclear Detection Office, Joint Analysis Center was an important component in the analysis of radiological/nuclear issues. According to one official, the Joint Analysis Center, in cooperation with the National Operations Center and other interagency assets, put "radiological/nuclear into any situational picture" by serving as the "window to the Global Nuclear Detection Architecture." In addition to alarm adjudication, this organization analyzed the Global Nuclear Detection Architecture and consolidated intelligence reports, data, and other related products to provide an assessment of any radiological or nuclear considerations that might occur. For example, during extreme weather conditions, the Joint Analysis Center provided the U.S. government with situational awareness for any permanent or mobile radiological or nuclear asset in affected areas. Department of Homeland Security, *Department of Homeland Security" Domestic Nuclear Detection Office: Progress in Integrating Detection Capabilities and Response Protocols,* Inspector General Report, December 2007, pp. 20-24; Interview with Department of Homeland Security, Domestic Nuclear Detection Office, Joint Analysis Center Official, October 26, 2010; Department of Homeland Security, "Fact Sheet: Joint Analysis Center," Domestic Nuclear Detection Office.

exceeded during an event, or if a response is required, the Department of Homeland Security relies on additional capabilities provided by Lawrence Livermore, Sandia, or Los Alamos National Laboratories.

Customs and Border Protection would prepare the area if an incident called for response teams from the Federal Bureau of Investigation and the Department of Energy. The leads, experts, and procedures are different for pre-detonation device and material events. For example, in the case of a device, the main difference emanates from the time-sensitive render-safe requirement before any technical nuclear forensics sampling, characterization, or investigations can begin.[634] For nuclear materials, where detonation is not a concern, once the area has been prepared from a safety and investigative standpoint, initial expert analysis is conducted at the scene by nuclear emergency response teams from the Department of Energy under the operational control of the Department of Homeland Security.[635] If material is deemed to be a non-benign source during field analysis, then joint sample collection begins, and the Federal Bureau of Investigation would take operational control from an investigative standpoint.[636]

---

634   Post-detonation scenarios were completely different. These events required simultaneous consequence management operations and attribution assessment, in a hazardous, time-sensitive environment. Collection techniques were also different from the two types of pre-detonation mission areas, because of differences in physical evidence. Interview with Department of Homeland Security, Domestic Nuclear Detection Office Director Vayl Oxford, September 13, 2010.

635   Procedures assigning operational control to Department of Homeland Security were outlined in the original Homeland Security Act, but additional memoranda of understanding provided procedures for the Federal Bureau of Investigation to assume lead authorities earlier in the incident if necessary. Interview with Department of Homeland Security, Domestic Nuclear Detection Office Director Vayl Oxford, September 13, 2010; *Homeland Security Act of 2002* (H.R. 5005, P.L. 107-296), Title V, Sec. 504; Department of Energy, "Fact Sheet: Nuclear Emergency Support Team (NEST)," and "Fact Sheet: Radiological Assistance Program (RAP)," National Nuclear Security Administration, 2010.

636   This includes supervision of the chain of custody for all samples.

Sample collection is followed by off-site joint analysis by the Federal Bureau of Investigation at the Savannah River National Laboratory's Radiological Evidence Examination Facility, and the Department of Homeland Security through Lawrence Livermore National Laboratory.[637] This dual-approach means that separate laboratories are used to confirm results from two sample sources. Each laboratory would conduct a thorough analysis of their respective samples, and produce periodic reports to support on-going investigations and policy decisions.[638] Other national laboratories are available if assistance is needed, and for secondary analysis of initial findings. The principle laboratories for secondary analysis include Oak Ridge for uranium, Los Alamos for plutonium, and Pacific Northwest for nuclear reactor designs and the fuel process.[639] Reports and conclusions are then forwarded to the Attribution Assessment Working Group, and the laboratories remain prepared to answer any technical questions that might arise during deliberations.

While traditional and nuclear forensics efforts are conducted simultaneously, the two investigative methods are distinctly different. Nuclear forensics focuses "on the information inherent to the materials," and traditional forensics focuses "on the information adherent to the materials."[640] In nuclear forensics, the

---

637   According to a 2009 Federal Bureau of Investigation Laboratory Division article, Lawrence Livermore National Laboratory and Savannah River National Laboratory were the primary national laboratories accredited (International Organization for Standardization 17025) for certain nuclear forensics functions. Leggitt, J., K. Inn, S. Goldberg, R. Essex, S. LaMont, and S. Chase, "Nuclear forensics-metrological basis for legal defensibility," *Journal of Radioanalytical and Nuclear Chemistry*, 2009, pp. 997-1001.

638   Routine reports would appear at the 24-hour, one week, and two-month marks. International Atomic Energy Agency, "Technical Guidance Reference Manual: Nuclear Forensics Support," *International Atomic Energy Agency Nuclear Security Series No. 2*, 2006, p. 27.

639   Rennie, Gabriele, "Tracing the Steps in Nuclear Material Trafficking: Forensic scientists are combining an array of technologies to track illicit nuclear materials to their sources," *Science and Technology Review*, March 2005, p. 16.

640   Mayer, K., M. Wallenius, and T. Fanghanel, "Nuclear forensic

material signature or characteristic parameters must be identified before the material is connected to or excluded from possible sources. Simultaneously, traditional forensic techniques, which may require specially equipped laboratories for contaminated items, also aid in attribution.[641] For pre-detonation material and device analysis, both forms of forensics bring powerful scientific tools to bear as part of the attribution process.[642] In the case of inherent information from nuclear materials, scientists can derive significant amounts of data from established parameters using technical nuclear forensics methodologies and techniques.[643] Figure 5.2 provides examples of parameters and corresponding information for existing nuclear forensics capabilities.

Parameter	Information
Appearance	Material Type
Dimensions	Reactor Type
Uranium, Plutonium Content	Chemical Composition
Isotopic Analysis	Reactor Type, Enrichment
Time Since Last Chemical Separation	Age
Impurities	Production Process
Oxygen Isotope Ratio Cycles	Geolocation
Surface Roughness	Production Plant
Microstructure	Production Process

FIGURE 5.2. URANIUM AND PLUTONIUM INHERENT FORENSIC INFORMATION[644]
(PARAMETERS DENOTE INFORMATION TYPE)

science-From cradle to maturity," *Journal of Alloys and Compounds*, 2007, pp. 50-56.
641   Ibid.
642   In the case of pre-detonation devices, reverse engineering also added a significant attribution capability.
643   While techniques from nuclear testing and safeguards provided the basis for technical nuclear forensics, the mission area expanded into a specific scientific discipline, complete with evolving methodologies and techniques for pre- and post-detonation cases. Wallenius, Maria, et al., "Nuclear forensic investigations with a focus on plutonium," *Journal of Alloys and Compounds*, 2007, pp. 57-62.
644   Wallenius, M., K. Mayer, I. Ray, "Nuclear forensic investigations: Two case studies," *Forensic Science International*, 2006, p. 56.

A real-world example of a pre-detonation response that impacted planning and execution occurred in Sri Lanka in October 2005. In this incident, a maintenance team found that pre-operational Megaports Initiative detectors had experienced nuclear alarms. The alarms appeared on the previous 48-hour data logs of the unmanned detection units. As a result of several forms of input information, officials were able to ascertain which ships and containers possibly posed a threat. Deemed a potentially serious alarm, this incident set in motion the global response network for the next six weeks as the ships headed for India, Germany, and the United States. This event generated two to three situation updates a day at the Domestic Nuclear Detection Office, and tested national response preparations and coordination. The alarm turned out to involve a scrap metal container, but the after action-review indicated that domestic and international alarm resolution protocols did not exist.[645]

NUCLEAR MATERIALS DATABASE

A standing database of nuclear materials and designs is often described as the linchpin between technical nuclear forensics and attribution.[646] However, a major problem confronting technical nuclear forensics in support of rapid attribution was the lack of participation in pre-existing domestic and international

---

645   Megaports Initiative detectors had other similar incidents of non-operational detectors displaying readings. This type of pre-handover event was one of the unresolved issues concerning the Megaports program. Huizenga, David, "Radiation Detection," testimony, September 18, 2007; Huizenga, David, "National Nuclear Security Administration's Megaports Initiative and Its Role in the Secure Freight Initiative (SFI)," testimony, June 12, 2008; Interviews with Department of Homeland Security, Domestic Nuclear Detection Office Director Vayl Oxford, and Joint Analysis Center Official, September 13, and October 26, 2010.
646   Oxford, Vayl, "Needed: A Comprehensive Nuclear Forensics and Attribution Act," *Domestic Preparedness*, June 30, 2010; May, Michael, Chair, *Nuclear Forensics: Role, State of the Art, Program Needs*, Joint Working Group of the American Physical Society and the American Association for the Advancement of Science Report, 2008, pp. 26-30.

databases. Domestically, the Department of Energy was the lead for the Nuclear Materials Information Program with the Department of Homeland Security responsible for pre-detonation materials catalogue support.[647] The United States nuclear materials database was dependent on available information collected over time by the laboratories, and from agreements negotiated with international partners. The database is described as the linchpin because these known samples, and designs in the case of weapons, are required for matching once initial technical nuclear forensics analysis has been conducted. Without known samples and designs, scientists can identify, but not necessarily connect findings to an originating source. The national laboratories incrementally supplied historic samples of materials and designs accumulated over several decades, but these efforts did not result in a complete database.

An example of national laboratory database participation was provided by the Fermi National Accelerator Laboratory. In a memorandum from February 2009, the laboratory responded to a January 2009, Department of Energy request for Nuclear Materials Information Program archive assistance concerning the following materials:

1) Early U.S. highly enriched uranium (HEU) that is essentially free of U-236
2) Modern U.S. HEU
3) HEU enriched by processes other than gaseous diffusion
4) Early U.S. Weapons Grade Plutonium (WGPu)
5) Modern U.S. WGPu, both from Los Alamos National Laboratory, Hanford, and Savannah River
6) Blended U.S. WGPu produced from high assay Hanford N-reactor fuel and low-assay Savannah River Site (SRS) targets
7) Examples of special nuclear material (SNM) produced by different metallurgical process
8) Alloyed SNM

---

647   Interview with Department of Homeland Security, Domestic Nuclear Detection Office Director Vayl Oxford, September 13, 2010.

9) Other materials deemed valuable to NMIP [Nuclear Materials
   Information Program][648]

While the Fermi National Accelerator Laboratory did
not possess any of the requested archival materials, the
memorandum pointed to basic gaps in a centralized database
even among U.S. government participants as late as 2009.
The United States relied on individual and collective agreements for nuclear forensic related samples, data, and expertise,
and assisted foreign partners when possible.[649] International
partners that did not have the facilities or expertise for technical nuclear forensics routinely used American capabilities. In
1999, this was the case in a Bulgarian incident where Lawrence
Livermore National Laboratory traced the contents of a 2.4 ki-
logram lead container back to Eastern Europe.[650] In these types
of proceedings, where pre-existing agreements were not present,
the Department of State acted as a link between countries.[651]

The national laboratories also leveraged existing working
relationships with foreign partners such Kazakhstan's
Kazatomprom, the state-owned source for Russian and former
Soviet uranium ore. In 2006, Kazatomprom agreed to provide
samples, data, and expert nuclear forensic consultation to

---

648   Fermi National Accelerator Laboratory, "Subject: Nuclear
Materials Information Program (NMIP)," memorandum from Fermi National
Accelerator Laboratory to Department of Energy, National Nuclear Security
Administration Site Manager, February 5, 2009.
649   This area was targeted for advancement in the Nuclear Forensics
and Attribution Act. *Nuclear Forensics and Attribution Act of 2010* (H.R.
730, P.L. 111-140), Sec. 3.
650   Rennie, Gabriele, "Tracing the Steps in Nuclear Material Trafficking:
Forensic scientists are combining an array of technologies to track illicit
nuclear materials to their sources," *Science and Technology Review*, March
2005, p. 17.
651   Additionally, the European Commission Joint Research Center,
and the International Science and Technology Center (ISTC) both had mature nuclear forensic foundations that worked toward internationalizing the
field. International efforts included events such as the June 2009 Science and
Technology Center in Ukraine, Nuclear Forensics Experts' Workshop.

Lawrence Livermore National Laboratory for a five-year period. Since the creation of the National Technical Nuclear Forensics Center, similar efforts in support of the pre-detonation materials database was funded by Department of Homeland Security, with legal and technical support provided by the National Nuclear Security Administration.[652] However, in the absence of significant incentives, the degree of international database participation remained low.

TRAINING AND EXERCISES

Prior to the creation of the National Technical Nuclear Forensics Center, nuclear response was managed at the department and agency levels, and as part of larger national exercises.[653] The National Technical Nuclear Forensics Center began to consolidate existing preparation programs such as the Department of Defense's post-detonation capabilities program, and aligned combined technical nuclear forensics training with the emerging national level exercise two-year cycle.[654] This approach facilitated integrated participation for technical and non-technical nuclear forensics personnel, and allowed sufficient time between exercises to identify lessons learned and implement corrections. An elevated priority helped the conduct of exercises involving the full range of technical nuclear forensics

---

652   Heller, Arnie, "Identifying the Source of Stolen Nuclear Materials: Livermore scientists are analyzing interdicted illicit nuclear and radioactive materials for clues to the materials" origins and routes," *Science and Technology Review*, January/February 2007, p. 16.

653   National Planning Scenario #1 was the detonation of a 10Kt improvised nuclear device, and scenario #11 was a radiological attack using a radiological dispersal device, but nuclear incident-related exercises had been in existence for many years. For more information on exercises involving nuclear and radiological incidents such as Mile Shakedown or the various Top Officials (TOPOFF) events, see Richelson, Jeffrey T., *Defusing Armageddon: Inside nuclear emergency support teams, America's Secret Nuclear Bomb Squad*, 2009.

654   Evenson, Michael K., "Hearing on H.R. 2631, the Nuclear Forensics and Attribution Act," statement, October 10, 2007.

procedures in support of attribution, instead of just highlighting interdiction and consequence management tasks, as previously occurred.

While large scale exercises were associated with the federal government, technical nuclear forensics also required smaller, more frequent scientific events to maintain the individual skills of participating scientists and laboratories. Part of the interagency technical nuclear forensics quality assurance program was the requirement that "laboratories operate an internal quality assurance (QA) program, impose an appropriate level of internal quality control (QC), and participate in proficiency testing schemes (external QC)."[655] Because technical nuclear forensics was, in many cases, not a full-time job, those involved had to conduct internal and external exercises to augment existing laboratory functions. In its role as the national nuclear forensics system integrator, the National Technical Nuclear Forensics Center provided "an external layer of quality management to existing internal quality control programs at participating laboratories" and ensured dissemination of best analytical and management practices across all facilities.[656]

The U.S. national laboratories had fewer real-world incidents than their European counterparts to draw from since the emergence of the nuclear black market. The lack of routine analysis requirements meant that multi-laboratory exercises with material samples were an important aspect of capability maintenance. It also meant that international engagement, and the International Technical Working Group's round robin exercises, provided valuable insight and technical training, and also built confidence with international partners.[657] In the expert-based

655   Department of Homeland Security, "National Technical Nuclear Forensics: Overview, QA, and Expertise Development," Domestic Nuclear Detection Office briefing, September 14, 2009.
656   Ibid.
657   Wallenius, Maria, et al., "Nuclear forensic investigations with a focus on plutonium," *Journal of Alloys and Compounds*, 2007, pp. 57-62.

system associated with technical nuclear forensics, it is paramount to produce peer review quality results and conclusions.
Without technically competent personnel, standardization, and
global interaction, conclusions based on technical nuclear forensics findings may not withstand legal and international scrutiny.

EXPERTISE DEVELOPMENT AND TECHNOLOGICAL ADVANCEMENT

Trained scientists and the supporting national laboratories
constituted the technical nuclear forensics knowledge and infrastructure base. Early on it was identified that a larger "brain
drain" issue was affecting the nuclear weapons complex as scientists with hands-on experience retired or neared retirement
age.[658] This eroding capability, according to the center, meant that
"a major mission area of National Technical Nuclear Forensics
Center is the academic pipeline initiative."[659] The pipeline was
formally known as the National Nuclear Forensics Expertise
Development Program, and was implemented in conjunction
with the Departments of Defense and Energy. The program provided funding and support for related university programs, fac-
ulty, students, and post-graduates working in applicable nuclear
sciences.[660] These domestic fellowships and grants concentrated

---

658   For more information on the state of nuclear science personnel
within the U.S. government, see Joseph Cerny, et al., *Education in Nuclear
Science: A Status Report and Recommendations for the Beginning of the
21st Century,* Department of Energy/National Science Foundation Nuclear
Science Advisory Committee, Subcommittee on Education, November 2004.
659   Department of Homeland Security, Domestic Nuclear Detection
Office, National Technical Nuclear Forensics Center Official [written re-
sponse], October 12, 2010.
660   According to the same official, the center started a formal program for initial and continuing training of federal personnel, following the
passage of the Nuclear Forensics and Attribution Act. Ibid.; Department of
Homeland Security, "National Technical Nuclear Forensics: Overview, QA,
and Expertise Development," Domestic Nuclear Detection Office briefing,
September 14, 2009.

on the development of technical nuclear forensics expertise in a dwindling and highly competitive training environment, where other fields such as nuclear energy were competing for limited manpower. For example, the Nuclear Regulatory Commission's Nuclear Education Program budget was $15 million in fiscal year 2008. This amount, dedicated solely to expertise development, was equal to the total budget for the National Technical Nuclear Forensics Center in fiscal year 2008 (Table 5.1).[661]

Technical nuclear forensics manpower requirements were limited, and in most cases relied on dual-use positions where forensics was only a small portion of an employee's duty description. According to Carol Burns, in 2007, only 20-30 personnel were working full-time on technical nuclear forensics at the national laboratories -- the majority of which were over 50 or retired -- with about 200 additional personnel serving in a part-time capacity.[662] Early attempts that addressed these expertise concerns were categorized as ad hoc by the Government Accountability Office.[663] In response, the center established an interagency working group dedicated to the National Nuclear Forensics Expertise Development Program, and solicited academic and laboratory expertise to deal with the forecasted manpower requirement of 35 new technical nuclear forensics scientists between 2009 and 2019.[664]

A distinct disadvantage for nuclear forensics was the reliance on a dual-use manpower base emanating from a politically controversial source, the nuclear weapons complex. The divisive

---

661   Government Accountability Office, *Nuclear Forensics: Comprehensive Interagency Plan Needed to Address Human Capital Issues,* April 30, 2009, pp. 6-9.

662   This general response during the member question and answer session following prepared testimony was based on laboratory "self-reporting data." Burns, Carol J., "Hearing on H.R. 2631, the Nuclear Forensics and Attribution Act," statement, October 10, 2007.

663   Government Accountability Office, *Nuclear Forensics: Comprehensive Interagency Plan Needed to Address Human Capital Issues,* April 30, 2009, pp. 6-8.

664   Ibid.

topic of the nuclear weapons complex in the post-Cold War era had a direct impact on the attraction and retention of nuclear forensic expertise at the national laboratories. Any aspiring scientist could discover with limited research that the national laboratories had consistently experienced reduced budgets and layoffs since the end of the Cold War.[665] Ineffective strategic communications by the national laboratories failed to convince elected officials and the public that a robust infrastructure was still necessary for other tasks, when the aging U.S. nuclear arsenal was scheduled to be reduced to a stockpile of 5,113 in 2009, down from a peak of 31,255 in 1967.[666]

---

665   For example, Ken Jacobson, "Budget cuts lead to layoffs of physicists at National Labs," *Manufacturing & Technology News*, May 6, 2005, "A minimum of 270 employees are expected to leave Brookhaven National Laboratory, Fermi National Accelerator Laboratory (Fermilab), Lawrence Berkeley National Laboratory and Stanford Linear Accelerator Center (SLAC) as a result of force reduction programs"; Sue Major Holmes, "Sandia Laboratories expects less than 100 layoffs for 2008," *Associated Press*, November 26, 2007, Sandia "looking at between 40 and 80 to meet expected federal budget cuts." This was in addition to the 350 to 400 people lost each year through attrition. The same article offered, "Los Alamos National Laboratory said it would eliminate 500 to 750 jobs because of anticipated budget cuts and other factors"; *Associated Press*, June 3, 2008, "Layoffs at nuke lab stir fears of a brain drain: Lawmakers fear loss of nation's top nuclear minds will benefit hostile rivals," "Because of budget cuts and higher costs, Lawrence Livermore National Laboratory laid off 440 employees. Over the past 2 1/2 years, attrition and layoffs have reduced the work force of 8,000 by about 1,800 altogether." Steve Maaranen also graphically illustrated that the complex was reduced from 70 million square feet in fiscal year 1990, to 35 million square feet by fiscal year 1997. Maaranen, Steve "Responsive Infrastructure," in James J. Wirtz, and Jeffrey A. Larsen, eds., *Nuclear Transformation: The New U.S. Nuclear Doctrine*, 2005, p. 89.
666   The Strategic Offensive Reductions Treaty levels of 1700-2200, and later the New Strategic Arms Reduction Treaty limit of 1,550, referred to strategically deployed weapons, not total inventories. U.S. Department of Energy, "Size of the U.S. Nuclear Stockpile and Annual Dismantlements," Office of Classification, May 6, 2010.

RESEARCH AND DEVELOPMENT

Near and long-term priorities for technical nuclear forensics research and development were paramount in a segmented technical mission area where multiple actors were interested in similar technologies. Much of the technical nuclear forensics research and development efforts were focused on mobility and time savings in support of rapid attribution. One of the center's initial undertakings -- as the chair of the National Science and Technology Council's Attribution Working Group -- was to assist in the development of a "Nuclear Defense Roadmap for Research and Development."[667] According to the Domestic Nuclear Detection Office director, the function of the Subcommittee on Nuclear Defense Research and Development was "to identify and recommend a prioritized investment strategy to continually increase the overall effectiveness and productivity of U.S. government research and development related to developing a robust nuclear defense capability."[668] By utilizing additional subcommittee working groups for "Nonproliferation, Interdiction, Render Safe, and Response and Recovery," the Nuclear Defense Research and Development Committee sought to integrate U.S. government "research and development needs analysis across the nuclear defense spectrum" through White House led interagency collaboration.[669]

The Attribution Working Group received the general tasks to catalogue current technical nuclear forensics research and development programs, create a prioritization methodology, conduct gap analysis, identify technology shortfalls, develop well-researched options, and to design a path forward that included milestones and assessments for future iterations. The resulting

---

667   This working group was part of the Subcommittee on Nuclear Defense Research and Development, Committee on Homeland Defense and National Security. Oxford, Vayl, "Hearing on H.R. 2631, the Nuclear Forensics and Attribution Act," statement, October 10, 2007.
668   Ibid.
669   Ibid.

"Nuclear Defense Roadmap for Research and Development" was a summary of all the working group input prioritized into three areas: nonproliferation, interdiction, and response and recovery. The Roadmap, completed in 2008, was written as a living, classified document of nuclear defense priorities and proposed programs, with the intention of a threat review every two years, and updates to the base document every five years. The nuclear defense research and development endeavor was chartered six months after the creation of the center and provided additional White House sponsorship for the National Technical Nuclear Forensics Center.[670]

This section highlighted the intricacies and challenges associated with integrating a national task in the absence of authority to control budgets or to supervise execution. It also identified benefits from collaborative planning, elevated research and development prioritization, and collective exercises to eliminate unnecessary redundancies. While support from the White House and Congress did not immediately expand resources beyond requirements, senior level interest facilitated initial interagency organization, and assisted with outreach. From a deterrent standpoint, the increased interest also led to limited publications on technical nuclear forensics.[671] However, these actions were not matched by a coordinated strategic communication campaign by the U.S. government to offset concerns over an unpredictable employment environment at the national laboratories. This section again demonstrated the impact of organizational barriers on collaborative policy execution in a federal government that is

---

670   Taylor, Tammy P., "Nuclear Defense Research and Development: Institute of Electrical and Electronics Engineers Keynote Address," May 12, 2008.

671   Moody, Kenton J., Ian D. Hutcheon, and Patrick M. Grant, *Nuclear Forensic Analysis*, 2005; Wallenius, Maria, et al., "Nuclear forensic investigations with a focus on plutonium," *Journal of Alloys and Compounds*, 2007, pp. 57-62; Heller, Arnie, "Identifying the Source of Stolen Nuclear Materials: Livermore scientists are analyzing interdicted illicit nuclear and radioactive materials for clues to the materials" origins and routes," *Science and Technology Review*, January/February 2007, p. 18.

structured for autonomous departmental implementation.[672] It established that participation in national nuclear forensics was voluntary because independent departments retained control of their programs, corresponding budgets, and execution authorities. Thus, as the Project on National Security Reform suggested, departments participating in national nuclear forensics were expected to "use their resources to support the capabilities they need to carry out their core mandates rather than national missions."[673]

PROGRAM EVALUATION

Of the three policy implementation studies, nuclear forensics is the most difficult area to evaluate. The 2007 formation only provides two years of data, while design complexities established the National Technical Nuclear Forensics Center as neither a production nor procedural organization. James Wilson used the term "coping organization" to describe when neither outputs nor outcomes of key operators can be observed.[674] In this regard, the center could not observe the designated departments and agencies conduct daily operations, nor could it evaluate routine outcomes across the interagency process. The center did present the opportunity to shift to what Wilson referred to as a "craft organization" – when activities are hard to observe, but outcomes are easy to evaluate -- following an incident, but there were no clear examples of collaborative nuclear forensics operations during the period of study.[675]

National nuclear forensics also differs from the two previous implementation studies because it was a non-acquisition-based

---

672   Wilson, James Q., *Bureaucracy: What Government Agencies Do and Why They Do It*, 2nd edition 2000, pp. 192-194.
673   Locher, James R. III, Executive Director, *Forging a New Shield*, Project on National Security Reform, 2008, p. 96.
674   Wilson, James Q., *Bureaucracy: What Government Agencies Do and Why They Do It*, 2nd edition 2000, pp. 168-171.
675   Ibid., pp. 165-168.

mission area. For example, from a resource standpoint the National Technical Forensics Center's annual budget of $15 million in 2008, paled in comparison to the $90.6 million budget of Cooperative Threat Reduction's Strategic Offensive Arms Elimination program and the Second Line of Defense Megaports" budget of $50 million. Moreover, when viewed within the broader context of total program budgets, the funding for federal nuclear forensics activities was estimated at $60 million in 2008, which was only a fraction of the budgets for Cooperative Threat Reduction at $425.9 million, and the Second Line of Defense at $257.6 million.[676] Nevertheless, the program evaluation criteria used for the previous studies do highlight important findings related to the organizational limitations of the U.S. government with regard to funding and operational control. Therefore, this section uses the standardized evaluation criteria from the initial studies related to: pace, interagency efforts, host nation responsibilities, realization of policy objectives, counterarguments, and theoretical applicability. The first criterion reveals differences between the planning and operation functions of national nuclear forensics. This disparity raises the question, what operational benefit is derived from centralized execution? The interagency criterion carries this theme through to identification of separate authorities and resources as the largest barriers to collaborative national nuclear forensics implementation. The host nation examination reinforces the importance of the international community in nuclear defense, but raises alarms over the absence of a comprehensive materials database for rapid attribution.

---

676   The Domestic Nuclear Detection Office budget was more appropriate for directorate comparison, but did not pertain to technical nuclear forensics beyond the National Technical Nuclear Forensics Center. According to the annual Department of Homeland Security *Homeland Security Budget-in-Brief,* Domestic Nuclear Detection Office budgets for fiscal years 2006-2008 were: 2006, $317,392 million (Fiscal Year 2008, p. 99), 2007, $615,968 million (Fiscal Year 2009, p. 111), and 2008, $484,750 million (Fiscal Year 2010, p. 146).

The Department of Homeland Security is used to evaluate the extent to which the National Technical Nuclear Forensics Center's policy objectives were realized, while greater federal activities are included in the remaining criteria. Policy objective evaluation suggests that the degree to which synchronization was realized depends on whether or not execution is included. While national planning benefited from the creation of the center, interagency operations and the second objective related to the pre-detonation material mission area were less successful. Counterarguments concentrate on duplication of effort and deterrence benefit. The degree of deterrence benefit is open for debate, but the impact of the National Technical Nuclear Forensics Center on federal redundancies is observable. While negative redundancies such as multiple sponsors for the same national laboratory projects required active oversight to prevent, other redundancies related to capabilities proved useful.[677] Theoretical applicability serves as the final evaluation criterion. Bureaucratic politics theory related to existing programs shaping policy implementation, maximization of organizational interests, and the impact of a large the number of actors, were all evident in the national nuclear forensics case study.

PACE

The integration of nuclear forensics work at the national level was more successful than similar integrative efforts such as those associated with the creation of the Director of National Intelligence. The reason for this was the size, scope, and pre-existing capabilities that were retained by participating interagency actors. Although disagreements remained, these factors, along with increased national priority and a common mission focus, allowed the center and participating actors to move toward a collaborative approach to technical nuclear forensics. The higher priority resulted in the identification of critical technical

677   Wilson, James Q., *Bureaucracy: What Government Agencies Do and Why They Do It*, 2nd edition 2000, p. 274.

and expertise requirements which were targeted for increased resources, and a methodological approach for developing both short and long-term capabilities.

While the national integrator design displayed positive results with regard to planning, fissures were evident during operations because of the reliance on independent federal organizations. A limited number of incidents, such as the Honduran detection of Cesium-137 in a container of scrap metal headed for a Far East smelting facility in November 2007, demonstrated that organizational interests remained more important to autonomous actors than newly approved national nuclear forensics plans.[678] For incidents such as this, Vayl Oxford, the initial director of the Domestic Nuclear Detection Office, offered that there was, "clear evidence of competition among agencies rather than the cooperation needed to drive the work being carried out to a satisfactory conclusion. Moreover, there are a number of recorded cases in which at least some elements of the forensics community have been cut out of the information flow altogether."[679]

INTERAGENCY INTEGRATION

The National Technical Nuclear Forensics Center adopted a collaborative interagency approach to nuclear defense planning. Instead of relying on the formal policy structure of the National and Homeland Security Councils, the National Technical Nuclear Forensics Center brought operational level interagency synchronization to a technical mission area. From 2007 to 2009, collective federal strides resulted in planning progress, although technical nuclear forensics remained in its infancy as an interagency endeavor. While policy and planning disagreements were kept to a minimum, previous pre-detonation

---

678   Huizenga, David, "National Nuclear Security Administration's Megaports Initiative and Its Role in the Secure Freight Initiative (SFI)," testimony, June 12, 2008.
679   Oxford, Vayl, "Needed: A Comprehensive Nuclear Forensics and Attribution Act," *Domestic Preparedness*, June 30, 2010.

material scenarios were varied; executed without national leadership, organizational incentives, or immediate threat.[680]

Lessons learned from limited real-world events and exercises helped to establish and improve procedures, but complete integration proved difficult to achieve through a national integrator approach because of separate resourcing lines, and distinct organizational cultures and interests across the federal government. For example, organizations such as the Department of Defense stood to lose budget priority if they provided too many departmental resources to an interagency operation without adequate reimbursement and/or recognition. Also, because several supporting actors related to intelligence had secretive operating cultures, incidents that were initially high-profile such as the Honduras detection in 2007, were quickly shifted from the spotlight, with little to no follow-up information for decision makers to act upon.[681]

The biggest factors in preserving a segregated approach were separate authorization and resourcing procedures. Individual department secretaries were responsible for their programs regardless of federal implementation efforts. From a budget standpoint, departments and agencies represented separate authorities that required dedicated program funding. This arrangement did not facilitate a consolidated national nuclear forensics budget, and prevented the National Technical Nuclear Forensics Center from directing policy execution. This lack of budget authority, according to officials from the National Technical Nuclear Forensics Center, meant that "if needed, they would have to

---

680   Ibid.
681   Even in classified, closed door sessions, much of the compartmentalized information was not provided. A problem also existed for congressional members that did not sit on classified committees, and for staffers that did not possess security clearances. This lack of information caused many members to vote based on resident subject matter opinion, or along party lines, with little background in highly technical subjects. Interview with Department of Homeland Security, Domestic Nuclear Detection Office Director Vayl Oxford, September 13, 2010.

"cajole and pressure" other agencies to make changes to certain aspects of their nuclear forensics budgets."[682] Because the mission area was split across multiple departments, and relied heavily on the support of existing infrastructure and manpower, it was impossible to determine the exact amount spent annually by the U.S. government on technical nuclear forensics. This remained a problem even as the center matured because there were no specific sub-categories within larger funding lines that identified the amount of annual budgets being dedicated to technical nuclear forensics.

HOST NATION RESPONSIBILITIES

International partners remained a vital requirement for a mature global nuclear forensics system. International agreements and catalogued materials aided in the linkage of samples to sources, and helped to standardize procedures for pre- and post-detonation events. However, large database gaps generated questions related to how the United States and the international community catalogued sensitive nuclear materials prior to an incident. An unwillingness to share nuclear materials for the creation of a viable international database continued to limit the timely attribution or elimination from inquiries of state actors based on pre-deposited comparative samples. While many countries were reluctant to share materials based on national security considerations, the lack of economic or political incentives for participation did not aid in the advancement of the American effort. Thus, the dearth of international cooperation and a credible catalogue placed significant limitations on U.S. government nuclear forensics programs.[683]

---

682   Government Accountability Office, *Nuclear Forensics: Comprehensive Interagency Plan Needed to Address Human Capital Issues,* April 30, 2009, p. 9.
683   Interview with Department of Homeland Security, Domestic Nuclear Detection Office Director Vayl Oxford, September 13, 2010.

REALIZATION OF POLICY OBJECTIVES

The National Technical Nuclear Forensics Center was originally created by an executive branch push to integrate national
nuclear forensics capabilities in the United States, with a second
objective emerging from initial assessments:

> **[Objective 1]** The National Technical Nuclear Forensics Center is
> to implement national level integration, centralized planning,
> exercising, evaluation, and stewardship across the full spectrum
> of U.S. government nuclear forensics capabilities, from pre- to
> post-detonation—in essence to serve as the "System Integrator"
> for the end-to-end national capabilities.
>
> **[Objective 2]** The National Technical Nuclear Forensics Center is
> intended to serve as the national "capability provider" to de-
> velop and advance capabilities to perform nuclear forensics on
> pre-detonation nuclear and radiological materials.[684]

Before the program could begin it had to be authorized and
resourced. The White House designated the Department of
Homeland Security as the originating organization of the National
Technical Nuclear Forensics Center, and a $13.3 million budget
was reprogramd for its formation in fiscal year 2007.[685] When
the Domestic Nuclear Detection Office approached the Office of
Management and Budget about interagency budgets related to
technical nuclear forensics, it was met with an additional setup
task of conducting a budget crosscut assessment. This interagency accounting exercise revealed different processes and
shared funding which in many cases could only be estimated.[686]
In complicated areas such as the Department of Energy's related
infrastructure and major activities, or the Department of State's

---

684   Oxford, Vayl, "Hearing on H.R. 2631, the Nuclear Forensics and
Attribution Act," statement, October 10, 2007.
685   Department of Homeland Security, Domestic Nuclear Detection
Office, National Technical Nuclear Forensics Center Official [written re-
sponse], October 12, 2010.
686   Interview with Department of Homeland Security, Domestic
Nuclear Detection Office Director Vayl Oxford, September 13, 2010.

outreach funding, approximations were excluded altogether. By the end of the exercise, the center estimated the interagency budgets related to technical nuclear were as follows:

	FY2008	FY2009
Department of Defense	14.8 million	15.5 million
Department of Energy*	22.3 million	18.4 million
Department of Homeland Security	15.0 million	16.9 million
Federal Bureau of Investigation	7.9 million	8.2 million
Total	60.0 million	59.0 million

TABLE 5.1. TECHNICAL NUCLEAR FORENSICS BUDGET CROSSCUT[687]

The Domestic Nuclear Detection Office fell under the budget procedures of the Department of Homeland Security which resembled the processes of the Departments of Defense and Energy described in the previous implementation studies. According to one official, the National Technical Nuclear Forensics Center participated "fully in and reports through the Department of Homeland Security and Domestic Nuclear Detection Office planning, programming, budgeting, and execution cycle and acquisition processes."[688] The long-range planning portion was guided by the Secretary of Homeland Security's Strategic Planning Guidance, and was submitted as the future years program and budget through the Office of Management and

---

687   *"Nuclear-forensics-related capabilities and readiness of facilities funded by Department of Energy's Nuclear Materials Information Program, Defense Programs, and Defense Nuclear Nonproliferation Program," not included in Department of Energy total. Original source, National Technical Nuclear Forensics Center, chart presented by Government Accountability Office, *Nuclear Forensics: Comprehensive Interagency Plan Needed to Address Human Capital Issues,* April 30, 2009, p. 9.
688   Department of Homeland Security, Domestic Nuclear Detection Office, National Technical Nuclear Forensics Center Official [written response], October 12, 2010.

Budget to Congress.[689] Research and development funding in the Domestic Nuclear Detection Office was generally for a three year period with limited no-year funding also available. In 2007 and 2008, minimal funding justification accomplishments listed for the National Technical Nuclear Forensics Center included:

2007
DNDO [Domestic Nuclear Detection Office] established the National Technical Nuclear Forensics Center as a national level interagency centralized planning and integration office for the Nation's nuclear forensic capabilities. In addition, the National Technical Nuclear Forensics Center is the principal capabilities provider for pre-detonation nuclear materials forensics. In fiscal year 2007, DNDO evaluated and developed several new isotopic, chemical, and physical forensic signatures to enhance this capability.[690]

2008
DNDO continued developing a validated set of unique characteristics, known as signatures, to be able to distinguish the origin and history of radioactive materials. DNDO developed tools for formulating rapid and credible technical conclusions which supported attribution assessments in a defensible manner. Additionally, DNDO initiated the "National Nuclear Forensics Expertise Development Program" to begin restoring the critical academic expertise pipeline for the nation. DNDO led a collaborative engagement with Canada on radiological materials forensics research and development.[691]

When the center was created the Department of Homeland Security had previously established policies and procedures for project management and acquisitions that mirrored those

---

689   Department of Homeland Security planning, programming, budgeting, and execution procedures were outlined in Management Directive 1330, dated February 14, 2005, and other resources such as the annual Department of Homeland Security Performance Budget Overview. Department of Homeland Security, "Planning, Programming, Budgeting, and Execution (PPBE)," Department brief, Fiscal Year 2005.
690   Department of Homeland Security, *Homeland Security Budget-in-Brief Fiscal Year 2009*, p. 110.
691   Department of Homeland Security, *Homeland Security Budget-in-Brief Fiscal Year 2010*, p. 145.

described in the previous studies. From a project management perspective, Department of Homeland Security Management Directive 0782 set the acquisition certification requirements for program managers, while Management Directive 1400 outlined the Department of Homeland Security's investment review process.[692] These directives established a federal acquisition foundation that, along with other standard operating procedures, constituted the department's federal acquisition approach to project management.[693] Prior to the formation of the National Technical Nuclear Forensics Center, the *Homeland Security Act of 2002* authorized transactions between the Departments of Homeland Security and Energy to facilitate the use of the national laboratories.[694] The center benefited from existing practices between the Domestic Nuclear Detection Office and the national laboratories, which included identification of differing accounting standards between the National Nuclear Security Administration field offices and the laboratories. These differences -- pertaining mainly to how funds were executed, tracked, and reported -- meant that active program management and multiple requests for financial reporting back to the Department of Homeland

---

692   U.S. Department of Homeland Security, Management Directive 0782, "Acquisition Certification Requirements for Program Manager," May 26, 2004, and Management Directive 1400, "Investment Review Process."
693   While Department of Homeland Security federal acquisition guidelines and systems proved sufficient for small National Technical Nuclear Forensics Center projects, the Government Accountability Office recommended in April 2008 that the department "develop measurable standards consistently linked to well-defined requirements, evaluate acquisition outcomes for major investments, and improve data quality to help identify and assess contracting methods and outcomes." Department of Homeland Security, *Acquisition Planning Requirements*, October 26, 2004, and *Capitol Planning Investment and Control Guide*, December 2005; Government Accountability Office, *Department of Homeland Security: Better Planning and Assessment Needed to Improve Outcomes for Complex Service Acquisitions*, April 2008.
694   *Homeland Security Act of 2002* (H.R. 5005, P.L. 107-296), Title III, Sec. 309.

Security were required of each project manager using national laboratory support.[695]

From a systems integration standpoint (Objective 1), the center served as a national planning body with interagency working groups to coordinate and develop technical nuclear forensics. The Department of Homeland Security approached its first objective by establishing an interagency center within the Domestic Nuclear Detection Office. The center assessed current U.S. government technical nuclear forensics capabilities and budgets, organized initial committees and working groups to eliminate redundant efforts, and streamlined procedures. These groups participated in national level planning that produced a "Strategic Five-Year Plan for Improving the Nuclear Forensics and Attribution Capabilities of the United States."[696]

Although these initial accomplishments were positive, several issues impeded national technical nuclear forensics efforts. The largest barrier was inconsistent adherence to and implementation of newly established procedures for routine incidents. The International Atomic Energy Agency provided a reference manual for global nuclear forensics support, and the center spearheaded the formation of a national technical nuclear forensics plan, but it was the responsibility of the participating agencies to follow these procedures. In this decentralized landscape, authors such as James Wilson have offered that "no agency head is willing to subordinate his or her organization to a procedure that allows other agencies to define its tasks or allocate its resources."[697] Thus, the director of the Domestic Nuclear Detection Office concluded:

---

695   Interview with Department of Homeland Security, Domestic Nuclear Detection Office Director Vayl Oxford, September 13, 2010.
696   Lute, Jane Holl, "Nuclear Terrorism: Strengthening Our Domestic Defenses, Part II," testimony, September 15, 2010.
697   Wilson, James Q., *Bureaucracy: What Government Agencies Do and Why They Do It*, 2nd edition 2000, p. 269.

To date, in the cases of interdiction of smuggled nuclear material, the report card is mixed – at best. In some cases, there has been a reasonable degree of cooperation with international partners, but the outcome has not always been definitive, particularly regarding the actual source of the material. In other cases, there has been less cooperation, leaving the intelligence community with more questions than answers. Moreover, the sense of urgency associated with many but not all of these cases has often been assessed as lacking in vigor – because at least some of those involved seem to believe that such smuggling cases do not pose an immediate terrorist threat.[698]

In regard to pre-detonation capabilities (Objective 2), the National Technical Nuclear Forensics Center conducted an assessment of manpower, technology, and database requirements, and developed the "Nuclear Defense Research and Development Roadmap." Beyond these labors, federal government participation in scientific recruitment and training, and database development, were hampered by separate organizational interests. In the absence of more effective communication -- both internally and externally -- the U.S. government faced challenges in attracting sufficient high-quality manpower and maintaining dual-use infrastructure. These problems were compounded by over-classification, compartmentalization, and bureaucratic competition for reduced resources. These impediments hampered collaborative endeavors and clear strategic communication to convince potential candidates and policymakers of the continued need to support the nuclear weapons complex.[699] According to the Executive Office of the President, Office of Science and Technology Policy:

---

698   Oxford, Vayl, "Needed: A Comprehensive Nuclear Forensics and Attribution Act," *Domestic Preparedness*, June 30, 2010.
699   Reference to the national laboratories and the nuclear weapons complex was used interchangeably. Recognizing continued association with nuclear weapons was detrimental to effective communication, the Nevada Test Site was renamed the Nevada National Security Site in August 2010. U.S. Department of Energy, "Fact Sheet: Nevada National Security Site," National Nuclear Security Administration, August 23, 2010.

...the NDRD [Nuclear Defense Research and Development] Subcommittee identified two needs common to all NDRD mission areas that are required to effectively conduct nuclear defense research and development: 1) the necessary human expertise and skill base and 2) the accompanying physical infrastructure. Both must be developed, maintained, and continually renewed. A stable workforce is essential, and programs that support the education of nuclear defense disciplines are required to replenish the workforce. The success of the Roadmap recommendations is equally dependent on adequate physical infrastructure to conduct research and development activities. It is necessary to generate a clear, concise, and consistent definition of what physical infrastructure is required for nuclear defense research and development and then support the sustenance or new construction of this infrastructure. The human expertise and physical infrastructure requirements are needs that cannot be resolved in a short time period. They require long-term planning and sustained support.[700]

Finally, the maturation of technical nuclear forensics to enable rapid attribution required international cooperation and standards. Beyond the inherent science of nuclear forensics, a viable international nuclear materials database was necessary to expedite attribution, and to reinforce global confidence in the accuracy of technical nuclear forensics results. For years, experts such as Michael May, Jay Davis, and Raymond Jeanloz argued for the creation of an international database.[701] Their recommendations centered on an international approach in conjunction with the Nonproliferation Treaty or through a United Nations Security Council Resolution, but neither proposal was adopted by the U.S. government.[702] The Department of State facilitated technical nuclear forensics training that highlighted issues unique to the international environment such as differing standards, extreme distances, and language difficulties.

---

700   Taylor, Tammy P., "Nuclear Defense Research and Development: Institute of Electrical and Electronics Engineers Keynote Address," May 12, 2008.
701   May, Michael, Jay Davis, and Raymond Jeanloz, "Preparing for the Worst," *Nature,* October 26, 2006, pp. 907-908.
702   Ibid.

However, as of 2009, the U.S. government did not participate in a full-scale international training exercise to test all aspects of nuclear forensics preparations and integration.

COUNTERARGUMENTS

Unnecessary duplication of effort was a concern in the context of national nuclear forensics. One of the primary functions of the center was to integrate the U.S. government approach to technical nuclear forensics. From the outset the center sought to limit duplication of effort, to standardize U.S. government procedures, and to influence international technical nuclear forensics efforts. Unlike the other acquisition-based policy implementation studies, the center was the national systems integrator charged with technical nuclear forensics interagency planning and implementation. However, because of segregated federal organization and resourcing, there were still unwanted redundancies at the national level. For example, because the laboratories were contracted through decentralized Department of Energy field offices, they routinely solicited business proposals to multiple department sponsors. This meant there was still the possibility that several departments would fund the same or similar proposals without realizing it. Clearer interagency communication facilitated by the National Technical Nuclear Forensics Center began to limit this practice, but without a central approval authority for nuclear forensics it remained a function of interagency coordination to prevent unwarranted duplication of effort.[703]

Manpower competition between related scientific fields outside of nuclear forensics and the national laboratories remained an impediment to progress. Other U.S. government entities, such as the Nuclear Regulatory Commission, had competing outreach plans equal to the entire National Technical Nuclear Forensics Center's annual budget. A diverse U.S. government

---

703   Downs, Anthony, *Inside Bureaucracy*, 1967, pp. 54-56.

strategic message, hampered by self-induced classification requirements, impacted negatively on the ability of the center to tell the positive story of the evolving field of nuclear forensics. While scientists published limited articles and texts such as *Nuclear Forensic Analysis* by Ken Moody, Ian Hutcheon, and Pat Grant of Lawrence Livermore National Laboratory, the wider technical nuclear forensics community was silent.[704] The literature that was available -- written mainly by reporters, non-governmental experts, and government investigators such as the Government Accountability Office -- carried a generally negative tone on manning, databases, and the lack of interagency cohesion. For example, numerous reports and articles were available on the scientific "brain drain" that must be arrested in order for technical nuclear forensics to advance.[705] For a young person trying to identify a field of graduate research leading to a future career, this message did not sound very appealing.

An area where duplication of effort was required involved dispersed technical capabilities, including those of international partners. In order to have accepted technical nuclear forensics results it was necessary to have dual-analysis with additional verification. At a minimum this meant that four laboratories needed to have redundant capabilities, and for more responsive operations, multiple laboratories and mobile techniques were required. Likewise, independent international technical analysis was desirable in an area where political debate overshadowed scientific findings. It was imperative to have verifiable forensic evidence as political leaders justified retaliation proposals,

---

704   Moody, Kenton J., Ian D. Hutcheon, and Patrick M. Grant, *Nuclear Forensic Analysis*, 2005.
705   Cerny, Joseph, et al., *Education in Nuclear Science: A Status Report and Recommendations for the Beginning of the 21ˢᵗ Century,* Department of Energy/National Science Foundation Nuclear Science Advisory Committee, Subcommittee on Education, November 2004; *Associated Press*, "Layoffs at nuke lab stir fears of a brain drain: Lawmakers fear loss of nation's top nuclear minds will benefit hostile rivals," June 3, 2008.

particularly in the case of a post-detonation event where tensions would be high, and timelines perceived to be short.

Experts such as Matthew Phillips questioned the deterrence benefits of attribution-facilitated threats of retaliation, given the developing state of technical nuclear forensics, and the enormous challenges associated with a post-detonation event.[706] The complexities of all areas of nuclear forensics could not be understated, but the levels of confidence related to retaliation and legal action were distinctly different. Nuclear forensics information may or may not have justified a legal argument, but post-event response policies and potential retaliation operations arguably do not require the same criteria for admissibility as a court of law.[707]

THEORETICAL APPLICABILITY

Three relevant areas of bureaucratic politics theory related to national technical nuclear forensics actions were as follows: 1) action associated with major policy departures is determined by existing programs and standard operating procedures; 2) the bureaucracy maximizes organizational interests; and 3) the larger the number of actors the less implementation reflects policy decisions.[708] Although the White House directed that the center be formed to integrate national technical nuclear forensics, existing programs dictated interagency organization and continued independent execution. This arrangement allowed organizations to maximize internal departmental interests and benefit from increased national priority, without being held accountable

---

706   Phillips, Matthew, "Uncertain Justice for Nuclear Terror: Deterrence of Anonymous Attacks Through Attribution," *Orbis*, Summer 2007, pp. 429-446.
707   Leggitt, J., K. Inn, S. Goldberg, R. Essex, S. LaMont, and S. Chase, "Nuclear forensics-metrological basis for legal defensibility," *Journal of Radioanalytical and Nuclear Chemistry*, 2009, pp. 997-1001.
708   Allison, Graham T., and Morton H. Halperin, "Bureaucratic Politics: A Paradigm and Some Policy Implications," *World Politics*, Vol. 24, Spring 1972, pp. 54-56.

for collaborative execution. This result could have been antic-ipated based on the number of actors from major organizations involved who were able to use departmental authorities to stave off collaborative implementation agreements and requirements.

This evaluation of the National Technical Nuclear Forensics Center identified several important points. The utilization of a national integrator certainly benefited planning, and research and development visibility for technical nuclear forensics. With the implementation level forums and central planning direction, the integration of national nuclear forensics improved in the two short years of this study's focus. A reverse planning approach that identified rapid attribution as the primary objective assisted with the coordination and synchronization of separate scientif-ic programs. The resulting standardized response techniques, timelines, and reporting all assisted information dissemination and scientific credibility. However, continued bureaucratic competition stunted progress in terms of collaborative execu-tion.[709] Autonomous departments voluntarily supported the center's planning mission but refused to follow these national plans during limited operations. The chapter also identified the high degree of dependence on international actors which prevented completion of a pre-existing materials and design database. Without such a database to conduct materials match-ing, the U.S. government remained reliant on limited existing samples, and the desire of states of interest to clear their name following a significant incident.

CONCLUSION

The implementation case study research question asked, "How has the U.S. government implemented post-Cold War nuclear defense policy, and to what extent have corresponding objectives been realized?" The hypothesis offered was that,

---

709   Wilson, James Q., *Bureaucracy: What Government Agencies Do and Why They Do It*, 2nd edition 2000, pp. 192-194.

"The U.S. government was not organized to address nuclear defense, and as a result did not collaboratively implement evolving national policies." While the segregated, multi-departmental approach to nuclear defense remained consistent in this area, the use of a national integrator design was an attempt to shift to a whole-of-government emphasis.[710] Unlike the previous studies where White House policy staffs and coordination forums were leveraged, the National Technical Nuclear Forensics Center concept added a standing implementation body to coordinate and develop federal plans and priorities. However, limitations imposed by autonomous U.S. government design remained a barrier to progress. Organizational interests were accorded a higher internal priority than national implementation in all instances, and this phenomenon was readily apparent during execution.

Pre-existing capabilities related to technical nuclear forensics proved to be a valuable resource during the formation of the National Technical Nuclear Forensics Center, but they constrained possible departures from existing programs.[711] Existing decentralized programs and funding meant that the center was founded for only $13.3 million in fiscal year 2007, and a design that allowed departmental actors to retain control of their programs with elevated national priority facilitated initial progress.[712] Inclusion of interagency actors in the center at every level, while not always smooth, allowed it to organize technical nuclear forensics planning efforts and to develop out-year requirements. The collaborative committee and working group approach helped to minimize unnecessary redundancies, advance technical capabilities, and improve organizational memory.[713]

---

710   For more on these centralization efforts see Joseph R. Cerami, and Jeffrey A. Engel, eds., *Rethinking Leadership and "Whole-of-Government" National Security Reform: Problems, Progress, and Prospects*, May 2010.
711   Allison, Graham T., and Morton H. Halperin, "Bureaucratic Politics: A Paradigm and Some Policy Implications," *World Politics,* Vol. 24, Spring 1972, p. 54.
712   Downs, Anthony, *Inside Bureaucracy*, 1967, pp. 212-218.
713   Ibid., p. 18.

Unfortunately, several barriers existed which limited the maturation of national nuclear forensics efforts. The progress of national and international database expansion did not keep pace with the evolving scientific discipline of nuclear forensics. In 2008, the American Physical Society and the American Association for the Advancement of Science found that, "At present, international databases are not nearly extensive or usable enough to fulfill the potential utility of nuclear forensics."[714] The integrator design also lacked centralized command and control of incidents, and relied on dual-use personnel and infrastructure outside the direction of the National Technical Nuclear Forensics Center. The committee and working group structure improved routine coordination, collective planning, and research and development priorities, but real-world incidents were characterized by individual departmental responses to interagency scenarios that now had operational guidance associated with them. Thus, by 2010, the National Academy of Sciences described the state of national technical nuclear forensic as:

> DHS [Department of Homeland Security] and the other cooperating agencies have not yet devised or institutionalized a program that is optimized with respect to readiness, operational effectiveness, sustainment, and improvement. There is extensive and effective information sharing among several of the parties that constitute the National Technical Nuclear Forensics Center. Part of this success results from the sense of common purpose shared by the principals involved, and some arises from the short-term exchanges and extensive use of detailees among agencies. However, DHS does not direct resources or actions in program elements outside of the pre-detonation nuclear materials mission area, and agencies are more likely to optimize within their mission areas than across the mission areas. With this structure, it is difficult to form a coherent program with

---

714   May, Michael, Chair, *Nuclear Forensics: Role, State of the Art, Program Needs*, Joint Working Group of the American Physical Society and the American Association for the Advancement of Science Report, 2008, p. 27.

a single set of common goals and funds aligned appropriately and consistently to meet those goals.[715]

In sum, the three policy implementation studies demonstrated a patchwork landscape of U.S. government nuclear defense programs that aligned themselves with the uncoordinated policies on which they were based. Each of these programs represented the evolution of nuclear defense away from nuclear weapons toward combined security efforts to prevent, protect, and respond to a nuclear attack. Together they depicted three layers of the U.S. government's nuclear defense-in-depth strategy articulated by the end of the George W. Bush administration.[716] While the programs complied with the intent of a layered approach they did so in a segregated manner with multiple autonomous efforts pursued within and among various departments. This loose confederation of programs participated in senior level policy coordination, but did not demonstrate a collaborative approach to any of the nuclear defense tasks presented in the implementation studies.

---

715   Carnesale, Albert, Chair, *Nuclear Forensics: A Capability at Risk (Abbreviated Version)*, National Academy of Sciences, Committee on Nuclear Forensics report, 2010, p. 5.
716   *National Military Strategy to Combat Weapons of Mass Destruction*, 2006, p. 4; U.S. Department of State, "Defense-in-Depth," retrieved January 22, 2012.

CHAPTER 6

CONCLUSIONS

This book set out to examine how United States nuclear defense policy evolved during the post-Cold War period. It was divided into two parts with the first examining policy formulation and the second policy implementation. The first portion of the book analyzed two nuclear defense areas related to prevention and protection to evaluate the policy formulation process in the United States. These strategic arms reduction and national missile defense case studies were largely remnants of the Cold War. Multiple stakeholders that participated in a decentralized policy development process influenced policy in both areas. The continuation of strategic arms reduction and missile defense debates beyond initial decisions demonstrated the complexities of policy formulation in the United States and confirmed the dominance of stakeholder and actor variables in a decentralized development process.

The second portion of the book examined policy implementation in three areas: threat reduction, maritime radiation detection, and nuclear forensics. These implementation studies covered the prevention, protection, and response strands of American nuclear defense policy, respectively. It was demonstrated that the bureaucratic organizations involved in implementing policy in these areas worked through differences and reached further compromises, ultimately establishing programs in accordance with organizational interests and standard operating procedures. The case studies examined issues that characterized the reorientation of nuclear defense efforts toward proliferation following the Cold War. They represented the post-Cold War approach of layered nuclear defense-in-depth and demonstrated that, despite efforts by post-Cold War administrations to shift to a whole-of-government approach, systemic barriers prevented collaborative policy execution.[717]

POLICY DEVELOPMENT

Chapters 1 and 2 set out to examine "how and why U.S. nuclear defense policy evolved following the Cold War." This was a complex topic nested in broader national security issues. Policy decisions, which equated to "how" U.S. nuclear defense policy evolved, represented compromised outcomes with sufficient ambiguity to facilitate the continuation of opposing positions. For strategic arms control, the treaty process established reductions in Cold War excesses that continued through each administration, while deployment of national missile defense was declared the policy of the United States as soon as technologically possible. Although the decisions may have appeared "rational" at first glance, an examination of policy development in each area identified systemic variables that facilitated the continuation of arguments.

The examination of strategic arms reduction and national missile defense efforts during the George H. W. Bush and William J. Clinton administrations reinforced the view that multiple stakeholders influenced national policy development. These stakeholders – the president, Congress, and the bureaucracy -- each exercised significant influence on policy development to the point that no single actor dominated the process. Instead, stakeholders were forced to form coalitions to participate in a continual discussion that allowed dissatisfied actors to carry on arguments through different mechanisms. These differing

717   *National Military Strategy to Combat Weapons of Mass Destruction,* 2006, p. 4; U.S. Department of State, "Defense-in-Depth," retrieved January 22, 2012.

action channels facilitated the formulation of alternate policies to benefit numerous personal and organizational interests. This conclusion suggests there was not a unitary policy outcome at the end of the development process.

The explanation of "why" nuclear defense policy evolved as it did following the Cold War highlighted the relevance of bureaucratic politics theory to understanding the process of formulating nuclear defense policy. Changes in administrations, stakeholder disagreement, the continuation of norms related to maximum nuclear deterrence, external actor input from contracting firms, and an apathetic public, all contributed to the complexity of policy development. In the case of strategic arms reduction, the first and second treaties represented different approaches and circumstances. The first Strategic Arms Reduction Treaty was a continuation of Reagan-era negotiations. Despite the declared intent of the George H. W. Bush administration to develop a coherent approach to arms control policy and nuclear strategy during a period of strategic paradigm change, the normal interagency process within the executive branch resulted in recommendations remarkably similar to the previous administration. This situation was bolstered by the legislative branch, which had consistently increased its involvement in strategic arms negotiations over the previous decade. Although the strategic circumstances and the administration had changed, bureaucratic and legislative actors remained in place from the earlier period. These enduring stakeholders employed constitutional and statutory rules to ensure continuity in the American approach to strategic arms reduction.

This process was briefly modified for the second Strategic Arms Reduction Treaty that began with President Bush's unilateral nuclear initiatives. These initiatives, and the subsequent abbreviated negotiations for the second Strategic Arms Reduction Treaty, demonstrated the power of the presidency. In this case, a reduced number of advisors, with very specific guidance and pressure from the president, developed an arms control approach outside of existing interagency process. However, this abbreviated procedure was short-lived because the bureaucracy and legislature again asserted their positions following the initial announcement of the presidential nuclear initiatives. The bureaucracy ensured that large reserves of nuclear weapons were not included in treaty totals and attempted to delay negotiations until the president-elect stated his support for treaty signature prior to inauguration.[718] Portions of the bureaucracy that were not satisfied with this outcome continued to advocate pro-nuclear weapon positions well into the future.

While the president did not have the final word on nuclear weapon levels, this example supports Morton Halperin's argument that, "the president is qualitatively different – not simply a very powerful player among powerful players."[719] Neither the legislature nor the bureaucracy could have unilaterally mandated reductions comparable to those pushed by the White House. Congress would have had to follow prescribed rules by submitting a bill for consideration through the committee and full chamber process, reconciling Senate and House versions, and ultimately requesting the president's signature. Although the bureaucracy was able to establish lower-level policies within the confines of existing national policies, regulations, and procedures, it did not exercise this ability on high-profile national policy issues.

In contrast to strategic arms negotiations, national missile defense represented the alternate policymaking authority of Congress. Powers under existing rules ranged from redirection of administration policies through amendments and funding authorities, to the establishment of an alternative policy approach. During the Bush administration and the initial portion of the Clinton administration, Congress lacked consensus on the

718   Talbott, Strobe, *The Russia Hand: A Memoir of Presidential Diplomacy*, 2003, p. 34.
719   Halperin, Morton H., "The Decision to Deploy the ABM: Bureaucratic and Domestic Politics in the Johnson Administration," *World Politics*, Vol. 25, October 1972, pp. 90-91.

direction of missile defense. But even in this environment, key legislative actors were able to influence national missile defense policy by denying or adding funding, and proposing counter legislation. These mechanisms ensured the president understood that Congress was a full stakeholder in missile defense policy. Advocates of national missile defense in Congress were able to outlast both administrations and eventually leveraged opposition weakness, and newly perceived threats, to advance their positions. Once Congress was able to reach a consensus on alternate national missile defense policy it was able to forward veto-proof legislation to the president for signature.

Missile defense highlighted the influence of external actors in the policy development process. In this case defense contractors and advocates of national missile defense had unrestricted access to the president, Congress, and the bureaucracy. Active external actors held deep-seated beliefs or significant financial interests, while the public was not engaged in the topic. Congressional and Defense Department actors stood to benefit from sustained and increased funding as contracting firms represented multiple constituencies and a large portion of the national missile defense workforce. These actors were able to outlast resistant administrations and Congressional majorities until pro-national missile defense actors held key positions and timing facilitated the passage of alternative congressional policy.

In the case of both strategic arms control and missile defense, path dependence marginalized incremental responses to the shifting nuclear landscape. Despite the absence of the Cold War Soviet threat, actors were not prepared to alter traditional nuclear defense positions. For example, the Department of Defense represented the portion of the bureaucracy with the most supporting infrastructure and potential for tangible loss in terms of personnel, weapons, and other equipment. However, the Department of State also represented this line of reasoning. While it did not stand to lose large numbers of personnel or equipment, the arms control community understood one standard approach to nuclear weapon issues and negotiations with the Soviet Union. State's position had evolved over several decades and represented departmental influence and the essence of the arms control community. The resulting rigidity based on constraints and existing capabilities saw bureaucratic actors continuing to recommend Cold War approaches despite the absence of the Soviet Union.

Based on these research findings the first hypothesis -- "U.S. nuclear defense policy formulation during the post-Cold War administrations of George H. W. Bush and William J. Clinton was anchored in bureaucratic politics, not collective defense" -- was confirmed. The policy development case studies suggest that the formulation of post-Cold War nuclear defense policy was driven primarily by bureaucratic politics rather than national defense needs. While current and emerging threats were taken into account in the development process, policy recommendations and solutions primarily represented existing stakeholder positions and capabilities. Policy decisions emerged incrementally and were not part of a single, calculated national approach. Instead, decisions were the result of compromises designed to accommodate stakeholder positions, rather than a unitary outcome of the national nuclear defense policy development process. As a result, stakeholders dissatisfied with the policy outcomes continued to argue for their positions long after decisions had been made.

POLICY IMPLEMENTATION

Policies that emerged haphazardly due to compromises between stakeholders still had to be implemented once the dust settled. The second set of case studies considered whether the bureaucracy faithfully implemented policy decisions in a collaborative manner, or whether implementation constituted a continuation of the aggregation and compromise that characterized policy formulation? Bureaucratic politics theory suggests that policy decisions are not faithfully implemented, and that resulting efforts rarely reflect the policymaker's original intent.[720] Graham Allison and Morton Halperin have argued that in instances where orders are clear, and senior officials remained involved, there is a good chance that decisions are carried out.[721] In an environment characterized by limited time, tenure, and decentralized authority, however, this is seldom the case. Instead, vague policy decisions, numerous bureaucratic actors, competing interests, standard operating procedures, and a lack of national oversight suggest that policy arguments are carried through into execution by the implementing organizations. Indeed, the policy implementation studies examined in this book demonstrate that organizational interests gained precedence over collaborative federal execution. Instead of approaching nuclear defense from a unitary standpoint, research showed that multiple policies, the absence of national oversight, and the segregated structure of the U.S. government, all contributed to autonomous department policy implementation during the period of study.

The Cooperative Threat Reduction, Second Line of Defense, and National Technical Nuclear Forensics Center studies clearly demonstrated a segmented U.S. government approach to nuclear defense policy implementation. This independent federal design -- where authorities and resources were given directly to department secretaries -- did not match broader political priorities related to combined execution. While each of the programs supported the post-Cold War approach of layered nuclear defense strategy, it was evident that gaps, redundancies, and impeded performance were significant problems. While the measurable benefit of Cooperative Threat Reduction efforts stood out, the capabilities associated with the Megaports Initiative and the National Technical Nuclear Forensics Center, although

---

720   Allison, Graham T., and Morton H. Halperin, "Bureaucratic Politics: A Paradigm and Some Policy Implications," *World Politics,* Vol. 24, Spring 1972, pp. 53-54.
721   Ibid.

harder to quantify, had important but underdeveloped roles in the American nuclear defense architecture. The implementation studies represented standard federal government approaches to implementation: interagency, lead agency, and national integrator. In the first interagency approach departments conducted independent execution with minimal White House led coordination. In the second approach a specific agency was designated the mission area lead, while additional departments coordinated supporting efforts through the selected organization. The final approach delegated interagency coordination from the White House to a specific department. This arrangement was meant to facilitate integrated federal implementation from equally participating members. For each arrangement departments used available interagency coordination systems and leveraged general capabilities such as State Department diplomatic missions or the national laboratories science and technical infrastructure.

In all three studies the final nuclear defense function was executed by contractors or host nation partners, and not by federal officials fulfilling a direct policy implementation role.[722] There was a close interrelationship between Department of Defense and Department of Energy programs that highlighted foreign, acquisition-based project management. The Department of Homeland Security study differed slightly, but national laboratory contractors were still the principal domestic work force for technical nuclear forensic analysis. The first two studies were concerned with department programs while the third met with frustration at the lack of authority accompanying the task of federal systems integration.

While the implementation studies highlighted numerous aspects of bureaucratic politics theory, three areas were particularly pronounced in each. First, action associated with major policy departures was determined by existing programs and standard operating procedures. Second, the larger the number

---

722   Reference to contractors includes the national laboratories.

of actors, the less implementation reflected policy decisions. Third, the bureaucracy sought to maximize organizational interests.[723] Moreover, national policy decisions in each area were vague and this allowed implementing organizations to follow internal operating procedures as they designed programs to highlight departmental strengths. Each department was adept at maintaining a minimum degree of interagency communication, but this existing process was narrowly focused at the senior policy coordination-level.[724]

In the case of Cooperative Threat Reduction, it was demonstrated that even if an implementing organization -- the Department of Defense -- wanted to move into a new policy area, it found itself confined to existing roles, missions, and associated capabilities. In this example, the Defense Department required expertise and capabilities specific to the Departments of Energy and State in order to conduct threat reduction operations. In order to accomplish the threat reduction mission as a single department, the national security capabilities of the Departments of Energy and State would have needed to shift back to the Defense Department. However, this central course of action would have met considerable resistance from the legislative branch and departmental actors unwilling to cede roles and responsibilities directly related to their organizational raison d'etre.

The initial lead agency effort proved cumbersome and provided a centralized target for opposition actors. The answer for many of the impediments to early threat reduction was to separate the program from lead agency to independent departmental execution. The resulting interagency design used a decentralized format to disperse budgets and authorities, and provided motivation for independent departments to improve execution

---

723   Allison, Graham T., and Morton H. Halperin, "Bureaucratic Politics: A Paradigm and Some Policy Implications," *World Politics*, Vol. 24, Spring 1972, pp. 54-56.
724   Deutch, John M., "Combating Proliferation of Weapons of Mass Destruction," Commission Report, July 14, 1999, pp. 5-6.

to ensure smaller program survival. The decentralized budget enlisted diverse support from habitual department committees, and in turn shielded the smaller programs from congressional funding adjustments.

It is apparent from the research that the fulfillment of policy decisions was not the primary concern of the implementing organizations and, when two or more actors were involved, policy execution only remotely reflected the original policymaker's intent. The Megaports Initiative was one example of the 72 programs that the Domestic Nuclear Defense Office discovered to be involved in nuclear detection during its initial analysis of existing federal efforts. These programs were scattered throughout the U.S. government, often in support of different mission areas such as maritime security. Assigned policy objectives repeatedly included statutory authorities for different secretaries and administrators that prevented central direction from a lead agency. In the case of the Department of Homeland Security, the secretary was charged with the Global Nuclear Detection Architecture and 100% screening and scanning of maritime cargo containers under the *Security and Accountability for Every (SAFE) Port Act of 2006*. These responsibilities rested with different intra-departmental entities that lacked the authority to direct interagency actors outside of the department. The result was that separate programs such as the Megaports Initiative were able to execute independent efforts designed to benefit their parent department.

The threat reduction and nuclear detection studies demonstrated that bureaucratic actors placed organizational interests over collaborative execution. This finding was also highlighted by the examination of national nuclear forensics efforts. Increased priority that benefited existing programs served as an incentive for departments to participate in planning, and research and development, but there were no comparable incentives for collaborative operations. In this last area, departments risked being associated with unsuccessful operations, and the possibility of not receiving credit for participating in successful interagency efforts. Either way, no inducement existed to follow National Technical Nuclear Forensics Center led plans that did not include operational authorities for the designated integrator or a lead agency.

Based on research, the second hypothesis -- "The U.S. government was not organized to address nuclear defense, and as a result did not collaboratively implement evolving national policies" -- was also confirmed. The implementation studies examined three different departments but highlighted multiple similarities. Moreover, while interagency coordination was evident, collaborative design and policy execution was absent. Each study demonstrated different operational arrangements. Cooperative Threat Reduction began as a lead depart program and then shifted to interagency execution along existing lines of responsibility. While departments maintained communication they did not approach threat reduction planning and implementation from a national or unified perspective. The Megaports Initiative displayed a supporting department design that highlighted the importance for lead agencies to maintain situational awareness. The initiative demonstrated that when lead agencies do not have planning input or operational control, the focus is on self-preservation instead of collective objective accomplishment. The National Technical Nuclear Forensics Center case demonstrated the limits of a national integrator design that lacked a budget and was characterized by the operational control of supporting actors.

The analogy of "Swiss cheese," with the holes representing gaps, was used by the former Deputy Homeland Security Advisor to the President to describe the current state of U.S. government nuclear defenses that lack central national direction.[725] This assessment was supported by the Weapons of Mass Destruction Commission which found that, "Members of Congress and

---

725   Interview with Deputy Homeland Security Advisor to the President Kenneth Rapuano, November 8, 2010.

experts inside and outside of government have noted that no single person is in charge of and accountable for preventing weapons of mass destruction proliferation and terrorism, with insight into all the committees and interagency working groups focused on these issues."[726] The implementation studies supported the assertion that nuclear defense did not have a single point of federal direction, and was instead a loose confederation of individual departmental programs. Simply put, despite the priority accorded to nuclear defense, no single national staff, department, or office was charged with defending the United States from nuclear attack.

FINDINGS

The key findings suggest why the Deutch Commission Report's description of American counterproliferation efforts was accurate.

> There is no proliferation-related architecture -- an end-to-end plan for policy development, program planning, and budget formulation -- nor does any person or staff have the power or responsibility to develop one... Neither the President, Congress, nor any executive branch official knows how much the various agencies have spent on these efforts or how much they plan to spend in the future... Without an explicit financial plan tied to programmatic objectives, individual agencies and the corresponding sub-committees [of which there were 23 sub-committees related to proliferation in 1999] on Capitol Hill made their program and resource decisions independently of any overall plan or objective. The result was not only inefficiency and duplication but also potentially catastrophic delay.[727]

They also illustrate why -- despite the repeated identification of segregated organizational impediments since the

---

726   Graham, Bob, Jim Talent, et al., *World at Risk: The Report of the Commission on the Prevention of Weapons of Mass Destruction Proliferation and Terrorism*, 2008, p. 82.
727   Deutch, John M., "Combating Proliferation of Weapons of Mass Destruction," Commission Report, July 14, 1999, p. 9.

report was published -- the U.S. government has continued to resist collaborative nuclear defense policy development and implementation.[728]

The book demonstrated that competition for control of the national government ensured a haphazard approach to nuclear defense with a segregated federal bureaucracy impeding collaborative policy development and implementation.[729] Ultimately, personal and organizational interests were of greater concern to stakeholders and actors than the pursuit of integrated nuclear defense policy. These findings were consistent with bureaucratic politics theory and suggest there was no effective method to ensure collaborative federal execution under existing U.S. government rules and structure.[730]

Competition between the executive and legislative branches provided an opportunity for the bureaucracy to influence national policy.[731] While the president and Congress are depicted as major stakeholders in bureaucratic politics theory, the research for this book suggests the actual power wielded by the bureaucracy is underestimated.[732] The majority of the literature on nuclear defense policy has previously focused on the policy development

---

728   Kean, Thomas H., and Lee H. Hamilton, Chairs, *9/11 Commission Report: Final Report of the National Commission on Terrorist Attacks Upon the United States*, 2004, pp. 399-428; Murdock, Clark A., and Michele A. Flournoy, "Beyond Goldwater-Nichols: U.S. Government and Defense Reform for a New Strategic Era (Phase II)," Center for Strategic and International Studies Report, July 28, 2005, pp. 26-54.
729   Wilson, James Q., *Bureaucracy: What Government Agencies Do and Why They Do It*, 2nd edition 2000, p. 257.
730   Graham, Bob, Jim Talent, et al., *World at Risk: The Report of the Commission on the Prevention of Weapons of Mass Destruction Proliferation and Terrorism*, 2008, pp. 82-98.
731   Hammond, Thomas H., and Jack H. Knott, "Who Controls the Bureaucracy?: Presidential Power, Congressional Dominance, Legal Constraints, and Bureaucratic Autonomy in a Model of Multi-Institutional Policy-Making," *The Journal of Law, Economics, and Organization*, Vol. 12, No. 1, 1996, pp. 119-126.
732   Halperin, Morton H., and Priscilla A. Clapp, *Bureaucratic Politics and Foreign Policy*, 2nd edition 2006, pp. 16-19.

process. When formulation and implementation are examined together, however, the bureaucracy emerged as a major stakeholder because of expert continuity, operational autonomy, and the flexibility permitted by vague policy decisions.[733] The president and Congress allowed this elevation of the bureaucracy to occur because neither stakeholder was prepared to cede limited control granted to them under existing rules and procedures.[734]

The divided federal bureaucracy mirrored constitutional philosophies on the separation of powers. Each department and agency represented independent agendas in a structure where various bureaucratic actors used different authorities and channels to advance their organizational interests. The implementation studies examined similar programs spread across multiple departments for threat reduction, maritime radiation detection, and nuclear forensics. In each case, threat concerns and senior stakeholder priorities spawned similar, independent programs across the federal government. In the case of nuclear forensics, once ad hoc inefficiencies were identified, departments resisted national coordination efforts based on existing authorities and multiple action channels. Continued independent actions were facilitated by a federal design that lacked the ability to centrally direct or execute the segregated bureaucracy.[735]

Finally, no shared vision existed across the U.S. government for the direction of nuclear defense. Instead, each perceived threat

---

733   This finding went beyond the bureaucratic politics description of senior players, which included heads of major national security organizations. Subordinate bureaucratic officials from each of the implementation studies demonstrated the ability of junior actors to shape policy development and implementation in their areas. Allison, Graham T., and Morton H. Halperin, "Bureaucratic Politics: A Paradigm and Some Policy Implications," *World Politics,* Vol. 24, Spring 1972, p. 47; Nicholson-Crotty, Jill, and Susan M. Miller, "Bureaucratic Effectiveness and Influence in the Legislature," *Journal of Public Administration and Research Theory*, August 22, 2011, pp. 1-21, retrieved December 10, 2011.
734   Wilson, James Q., *Bureaucracy: What Government Agencies Do and Why They Do It*, 2nd edition 2000, pp. 274-276.
735   Ibid., pp. 268-274.

or issue was addressed as a separate matter. Each stakeholder initiated reactive policies using various channels permitted by existing rules. For example, the president and Congress had the authority to originate national policies while the bureaucracy could use either executive or legislative channels to advance separate actor positions. Once policy decisions progressed into implementation, separate bureaucratic actors had the autonomy to further organizational interests through supporting programs.

The principal considerations of participating actors and stakeholders during the policy development and implementation processes were not threat-based. Instead, personal and organizational interests drove the nuclear defense policy process. In the current structure, actors competed with one another to advance individual and organizational positions. This procedure was repeated by stakeholders prior to agreement on policy decisions. Resulting decisions were an aggregation of multiple positions that lacked specificity or unified implementation requirements. As a result, competition continued into policy execution and along different formulation channels for alternate policies.[736]

In summary, the book demonstrated that an awkward, ad hoc nuclear defense policy development process extended into the policy implementation area. Even when officials recognized process and organizational shortfalls, it was impossible to forge a unified U.S. government approach given existing statutory authorities, multiple development and action channels, and segregated capabilities. Consequently, the national approaches represented in this book made only limited headway in collaborative nuclear defense implementation, as none of these mechanisms proved capable of addressing the root problem of segregated government design.

---

736   Nicholson-Crotty, Sean, "Bureaucratic Competition in the Policy Process," *Policy Studies Journal*, Volume 33, Number 3, 2005, pp. 341-357.

APPENDIX A

DEFINITIONS

The Office of the Deputy Assistant to the Secretary of Defense for Nuclear Matters defined nuclear defense as "the sum of activities that lead to the prevention of a nuclear or radiological incident on U.S. soil or against U.S. interests, or failing that, ensuring capabilities exist to manage the consequences and attribute the source."[737] While the White House had an Office of Nuclear Defense Policy as part of the Homeland Security Council staff under President George W. Bush it did not define nuclear defense at the national level.[738] This office instead followed the National Security Presidential Directive-43/ Homeland Security Presidential Directive-14 charge to "protect against the unauthorized importation, possession, storage, transportation, development, or use of a nuclear explosive device, fissile material, or radiological material in the United States, and to protect against attack using such devices or materials against the people, territory, or interests of the United States."[739]

The book uses the areas of prevention, protection, and response as the format for examining nuclear defense efforts in

---

737   Ibid.

738   Interview with Homeland Security Council Staff, Office of Nuclear Defense Policy Director Timothy Nank, April 24, 2010.

739   Bush, George W., "National Security Presidential Directive-43/ Homeland Security Presidential Directive-14: Domestic Nuclear Detection," April 15, 2005.

the post-Cold War era. Prevention consists of diplomacy, multilateral regimes, nuclear materials controls, threat reduction, partner activities, export controls, and sanctions to prevent the spread of nuclear weapons, materials, and expertise. Protection is designed to "deter and defend against the [nuclear] threat before it is unleashed."[740] This area includes deterrence, interdiction, defense, and mitigation. Response at home or abroad is intended to address the effects of a nuclear detonation, identify responsible parties, initiate appropriate actions to ensure aggressors are held accountable, and to dissuade future attacks.

U.S. government departments and agencies have defined weapons of mass destruction, and interpreted the corresponding combating weapons of mass destruction pillars, differently. These organizations have released subordinate policies for mission area articulation and dissemination independently of one another.[741] This lack of common definitions creates opportunities for policy gaps, overlap, redundancy, and confusion. Weapons of mass destruction were commonly defined as chemical, biological, radiological, nuclear, and high-yield explosives.[742] However, this definition of the term "weapons of mass destruction" was too broad to be useful. Throughout this book the term weapons of mass destruction is used to refer to nuclear weapons unless otherwise stated. Nuclear weapons are those weapons that cause an explosion based on fission or fusion chain-reactions. These weapons are often confused or

---

740   *National Security Strategy of the United States of America*, 2002, p. 14.

741   For example, Department of Defense places nuclear terrorism into a separate pillar and assigns responsibility for nuclear surety and deterrence separately. They also align forensics and attribution with counterproliferation instead of response as part of their "Nuclear Defense Umbrella." Department of Defense, "U.S. Nuclear Defense," Office of the Deputy Assistant to the Secretary of Defense for Nuclear Matters, retrieved November 5, 2009.

742   The term weapon of mass destruction is also defined by effect. For a thorough examination of the acronym weapons of mass destruction, see W. Seth Carus, *Defining "Weapons of Mass Destruction,"* Center for the Study of Weapons of Mass Destruction, Occasional Paper 4, January 2006.

paired with radiological dispersal and radiation emission devices, but as these two types of weapons do not initiate a nuclear chain-reaction they are not addressed here. References are made to radiological detection throughout the book because the same systems are used to scan for general radiological and special nuclear materials. The remaining chemical, biological, and high-yield conventional explosive weapons are excluded from this discussion.

For uniformity the book follows the Office of the Deputy Assistant Secretary of Defense for Nuclear Matters" definition of nuclear defense pertaining to nuclear weapons, while using the areas of preventing, protecting, and responding to nuclear attack to conceptually align nuclear defense with the three pillars of combating weapons of mass destruction (Figure A.1).

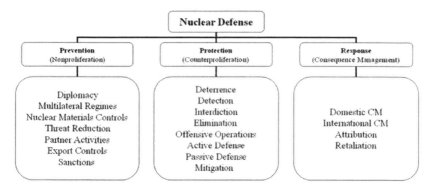

FIGURE A.1. U.S. GOVERNMENT NUCLEAR DEFENSE CONSTRUCT[743]

Nuclear defense was by no means a linear affair with some policies and programs spanning all three areas simultaneously. In this regard, the Department of Homeland Security's nuclear defense spectrum (Figure A.2) helps to illustrate the crosscutting representation of departmental mission areas.

---

743   This figure was derived from multiple sources, for a full list see the bibliography.

Deter-Dissuade	Secure	Detect	Interdict	Render Safe	Consequence Management	Recovery	Attribution

**FIGURE A.2. DEPARTMENT OF HOMELAND
SECURITY NUCLEAR DEFENSE SPECTRUM**[744]

The term "policy" appears repeatedly in this text. To limit the scope of the term this book concentrates on formal national policies. National level policies were either statutory or non-statutory depending on their origin. Statutory policies were those that originated in the legislative branch and were signed into law by the president. Non-statutory national policies were those that originated in the executive branch -- the White House or a separate department or agency. Often there were multiple policies of both types pertaining to an individual area of nuclear defense. Policies of either type represent a policy decision that includes or justifies resources for subsequent program development.

In the context of policy development domestic nuclear defense stakeholders consisted of the president, Congress, and the bureaucracy. Each group had multiple actors participating in both policy development and implementation. For example, the president was supported by various staffs and functionally aligned entities for national security, budget, science and technology, and so on. Congress comprised two chambers, supporting staffs, and lobbyists. External actors, such as the media, constituents, and foreign political actors, played important roles in both presidential and congressional policy formulation. The bureaucracy consisted of multiple departments and agencies each with numerous subordinate actors.[745] For example, the Department of Defense comprised the Office of the Secretary

744   Department of Homeland Security, "National technical nuclear forensics: Overview, QA, and Expertise Development," Domestic Nuclear Detection Office Brief, September 14, 2009.
745   During execution, bureaucratic actors are also referred to as implementing organizations.

of Defense, the Joint Chiefs of Staff, separate military services, supporting agencies, and contractors that served in various internal and external roles.

References to the nuclear defense community refer to the large portion of the U.S. government with duties and responsibilities related to defending America from nuclear attack.[746] This loose conglomeration of programs lacks a single authority charged with the direction and execution of related nuclear defense efforts. Instead, it is characterized by legislative and executive policy bodies with separate departmental and agency programs responsible for implementing a diverse portfolio of polices pertaining to prevention, protection, and response. Within the portfolio additional geographic, functional, and statutory authority considerations are present in a federal design dating back to post-World War II reorganization efforts.

U.S. government nuclear defense implementing organizations comprise the majority of executive branch departments, although this book concentrates on the U.S. Departments of State, Defense, Energy, and Homeland Security. These four departments were responsible for executing the majority of nuclear defense policy efforts. For example, the Department of State was the lead department for the overall nonproliferation agenda but has responsibilities in each nuclear defense area; interaction with foreign governments was an ongoing task that required coordination of reduction activities, partner facilitated interdiction, or organization of foreign assistance in the event of response operations. The Department of Defense was a leader in counterproliferation efforts but, like State, it also had far reaching responsibilities in each nuclear defense area. From Cooperative

---

746   Unlike the intelligence community, which is defined in documents such as Executive Order 12333, there are no comparable definitions of a nuclear defense community. Although referred to as a "community," the intelligence community remains a conglomeration of 16 separate intelligence entities with multiple reporting and budget sources. Because of classification limitations, the intelligence community role in nuclear defense has been omitted from this book.

Threat Reduction, missile defense, and elimination operations, to foreign consequence management, or post-detonation technical nuclear forensics, Defense was the largest of the executive departments and had the available manpower, equipment, and resources to participate in a plethora of nuclear defense missions. While the Department of Energy fulfilled a supporting role, the Materials Protection, Controls, and Accounting program, the Second Line of Defense program, and national laboratory expertise and infrastructure meant the department played an essential role within the nuclear defense community. The Department of Homeland Security was the primary domestic department for nuclear defense with a broad structure that facilitated participation in each area. The department's forward immigration and customs efforts, border and coastline security, and federal emergency management divisions, positioned Homeland Security as a primary actor in international and domestic nuclear defense efforts.

APPENDIX B

LITERATURE REVIEW

There is a large amount of work dedicated to policy development and nuclear subjects, but there is comparatively less literature devoted to collective nuclear defense and policy implementation. Much like nuclear defense policy itself, the related literature tends to be a patchwork of different research areas. The two most prolific areas encompass nuclear strategy and proliferation, not the collective assessment of nuclear defense, which accounts for a broad range of prevention, protection, and response measures to safeguard the United States and its allies from nuclear attack. The Cold War dominates nuclear defense literature. Works written during this period described the early years of nuclear theory and weapons development, with an emphasis on deterrence and associated nuclear war-fighting requirements.[747] Proliferation theory and corresponding country studies account for a large body of work that migrated into

---

747   Kelly, Cynthia C., ed., *The Manhattan Project: The Birth of the Atomic Bomb in the Words of Its Creators, Eyewitnesses, and Historians*, 2007; Clark, Ronald W., *The Greatest Power on Earth: The Story of Nuclear Fission*, 1980, *The Greatest Power on Earth: The International Race for Nuclear Supremacy*, 1980, and *The Birth of the Bomb*, 1961; Allison, Graham T. and Philip Zelikow, *Essence of Decision: Explaining the Cuban Missile Crises*, 2nd edition 1999; Halperin, Morton H., "The Decision to Deploy the ABM: Bureaucratic and Domestic Politics in the Johnson Administration," *World Politics*, Vol. 25, No. 1, October 1972, 62-96.

non-state actor concerns in the post-Cold War era.[748] A third area of related literature originated in the fields of public policy and international relations.

NUCLEAR STRATEGY

This area of nuclear defense literature is extensive and covers strategy, weapons, and defenses. Renowned experts such as Bernard Brodie and Lawrence Freedman facilitated discussions of deterrence, and the evolution of nuclear strategy from the earliest days of the Cold War.[749] These discussions carried forward to a new generation of nuclear theorists that returned to the utility of nuclear weapons in the post-Cold War landscape.[750] Resulting contemporary works debate the appropriate nuclear force structure necessary for new deterrence requirements that include regional and non-state actors, and question whether emerging threats can actually be deterred.[751] Administration-

748   Younger, Stephen M., *The Bomb: A New History*, 2009; Cirincione, Joseph, *Bomb Scare: The History & Future of Nuclear Weapons*, 2008; Reed, Thomas C., and Danny B. Stillman, *The Nuclear Express: A Political History of the Bomb and its Proliferation*, 2009; Nolan, Janne E., *An Elusive Consensus: Nuclear Weapons and American Security After the Cold War*, 1999; Powaski, Ronald E., *Return to Armageddon: The United States and the Nuclear Arms Race, 1981-1999*, 2000.

749   Brodie, Bernard, "The Anatomy of Deterrence," *World Politics*, Vol. 11, No. 2, January 1959; Brodie, Bernard, ed., *The Absolute Weapon: Atomic Power and World Order*, 1946; Freedman, Lawrence, *The Evolution of Nuclear Strategy*, 3rd edition 2003; Sagan, Scott D., *Moving Targets: Nuclear Strategy and National Security*, 1989.

750   Paul, T.V., Richard J. Harknett, and James J. Wirtz, eds., *The Absolute Weapon Revisited: Nuclear Arms and the Emerging International Order*, 2000; Jervis, Robert, "The Dustbin of History: Mutual Assured Destruction," *Foreign Policy*, November/December 2002, pp. 34-48; Record, Jeffrey, "Nuclear Deterrence, Preventive War, and Counterproliferation," *Policy Analysis*, No. 519, July 2004.

751   Paul, T.V., Patrick M. Morgan, and James J. Wirtz, eds., *Complex Deterrence: Strategy in the Global Age*, 2009; Phillips, Matthew, "Uncertain Justice for Nuclear Terror: Deterrence of Anonymous Attacks Through Attribution," *Orbis*, Vol. 51, Issue 3, Summer 2007; Dunn, Lewis A., *Can al Qaeda Be Deterred from Using Nuclear Weapons?*, Center for the Study of

specific literatures addressing evolving strategy and doctrine highlight the shift away from nuclear war-fighting. The first example, *Preventive Defense*, was written by Clinton administration officials to articulate the importance of new nuclear defense areas such as threat reduction and counterproliferation, in a security landscape void of a peer competitor. The second example, *Nuclear Transformation*, was an edited assessment of George W. Bush administration nuclear defense policies. This volume highlighted the progression of nuclear policy under George W. Bush, assessing the impact of nuclear policies and programs, such as global strike and missile defense.[752]

Nuclear weapons policy has been covered at length as a stand-alone topic. One such work that highlighted the three administrations of the post-Cold War periods is *U.S. Nuclear Weapons Policy after the Cold War*.[753] In this book the author presented a thorough analysis of each administration from 1989-2007. He explored the nuclear weapons specific policy process, offering three nuclear weapon idea sets for the era along with an examination of domestic politics. Many key themes were similar concerning nuclear weapons related policy and idea sets, but this work did not account for the greater nuclear defense areas beyond weapons and arms control, and made no attempt to analyze implementation other than limited issues concerning the nuclear weapons complex. A related volume, aptly named *Tactical Nuclear Weapons,* dealt with the often overlooked issue of sub-strategic nuclear weapons, and their impact on the post-Cold War security environment.[754]

Weapons of Mass Destruction, Occasional Paper 3, July 2005.
752   Carter, Ashton B., and William J. Perry, *Preventive Defense: A New Security Strategy for America,* 1999; Payne, Keith B., et al., *Rationale and Requirements for U.S. Nuclear Forces, Vol. I, Executive Report,* National Institute for Public Policy, January 2001; Wirtz, James J., and Jeffrey A. Larsen, eds., *Nuclear Transformation: The New U.S. Nuclear Doctrine,* 2005.
753   Ritchie, Nick, *U.S. Nuclear Weapons Policy after the Cold War: Russians, "rogues," and domestic division,* 2009.
754   Alexander, Brian, and Alistair Millar, eds., *Tactical Nuclear*

A large portion of literature focused on missile defense.[755] Missile defense has been a polarizing topic in nuclear defense debates since it was re-introduced by President Reagan. These arguments were captured in divergent works such as *The Phantom Defense* and *Defending America*.[756] *The Phantom Defense* authors argued that the missile threat is exaggerated and that, even if the threat were viable, national missile defense is unachievable given current technologies.[757] Differing opinions on the necessity and feasibility of missile defense were offered by James Lindsay and Michael O'Hanlon. These authors cited a growing missile threat in *Defending America*, and argue for a limited national missile defense based on existing and developing technologies.[758] Other limited protection works, such as *Combating Proliferation,* looked at the shift to counterproliferation policy.[759] This book, published in 2004, used post-Cold War and early post-9/11 weapons of mass destruction examples and intelligence case studies. Although concerned with broader weapons of mass destruction intelligence issues, the nuclear specific counterproliferation intelligence information on North

Weapons: Emerging Threats in an Evolving Security Environment, 2003.

755   Wirtz, James J., and Jeffrey A. Larsen, eds., *Rockets" Red Glare: Missile Defenses and the Future of World Politics*, 2001; Korb, Lawrence J., "Republicans, missile defense, and the Reagan legacy," *Bulletin of the Atomic Scientists,* 25 April 2008, retrieved May 2, 2009; Lewis, George N., and Theodore A. Postol, "The European Missile Defense Folly," *Bulletin of the Atomic Scientists*, May/June 2008, pp. 33-39.

756   Eisendrath, Craig, Melvin A. Goodman, and Gerald E. Marsh, *The Phantom Defense: America's Pursuit of the Star Wars Illusion*, 2001; Lindsay, James M., and Michael E. O'Hanlon, *Defending America: The Case for Limited National Missile Defense*, 2001.

757   Eisendrath, Craig, Melvin A. Goodman, and Gerald E. Marsh, *The Phantom Defense: America's Pursuit of the Star Wars Illusion*, 2001.

758   Lindsay, James M., and Michael E. O'Hanlon, *Defending America: The Case for Limited National Missile Defense*, 2001.

759   Ellis, Jason D., and Geoffrey D. Kiefer, *Combating Proliferation: Strategic Intelligence and Security Policy*, 2004; Goodpaster, Andrew, *Dealing with Weapons of Mass Destruction: Framing a Strategy,* The Eisenhower Institute, retrieved April 8, 2009.

Korea, India, and Pakistan was insightful. This weapon of mass destruction theme was representative of post-9/11 works that aggregated these weapons into a single category, and used available chemical and biological cases to support their arguments.

NUCLEAR PROLIFERATION

A great deal of nuclear defense literature has been devoted to proliferation theory, country specific weapons programs, and nuclear terrorism. Each proliferation area was important to the construction of a complete defense framework that addressed the full-range of nuclear threats, but historically these areas were examined separately. Proliferation theory as espoused by authors such as Scott Sagan and Kenneth Waltz was a long-standing topic that carried forward into the post-Cold War.[760] State debates over security, domestic politics, and prestige extended into the exportation of technologies for profit, and the potential transfer of nuclear capabilities to non-state actors. While theoretical nuclear proliferation frameworks served an important role in the understanding of nuclear defense issues, these works were not routinely consulted by federal officials charged with policy implementation.[761] Worries over the changing landscape of post-Cold War proliferation also prompted examination of existing nonproliferation frameworks. Works such as *Repairing the Regime* attempted to assess the state of the nonproliferation community and emerging requirements based on the first decade of the post-Cold War period.[762]

Literature concerning country programs continued the assessment of proliferation, with individual country studies leading this area. Works examining existing programs tended

---

760   Sagan, Scott D., and Kenneth N. Waltz, *The Spread of Nuclear Weapons: A Debate*, 1995; Sagan, Scott D., "Why Do States Build Nuclear Weapons?: Three Models in Search of a Bomb," *International Security*, Vol. 21, No. 3, Winter, 1996-1997.
761   For a full list of interviews, see the bibliography.
762   Cirincione, Joseph, ed., *Repairing the Regime: Preventing the Spread of Weapons of Mass Destruction*, 2000.

to describe state specific routes and capabilities.[763] These appraisals assisted with establishing development indicators and declaratory policy analysis, but given the lack of success with roll-back policies, descriptive country studies remained only part of nuclear defense considerations. Programs in various stages of development were the next set of works.[764] These sources again targeted specific countries and their emerging programs. This set of literature provided nuclear defense issues related to the programs, and their potential for greater proliferation to additional actors. Collective accounts of potential states rounded out country-oriented literature.[765] These works looked at states with reason to establish a nuclear weapons program or acquire nuclear weapons. This category of country study highlighted the evolving nature of proliferation concerns, and contributed to the discussion of prevention and protection priorities.

Interest in nuclear defense writing spiked several times following the Cold War. First were nonproliferation works concerning the potential for loose nuclear weapons and new regional nuclear weapons states, and then there was a shift to counterproliferation and terrorist nuclear scenarios, as al-Qaeda grew in notoriety toward the end of the Clinton administration and immediately following 9/11. Nonproliferation and remediation concerns created by the collapse of the Soviet Union benefited from scholarly analysis, but were presented as stand-alone issues, not as part of the nuclear defense problem set. Several authors linked nuclear energy and proliferation, or nuclear energy and

---

763   Cohen, Avner *Israel and the Bomb*, 1998; Perkovich, George, *India's Nuclear Bomb: The Impact on Global Proliferation*, 2001.

764   Obeidi, Mahdi and Kurt Pitzer, *The Bomb in My Garden: The Secrets of Saddam's Nuclear Mastermind*, 2004; Chubin, Shahram, *Iran's Nuclear Ambitions*, 2006 Corera, Gordon, *Shopping for Bombs: Nuclear Proliferation, Global Insecurity, and the Rise and Fall of the A. Q. Khan Network*, 2006; Corsi, Jerome, *Atomic Iran: How the Terrorist Regime Bought the Bomb and American Politicians*, 2005.

765   Campbell, Kurt, Robert Einhorn, and Mitchell B. Reiss, eds. *The Nuclear Tipping Point: Why States Reconsider Their Nuclear Choices*, 2004; Venter, Al J., *Allah's Bomb: The Islamic Quest for Nuclear Weapons*, 2007.

weapons, but again they did not deal with the analysis of layered nuclear defense policy.[766] For example, the first implementation study topic on threat reduction saw numerous articles, books, reports, and other references dedicated to the subject. Initially, works argued for or against threat reduction, and covered the problematic first years of implementation, as the program shifted from a lead to an interagency design to address combative political environments in the United States and Russia.[767] Once the Cooperative Threat Reduction program was up and running, nonproliferation writings shifted to the nuclear black market.[768]

In 2001, the non-state actor nuclear threat suddenly shot to the top of U.S. government nuclear defense priorities, and generated excitement in the academic community.[769] Authors in this area of nuclear defense research were hampered by the lack of source materials, and often the absence of a pre-9/11 background in terrorism studies. Since a nuclear terrorist event had never taken place, many existing writings revolve around speculative scenarios, or on the same limited information such as al-Qaeda's infamous meetings with Pakistani nuclear officials. Authors

---

766   Mozley, Robert F., *The Politics and Technology of Nuclear Proliferation*, 1998; Garwin, Richard L., and Georges Charpak, *Megawatts and Megatons: The Future of Nuclear Power and Nuclear Weapons*, 2002.

767   Shields, John and William Potter, et al. *Dismantling the Cold War: U.S. and newly independent state Perspectives on the Nunn-Lugar Cooperative Threat Reduction Program,* 1997; Allison, Graham T., Owen R. Cote, Jr., Richard A. Falkenrath, Steven E. Miller, *Avoiding Nuclear Anarchy: Containing the Threat of Loose Russian Nuclear Weapons and Fissile Material,* 1996; Kelly, Rich, "The Nunn-Lugar Act: A Wasteful and Dangerous Illusion," *Cato Foreign Policy Briefing no. 39,* March 18, 1996.

768   Lee, Rensselaer W. III, *Smuggling Armageddon: The Nuclear Black Market in the Former Soviet Union and Europe,* 1998; Langewiesche, William, *The Atomic Bazaar: Dispatches from the Underground World of Nuclear Trafficking,* 2007; Bunn, Matthew, *Securing the Bomb, 2007 and 2008.*

769   Allison, Graham T., *Nuclear Terrorism: The Ultimate Preventable Catastrophe,* 2004, 2005; Levi, Michael, *On Nuclear Terrorism,* 2007; Jenkins, Brian M., *Will Terrorists Go Nuclear?,* 2008; Ferguson, Charles D., and William C. Potter with Amy Sands, Leonard S. Spector, and Fred L. Wehling, *The Four Faces of Nuclear Terrorism,* 2005.

such as Brian Jenkins drew on technical or terrorist arguments, making cases why this type of attack could or could not take place.[770] Limited counterarguments that the U.S. government and like-minded conservative writers were blowing the possibilities of nuclear attacks out of proportion also appeared.[771] Works in this area, when paired with specific terrorist or broader weapons of mass destruction studies, helped policymakers that lacked a background in nuclear weapons and terrorism tactics understand the issues, but did not address the greater U.S. government responses to the changing nuclear defense landscape.[772]

POLICY DEVELOPMENT AND IMPLEMENTATION

Few efforts have been made to examine the link between the nuclear defense subset of national security policy, and follow-on implementation efforts. The approach to the study of public policy suggested that implementation is a less significant area in the literature. For example, Thomas Dye's ninth edition of *Understanding Public Policy* dedicated three pages to the topic of "Policy Implementation: The Bureaucracy," and one chapter to program evaluation with the majority of the text focused on analysis of the policy process.[773] This well-known work was indicative of the approach to policy examination, where a great deal of time was spent on the development process with limited efforts to address decentralized implementation and evaluation.

---

770   Jenkins, Brian M., *Will Terrorists Go Nuclear?*, 2008.
771   Mueller, John, *Overblown: How Politicians and the Terrorism Industry Inflate National Security Threats, and Why We Believe Them*, 2006.
772   Allison, Graham T., *Nuclear Terrorism: The Ultimate Preventable Catastrophe*, 2004, 2005; Levi, Michael, *On Nuclear Terrorism*, 2007; Jenkins, Brian M., *Will Terrorists Go Nuclear?*, 2008; Ferguson, Charles D., and William C. Potter with Amy Sands, Leonard S. Spector, and Fred L. Wehling, *The Four Faces of Nuclear Terrorism*, 2005.
773   Dye, Thomas R., *Understanding Public Policy*, 9th edition 1998, pp. 329-333.

Theories pertaining to rational policy and bureaucratic politics have dominated the study of national security and foreign policy formulation. Of these two, the bureaucratic politics model pioneered by Graham Allison and Morton Halperin had an existing relationship with the examination of Cold War nuclear defense.[774] The seminal works on bureaucratic politics, *Essence of Decision* and "Conceptual Models and the Cuban Missile Crises," used the Cuban missile crises to demonstrate what Allison originally described as organizational process and bureaucratic politics models.[775] Halperin used the Johnson administration's decision to deploy an anti-ballistic missile shield as a follow-on bureaucratic politics study, while the two authors continued to refine the theory in another article that included the examination of nuclear deterrence positions between allies.[776]

While nuclear defense topics were included in early bureaucratic politics literature, the theory was developed to describe foreign policy development within the U.S. government, with limited reference dedicated to suggestive implementation propositions. Morton Halpern's book, *Bureaucratic Politics and Foreign Policy,* defined the major areas comprising the theory as interests and participants, decisions, and actions.[777] The first area defined stakeholders and their positions, demonstrating that there is not a unified U.S. government position. The second area described the process by which stakeholder positions were aggregated prior to the issuance of a decision. Finally,

---

774 Allison, Graham T. and Philip Zelikow, *Essence of Decision: Explaining the Cuban Missile Crises,* 2nd edition 1999; Allison, Graham T., "Conceptual Models and the Cuban Missile Crises," *The American Political Science Review,* Vol. 63, No. 3, September 1969, pp. 689-718.
775 Ibid.
776 Morton H. Halperin, "The Decision to Deploy the ABM: Bureaucratic and Domestic Politics in the Johnson Administration," *World Politics,* Vol. 25, October 1972, 62-96; Allison, Graham T., and Morton H. Halperin, "Bureaucratic Politics: A Paradigm and Some Policy Implications," *World Politics,* Vol. 24, Spring 1972, pp. 40-80.
777 Halperin, Morton H., and Priscilla A. Clapp, *Bureaucratic Politics and Foreign Policy,* 2nd edition 2006.

actions demonstrated the continued negotiation and independent organization activities associated with segregated implementation.[778] More recent bureaucratic politics literature assessed the applicability of the paradigm and attempted to build on previous works, but did not offer drastically new insights on the topic.[779] While bureaucratic politics literature targeted nuclear defense topics, it represented the Cold War era and gravitated toward the development process.

General policy literature provides valuable insights into the dynamics of the U.S. policy process and some of the obstacles, but these works are not specific to nuclear defense.[780] Policy implementation literature, which has grown in popularity over the past two decades, is separated into two wide-ranging approaches that examine systems and political actors, or implementing organizations and target groups.[781] Much of the literature deals

778   Allison, Graham T., and Morton H. Halperin, "Bureaucratic Politics: A Paradigm and Some Policy Implications," *World Politics,* Vol. 24, Spring 1972, pp. 46-56.

779   Art, Robert J., "Bureaucratic Politics and American Foreign Policy: A Critique," *Policy Sciences,* Vol. 4, December 1973, pp. 467-490; Krasner, Stephen D., "Are Bureaucracies Important? (Or Allison Wonderland)," *Foreign Policy,* Vol. 7, Summer 1972, pp. 159-179; Ball, Desmond J., "The Blind Men and the Elephant: A Critique of Bureaucratic Politics Theory," *Australian Outlook,* Vol. 28, No. 1, April 1974, pp. 71-92; Bendor, Jonathan and Thomas H. Hammond, "Rethinking Allison's Models," *American Political Science Review,* Vol. 86, No. 2, June 1992, pp. 301-322.

780   Kernell, Samuel and Steven Smith, *Principles and Practice of American Politics,* 3rd edition 2007; Van Horn, Carl E., Donald C. Baumer and William T. Gormley Jr., *Politics and Public Policy,* 3rd edition 2001; Dye, Thomas R., *Understanding Public Policy,* 9th edition 1998; Sarkesian, Sam C., John Allen Williams, and Stephen J. Cimbala, *U.S. National Security: Policymakers, Processes, and Politics,* 4th edition 2002, Wilson, James Q., *Bureaucracy: What Government Agencies Do and Why They Do It,* 2nd edition 2000.

781   Hill, Michael James, and Peter L. Hupe, *Implementing Public Policy: Governance in Theory and Practice,* 2002; Matland, Richard E., "Synthesizing the Implementation Literature: The Ambiguity-Conflict Model of Policy Implementation," *Journal of Public Administration Research and Theory,* Vol. 5, No. 2: pp. 145-174, 1995; O'Toole, Laurence J. Jr. and Robert S. Montjoy, "Interorganizational Policy Implementation: A Theoretical

with theoretical models derived from implementation studies in different public policy areas.[782] These general references to bureaucratic organizations describe them as resistant to change and protective of resources, autonomy, and influence.

In recent history, the U.S. government has spent considerable resources on policy evaluation. Peter Rossi and his colleagues described the "boom period in evaluation research" as post-World War II through the establishment of the field in the 1970s.[783] This newer importance placed on evaluation created a market for evaluation contracting and consulting firms, and has contributed to shaping complex policies into measurable formats. The majority of literature in this area however came from government sponsored studies and reports, not academia.[784] These U.S. government evaluations tended to remain focused on individual programs and not the broader use of findings to improve federal nuclear defense performance, or the use of multiple studies to identify systemic issues.

In the area of nuclear defense policy implementation two U.S. government reports stand out.[785] The Report of the Commission

Perspective," *Public Administration Review*, Vol. 44, No. 6, Nov. - Dec., 1984, pp. 491-503.

782   Dye, Thomas R., *Understanding Public Policy*, 9th edition 1998, pp. 13-38.

783   Rossi, Peter H., Mark W. Lipsey, and Howard E. Freeman, *Evaluation: A Systematic Approach,* 7th edition 2004, pp. 8-11.

784   Schwartz, Stephen I., ed., *Atomic Audit: The Costs and Consequences of U.S. Nuclear Weapons since 1940,* Government Accountability Office, *Cooperative Threat Reduction: Department of Defense Has Improved Its Management and Internal Controls, but Challenges Remain,* June 2005; Government Accountability Office, *Preventing Nuclear Smuggling: Department of Energy Has Made Limited Progress in Installing Radiation Detection Equipment at Highest Priority Foreign Seaports,* March 2005; Shea, Dana A., "The Global Nuclear Detection Architecture: Issues for Congress," *Congressional Research Service Report for Congress*, September 23, 2008.

785   Deutch, John M., Chair, "Combating Proliferation of Weapons of Mass Destruction," Commission Report, July 14, 1999; Graham, Bob, Jim Talent, et al., *World at Risk: The Report of the Commission on the Prevention of weapons of mass destruction Proliferation and Terrorism*, 2008.

to Assess the Organization of the Federal Government to Combat the Proliferation of Weapons of Mass Destruction (known as the Deutch Commission Report) was directly applicable to the book, as it attempted to describe the organization of the U.S. government to combat the proliferation of weapons of mass destruction. For example, the commission found:

> There is no proliferation-related architecture -- an end-to-end plan for policy development, program planning, and budget formulation -- nor does any person or staff have the power or responsibility to develop one... Neither the President, Congress, nor any executive branch official knows how much the various agencies have spent on these efforts or how much they plan to spend in the future... Without an explicit financial plan tied to programmatic objectives, individual agencies and the corresponding sub-committees [of which there were 23 sub-committees related to proliferation in 1999] on Capitol Hill make their program and resource decisions independently of any overall plan or objective. The result is not only inefficiency and duplication but also potentially catastrophic delay.[786]

The Deutch Commission Report went beyond the major departmental actors and included recommendations for justice, commerce, treasury, health and human services, agriculture, and the intelligence community. The report discussed issues with current interagency coordination including the lack of collaborative planning and execution, and provided recommendations for how to improve federal policy implementation. However, this report was primarily a survey of general U.S. government implementation efforts and not a systematic study of the collective nuclear defense policy development and implementation processes.

The second work, *World at Risk*, was prepared by the Commission on the Prevention of Weapons of Mass Destruction Proliferation and Terrorism.[787] This report offered updated

---

786   Deutch, John M., Chair, "Combating Proliferation of Weapons of Mass Destruction," Commission Report, July 14, 1999, p. 9.
787   Graham, Bob, Jim Talent, et al., *World at Risk: The Report of the*

post-9/11 recommendations focused on weapons of mass destruction and terrorism concerns for the incoming Obama administration. Two sections of the report dealt with government organization and culture, and the role of the public, while an informative appendix tracked the implementation efforts of the 2001 Baker-Cutler Report recommendations.[788] Unlike the earlier Deutch commission report, the *World at Risk* focused on policy development concerning the White House, Congress, and the intelligence and greater national security communities. It offered general recommendations such as the need to create "a more efficient and effective policy coordination structure."[789] The report also recommended that multiple department or agency service should be "a prerequisite for advancement to the National Security Council or to department or agency leadership level," to combat existing single department mindsets.[790]

Commission on the Prevention of weapons of mass destruction Proliferation and Terrorism, 2008.

788   Baker, Howard, and Lloyd Cutler, Chairs, *A Report Card on the Department of Energy's Nonproliferation Programs with Russia*, The Secretary of Energy Advisory Board, U.S. Department of Energy, January 10, 2001.

789   Graham, Bob, Jim Talent, et al., *World at Risk: The Report of the Commission on the Prevention of weapons of mass destruction Proliferation and Terrorism*, 2008, p. 84.

790   Ibid., p. 103.

APPENDIX C

METHODOLOGY

Given the patchwork nature of existing nuclear defense literature, this book addresses two gaps: analysis of nuclear defense as a complete framework; and analysis of policy development through to implementation. The first part of the book examines how and why nuclear defense policy evolved during the George H. W. Bush and William J. Clinton administrations. The bureaucratic politics model is applied to two post-Cold War nuclear defense case studies involving strategic arms reduction and missile defense. The second part of the book examines how the U.S. government implemented prevention, protection, and response policies, and the extent to which corresponding objectives were realized. This part of the book employs three policy implementation case studies -- threat reduction, maritime radiation detection, and nuclear forensics -- to analyze systemic barriers to collaborative policy execution.

National nuclear defense policy serves as the dependent variable in this study. It is a complex topic influenced by numerous independent variables that include but are not limited to issues involving stakeholders, actors, politics (domestic and international), organization, threat, norms, technology, resources, vulnerabilities, capabilities, and intentions. The book focuses primarily on stakeholder and organization variables framed by prevention, protection, and response case studies. These were designed so that the analysis could logically progress from nuclear defense policy development through to implementation.

POLICY DEVELOPMENT CASE STUDIES

Chapters 1 and 2 draw on the bureaucratic politics model to examine the key stakeholders taking part in the nuclear defense policy development process. The hypothesis being tested in these chapters asserts that, "U.S. nuclear defense policy formulation during the post-Cold War administrations of George H. W. Bush and William J. Clinton was anchored in bureaucratic politics, not collective defense." This hypothesis was tested by asking the following questions: Did the policy formulation process reflect rational policy theory, which portrays the state as a unitary entity that employs a rational decision-making process designed to maximize outcomes resulting from policy decisions and actions?[791] Or, did policy development represent the incremental compromises associated with the aggregation of competing interests and positions presented by multiple stakeholders participating in bureaucratic politics?

If the hypothesis is disconfirmed, this would mean that rational policy theory has prevailed. More specifically, the research would show that the U.S. government collaboratively approached nuclear defense to maximize national responses. In this instance, a collective national interest would focus stakeholders during policy formulation. The researcher could then deduce that defense against immediate or potential nuclear threats would be the dominant independent variable. This threat-based unity would suggest that stakeholders placed a greater emphasis on national interests. However, the opposite would apply if the hypothesis is confirmed. If this is the case, independent variables related to stakeholder positions would prevail during the development process. The threat-based argument is often used to justify national security policy decisions, but research has indicated that collaborative response to emerging threats is not the primary

---

791   For more information on the rational policy model see Graham T. Allison and Philip Zelikow, *Essence of Decision: Explaining the Cuban Missile Crises*, 2nd edition 1999, pp. 13-75.

concern of national stakeholders.[792] Instead, stakeholders have been shown to place personal and organizational interests above national security and nuclear defense considerations.[793]

SELECTION

Chapters 1 and 2 examine two post-Cold War nuclear defense policies in order to analyze the policy formulation process. The approach concentrates on formal national level policies related to strategic arms reduction and national missile defense. These prevention and protection policies were selected using five criteria:

1. Was this a national level policy? Both areas required national level policy formulation that included all three stakeholders. Strategic arms reduction was anchored in treaty authorities outlined in the constitution, while national missile defense underscored the evolutionary nature of the formulation process that has facilitated alternate policymaking challenges from the legislative branch. Thus, the national missile defense case study demonstrated the ability of Congress to establish national policies counter to administration positions.

2. Did the policy demonstrate the transition between eras? Arms control and missile defense efforts had long Cold War histories that carried forward into the post-Cold War era. In both cases, these arguments were highlighted under the preceding Reagan administration, and possessed the potential to demonstrate path dependencies related to rules, norms, and capabilities. For example,

---

792   Jordan, Amos A., William J. Taylor, Jr., and Michael J. Mazarr, *American National Security,* 1999, pp. 93-236.
793   Allison, Graham T. and Philip Zelikow, *Essence of Decision: Explaining the Cuban Missile Crises,* 2nd edition 1999; Halperin, Morton H., and Priscilla A. Clapp, *Bureaucratic Politics and Foreign Policy,* 2nd edition 2006.

Barry Blechman and Morton Halperin provided Cold War assessments of arms control and anti-ballistic missile defense to highlight that, while actors and strategic considerations may have changed, the rules of the game remain the same.[794]

3. Was the topic a major post-Cold War nuclear defense theme? Strategic arms reduction and national missile defense were major themes from post-Cold War nuclear defense labors.

4. Did the policy represent a prevention or protection effort from the George H. W. Bush or William J. Clinton administrations? Strategic arms reduction represented a key prevention policy under both, but successful policy decisions were realized during the presidency of George H. W. Bush. Missile defense was a central protection policy present in both administrations, with national missile defense policy decisions made during the William J. Clinton administration.

5. Was sufficient data available? Strategic arms reduction and national missile defense represented a large portion of the nuclear defense literature. Both polices have been covered extensively by non-governmental and governmental experts. While there was extensive coverage, nothing in the literature approached either prevention or protection policies from a bureaucratic politics standpoint.

Other policies that were assessed for examination in the book, but not finally selected, include: the Nonproliferation Treaty extension decision of 1995; the Missile Technology Control Regime the United States-Democratic People's Republic of

---

794 Blechman, Barry M., *The Politics of National Security: Congress and Defense Policy*, 1990, pp. 63-111; Halperin, Morton H., "The Decision to Deploy the ABM: Bureaucratic and Domestic Politics in the Johnson Administration," *World Politics*, Vol. 25, October 1972, 62-96.

Korea Agreed Framework of 1994; and the Comprehensive Test
Ban Treaty. The Nonproliferation Treaty extension decision, the
Missile Technology Control Regime, and Agreed Framework
were limited foreign policy actions that required different levels
of stakeholder participation. Each was an executive branch driv-
en effort with mixed or limited outcomes. The Nonproliferation
Treaty had already been ratified by Congress so the review
and indefinite extension conference of 1995, was an executive
branch action where the U.S. policy decision of indefinite extension was not contested by the two applicable stakeholders -- the
president and the bureaucracy.

The Missile Technology Control Regime was a voluntary
initiative and not a treaty. While all stakeholders were present,
policy decisions were compartmentalized based on departmental
authorities. In this instance, the executive branch was responsible for negotiations while the legislative branch was responsible
for the supporting U.S. legislation. The 1994 Agreed Framework
was a short-term executive branch effort. It was neither a treaty, nor a legally binding document. As such, Congress was not
included in the policy development process, and later refused
to support the agreement. The Comprehensive Test Ban Treaty
was a formal prevention action preceded by domestic alternative
policy in the form of a testing moratorium implemented in 1992.
While the treaty represented a key aspect of national nuclear
defense policy development under President Clinton, this agreement was not ratified during the period of study.

STRUCTURE

Chapters 1 and 2, titled, "Strategic Arms Reduction
Development Study," and "National Missile Defense
Development Study," follow the same format comprising the following sections: policy introduction; stakeholders; history; decision; development; barriers; and conclusions. Each case study
demonstrates the continued reliance of the U.S. government on

prior policy decisions. For arms control this was a direct link to previous negotiations and, in the case of missile defense, it was the result of prior policy decisions and resulting norms. Arguments related to the historical impact of prior decisions are framed by the theory of path dependence which originated in the field of economics in the mid-1980's and has since migrated to other disciplines.[795] Although the exact definition is still open to debate, the general context suggests that "history matters."[796] Both case studies draw heavily on path dependence theory to explain similar decisions across different periods despite drastically different strategic circumstances and the likelihood of nuclear war.

The stakeholder sections identify who was involved in the policy development process, what their interests were, and what rules applied to each.[797] James Keagle emphasizes the importance of what Graham Allison and Morton Halperin refer to as "rules of the game."[798] For the president and Congress, rules are derived from the constitution, but for the bureaucracy rules are primarily the result of non-statutory and statutory authorities. These rules establish responsibilities, action channels, and frameworks that carried forward into policy implementation. In the case of the U.S. government competing rules facilitated

---

795   For more information on emerging types of path dependence see Scott E. Page, "Path Dependence," *Quarterly Journal of Political Science,* Vol. 1, 2006, pp. 87-115.
796   Pierson, Paul, "Increasing Returns, Path Dependence, and the Study of Politics," *The American Political Science Review,* Vol. 94, No. 2, June 2000, p. 252.
797   Allison, Graham T., and Morton H. Halperin, "Bureaucratic Politics: A Paradigm and Some Policy Implications," *World Politics,* Vol. 24, Spring 1972, pp. 47-48.
798   James Keagle defines rules of the game as, "assorted customs, statutes, and constitutional requirements" that establish "responsibility, paper flows, and the direction of debate." Keagle, James M., "Introduction and Framework," in David C. Kozak, and James M. Keagle, eds., *Bureaucratic Politics and National Security: Theory and Practice,* 1988, p. 21.

multiple policy development routes along different action channels.[799]

Each case study begins by focusing on the policy's origin and major decisions. The origins of both policy areas during the Cold War demonstrate the longevity of each issue while the decisions represent how national policy specifically evolved in these areas. This approach allows the analysis sections to focus on why U.S. nuclear defense policy evolved in the manner that it did after the Cold War. Graham Allison has offered that, "different groups pulling in different directions yield a resultant distinct from what anyone intended" at the beginning of the policy development process.[800] With this in mind questions driving the analysis in this chapter include: did different groups pull in different directions and what was the general result? Did the Strategic Arms Reduction Treaties successfully enter into force? Was the U.S. government able to reach a decision on the direction of national missile defense? The book argues that in each issue area, policy decisions during the George H. W. Bush and William J. Clinton administrations proved to be incremental in nature, and in response to the underlying issues. The responses were highly debated -- both domestically and internationally -- to the point that compromised policy decisions left multiple stakeholders unsatisfied.

The case studies examine how stakeholder positions were defined and aggregated to produce policy decisions. In the literature, "Miles Law" of "where you stand depends upon where you sit," is often cited to describe the formulation of policy positions.[801] Stakeholder positions comprise multiple actor positions

---

799   Allison and Halperin define action channels as "regularized sets of procedures for producing particular classes of actions." Allison, Graham T., and Morton H. Halperin, "Bureaucratic Politics: A Paradigm and Some Policy Implications," *World Politics,* Vol. 24, Spring 1972, pp. 45, 50-53.
800   Allison, Graham T., "Conceptual Models and the Cuban Missile Crises," *The American Political Science Review,* Vol. 63, No. 3, September 1969, p. 707.
801   Kozak, David C., "The Bureaucratic Politics Approach: The

pertaining to national security, organizational, political, and/or personal considerations. For example, the independent positions of congressional members take into account personal ambitions, constituency impact, and lobbyist positions. Each actor position is then aggregated to form a majority position representative of Congress as a single stakeholder. This process is repeated between stakeholders for national level policy development in an environment where each stakeholder -- the president, Congress, and the bureaucracy -- have a different position based on multiple variables.[802] The objective is to determine how stakeholder positions were defined and aggregated in order to demonstrate whether or not the U.S. government formulated and presented unitary nuclear defense policy decisions. Questions that drive this part of the analysis include: was the national policy development process involving the president, Congress, and the bureaucracy collegial or competitive in nature? Did rationality compel a collective vision for nuclear defense beyond prevention of a nuclear attack against the United States or its allies, or did bureaucratic politics place actor and stakeholder positions above national security considerations?

Each policy development case study ends with a barriers section on shared attitudes, flexibility, and organizational constraints. The aim is to determine if there existed a collective national vision related to the issues in question, and the degree of flexibility enjoyed by stakeholders that inherited ongoing policy actions in these areas. A key question here is how did the rules impact the policy development process? For treaties, the constitution established specific roles for the president and the

---

Evolution of the Paradigm," in David C. Kozak, and James M. Keagle, eds., *Bureaucratic Politics and National Security: Theory and Practice,* 1988, p. 7.

802   For example, external variables may relate to the office, former group affiliations, and in the case of the president and Congress, domestic politics. For further discussion of organizational interests and positions reference Morton H. Halperin, "Why Bureaucrats Play Games," *Foreign Policy,* Number 2, Spring 1971, pp. 70-90.

Senate, but for national missile defense, what rules facilitated alternate policymaking in the legislative branch? Norms are also an important concept in this section with the potential to highlight path dependence theory. In this regard, as the strategic environment evolved, what determines if norms prevailed despite the changing circumstances?

Research for this book suggests that actors associating their organizational essence with nuclear weapons or missile defense did not accept policy decisions to reduce stockpiles or to shift national missile defense priorities. Instead, these actors continued to argue for their positions along alternate action channels in the policy development and implementation arenas. The continuation of position debates beyond initial decisions suggested that national nuclear defense policy decisions did not represent unitary outcomes.

IMPLEMENTATION CASE STUDIES

Chapters 1 and 2 demonstrate the complex nature of nuclear defense policy development, and explore the processes that have led to decades of incremental policy compromise in specific issue areas. But the policy process involves more than just formulation. Questions of how the government bureaucracy implemented policy decisions, and the extent to which corresponding objectives were realized, are the focus of chapters 3, 4, and 5. Regulated by systemic constraints implementing organizations, are responsible for translating policy decisions into action. The question therefore arises: to what extent did such actions reflect the unity of effort associated with stated policy goals or did the influence of bureaucratic politics also extend into implementation?

Graham Allison and Morton Halperin outlined a series of constraints and predisposed actions regarding bureaucracies and policy implementation.[803] They argued that ill-defined policy

803   Allison, Graham T., and Morton H. Halperin, "Bureaucratic Politics: A Paradigm and Some Policy Implications," *World Politics,* Vol. 24, Spring

direction, and a lack of oversight from political actors, provides freedom of maneuver for independent implementing organizations. James Keagle offered, "For many the game has just begun." He asserted that, "Particularism and parochialism are reborn, with resultant organizational twists to implementation that can take actors in numerous directions, each trying to apply the general prescription to the specific malady as viewed through different lenses."[804] In light of these arguments, the question of the impact of a shared attitude to prevent, protect, or respond to a nuclear incident in the United States or against U.S. interests or allies arises. Was the common goal to stop this type of attack a sufficient driver to foster collaborative execution from a normally segregated bureaucracy?

The three policy implementation case studies employ formative evaluations to examine the U.S. government's policy implementation process. The hypothesis tested in this portion of the book states that, "The U.S. government was not organized to address nuclear defense, and as a result did not collaboratively implement evolving national policies." If the hypothesis was disconfirmed, this would suggest that the U.S. government was organized sufficiently to conduct collaborative work. The key definition for this portion revolved around the concept of collaborative work. This notion would require implementers to participate in an interagency process that accounted for combined policy planning, resourcing, and execution. In this case, various departments and agencies would work together to implement national nuclear defense policies for the good of the nation. This would remain constant even when the interests of the implementing organization did not align with policy decisions. However, if the hypothesis is confirmed, the formulation studies would depict parochial implementation that places individual

---

1972, pp. 51-56.
804   Keagle, James M., "Introduction and Framework," in David C. Kozak, and James M. Keagle, eds., *Bureaucratic Politics and National Security: Theory and Practice,* 1988, p. 22.

organization and program concerns above collaborative implementation. In this case, senior level officials would participate
in interagency coordination, and return to individually implemented programs with guidance. Despite interagency coordination, departments and agencies would place organizational
interests above collaborative execution in an effort to maximize
organizational resources, influence, and autonomy.[805]

Research for the book suggests that as a sub-set of national
security policy, nuclear defense was independently implemented. For example, previous studies such as "Beyond Goldwater-
Nichols" found that, "Cabinet agencies continue to be the principal organizational element of national security policy, and each
agency has its own strategies, capabilities, budget, culture, and
institutional prerogatives to emphasize and protect."[806] This
finding was consistent throughout the implementation study
chapters where multiple organizations displayed these characteristics as they interacted in the shared policy spaces of threat
reduction, radiation detection, and nuclear forensics.

SELECTION

Chapters 3, 4, and 5 examine three post-Cold War nuclear
defense policy areas to analyze policy execution. Each implementation case study was designed as a one-time evaluation
conducted by an outside evaluator, drawing on field research,
interviews, reports and internal documents, and archival data,
to establish how the U.S. government implemented select nuclear defense policies following the Cold War. The case studies
selected include: the Cooperative Threat Reduction program
under the U.S. Department of Defense; the Megaports Initiative

---

805   Anthony Downs described these areas as power, income, and prestige. Downs, Anthony, *Inside Bureaucracy*, 1967, pp. 58-59.
806   Murdock, Clark A., and Michele A. Flournoy, "Beyond Goldwater-
Nichols: U.S. Government and Defense Reform for a New Strategic Era
(Phase II)," Center for Strategic and International Studies Report, July 28,
2005, p. 26.

located in the Department of Energy; and the National Technical Nuclear Forensics Center under the Department of Homeland Security.[807] These policy implementation cases were selected based on seven criteria:

1. Was the topic a key nuclear defense policy theme? In the post-Cold War era Cooperative Threat Reduction and Second Line of Defense activities stood out as distinct areas emphasized by the administrations and Congress, with the third, technical nuclear forensics, increasing in priority by the end of the George W. Bush administration.
2. Could the case be evaluated? Each of the topics examined here had defined political objectives outlined by formal national policies.[808]
3. Was there sufficient data and access? While involving sensitive security policy areas all three issue areas were headquartered in Washington, D.C., with suitable material for unclassified primary and secondary source analyses.
4. Were there clear lines of delineation between nuclear defense areas? Although benefits and operational intricacies may extend into other areas, each implementation study could be associated with a defined area. The Second Line of Defense Megaports Initiative was the most debatable, if argued from a partner capacity standpoint, but the purpose to "deter, detect, and interdict illicit trafficking in nuclear and other radioactive materials...

---

807   The studies concentrate on the Strategic Offensive Arms Elimination branch within the U.S. Department of Defense Cooperative Threat Reduction program, the Department of Energy Megaports Initiative within the National Nuclear Security Administration Second Line of Defense program, and the Department of Homeland Security National Technical Nuclear Forensics Center within the Domestic Nuclear Defense Office.

808   Smith, Thomas B., "The Policy Implementation Process," *Policy Sciences*, June 1973, pp. 203-204.

through the global maritime shipping system" lent itself to prevention.[809]

5.   Did the case represent a post-Cold War approach? Threat reduction, while beginning under George H. W. Bush, centered primarily on Presidents Clinton and George W. Bush for implementation. The Second Line of Defense program was formed at the end of the Clinton administration to address former Soviet borders, and added the Megaports Initiative to its portfolio under George W. Bush. The National Technical Nuclear Forensics Center, formed in 2007, built on attribution concerns that began to arise following the collapse of the Soviet Union.

6.   Did it represent a major department? Each program was implemented by a different cabinet department. Cooperative Threat Reduction was executed by the Department of Defense, the Megaports Initiative fell under the Department of Energy, and the National Technical Nuclear Forensics Center was housed in the Department of Homeland Security.

7.   Did it present distinct conclusions? Cooperative Threat Reduction was characterized by an interagency design and the complex adaptive nature of nuclear defense when left to U.S. government implementing organizations. The Megaports Initiative represented a lead agency design and was typified by the difficulties associated with integrating a supporting program into the greater U.S. government architecture. The National Technical Nuclear Forensics Center demonstrated both advantages and limitations associated with a national integrator design. Together, these implementation studies provide examples of the difficulties associated with the collective

---

809   Department of Energy, "Fact Sheet: National Nuclear Security Administration's second line of defense," National Nuclear Security Administration, December 2008.

execution of national nuclear defense policies under the current U.S. government structure.

Because of the breadth of nuclear defense many potential topics could have been chosen as the basis for implementation studies. Topics evaluated but not selected include security schemes such as the proliferation security, container security, counterproliferation, and presidential nuclear initiatives. These policy areas were found to be too broad in character, and tied too closely to specific administrations, to constitute effective implementation studies. Similarly, export controls and sanctions were also deemed to be extremely broad in scope with specific examples tied to individual administrations. Deterrence was also considered, but at the operational level this is a highly-classified area. Legacy organizations in this area represented status quo programs, and the breadth of nuclear and conventional deterrence was deemed to be much too large for a detailed implementation study.

Nuclear interdiction and elimination fields were also considered but both are sensitive subject areas with diverse international participation. Because operations in these areas rely heavily on intelligence and specialized forces, security issues would have significantly constrained a formative evaluation drawing purely on open source material. Retaliation and pre-emption were also considered but offensive operations such as the invasions of Afghanistan and Iraq did not lend themselves to limited-scope organizational analyses of nuclear defense policy implementation. Passive defense efforts such as fortified preparedness extended into domestic consequence management, while foreign consequence management relied heavily on general U.S. government assets and lacked supporting data for the period.

STRUCTURE

Each implementation case study is framed by a standardized format beginning with an introduction to the specific topic. This is followed by an explanation of the policy decision and corresponding political objectives, before key actors are identified. Once the context, policy decision, and actors are defined, the chapters examine the implementation process pertaining to the issue areas: Cooperative Threat Reduction, the Megaports Initiative, and the National Technical Nuclear Forensics Center. The studies trace implementation from the working level to the national policy source. This equates to walking policy implementation from the federal project manager back to the policy's point, or points, of origin. The final part of each study examines program performance and the realization of policy objectives. Criteria from prior reports and studies, stated policy objectives, counterarguments, and theoretical applicability provide the framework for this program evaluation.

Chapter 3, titled "Threat Reduction Implementation Study," examines the first implementation area. Threat reduction was a key prevention policy in the post-Cold War era and represented a clear transition from previous nuclear defense strategies. It was characterized by lead agency and interagency approaches to federal policy implementation. Cooperative Threat Reduction began with early Department of Defense efforts. The initial structure was centered on a single department budget with resources transferred from the Defense Department to supporting governmental and non-governmental organizations. Under President Clinton, the effort shifted to an interagency approach with independent departmental budgets and execution. The Department of Defense's Cooperative Threat Reduction program represented a case of individual department implementation inside a larger interagency construct. Within the Cooperative Threat Reduction directorate, the Strategic Offensive Arms Elimination branch provided the opportunity for a detailed examination of threat reduction implementation down to the federal project officer level. This case study characterizes implementation as an independent acquisition-based program that was not integrated into a national strategic plan.

Chapter 4, titled "Maritime Radiation Detection Implementation Study," examines the second implementation area of protection. The Department of Energy played the role of a supporting department inside a federal lead agency structure. Within the department, the Second Line of Defense Office's Megaports Initiative is the subject of detailed analysis. The supporting department approach to maritime radiation detection is characterized as an independent acquisition-based program similar to Cooperative Threat Reduction. The chapter identifies a strong internal bureaucracy positioned to champion a program that was not integrated into the larger U.S. government nuclear defense architecture. Research for the book found that the Department of Homeland Security -- the lead agency for global radiation detection -- was not able to fully incorporate Department of Energy capabilities because of conflicting statutory authorities.

Chapter 5, titled "Nuclear Forensics Implementation Study," presents the third and final nuclear defense area of response. This chapter differs from the previous implementation studies because of the national integrator role played by the Department of Homeland Security's National Technical Nuclear Forensics Center, and which represented a distinct approach to federal policy implementation. The national integrator design was demonstrative of an understanding within the U.S. government that separate departmental execution is prone to gaps, redundancies, and waste in policy implementation. However, despite attempts to unify nuclear attribution the case study demonstrates that independent policy execution based on existing organizational capabilities and authorities continued to be the norm.

The policy implementation studies suggest that organizational interests are of a higher priority than collaborative national policy execution to individual departments. Each case study was characterized by a different operational arrangement – interagency, lead agency, and national integrator. These designs are represented by different departments but all three display similarities related to independent execution. The Cooperative Threat Reduction study demonstrates that while there was a great deal of interagency communication, autonomous execution took place which supported separate departmental interests. The Megaports Initiative study illustrates that the focus of supporting departments in the context of a lead agency design is one of self-preservation rather than the accomplishment of a collective objective. The National Technical Nuclear Forensics Center study demonstrates the limits of a national integrator design where there is no budget and a lack of operational authority over supporting actors.

The research for the book suggests that competition for control of the U.S. government ensured an unsystematic approach to nuclear defense with a separate federal bureaucracy obstructing collaborative policy development and implementation. The case studies reveal that no shared vision existed across the U.S. government for nuclear defense. Instead, each perceived threat or issue area was dealt with independently. Reactive policies originated with each stakeholder using various channels permitted by existing rules. The principal considerations of participating actors and stakeholders during the policy process were not threat-based. Instead, personal and organizational interests were the primary drivers of post-Cold War nuclear defense efforts.

DATA COLLECTION

Qualitative data collection techniques consisted of semi-structured and structured interviews, discussions, field research, direct and participant observation, and analyses of written sources. Throughout the duration of the research, the author spent substantial periods at the Defense Threat Reduction

Agency interviewing multiple personnel in the Cooperative Threat Reduction directorate and related offices such as the agency historian, the On-Site inspection interagency liaison division, the Strategic Arms Reduction Treaty inspection office, and the Open Skies Treaty office. The Office of the Secretary of Defense provided access and interviews with the personnel from the Under Secretary of Defense for Policy and the Under Secretary of Defense for Acquisition, Technology, and Logistics offices. The National Nuclear Security Administration's public affairs office was instrumental in facilitating the Second Line of Defense research, but access restrictions did not seem to reflect the large amount of open source information available from press releases, briefings, brochures, and other materials already available that provided information as specific as the names, positions, and contact information for Department of Energy and National Nuclear Security Administration officials. A site visit to the Port of Southampton provided a first-hand account of the size and complexities associated with the aptly named "Megaports."

The Department of Homeland Security was an excellent resource throughout the research process. Officials coordinated access and provided expert assistance for the National Targeting Center, the National Operations Center, the Joint Analysis Center, and other applicable offices and initiatives. The Domestic Nuclear Detection Office led the internal research effort for the National Technical Nuclear Forensics Center where, again, access restrictions did not seem to reflect the amount of information from press releases, briefings, testimony, and numerous other open source materials available to the public. The response from multiple departments that played a supporting role related to the topics under examination was overwhelmingly positive. These other government officials assisted with access to current and former nuclear defense representatives up to the deputy assistant secretary level. Their collective willingness to facilitate research was pivotal to the project's completion. This category of assets ranged from White House officials from the National and Homeland Security Council staffs, to Capitol Hill, where Congressman Glenn Thompson's office was extremely accommodating for discussions concerning non-expert background on key resources, schedule restrictions, and House procedures. Finally, U.S. government sponsored studies and reports pertaining to Cooperative Threat Reduction, Second Line of Defense, and the National Technical Nuclear Forensics Center aided in framing an understanding of program issues and organizational cultures.

The Defense Threat Reduction Agency's unpublished Cooperative Threat Reduction history, *With Courage and Persistence,* was rich in detail. Other pertinent documents such as the Department of Energy's "Office of International Material Protection and Cooperation 2006 Strategic Plan" provided a window into departmental operations. Press releases such as "National Nuclear Security Administration and the Vietnamese Ministry of Finance Agreement," testimonies, and the *Congressional Record* also supplied a large amount of data for the book.[810] The same was true for reports from the Government Accountability Office and the Congressional Research Service, as well as singular products from designated commissions and panels.[811] A large volume of secondary sources covering the

---

810   Harahan, Joseph P., *With Courage and Persistence: The United States, Russia, Belarus, Kazakhstan, and Ukraine and the Cooperative Threat Reduction Program,* 2010; U.S. Department of Energy, "Office of International Material Protection and Cooperation 2006 Strategic Plan," National Nuclear Security Administration; U.S. Department of Energy, "NNSA and the Vietnamese Ministry of Finance Agreement," U.S. Department of State Foreign Press Center Briefing by Director of Megaports Initiative William Kilmartin, July 2, 2010.
811   Deutch, John M., Chair, "Combating Proliferation of Weapons of Mass Destruction," July 14, 1999; Woolf. Amy F., *"Nuclear Weapons in U.S. National Security Policy: Past, Present, and Prospects,"* CRS Report for Congress, January 28, 2008; U.S. Government Accountability Office,

Cold War period and specific areas of post-Cold War nuclear defense, such as technical nuclear forensics, also contributed to the analysis.[812] Interviews filled the remaining research gaps. Triangulation of existing primary sources, secondary sources, and field work allowed the researcher to overcome limitations associated with single data collection methods, and validate book findings.

While federal acquisition, planning, programming, budgeting, and execution operating similarities were identified in the studies, the informal security cultures associated with each primary department were strikingly different but difficult to depict in this format. Studying and presenting nuclear defense material in an open source design was a challenge. Based on classification, U.S. government policies, and the generally sensitive nature of the topics, several interviewees chose to remain anonymous, while current U.S. government officials were listed only by position to comply with public affairs requirements.

The Defense Threat Reduction Agency and the greater Department of Defense were open and accommodating, with public affairs approval taking place at the end of the project. This included interviews, documents, site visits, and further points of contact. By contrast Department of Energy supported the

---

Preventing Nuclear Smuggling: Department of Energy Has Made Limited Progress in Installing Radiation Detection Equipment at Highest Priority Foreign Seaports, March 2005; May, Michael, Chair, *Nuclear Forensics: Role, State of the Art, Program Needs,* Joint Working Group of the American Physical Society and the American Association for the Advancement of Science, 2008.
812   Heller, Arnie, "Identifying the Source of Stolen Nuclear Materials: Livermore scientists are analyzing interdicted illicit nuclear and radioactive materials for clues to the materials" origins and routes," *Science and Technology Review,* January/February 2007, pp. 12-18; Rennie, Gabriele, "Tracing the Steps in Nuclear Material Trafficking: Forensic scientists are combining an array of technologies to track illicit nuclear materials to their sources," *Science and Technology Review,* March 2005, pp. 14-21; Moody, Kenton J., Ian D. Hutcheon, and Patrick M. Grant, *Nuclear Forensic Analysis,* 2005.

research, but with further restrictions and delays. Department of Energy, National Nuclear Security Administration public affairs officials insisted on being the single point of contact to schedule and coordinate interviews. They scheduled multiple simultaneous interviews, and sat-in on all contact with program officials once they had been notified of the study. While the department provided the necessary information to conduct the study, they withheld random documents, and restricted Megaports interviews to the deputy director level and above.[813] The Department of Homeland Security and Domestic Nuclear Detection Office were extremely helpful throughout the book, but when it was time for the National Technical Nuclear Forensics Center implementation study, security restrictions and the newness of the program hampered dissemination. While the center cannot control open source briefings, testimonies, reports, and other similar unclassified documents, they placed a minimum "for official use only" restriction on internally generated products provided to the author, including their basic fact sheets. From an official background standpoint, the center was extremely accommodating for site visits, orientation and overview, and discussions with program officials. But, for dissemination the National Technical Nuclear Forensics Center's public affairs office dictated that all officials provide pre-cleared written responses to study questions. The newness of the program was also a limitation because the majority of the original National Technical Nuclear Forensics Center staff was still serving in active roles, thus eliminating the potential for interviews of former program officials.

---

813   This did not negatively impact data collection because the limited Megaports Initiative staff requires the director and deputy director to simultaneously serve as country and regional program managers.

Selected Bibliography

Primary Sources:

Interviews[814]

Ferguson, Charles (Council on Foreign Relations, Fellow for Science and Technology), February 15, 2008.

Ford, Christopher (Department of State, Principal Deputy Assistant Secretary of State, Bureau of Verification, Compliance, and Inspection), April 19, 2010

Foster, Mark (Department of Defense, Defense Threat Reduction Agency, Cooperative Threat Reduction Deputy Director), April, 16 2010.

Gallagher, John (National Security Council Staff, Director, Office of Iraq and Afghanistan Affairs), August 6, 2009.

---

814   Many interviewees held multiple positions during the three administrations and provided input on areas outside of the duty position with which they are associated in the bibliography. In accordance with public affairs requests personnel still serving in the government position for which they were interviewed were listed by position to protect their identities.

Harahan, Joseph P. (Department of Defense, Defense Threat Reduction Agency, Historian), April 26, 2010.

Joseph, Robert (Special Assistant to the President, National Security Council Staff Senior Director for Proliferation Strategy, Counterproliferation, and Homeland Defense), June 14, 2010.

Kluchko, Luke J. (Department of Defense, Defense Threat Reduction Agency, Defense Threat Reduction Office, Cooperative Threat Reduction Division Chief, Moscow), May 21, 2010.

Koch, Susan J. (National Security Council Staff, Director, Proliferation Strategy), May 10, 2010.

Leitner, Peter M., (Department of Defense, Defense Technology Security Administration, Senior Strategic Trade Advisor), January 22, 2011.

Lowman, Ray (Department of Defense, Defense Threat Reduction Agency, Open Skies Treaty Pilot), January 25, 2010.

Nank, Timothy D. (Homeland Security Council Staff, Director, Office of Nuclear Defense Policy), April 24, 2010.

Nelson, Rick, (National Security Council Staff, Associate Director for Maritime Security, Office of Combating Terrorism), August 25, 2010.

Oxford, Vayl (Department of Homeland Security, Director, Domestic Nuclear Detection Office), September 13, 2010.

Rapuano, Kenneth (Deputy Homeland Security Advisor to the President), November 8, 2010.

Reid, James (Department of Defense, Under Secretary of Defense for Policy, Director, Cooperative Threat Reduction Policy Office), April 29, 2010.

Roundy, Jason (Department of Defense, Joint Staff Special Operations Division Official), July 29, 2009.

Semmel, Andrew (Senior Legislative Assistant for Foreign Policy to Senator Lugar), November 17, 2010.

Sloan, Keith (Department of Defense, Defense Threat Reduction Agency, Strategic Arms Reduction Treaty Mission Commander), January 29, 2010.

Slocombe, Walter (Department of Defense, Under Secretary of Defense for Policy), November 18, 2010.

Taylor, Dale (Department of Defense, Defense Threat Reduction Agency, Cooperative Threat Reduction, Strategic Offensive Arms Elimination Project Manager), February 21, 2010.

West, Mark (Department of Defense, Under Secretary of Defense for Acquisition, Technology, and Logistics, Director, Cooperative Threat Reduction Oversight Office), May 20, 2010.

U.S. Department of Defense
----, Defense Threat Reduction Agency, Cooperative Threat Reduction, Advice and Assistance Contractor, January 29, 2010.

----, Defense Threat Reduction Agency, Cooperative Threat Reduction, Director, June 18, 2010.

----, Defense Threat Reduction Agency, Cooperative Threat Reduction, Strategic Offensive Arms Elimination Program Official, February 19, 2010.

----, Defense Threat Reduction Agency, Cooperative Threat Reduction, Strategic Offensive Arms Elimination Project Manager, January 29, 2010.

----, Defense Threat Reduction Agency, Interagency Liaison Division, Chief, Strategic Arms Reduction Treaty/Nuclear Branch, May 14, 2010.

U.S. Department of Energy

----, National Nuclear Security Administration, International Material Protection and Cooperation Budget Official, October 5, 2010.

----, National Nuclear Security Administration, Second Line of Defense, Core Program Official, June 25, 2010.

----, National Nuclear Security Administration, Second Line of Defense, Megaports Program Official, June 25, 2010.

----, National Nuclear Security Administration, Second Line of Defense, Megaports Program Official, July 21, 2010.

----, National Nuclear Security Administration, Second Line of Defense, Program Official, October 5, 2010.

U.S. Department of Homeland Security

----, Customs and Border Protection, Container Security and Secure Freight Initiatives Director, September 15, 2010.

----, Domestic Nuclear Detection Office, Joint Analysis Center Official, October 26, 2010.

----, Customs and Border Protection, National Targeting Center, Assistant Director for Cargo, September 1, 2010.

----, Customs and Border Protection, National Targeting Center, Container Security Initiative Watch Commander, September 1, 2010.

----, Domestic Nuclear Detection Office, National Technical Nuclear Forensics Center Official [written response], October 12, 2010.

----, Domestic Nuclear Detection Office, National Technical Nuclear Forensics Center Official [written response], October 13, 2010.

U.S. Department of State, Bureau of Economic, Energy, and Business Affairs, Directorate and Office of Transportation Policy, Director, Maritime Security, August 25, 2010.

SPEECHES, LETTERS, DIRECTIVES, DECLARATIONS, DEBATES, INTERVIEWS, AND TESTIMONY

Aoki, Steven, "Hearing on H.R. 2631, the Nuclear Forensics and Attribution Act." Statement before the House Committee on Homeland Security Subcommittee on Emerging Threats, Cybersecurity, and Science and Technology, October 10, 2007.

Aspin, Les, "Defense Secretary Aspin speech to the National Academy of Sciences." December 7, 1993.

Biegun, Stephen E., Presider, and Richard G. Lugar, and Barrack Obama, Speakers, "Challenges Ahead for Cooperative Threat Reduction." Rush Transcript, Federal News Service, Inc., Council on Foreign Relations, Washington, D.C., November 1, 2005.

Bronson, Lisa, "Cooperative Threat Reduction Program." Testimony before the Senate Armed Services Committee Subcommittee on Emerging Threats and Capabilities, March 10, 2004.

Burns, Carol J., "Hearing on H.R. 2631, the Nuclear Forensics and Attribution Act." Statement before the House Committee on Homeland Security Subcommittee on Emerging Threats, Cybersecurity, and Science and Technology, October 10, 2007.

Bush, George H. W., "Address to the Nation Announcing United States Military Action in Panama." December 20, 1989.
----, "Address to the Nation on Reducing United States and Soviet Nuclear Weapons." September 27, 1991.
----, "Letter to Congressional Leaders Reporting on Nuclear Nonproliferation." January 19, 1993.
----, "National Security Directive-40: Decisions on START Issues." May 14, 1990.
----, "National Security Directive-43: FY 90-95 Nuclear Weapons Stockpile Plan." July 12, 1990.
----, "National Security Directive-54: Responding to Iraqi Aggression in the Gulf." January 15, 1991.
----, "National Security Review-14: Review of United States Arms Control Policies." April 3, 1989.
----, "Remarks at the Associate Press Business Luncheon in Chicago, Illinois." April 24, 1989.

Bush, George H. W., Boris Yeltsin, "Joint Understanding." June 17, 1992.

Bush, George W., "Homeland Security Presidential Directive-1: Organization and Operation of the Homeland Security Council." October 29, 2001.
----, "Homeland Security Presidential Directive-8: National Preparedness." December 17, 2003.
----, "Memorandum for the Secretary of State, Subject: Waiver of Nuclear-Related Sanctions on India and Pakistan (Presidential Determination No. 2001-28)." September 22, 2001.

----, "National Security Presidential Directive-1: Organization of the National Security Council System." February 13, 2001.

----, "National Security Presidential Directive-43/Homeland Security Presidential Directive-14: Domestic Nuclear Detection." April 15, 2005.

----, "National Security Presidential Directive-44: Management of Interagency Efforts Concerning Reconstruction and Stabilization." December 7, 2005.

----, "Remarks at the National Defense University," May 1, 2001.

Bush, George W., V. V. Putin, "Joint Statement by U.S. President George Bush and Russian Federation President V.V. Putin Announcing the Global Initiative to Combat Nuclear Terrorism." Office of the White House Press Secretary, July 15, 2006.

Caldwell, Stephen L. "The SAFE Port Act: Status and Implementation One Year Later." Testimony before the House Subcommittee on Border, Maritime and Global Counterterrorism; Committee on Homeland Security, October 30, 2007.

Carter, Ashton B., "U.S. assistance to the New Independent States of the Former Soviet Union (FSU) in dismantling their weapons of mass destruction." Testimony before the House Foreign Affairs Committee, September 21, 1993.

Carter, James E., "Nuclear Nonproliferation Act of 1978 Statement on Signing H.R. 8638 Into Law." March 10, 1978.

----, "Executive Order 12148- Federal Emergency Management." July 20, 1979.

Cerny, Joseph, et al., *Education in Nuclear Science: A Status Report and Recommendations for the Beginning of the 21ˢᵗ Century.* Department of Energy/National Science Foundation Nuclear Science Advisory Committee, Subcommittee on Education, November 2004.

Cirincione, Joseph, "Assessing the Ballistic Missile Threat." Testimony before the Senate Committee on Governmental Affairs, February 9, 2000.

Clarke, Richard A., "Testimony of Richard A. Clarke before the National Commission on Terrorist Attacks upon the United States." March 24, 2004.

Clinton, William J., "Presidential Decision Directive/National Security Council-15: U.S. Policy on Stockpile Stewardship Under an Extended Moratorium and a Comprehensive Test Ban." November 3, 1993.
----, "Presidential Decision Directive/National Security Council-39: U.S. Policy on Counterterrorism." June 21, 1995.
----, "Presidential Decision Directive/National Security Council-56: Managing Complex Contingency Operations." May 1997.
----, "Statement on Signing the National Missile Defense Act of 1999." July 22, 1999.
----, "Statement on the National Security Strategy Report." July 21, 1994.
----, "The President's Radio Address." July 3, 1993.

Clinton, William J., and Boris Yeltsin, "Joint Statement Concerning the Anti-Ballistic Missile Treaty." Office of the White House Press Secretary, March 21, 1997.

----, "Joint Statement on Nonproliferation of Weapons of Mass Destruction and the Means of Their Delivery." January 14, 1994.

Cochran, Thad, "Lott, Daschle Announce Bipartisan National Security Working Group." Press Release, April 29, 1999.

Coyle, Philip E. III., "Oversight of Ballistic Missile Defense (Part 3): Questions for the Missile Defense Agency." Testimony before the House Committee on Oversight and Government Reform, Subcommittee on National Security and Foreign Affairs, April 30, 2008.

CONGRESSIONAL RECORD

101st Congress (1989-1990), "Senate Resolution 149 – Relating to the Resumption of START Talks." Senate, June 21, 1989.

102nd Congress (1991-1992), "Committee Approval of the START Treaty." Senate, July 2, 1992.

----, "START Is No Place to Stop." Senate, September 10, 1991.

----, "The START Treaty." Senate, October 5.

----, "The START Treaty Must Be Postponed." Senate, October 25, 1991.

103rd Congress (1993-1994), "START II Treaty." Senate, May 12, 1993.

104th Congress (1995-1996), "Defend America Act increases nuclear threat." Senate, May 23, 1996.

----, "Missile proliferation: one of the greatest threats to America in the 21st-Century." House of Representatives, April 3, 1995.

----, "National Defense Authorization Act for Fiscal Year 1996- Veto message from the President of the United States (H. Doc. No. 104-155)." House of Representatives, January 3, 1996.

----, "Star Wars or Maginot Line? Contract to Bankrupt America." Senate, January 6, 1995.

----, "Threat of Missile attack on the United States and our Allies." Senate, March 15, 1996.

----, "Treaty with the Russian Federation on Further Reduction and Limitation of Strategic Offensive Arms (The START II Treaty)." Senate, December 22, 1995.

106th Congress (1999-2000), "National Missile Defense." Senate, May 25, 2000.

----, "The National Missile Defense Act." Senate, July, 26, 1999.

Croft, Steve, "Secretary Rumsfeld Live Interview with Infinity CBS Radio." November 14, 2002.

Crouch, J.D. II, "Cooperative Threat Reduction Program." Testimony before the Senate Armed Services Committee Subcommittee on Emerging Threats, March 6, 2002.

----, "Cooperative Threat Reduction Program." Statement before the House Armed Services Committee, March 4, 2003.

D'Agostino, Davi M., "Homeland Defense: Preliminary Observations on Defense Chemical, Biological, Radiological, Nuclear, and High-Yield Explosives Consequence Management Plans and Preparedness." Testimony before the House Subcommittee on Terrorism and Unconventional Threats and Capabilities, Committee on Armed Services, July 28, 2009.

Deutch, John M., "Briefing on Results of the Nuclear Posture Review." Hearing before the Senate Committee on Armed Services (S. HRG. 103-870), September 22, 1994.

Eisenhower, Dwight D., "Farewell Address, January 17, 1961." Dwight D. Eisenhower Memorial Commission.

Evenson, Michael K., "Hearing on H.R. 2631, the Nuclear Forensics and Attribution Act." Statement before the

House Committee on Homeland Security Subcommittee on Emerging Threats, Cybersecurity, and Science and Technology, October 10, 2007.

Feith, Douglas J., "Hearing on the Nuclear Posture Review." Statement before the Senate Armed Services Committee, February 14, 2002.

Ford, Jess T., "U.S. Public Diplomacy: State Department Efforts Lack Certain Communication Elements and Face Persistent Challenges." Testimony before the Subcommittee on Science, the Departments of State, Justice, and Commerce, and Related Agencies, House Committee on Appropriations, May 3, 2006.

Ford, Gerald R. Jr., "Statement on Nuclear Policy." October 28, 1976.

Fuentes, Thomas V., "The FBI's Legal Attaché program." Statement before the Subcommittee on Border, Maritime, and Global Counterterrorism House Homeland Security Committee, October 4, 2007.

Gates, Robert, "Nuclear Weapons and Deterrence in the 21st Century." Speech to the Carnegie Endowment for International Peace Speech, Washington, D.C., October 28, 2008.

Grant, Andrew, "Hearing on H.R. 2631, the Nuclear Forensics and Attribution Act." Statement before the House Committee on Homeland Security Subcommittee on Emerging Threats, Cybersecurity, and Science and Technology, October 10, 2007.

Huizenga, David, "NNSA's Megaports Initiative and Its Role in the Secure Freight Initiative (SFI)." Testimony before the Senate Commerce, Science, and Transportation Subcommittee, June 12, 2008.

----, "Radiation Detection." Testimony before the House Energy and Commerce Subcommittee on Oversight and Investigations September 18, 2007.

Langevin, James, "Markup of H.R. 2631, the Nuclear Forensics and Attribution Act." Opening Statement Chairman House Committee on Homeland Security Subcommittee on Emerging Threats, Cybersecurity, and Science and Technology, October 10, 2007.

Lewis, John, "Detecting and Neutralizing Potential Terrorist Threats Involving Nuclear Weapons." Statement before the House of Representatives Committee on Homeland Security Subcommittee on Prevention of Nuclear and Biological Attack, October 27, 2005.

Lugar, Richard G., "The Nunn-Lugar Threat Reduction Program." Retrieved June 10, 2010, from http://lugar.senate.gov/nunnlugar/.

Lute, Jane Holl, "Nuclear Terrorism: Strengthening Our Domestic Defenses, Part II." Testimony before the United States Senate Committee on Homeland Security and Governmental Affairs, September 15, 2010.

Jones, Gary L., "Nuclear Nonproliferation: Coordination of U.S. Programs Designed to Reduce the Threat Posed by Weapons of Mass Destruction." Testimony before the Senate Subcommittee on International Security, Proliferation, and Federal Services, Committee on Governmental Affairs, November 14, 2001.

----, "U.S. Efforts to Combat Nuclear Smuggling." Testimony before the Senate Subcommittee on Emerging Threats and Capabilities, Committee on Armed Services, July 30, 2002.

Kennedy, Edward M., "EMK Address at the Brown University Commencement Forum." June 4, 1983.

Kennedy, John F., "The President's News Conference." March 21, 1963.

Kennedy, John F., and Richard M. Nixon, "Kennedy-Nixon Presidential Debate Broadcast from New York and Los Angeles." October 13, 1960.
----, "Kennedy-Nixon Presidential Debate in New York." October 21, 1960.

Lake, Anthony, "Laying the Foundation for a Post-Cold War World- National Security in the 21st Century." Speech to the Council on Foreign Relations, May 24, 1996.

Majidi, Vahid, "Hearing on H.R. 2631, the Nuclear Forensics and Attribution Act." Statement before the House Committee on Homeland Security Subcommittee on Emerging Threats, Cybersecurity, and Science and Technology, October 10, 2007.

McCain, John, "Statement by Senator McCain Expressing Concerns about the Senate Vote on the Comprehensive Test Ban Treaty." Press Release, October 12, 1999.

Mines, Michael, "The FBI and Fusion Centers." Statement before the House Committee on Homeland Security, Subcommittee on Intelligence, Information Sharing, and Terrorism Risk Assessment, September 27, 2007.

Mowatt-Larsen, Rolf, "The Threat of Nuclear Terrorism." Statement before the Senate Homeland Security and Government Affairs Committee, April 2, 2008.

Mueller, Robert S. III, "Nuclear Terrorism: Prevention is our Endgame." Global Initiative Nuclear Terrorism Conference Speech, Miami, Florida, June 11, 2007.

Oxford, Vayl, "Hearing on H.R. 2631, the Nuclear Forensics and Attribution Act." Statement before the House Committee on Homeland Security Subcommittee on Emerging Threats, Cybersecurity, and Science and Technology, October 10, 2007.

Perry, William J., "Defense Secretary Perry address to the Aspin Institute on U.S. National Strategy in the Middle East." February 6, 1996.

Powell, Colin L., "U.S. Secretary of State Colin Powell Address to the UN Security Council Transcript." February 5, 2003.

Reagan, Ronald W., "Address to the Nation on Defense and National Security." March 23, 1983.
----, "National Security Decision Directive-325: FY89-94 Nuclear Weapon Stockpile Plan." January 19, 1989.

Sagan, Scott, "Introductory Statement at the Sagan-Payne debate on U.S. Nuclear Declaratory Policy." Center for International Security and Cooperation, May 25, 2010.

Schiff, Adam, "Hearing on H.R. 2631, the Nuclear Forensics and Attribution Act." Statement before the House Committee on Homeland Security Subcommittee on Emerging Threats, Cybersecurity, and Science and Technology, October 10, 2007.

Steensma, David K., "U.S.-Russian Cooperative Threat Reduction and Nonproliferation Programs." Testimony before the House Committee on Armed Services, March 4, 2003.

Tannenhaus, Sam, "Deputy Secretary Wolfowitz Interview Transcript." *Vanity Fair*, May 9, 2003.

Taylor, Tammy P., "Nuclear Defense Research and Development: Institute of Electrical and Electronics Engineers Keynote Address." Office of Science and Technology Policy, Executive Office of the President, May 12, 2008.

Tenet, George J., "DCI Remarks on Iraq's WMD Programs." Georgetown University, February 5, 2004.

Towns, Edolphus, "Letter to U.S. Government Accountability Office requesting a new review of the Megaports Initiative." Chairman, House Committee on Oversight and Government Reform, January 13, 2010.

Visclosky, Peter J., "Subcommittee Markup: Fiscal Year 2009 Energy and Water Development Appropriations Act." Statement of Chairman, June 17, 2008.

Weldon, Curt, "Open session on KGB operations and Soviet-era and contemporary Russian threat perceptions." Opening statement of the Chairman, Subcommittee on Research and Development, October 26, 1999.

Zemin, Jiang and Vladimir Putin, "Joint Statement by the Presidents of the People's Republic of China and the Russian Federation on Anti-Missile Defense." Beijing, China, July, 18, 2000.

LEGISLATION, TREATIES, AND AGREEMENTS

"Agreed Framework Between The United States of America and The Democratic People's Republic of Korea." October 21, 1994.

"Agreement Between The United States of America and The Union of Soviet Socialist Republics on the Establishment of Nuclear Risk Reduction Centers (and Protocols Thereto)." September 15, 1987.

"Amendment to the Agreement Between the Department of Defense of the United States of America and the Federal Space Agency Concerning Cooperation in the Elimination of Strategic Offensive Arms." May 2009.

Atomic Energy Act of 1946 (P.L. 585). The Library of Congress.

Atomic Energy Act of 1954 (P.L. 83-703), *as Amended.* The Library of Congress.

Authorization for Use of Military Force Against Iraq Resolution of 2002 (P.L. 107-243). The Library of Congress.
----, 107th Congress-2nd Session 455th Roll Call Vote of by members of the House of Representatives.
----, 107th Congress-2nd Session 237th Roll Call Vote by members of the Senate.

Department of Defense Appropriations Act, 2006 (H.R. 2863, P.L. 109-148). The Library of Congress.

Energy and Water Development Appropriations Act, 2006 (H.R. 2419, P.L. 109-103). The Library of Congress.

Energy Reorganization Act of 1974 (P.L. 93-438). The Library of Congress.

Henry J. Hyde United States-India Peaceful Atomic Energy Cooperation Act of 2006 (H.R. 5682). The Library of Congress.

Homeland Security Act of 2002 (H.R. 5005, P.L. 107–296). The Library of Congress.

Implementing Recommendations of the 9/11 Commission Act of 2007 (H.R. 1, P.L. 110-53). The Library of Congress.

Intelligence Reform and Terrorism Prevention Act of 2004 (P.L.108-458). The Library of Congress.

John Warner National Defense Authorization Act for Fiscal Year 2007 (H.R. 5122). The Library of Congress.

"Memorandum of Understanding Relating to the Treaty between the United States of America and the Union of Soviet Socialist Republics on the Limitation of Anti-Ballistic Missile Systems on May 26, 1972." September 26, 1997.

National Defense Authorization Act for Fiscal Year(s) 1992 and 1993, 1994, 1996, 1997, 1998, 1999, 2000, 2001, 2004, and 2008. The Library of Congress.

National Missile Defense Act of 1999 (P.L. 106-38). The Library of Congress.

National Science and Technology Policy, Organization, and Priorities Act of 1976 (P.L. 94-282). The Library of Congress.

National Security Restoration Act. United States House of
    Representatives. Retrieved November 15, 2011, http://
    www.house.gov/house/Contract/defenseb.txt.

Nuclear Forensics and Attribution Act of 2010 (H.R. 730, P.L.
    111-140). The Library of Congress.

Nuclear Waste Policy Act of 1982 (P.L. 97-425). The Library of
    Congress.

Post-Katrina Emergency Management Reform Act of 2006 (P.L.
    109–295). The Library of Congress.

"Republican Contract with America." United States House
    of Representatives. Retrieved November 15, 2011, http://
    www.house.gov/house/Contract/CONTRACT.html.

*Robert T. Stafford Disaster Relief and Emergency Assistance
    Act, as amended and Related to Authorities* (P.L. 93-288).
    The Library of Congress.

Security and Accountability for Every (SAFE) Port Act of 2006
    (H.R. 4954, P.L. 109-347). The Library of Congress.

Soviet Nuclear Threat Reduction Act of 1991 (H.R 3807, P.L.
    102-228, Title II). The Library of Congress.

The Constitution of the United States and The Declaration
    of Independence. 109th Congress, 2nd Session (Senate
    Document 109-17), 22nd printing 2006.

"Treaty Between The United States of America and The Russian
    Federation on Further Reduction and Limitation of Strategic
    Offensive Arms." January 3, 1993, Protocol September 26,
    1997.

"Treaty Between The United States of America and The Union of Socialist Republics on the Limitation of Anti-Ballistic Missile Systems." May 26, 1972.

"Treaty Between the United States of America and the Union of Soviet Socialist Republics on the Limitation of Strategic Offensive Arms, Together with Agreed Statements and Common Understandings Regarding the Treaty." June 18, 1979.

"Treaty Between The United States of America and The Union of Socialist Republics on the Reduction and Limitations of Strategic Offensive Arms." July 31, 1991, Protocol May 23, 1992.

U.S. Code, *Title 42- The Public Health and Welfare.* January 3, 2006. The Library of Congress.

STRATEGIES, DOCTRINE, AND PLANS

Baruch, Bernard, "Baruch Plan: Presented to the United Nations Atomic Energy Commission." June 14, 1946.

Environmental Protection Agency, "National Oil and Hazardous Substances Pollution Contingency Plan Overview." March, 17, 2009. Retrieved November 15, 2009, from http://www.epa.gov/OEM/content/lawsregs/ncpover.htm.

Federal Emergency Management Agency, *2008 Disaster Housing Plan.* Retrieved November 13, 2009, from http://www.fema.gov/pdf/media/2008/dhp_08.pdf.
----, *Federal Response Plan (9230.1-PL).* April 1999.

Homeland Security Council, *National Planning Scenarios: Executive Summaries.* Domestic Threat, Response, and

Incident Management Policy Coordination Committee, Scenarios Working Group, April 2005, Draft Version 20.2.
----, *Planning Guidance for Response to a Nuclear Detonation.* January 16, 2009.

Joint Publication 3-40, *Joint Doctrine for Combating Weapons of Mass Destruction.* July 8, 2004.

National Response Plan. U.S. Government Printing Office, Washington, D.C., 2003.

National Military Strategy. U.S. Government Printing Office, Washington, D.C., 2004.

National Military Strategy to Combat Weapons of Mass Destruction. U.S. Government Printing Office, Washington, D.C., 2006.

National Security Strategy for a New Century. U.S. Government Printing Office, Washington, D.C., 1998.

National Security Strategy of Engagement and Enlargement. U.S. Government Printing Office, Washington, D.C., 1995.

National Security Strategy of the United States of America. U.S. Government Printing Office, Washington, D.C., 1991, 2002, and 2006.

National Strategy for Combating Terrorism. U.S. Government Printing Office, Washington, D.C., 2003.

National Strategy for Homeland Security. U.S. Government Printing Office, Washington, D.C., 2002.

National Strategy to Combat Weapons of Mass Destruction. U.S. Government Printing Office, Washington, D.C., 2002.

National Strategy for Maritime Security. U.S. Government Printing Office, Washington, D.C., September 2005.

North Atlantic Treaty Organization, *NATO Handbook.* NATO Publications, October 15, 2002.

Nuclear Regulatory Commission, *Federal Radiological Emergency Response Plan.* May 1, 1996.

U.S. DEPARTMENT OF DEFENSE

----, *Defense Acquisition Guidebook.* Defense Acquisition University. Retrieved April 15, 2010, https://acc.dau.mil/CommunityBrowser.aspx?id=289207&lang=en-US.

----, *Defense Strategy for the 1990s: The Regional Defense Strategy.* January 1993.

----, Directive 5000.1, "Defense Acquisition System." November 20, 2007.

----, Directive 5111.14, "Assistant Secretary of Defense for International Security Policy (ASD (ISP))." March 22, 2005.

----, "Sample Acquisition Plan Format." Defense Acquisition University. Retrieved April 15, 2010, https://acc.dau.mil/CommunityBrowser.aspx?id=31482.

U.S. DEPARTMENT OF ENERGY

----, "Office of International Material Protection and Cooperation 2006 Strategic Plan." National Nuclear Security Administration.

----, "Office of the Second Line of Defense 2006 Strategic Plan." National Nuclear Security Administration.

U.S. DEPARTMENT OF HOMELAND SECURITY

----, *Acquisition Planning Requirements.* October 26, 2004.
----, *Capitol Planning Investment and Control Guide.* December 2005.
----, *Container Security Initiative: 2006-2011 Strategic Plan.* U.S. Customs and Border Protection, August 2006.
----, Management Directive 0782, "Acquisition Certification Requirements for Program Manager." May 26, 2004.
----, Management Directive 1400, "Investment Review Process."

----, *The Integrated Planning System.* January 2009.

U.S. Department of State, *International Outreach and Coordination Strategy for the National Strategy for Maritime Security.* November 2005.

U.S. Homeland Defense Strategy. U.S. Government Printing Office, Washington, D.C. 2005.

POLICIES, PRESS RELEASES, BRIEFINGS, AND REPORTS

Acheson, Dean, and David Lilienthal, "Acheson-Lilienthal: Report on the International Control of Atomic Energy." March 16, 1946.

Albright, David, Jacqueline Shire, and Paul Brannan, "IAEA Report on Iran: Centrifuge Operation Significantly Improving; Gridlock on Alleged Weaponization Issues."

Institute for Science and International Security Report, September 15, 2008.

Aspin, Les, "The End of the Star Wars Era." Department of Defense News Briefing, May 13, 1993.

Baker, Howard, and Lloyd Cutler, Chairs, *A Report Card on the Department of Energy's Nonproliferation Programs with Russia.* The Secretary of Energy Advisory Board, U.S. Department of Energy, January 10, 2001.

Beauchesne, Ann M., and Jerry Boese, *Cleaning Up America's Nuclear Weapons Complex: A Governors Guide.* National Governors" Association Center for Best Practices, 2000.

Bliley, Tom, "Rudman Report: Science at its Best, Security at its Worst." Hearing (Serial No. 106-57) before the House Committee on Commerce, June 22, 1999.

Carnegie Endowment for International Peace and the Russian-American Nuclear Security Advisory Council, *Reshaping U.S.-Russian Threat Reduction: New Approaches for the Second Decade.* Washington D.C., 2002.

Carnesale, Albert, Chair, *Nuclear Forensics: A Capability at Risk (Abbreviated Version).* National Academy of Sciences, Committee on Nuclear Forensics Report, Washington D.C.: The National Academies Press, 2010.

Central Intelligence Agency, "Estimate of the Effects of the Soviet Possession of the Atomic Bomb upon the Security of the United States and upon the Probabilities of Direct Soviet Military Action." April 6, 1950.

Central Intelligence Group, "Soviet Capabilities for the Development and Production of Certain Types of Weapons and Equipment." October 31, 1946.

Cerami, Joseph R., and Jeffrey A. Engel, eds., *Rethinking Leadership and "Whole-of-Government" National Security Reform: Problems, Progress, and Prospects.* Carlisle, Pennsylvania, Strategic Studies Institute, May 2010.

Congressional Research Service
----, *Treaties and Other International Agreements: The Role of the United States Senate.* Washington D.C.: Library of Congress, January 2001.
Bea, Keith, "Federal Stafford Act Disaster Assistance: Presidential Declarations, Eligible Activities, and Funding." *CRS Report for Congress*, August 15, 2008.
Best, Richard A. Jr., "The National Security Council: An Organizational Assessment." *CRS Report for Congress*, April 21, 2008.
Best, Richard A. Jr., Alfred Cumming, and Todd Masse, "Director of National Intelligence: Statutory Authorities." *CRS Report for Congress*, April 11, 2005.
Chanlett-Avery, Emma, and Sharon Squassoni, "North Korea's Nuclear Test: Motivations, Implications, and U.S. Options." *CRS Report for Congress,* October 24, 2006.
Daggett, Stephen, and Robert D. Shuey, "National Missile Defense: Status of the Debate." *CRS Report for Congress,* May 29, 1998.
Dale, Cathrine, "National Security Strategy: Legislative Mandates, Execution to Date, and Considerations for Congress." *CRS Report for Congress*, September 23, 2008.
Hildreth, Steven A., "Ballistic Missile Defense: Historical Overview." *CRS Report for Congress*, July 9, 2007.
----, "North Korean Ballistic Missile Threat to the United States." *CRS Report for Congress*, October 18, 2006.

Medalia, Jonathan, "Nuclear Earth Penetrator Weapons." *CRS Report for Congress*, January 27, 2003.

----, "Nuclear Weapons: Comprehensive Test Ban Treaty." *CRS Report for Congress*, October 11, 2006.

----, "The Reliable Replacement Warhead Program: Background and Current Developments." *CRS Report for Congress*, September 12, 2008.

Nikitin, Mary Beth, "Proliferation Security Initiative." *CRS Report for Congress*, September 10, 2009.

Niksch, Larry A., "North Korea's Nuclear Weapons Development and Diplomacy." *CRS Report for Congress*, January 21, 2008 and May 27, 2009.

Relyea, Harold C., "Organizing for Homeland Security: The Homeland Security Council Reconsidered." *CRS Report for Congress*, March 19, 2008.

Rennack, Dianne E., "North Korea: Economic Sanctions." *CRS Report for Congress*, October 17, 2006.

Shea, Dana A., "The Global Nuclear Detection Architecture: Issues for Congress." *CRS Report for Congress*, September 23, 2008.

Shea, Dana A., John D. Moteff, and Daniel Morgan, "The Advanced Spectroscopic Portal Program: Background and Issues for Congress." *CRS Report for Congress*, December 30, 2010.

Squassoni, Sharon, "North Korea's Nuclear Weapons: Latest Developments." *CRS Report for Congress*, October 18, 2006.

Squassoni, Sharon, and Carl E. Behrens "The Nuclear Nonproliferation Treaty Review Conference: Issues for Congress." *CRS Report for Congress*, May 16, 2005.

Woolf, Amy F., "Nonproliferation and Threat Reduction Assistance: U.S. Programs in the Former Soviet Union." *CRS Report for Congress*, February 4, 2010.

----, "Nuclear Weapons in U.S. National Security Policy: Past, Present, and Prospects." *CRS Report for Congress*, January 28, 2008.

----, "Nunn-Lugar Cooperative Threat Reduction Programs: Issues for Congress." *CRS Report for Congress*, March 23, 2001 and March 6, 2002.

----, "Strategic Arms Reduction Treaties (START I&II): Verification and Compliance Issues." *CRS Issue Brief*, November 22, 1996.

----, "The Nuclear Posture Review: Overview and Emerging Issues." *CRS Report for Congress*, January 31, 2002.

Cox, Christopher, Chair, "U.S. National Security and Military/ Commercial Concerns with the People's Republic of China." U.S. House of Representatives Select Committee Report (105-851) on U.S. National Security and Military/ Commercial Concerns with the Peoples Republic of China, May 1999.

Deutch, John M., Chair, "Combating Proliferation of Weapons of Mass Destruction." Report of the Commission to Assess the Organization of the Federal Government to Combat the Proliferation of Weapons of Mass Destruction, July 14, 1999.

Federal Bureau of Investigation, "FBI and Savannah River National Laboratory Put Science to Work to Protect the Nation." FBI National Press Office, June 3, 2010.

Fermi National Accelerator Laboratory, "Subject: Nuclear Materials Information Program (NMIP)." Memorandum from Fermilab to Department of Energy/NNSA Site Manager, dated February 5, 2009.

Franck, James, et al., "Franck Report: A Report to the Secretary of War." June 1945.

Franz, David R., and Ronald Lehman, Chairs, *Global Security Engagement: A New Model for Cooperative Threat Reduction*. National Academy of Sciences, Committee Report on Strengthening and Expanding the Department of Defense Cooperative Threat Reduction Program Report, Washington D.C.: The National Academies Press, 2009.

Gilmore, James S. III, Chair, *II. Toward a National Strategy for Combating Terrorism*. Advisory Panel to Assess Domestic Response Capabilities for Terrorism Involving Weapons of Mass Destruction, RAND Report, December 15, 2000.

Hobson, David, "Committee on Appropriations accompanying report to the FY 2004 Energy and Water Development Appropriations Bill (H.R. 2754, 108-212)." The Library of Congress, July 16, 2003.

Kean, Thomas H., and Lee H. Hamilton, Chairs, *9/11 Commission Report: Final Report of the National Commission on Terrorist Attacks Upon the United States*. New York and London: W.W. Norton and Company, 2004.

Locher, James R. III, Executive Director, *Forging a New Shield.* Project on National Security Reform, 2008.

May, Michael, Chair, *Nuclear Forensics: Role, State of the Art, Program Needs*. Joint Working Group of the American Physical Society and the American Association for the Advancement of Science, United States of America: AAAS Publication Services, 2008.

Kunsman, David M., and Douglas B. Lawson, "A Primer on U.S. Strategic Nuclear Policy." Sandia Report (SAND2001-0053), January 2001.

Murdock, Clark A., "Beyond Goldwater-Nichols: Defense Reform for a New Strategic Era (Phase I)." Center for Strategic and International Studies Report, March 1, 2004.

Murdock, Clark A., and Michele A. Flournoy, "Beyond Goldwater-Nichols: U.S. Government and Defense Reform for a New Strategic Era (Phase II)." Center for Strategic and International Studies Report, July 28, 2005.

National Intelligence Council, "Iran: Nuclear Intentions and Capabilities." National Intelligence Estimate, November 2007.

National Security Council, "Instructions for the Expenditure of Nuclear Weapons in Accordance with the Presidential Authorization." May 22, 1957.
----, "NSC 68: United States Objectives and Programs for National Security." April 7, 1950.
----, "NSC 162/2: Basic National Security Policy." October 30, 1953.

Office of the Director of National Intelligence, "Fact Sheet: Real Progress in Reforming Intelligence." Public Affairs Office, January 23, 2007.

Oxford, Vayl, "Energy Facility Contractors Group (EFCOG) 2007 Executive Council Meeting." February 21-22, 2007.

Payne, Keith B., et al., *Rationale and Requirements for U.S. Nuclear Forces, Vol. I, Executive Report.* National Institute for Public Policy, January 2001.

Perry, William J., and Brent Scowcroft, Chairs, "U.S. Nuclear Weapons Policy." Council on Foreign Relations Independent Task Force Report No. 62, 2009.

Rumsfeld, Donald, Chair, "Report of the Commission to Assess the Ballistic Missile Threat to the United States." Commission to Assess the Ballistic Missile Threat to the United States, July 15, 1998.

Speaker's Advisory Group on Russia, *Russia's Road to Corruption: How the Clinton Administration Exported Government Instead of Free Enterprise and Failed the Russian People.* U.S. House of Representatives 106th Congress, September 2000.

Spence, Floyd D., *The Clinton Administration and Nuclear Stockpile Stewardship: Erosion by Design.* House National Security Committee Report, October 30, 1996.

U.S. Census Bureau, "Trade in Goods (Import, Export and Trade Balance) with China." Retrieved July 30, 2009, from http://www.census.gov/foreign-trade/balance/c5700.html#2009.

U.S.-China Business Council, "U.S.-China Trade Statistics and China's World Trade Statistics." Retrieved July 30, 2009, from http://www.uschina.org/statistics/tradetable.html.

U.S. Department of Defense

----, *An Executive Primer: Department of Defense Planning, Programming, Budgeting, and Execution (PPBE) Process/Army Planning, Programming, Budgeting, and Execution (PPBE) Process.* Army Force Management School, May 2006.

----, *Annual Report to the President and the Congress.* February 1995.

----, *Contracts Awarded by the Defense Threat Reduction Agency In Support of the Cooperative Threat Reduction*

Program. Inspector General Report (No. D-2004-111), August 25, 2004.

----, *Cooperative Threat Reduction Annual Report to Congress.* Defense Threat Reduction Agency, Fiscal Years 2006, 2007, 2008, and 2009.

----, *Cooperative Threat Reduction Budget Estimates.* Defense Threat Reduction Agency, Fiscal Years 2009 and 2010.

----, *Cooperative Threat Reduction Construction Projects.* Inspector General Report (No. D-2004-039), December 18, 2003.

----, "Cooperative Threat Reduction Integrating Contracts (CTRIC)." Defense Threat Reduction Agency. Retrieved April 15, 2010, http://ctric.dtra.saic-trsc.com/.

----, *Cooperative Threat Reduction Program: Audit Report.* Inspector General Report (No. D-2001-074), March 9, 2001.

----, *Cooperative Threat Reduction Program Liquid Propellant Disposition Project.* Inspector General Report (No. D-2002-154), September 30, 2002.

----, *Cooperative Threat Reduction Solid Rocket Motor Disposition Facility Project.* Inspector General Report (No. D-2003-131), September 11, 2003.

----, *Defense Science Board Summer Study Task Force on Department of Defense Responses to Transnational Threats—Volume III Supporting Reports.* Office of the Under Secretary of Defense for Acquisition and Technology, February 1998.

----, "Defense Threat Reduction Agency FY2008 Supplemental Funding Request." Retrieved April 15, 2010 http://comptroller.defense.gov/defbudget/fy2008/fy2007_supplemental/FY2008_Global_War_On_Terror_Request/pdfs/operation/13_DTRA_Supp_OP-5.pdf.

----, *Department of Defense Key Officials 1947-2004.* Historical Office of the Secretary of Defense, 2004.

----, "Department of Defense Launches Threat Reduction Advisory Committee." Office of the Assistant Secretary of Defense (Public Affairs) News Release (No. 366-98), July 15, 1998.

----, "Fact Sheet: Air Force Technical Applications Center." U.S. Air Force, November 2008.

----, "Historical Funding for MDA FY85-10." Missile Defense Agency. Retrieved May 15, 2010, from http://www. mda.mil/global/documents/pdf/histfunds.pdf.

----, "History of the Custody and Deployment of Nuclear Weapons (U), July 1945 through September 1977." National Security Archives. Retrieved April 9, 2009, from http://www.gwu.edu/~nsarchiv/news/19991020/index.html.

----, "Missile Defense Agency Completes Change of Responsibility Ceremony." Missile Defense Agency News Release, November 21, 2008.

----, *Management Structure of the Cooperative Threat Reduction Program.* Inspector General Report (No. D-2004-050), February 4, 2004.

----, "Nuclear Forensics and Attribution." Defense Threat Reduction Agency and U.S. STRATCOM Center for Combating WMD. Retrieved October 25, 2010, from http://www.dtra.mil/missions/NuclearDetectionForensics/Forensics.aspx.

----, "Nuclear Posture Review Brief." September 22, 1994.

----, *Nuclear Posture Review Report: Forward.* January 2002.

----, *Quadrennial Defense Review Report,* September 30, 2001, February 6, 2006, and February 2010.

----, "Report on the Bottom-Up Review." October 1993.

----, "U.S. Nuclear Defense." Office of the Deputy Assistant to the Secretary of Defense for Nuclear Matters. Retrieved November 5, 2009, from http://www.acq.osd. mil/ncbdp/nm/U.S.NuclearDefense.html.

U.S. DEPARTMENT OF ENERGY

----, "Beyond Guns, Gates and Guards: An Integrated Approach to Nuclear Material Security." National Nuclear Security Administration Briefing, 2008.

----, "Fact Sheet: Nevada National Security Site." National Nuclear Security Administration, August 23, 2010.

----, "Fact Sheet: NNSA's Second Line of Defense." National Nuclear Security Administration, December 2008.

----, "Fact Sheet: Nuclear Emergency Support Team (NEST)." National Nuclear Security Administration, 2010.

----, "Fact Sheet: Radiological Assistance Program (RAP)." National Nuclear Security Administration, 2010.

----, "Megaports Initiative Homepage." National Nuclear Security Administration. Retrieved July 15, 2010, from http://nnsa.energy.gov/aboutus/ourprograms/nonproliferation/programoffices/internationalmaterialprotectionandcooperation/s-1.

----, "Megaports Initiative: Morocco Transshipment Conference." National Nuclear Security Administration Briefing, May 2008.

----, "NNSA and the Vietnamese Ministry of Finance Agreement." U.S. Department of State Foreign Press Center Briefing by Director of Megaports Initiative William Kilmartin, July 2, 2010.

----, Nuclear Weapons Complex Reconfiguration Study. Springfield VA: National Technical Information Service, U.S. Department of Commerce, January 1991.

----, "Office of the Second Line of Defense Megaports Initiative." National Nuclear Security Administration Briefing, July 2006.

----, "Organization Chart." National Nuclear Security Administration, May 2010.

----, "Planning, Programming, Budgeting, and Evaluation (PPBE) Briefing." National Nuclear Security Administration, February 3, 2010

----, "Program Overview: Office of the Second Line of Defense." National Nuclear Security Administration, March 2010.

----, "Richardson, Russian Federation Dedicate 'Second Line of Defense' U.S. Nuclear Detection Technology to Help Secure Russian Borders." Office of the Press Secretary, September 2, 1998.

----, "Size of the U.S. Nuclear Stockpile and Annual Dismantlements." Office of Classification, May 6, 2010.

----, "Summary of Declassified Nuclear Stockpile Information." Office of the Press Secretary, June 27, 1994.

----, *United States Nuclear Tests July 1945 through September 1992.* Las Vegas, NV: Department of Energy Nevada Operations Office (Department of Energy/NV—209-REV 15), December 2000.

U.S. DEPARTMENT OF HOMELAND SECURITY

----, *CBP's Container Security Initiative Has Proactive Management and Oversight but Future Direction Is Uncertain.* Inspector General Report (OIG-10-52), February 2010.

----, "Container Security Initiative Ports." U.S. Customs and Border Protection, as of June 18, 2009. Retrieved July 15, 2010, from http://www.dhs.gov/files/programs/gc_1165872287564.shtm.

----, *DHS" Domestic Nuclear Detection Office: Progress in Integrating Detection Capabilities and Response Protocols.* Inspector General Report (OIG-08-19), December 2007.

----, "Fact Sheet: Container Security Initiative." U.S. Customs and Border Protection, October 2, 2007.

----, "Fact Sheet: Joint Analysis Center." Domestic Nuclear Detection Office.

----, "Fact Sheet: Secure Freight with CSI, Megaports." U.S. Customs and Border Protection, October, 2007.

----, *Homeland Security Budget-in-Brief Fiscal Year(s) 2006, 2007, 2008, 2009, and 2010.*

----, "National Targeting Center keeps terrorism at bay." *U.S. Customs and Border Protection Today*, March 2005.

----, "National Technical Nuclear Forensics: Overview, QA, and Expertise Development." Domestic Nuclear Detection Office Briefing, September 14, 2009.

----, "NSPD 41/HSPD 13 National Strategy for Maritime Security Supporting Plans," March 26, 2008. Retrieved July 15, 2010, from http://www.dhs.gov/files/programs/editorial_0608.shtm.

----, "Planning, Programming, Budgeting, and Execution (PPBE)." Department Brief, Fiscal Year 2005.

----, "Secure Freight Initiative: Vision and Operations Overview." Office of the Press Secretary, December 7, 2006.

U.S. DEPARTMENT OF STATE

----, "Atomic Diplomacy." Retrieved April 9, 2009, from http://www.state.gov/r/pa/ho/time/cwr/104434.htm.

----, "Defense-in-Depth." Retrieved January 22, 2012, from http://www.state.gov/t/isn/c16586.htm.

----, "Export Control and Related Border Security Program: Strategic Plan." Bureau of International Security and Nonproliferation, September 15, 2006.

----, "Fact Sheet on Open Skies Arms Control Treaty." May 18, 2009.

----, "Interdiction Principles for the Proliferation Security Initiative." Bureau of International Security and Nonproliferation, September 4, 2003. Retrieved November 15, 2009, from http://www.state.gov/t/isn/c27726.htm.

----, "Secretary Clinton and Argentine Foreign Minister Taiana Sign U.S.-Argentina Megaports Agreement to Prevent Nuclear Smuggling." Office of the Spokesman, Washington D.C., April 13, 2010.

----, "Strategic Arms Reduction II Chronology." U.S. Arms Control and Disarmament Agency, December 13, 1995. Retrieved November 13, 2011, from http://dosfan.lib.uic.edu/acda/factshee/wmd/nuclear/start2/strt-chr.htm.

----, "The Acheson-Lilienthal and Barauch Plans, 1946." Retrieved April 9, 2009, from http://www.state.gov/r/pa/ho/time/cwr/88100.htm.

----, "The G8 Global Partnership." Bureau of International Security and Nonproliferation. Retrieved November 15, 2009, from http://www.state.gov/t/isn/c12743.htm.

----, "The Global Initiative to Combat Nuclear Terrorism." Bureau of International Security and Nonproliferation. Retrieved November 15, 2009, from http://www.state.gov/t/isn/c18406.htm.

----, "UN Security Council Resolution 1540." Bureau of International Security and Nonproliferation, Retrieved November 15, 2009, from http://www.state.gov/t/isn/c18943.htm.

U.S. Department of Treasury, "Major Foreign Holders of Treasury Securities." Retrieved July 6, 2009, from http://www.treas.gov/tic/mfh.txt.

U.S. Government Accountability Office (formerly Accounting)
----, *Combating Terrorism: The United States Lacks Comprehensive Plan to Destroy the Terrorist Threat and*

Close the Safe Haven in Pakistan's Federally Administered Tribal Areas, April 2008.

----, *Container Security: Expansion of Key Customs Programs Will Require Greater Attention to Critical Success Factors,* July 2003.

----, *Cooperative Threat Reduction: Department of Defense Has Improved Its Management and Internal Controls, but Challenges Remain,* June 2005.

----, *Cooperative Threat Reduction Program Annual Report,* December 2, 2002.

----, *Department of Homeland Security: Better Planning and Assessment Needed to Improve Outcomes for Complex Service Acquisitions,* April 2008.

----, *Hurricane Katrina: Better Plans and Exercises Needed to Guide the Military's Response to Catastrophic Natural Disasters,* May 2006.

----, *Maritime Security: National Strategy and Supporting Plans Were Generally Well-Developed and Are Being Implemented,* June 2008.

----, *Military Personnel: High Aggregate Personnel Levels Maintained Throughout Drawdown,* June 1995.

----, *National Missile Defense: Even With Increased Funding Technical and Schedule Risks Are High,* June 1998.

----, *Nuclear Detection: Preliminary Observations on the Domestic Nuclear Detection Office's Efforts to Develop a Global Nuclear Detection Architecture,* July 16, 2008.

----, *Nuclear Forensics: Comprehensive Interagency Plan Needed to Address Human Capital Issues,* April 30, 2009.

----, *Nuclear Nonproliferation: Department of Energy Needs to Take Action to Further Reduce the Use of Weapons-Usable Uranium in Civilian Research Reactors,* July 2004.

----, *Nuclear Nonproliferation: Status of U.S. Efforts to Improve Nuclear Material Controls in Newly Independent States,* March 1996.

----, *Preventing Nuclear Smuggling: Department of Energy Has Made Limited Progress in Installing Radiation Detection Equipment at Highest Priority Foreign Seaports,* March 2005.

----, *Securing U.S. Nuclear Material: Department of Energy Has Made Little Progress Consolidating and Disposing of Special Nuclear Material,* October 2007.

----, *Weapons of Mass Destruction: Defense Threat Reduction Agency Addresses Broad Range of Threats, but Performance Reporting Can Be Improved,* February 2004.

----, *Weapons of Mass Destruction: Nonproliferation Programs Need Better Integration,* January 2005.

Welch, Larry, Chair, "Report of the Panel on Reducing Risk In Ballistic Missile Defense Flight Test Programs." Department of Defense, February 27, 1998.

WHITE HOUSE

----, "Background Information: START II Ratification." Office of the White House Press Secretary, January 26, 1996.

----, "Background Information: U.S. Policy on Nuclear Testing and a Comprehensive Test Ban." Office of the White House Press Secretary, July 3, 1993.

----, "Department of Defense: Cooperative Threat Reduction Program Assessment, 2006." Office of Management and Budget (ExpectMore.gov). Retrieved April 15, 2010, from http://www.financingstimulus.org/summary/10003219.2006.html.

----, "Fact Sheet: Administration Review of Nonproliferation and Threat Reduction Assistance to the Russian Federation." Office of the White House Press Secretary, December 27, 2001.

----, "Fact Sheet: Counterintelligence for the 21st Century." Office of the White House Press Secretary, January 5, 2001.

----, "Fact Sheet: Presidential Decision Directive-62, Combating Terrorism." Office of the White House Press Secretary, May 22, 1998.

----, "Fact Sheet: Presidential Decision Directive-63, Protecting America's Critical Infrastructures." Office of the White House Press Secretary, May 22, 1998.

----, "George W. Bush Administration: National Security Council." Office of the White House Press Secretary. Retrieved November 5, 2009, from http://www.whitehouse. gov/nsc/.

----, "Press Briefing by Mike McCurry and Robert Bell, Special Assistant to the President and Senior Director for Defense Policy and Arms Control, National Security Council." Office of the White House Press Secretary, April 11, 1996.

----, "Response to the Report of the Select Committee on U.S. National Security and Military/Commercial Concerns with The People's Republic of China." Office of the White House Press Secretary, May 25, 1999."

----, "Statement by Press Secretary Fitzwater on the START II Treaty." Office of the White House Press Secretary, January 15, 1993.

----, "Statement By The Press Secretary on U.S. Counterintelligence Effectiveness." Office of the White House Press Secretary, May 3, 1994."

----, "Text of the Strategic Offensive Reductions Treaty." Office of the White House Press Secretary, May 24, 2002.

----, *The Federal Response to Hurricane Katrina Lessons Learned.* U.S. Government Printing Office, Washington, D.C., February 2006.

----, "U.S.-Russia Joint Fact Sheet: Bratislava Initiatives." Office of the White House Press Secretary, February 24, 2005.

----, "White Paper: Presidential Decision Directive-56, The Clinton Administration's Policy on Managing Complex Contingency Operations." Office of the White House Press Secretary, May 1997.

----, "William J. Clinton Administration: National Security Council Staff." Office of the White House Press Secretary. Retrieved November 5, 2009, from http://clinton4.nara.gov/ WH/EOP/NSC/html/NSC_Staff.html.

SECONDARY SOURCES:

BOOKS/EDITED VOLUMES

Adams, Bianka J., and Joseph P. Harahan, *Responding to War, Terrorism, and WMD Proliferation: History of DTRA, 1998-2008*. Washington, D.C.: U.S. Department of Defense, 2008.

Alexander, Brian, and Alistair Millar, eds., *Tactical Nuclear Weapons: Emerging Threats in an Evolving Security Environment*. Washington D.C.: Brassey's, Inc., 2003.

Allison, Graham T., *Nuclear Terrorism: The Ultimate Preventable Catastrophe*. New York: Owl Books, 2004, 2005.

Allison, Graham T., Owen R. Cote, Jr., Richard A. Falkenrath, Steven E. Miller, *Avoiding Nuclear Anarchy: Containing the Threat of Loose Russian Nuclear Weapons and Fissile Material*. Cambridge: MIT Press, 1996.

Allison, Graham T., and Philip Zelikow, *Essence of Decision: Explaining the Cuban Missile Crises*. United States: Addison-Wesley Educational Publishers Inc., 2nd edition 1999.

Amstutz, Mark A., *International Ethics: Concepts, Theories, and Cases in Global Politics*. Lanham: Rowman and Littlefield Publishers, Inc., 3rd edition 2008.

Arnold, R. Douglas, *Congress and the Bureaucracy: A Theory of Influence*. New Haven and London: Yale University Press, 1979.

Ball, Desmond and Jeffrey Richelson, eds., *Strategic Nuclear Targeting*. Ithaca: Cornell University Press, 1986.

Bergner, Jefferey T., *The Next American Century: Essays in Honor of Richard G. Lugar.* Maryland: Rowman and Littlefield Publishers, Inc., 2003.

Beschloss, Michael R., and Strobe Talbott, *At the Highest Levels: The Inside Story of the End of the Cold War*. New York: Little, Brown and Company, 1993.

Betts, Richard K., *Nuclear Blackmail and Nuclear Balance*. Washington D.C.: The Brookings Institution, 1987.

Blechman, Barry M., *The Politics of National Security: Congress and Defense Policy*. New York: Oxford University Press, 1990.

Blix, Hans, *Why Nuclear Disarmament Matters*, Cambridge and London: MIT Press, 2008.

Bolt, Paul J., Damon V. Coletta, and Collins G. Shackelford, Jr., *American Defense Policy*. Baltimore: Johns Hopkins Press, 8th edition 2005.

Bowen, Wyn Q., *The Politics of Ballistic Missile Nonproliferation*, New York: Palgrave, 2000.

Brodie, Bernard, ed., *The Absolute Weapon: Atomic Power and World Order*. New York: Harcourt, Brace, 1946.

Bush, George H. W., and Brent Scowcroft, *A World Transformed*. New York: Vintage Books, 1998.

Campbell, Kurt M., Robert J. Einhorn, and Mitchell B. Reiss, eds., *The Nuclear Tipping Point: Why States Reconsider Their Nuclear Choices*. Washington, D.C.: Brookings Institution Press, 2004.

Carter, April, *Success and Failure in Arms Control Negotiations*. United States: Oxford University Press, 1989.

Carter, Ashton B., and William J. Perry, *Preventive Defense: A New Security Strategy for America*. Washington, D.C.: Brookings Institution Press, 1999.

Cheney, Dick, with Liz Cheney, *In My Time: A Personal and Political Memoir*. New York, New York: Threshold Editions, 2011.

Chaliand, Gerard and Arnaud Blin, eds., *The History of Terrorism: From Antiquity to Al Qaeda*. Berkeley and Los Angeles, California: University of California Press, 2007.

Chodhuri, Satyabrata Rai, *Nuclear Politics: Towards a Safer World*. United States, United Kingdom, India: New Dawn Press, Inc., 2005.

Chubin, Shahram, *Iran's Nuclear Ambitions*. Washington, D.C.: Carnegie Endowment, 2006.

Cirincione, Joseph, *Bomb Scare: The History & Future of Nuclear Weapons*. New York: Columbia University Press, 2008.

Cirincione, Joseph, ed., *Repairing the Regime: Preventing the Spread of Weapons of Mass Destruction.* New York and London: Routledge, 2000.

Cirincione, Joseph, Jon B. Wolfsthal, and Miriam Rajkumar, *Deadly Arsenals: Nuclear Biological, and Chemical Threats.* Washington, D.C.: Carnegie Endowment, 2nd edition 2005.

Clark, Ronald W., *The Birth of the Bomb.* New York: Horizon Press, 1961.
----, *The Greatest Power on Earth: The International Race for Nuclear Supremacy.* New York: Harper and Row, 1980.
----, *The Greatest Power on Earth: The Story of Nuclear Fission.* London: Sidgwick and Jackson, 1980.

Clarke, John L., *Armies in Homeland Security: American and European Perspectives.* Washington D.C.: National Defense University Press, 2002.

Cohen, Avner, *Israel and the Bomb.* New York: Columbia University Press, 1998.

Corera, Gordon, *Shopping for Bombs: Nuclear Proliferation, Global Insecurity, and the Rise and Fall of the A. Q. Khan Network.* Oxford: Oxford University Press, 2006.

Corsi, Jerome R., *Atomic Iran: How the Terrorist Regime Bought the Bomb and American Politicians.* Nashville, Tennessee: WND Books, 2005.

Defense Threat Reduction Agency, *Defense's Nuclear Agency 1947-1997: DTRA History Series.* Washington D.C.: U.S. Government Printing Office, 2002.

Downs, Anthony, *Inside Bureaucracy*. Boston: Little, Brown, and Company, 1967.

Dye, Thomas R., *Understanding Public Policy*, New Jersey: Prentice-Hall, 9th edition 1998.

Edwards, George C. III, Steven A. Shull, and Norman C. Thomas, eds., *The Presidency and Public Policy Making*. Pittsburgh, Pennsylvania: University of Pittsburgh Press, 1985.

Eisendrath, Craig, Melvin A. Goodman, and Gerald E. Marsh, *The Phantom Defense: America's Pursuit of the Star Wars Illusion*. Westport, Connecticut: Praeger, 2001.

Ellis, Jason D., and Geoffrey D. Kiefer, *Combating Proliferation: Strategic Intelligence and Security Policy*. Baltimore and London: Johns Hopkins University Press, 2004.

Feith, Douglas J., *War and Decision: Inside the Pentagon at the Dawn of the War on Terrorism*. New York: Harper, 2008.

Ferguson, Charles D., and William C. Potter with Amy Sands, Leonard S. Spector, and Fred L. Wehling, *The Four Faces of Nuclear Terrorism*. New York: Routledge, 2005.

Finkbeiner, Ann, *The Jasons: The Secret History of Science's Postwar Elite*. New York: The Penguin Group, 2006.

Fitzgerald, Frances, *Way Out There in the Blue: Reagan, Star Wars and the End of the Cold War*. New York: Touchstone, 2000.

Flynn, Stephen, *The Edge of Disaster: Rebuilding a Resilient Nation*. New York: Random House, 2007.

Fox, J. Ronald with James L. Field, *The Defense Management Challenge: Weapons Acquisition.* Boston, Massachusetts: Harvard Business School Press, 1988.

Frankfort-Nachmias, Chava and David Nachmias, *Research Methods in the Social Sciences.* New York: Saint Martin's Press, 5th edition 1996.

Freedman, Lawrence, *The Evolution of Nuclear Strategy.* New York: Palgrave MacMillan, 1981, 1983, 3rd edition 2003.

Garrison, Dee, *Bracing for Armageddon: Why Civil Defense Never Worked.* Oxford: Oxford University Press, 2006.

Garwin, Richard L., and Georges Charpak, *Megawatts and Megatons: The Future of Nuclear Power and Nuclear Weapons.* Chicago: University of Chicago Press, 2002.

Glasstone, Samuel, and Philip J. Dolan, *The Effects of Nuclear Weapons.* Washington D.C.: U.S. Department of Defense and Energy, 3rd edition 1977.

Graham, Bob, Jim Talent, et al., *World at Risk: The Report of the Commission on the Prevention of WMD Proliferation and Terrorism.* New York: Vintage Books, 2008.

Gregory, William H., *The Defense Procurement Mess*, Lexington, Massachusetts and Toronto: D.C. Heath and Company, 1989.

Groves, Leslie R. and Edward Teller, *Now it can be told: The story of the Manhattan Project.* Da Capo Press, 1983.

Halperin, Morton H., and Priscilla A. Clapp, *Bureaucratic Politics and Foreign Policy.* Washington D.C.: The Brookings Institution, 2nd edition 2006.

Hampson, Fen, *Unguided Missiles: How America Buys Its Weapons*. New York and London: W. W. Norton and Company, 1989.

Hersman, Rebecca K. C., *Friends and Foes: How Congress and the President Really Make Foreign Policy*. Washington, D.C.: Brookings Institution Press, 2000.

Hill, Michael James, and Peter L. Hupe, *Implementing Public Policy: Governance in Theory and Practice*. California, London, New Dehli: SAGE Publications, 2002.

Holland, Lauren, *Weapons Under Fire*. New York and London: Garland Publishing, Inc., 1997.

Hook, Steven W., and John Spanier, *American Foreign Policy Since World War II*. Washington D.C.: CQ Press, 17th edition 2007.

Jacobson, Harold Karan, and Eric Stein, *Diplomats, Scientists, and Politicians: The United States and the Nuclear Test Ban Negotiations*. Ann Arbor: University of Michigan Press, 1966.

Jenkins, Brian M., *Will Terrorists Go Nuclear?* New York: Prometheus Books, 2008.

Jones, Rodney W., and Mark G. McDonough, *Tracking Nuclear Proliferation: A Guide in Maps and Charts*. Washington, D.C.: Carnegie Endowment for International Peace, 1998.

Jordan, Amos A., William J. Taylor, Jr., and Michael J. Mazarr, *American National Security*. Baltimore and London: Johns Hopkins University Press, 5th edition 1999.

Kartchner, Kerry M., *Negotiating START: Strategic Arms Reduction Talks and the Quest for Stability*. New Jersey: Transaction Publishers, 1992.

Kaplan, David E., and Andrew Marshall, *The Cult at the End of the World*. New York: Crown Publishers Inc., 1996.

Kelly, Cynthia C., ed., *The Manhattan Project: The Birth of the Atomic Bomb in the Words of Its Creators, Eyewitnesses, and Historians*. New York: Black Dog and Leventhal, 2007.

Kernell, Samuel and Steven Smith, *Principles and Practice of American Politics*. Washington D.C.: CQ Press, 3rd edition 2007.

Kozak, David C., and James M. Keagle, eds., *Bureaucratic Politics and National Security: Theory and Practice*. Boulder, Colorado: Lynne Rienner, 1988.

Langewiesche, William, *The Atomic Bazaar: Dispatches from the Underground World of Nuclear Trafficking*. New York: Farrar, Straus, and Giroux, 2007.

Lee, Rensselaer W. III, *Smuggling Armageddon: The Nuclear Black Market in the Former Soviet Union and Europe*. New York: St. Martin's Griffin, 1998.

Leitner, Peter M., *Decontrolling Strategic Technology, 1990-1992: Creating the Military Threats of the 21st Century*. Lanham, Maryland: University Press of America, 1995.

Lettow, Paul, *Ronald Reagan and His Quest to Abolish Nuclear Weapons*. New York: Random House, 2006.

Levi, Michael, *On Nuclear Terrorism*. Cambridge, London: Harvard University Press, 2007.

Lindsay, James M., and Michael E. O'Hanlon, *Defending America: The Case for Limited National Missile Defense*. Washington D.C.: Brookings Institution Press, 2001.

Mankoff, Jeffrey, *Russian Foreign Policy: The Return of Great Power Politics*. United States of America: Rowman and Littlefield, 2009.

McClellan, Scott, *What Happened: Inside the Bush White House and Washington's Culture of Deception*. New York: Public Affairs, 2008.

McConnell, Campbell R., and Stanley L. Brue, *Economics: Principles, Problems, and Policies*. Boston: McGraw-Hill Irwin, 17th edition 2008.

McNaugher, Thomas L., *New weapons, old politics: America's military procurement muddle*. Washington D.C.: Brookings Institution Press, 1989.

McPhee, John, *The Curve of Binding Energy: A Journey into the Awesome and Alarming World of Theodore B Taylor*. United States: Farrar, Straus, and Giroux, 1974.

Moody, Kenton J., Ian D. Hutcheon, and Patrick M. Grant, *Nuclear Forensic Analysis*. Boca Raton, Florida: CRC Press, 2005.

Mowthorpe, Matthew, *The Militarization and Weaponization of Space*. Virginia: Lexington Books, 2003.

Mozley, Robert F., *The Politics and Technology of Nuclear Proliferation*. Seattle and London: University of Washington Press, 1998.

Mueller, John, *Overblown: How Politicians and the Terrorism Industry Inflate National Security Threats, and Why We Believe Them*. New York, London, Toronto and Sydney: Free Press, 2006.

Newmann, William W., *Managing National Security Policy: The President and the Process*. Pennsylvania: University of Pittsburgh Press, 2003.

Nolan, Janne E., *An Elusive Consensus: Nuclear Weapons and American Security After the Cold War*. Washington D.C.: Brookings Institution Press, 1999.

Obeidi, Mahdi and Kurt Pitzer, *The Bomb in My Garden: The Secrets of Saddam's Nuclear Mastermind*. Hoboken, New Jersey: John Wiley and Sons, 2004.

O'Hanlon, Michael E., *Defense Strategy for the Post-Saddam Era*. Washington, D.C.: Brookings, 2005.

Paul, T.V., Richard J. Harknett, and James J. Wirtz, eds., *The Absolute Weapon Revisited: Nuclear Arms and the Emerging International Order*. Ann Arbor: University of Michigan Press, 2000.

Paul, T.V., Patrick M. Morgan, and James J. Wirtz, eds., *Complex Deterrence: Strategy in the Global Age*. Chicago and London: University of Chicago Press, 2009.

Perkovich, George, *India's Nuclear Bomb: The Impact on Global Proliferation.* Berkeley: University of California Press, updated edition 2001.

Powaski, Ronald E., *Return to Armageddon: The United States and the Nuclear Arms Race, 1981-1999.* Oxford: Oxford University Press, 2000.

Powell, Colin L., *My American Journey.* New York: Random House, 1995.

Reed, Thomas C. and Danny B. Stillman, *The Nuclear Express: A Political History of the Bomb and Its Proliferation.* Minneapolis, Minnesota: Zenith Press, 2009.

Rowny, Edward L., *It Takes One to Tango.* Washington, New York, and London: Brassey's, 1992.

Richelson, Jeffrey T., *Defusing Armageddon: Inside NEST, America's Secret Nuclear Bomb Squad.* New York and London: W.W. Norton and Company, 2009.
----, Spying on the Bomb: American Nuclear Intelligence from Nazi Germany to Iran and North Korea. New York, New York: W.W. Norton and Company, 2007 and 2006.

Ricks, Thomas E., *Fiasco: The American Military Adventure in Iraq.* New York: Penguin, 2006.

Riisager, Thomas and Henry Sokolski, *Beyond Nunn-Lugar: Curbing the Next Wave of Weapons Proliferation Threats from Russia.* Carlisle, Pennsylvania: Strategic Studies Institute of the U.S. Army War College, 2002.

Ritchie, Nick, *U.S. Nuclear Weapons Policy after the Cold War: Russians, "rogues," and domestic division.* New York: Routledge, 2009.

Rose, Kenneth, *One Nation Under Ground: The Fall Out Shelter in American Culture.* New York: NYU Press, 2004.

Rossi, Peter H., Mark W. Lipsey, and Howard E. Freeman, *Evaluation: A Systematic Approach.* Thousand Oaks, London, New Delhi: SAGE Publications, 7th edition 2004.

Sagan, Scott D., *Moving Targets: Nuclear Strategy and National Security.* Princeton, New Jersey: Princeton University Press, 1989.

Sagan, Scott D., and Kenneth N. Waltz, *The Spread of Nuclear Weapons: A Debate.* New York and London: W.W. Norton and Company, 1995.

Sarkesian, Sam C., John Allen Williams, and Stephen J. Cimbala, *U.S. National Security: Policymakers, Processes, and Politics.* Boulder, Colorado: Lynne Rienner, 4th edition 2002.

Schell, Jonathan, *The Seventh Decade: The New Shape of Nuclear Danger.* New York: Metropolitan Books, 2007.

Schwartz, Stephen I., ed., *Atomic Audit: The Costs and Consequences of U.S. Nuclear Weapons since 1940.* Washington, D.C.: Brookings Institution Press, 1998.

Shambaugh, George E., IV, and Paul J. Weinstein Jr., *The Art of Policy Making: Tools, Techniques, and Processes in the Modern Executive Branch.* New York: Longman, 2003.

Shelton, Hugh, with Ronald Levinson and Malcolm McConnell, *Without Hesitation: The Odyssey of an American Warrior*. New York: St. Martin's Press, 2010.

Shields, John M., and William C. Potter, eds., *Dismantling the Cold War: U.S. and NIS Perspectives on the Nunn-Lugar Cooperative Threat Reduction Program*. Cambridge, Massachusetts and London, England: MIT Press, 1997.

Sigal, Leon V., ed., *The Changing Dynamics of U.S. Defense Spending*. Westport, CT: Praeger Publishers, 1999.

Siracusa, Joseph M., *Nuclear Weapons: A Very Short Introduction*. Oxford: Oxford University Press, 2008.

Snow, Donald M., *National Security for a New Era: Globalization and Geopolitics After Iraq*. New York: Pearson Education, Inc., 3rd edition 2008.

Sokolski, Henry, ed., *Getting MAD: Nuclear Mutual Assured Destruction, its Origins and Practice*. Carlisle, Pennsylvania: Strategic Studies Institute, November 2004.

Stober, Dan, and Ian Hoffman, *A Convenient Spy: Wen Ho Lee and the Politics of Nuclear Espionage*. New York: Simon and Schuster, 2002.

Talbott, Strobe, *The Russia Hand: A Memoir of Presidential Diplomacy*. New York: Random House, 2003.

Tenet, George, with Bill Harlow, *At the Center of the Storm: My Years at the CIA*. New York: Harper Collins Publishers, 2007.

Truman, Harry S., *Year of Decisions*. Garden City, New York: Doubleday and Company, 1955.

U.S. Senate Committee on Government Operations, *Negotiation and Statecraft: A Selection of Readings*. Washington, D.C.: Government Printing Office, 1970.

Van Horn, Carl E., Donald C. Baumer and William T. Gormley Jr., *Politics and Public Policy*. Washington D.C.: CQ Press, 3rd edition 2001.

Venter, Al J., *Allah's Bomb: The Islamic Quest for Nuclear Weapons*. Connecticut: The Lyons Press, 2007.

Weiner, Tim, *Legacy of Ashes: The History of the CIA*. New York: Anchor Books, 2007, 2008.

Wenger, Andreas, *Living with Peril: Eisenhower, Kennedy and Nuclear Weapons*. Lanham, Maryland: Rowman and Littlefield, 1997.

Williamson, Samuel R., Jr. and Steven L. Rearden, *The Origins of U.S. Nuclear Strategy, 1945-1953,* New York: Saint Martin's, 1993.

Wilson, James Q., *Bureaucracy: What Government Agencies Do and Why They Do It*. United States: Basic Books, 2nd edition 2000.

Wirtz, James J., and Jeffrey A. Larsen, eds., *Nuclear Transformation: The New U.S. Nuclear Doctrine*. New York: Palgrave MacMillan, 2005.
----, *Rockets" Red Glare: Missile Defenses and the Future of World Politics*. Colorado: Westview Press, 2001.

Woodward, Bob, *State of Denial: Bush at War Part III.* New York, London, Toronto and Sydney: Simon and Schuster, 2006.

Younger, Stephen M., *The Bomb: A New History.* New York: HarperCollins Publishers, 2009.

Zarate, Robert, and Henry Sokolski, eds., *Nuclear Heuristics: Selected Writings of Albert and Roberta Wohlstetter.* Carlisle, Pennsylvania: Strategic Studies Institute, January 2009.

UNPUBLISHED

Carrigan, Alisa L., *The Best Knowledge that Money Can Buy: Patterns of State-level Recruitment and Training of Nuclear Weapons Personnel and International Nonproliferation Policy Responses.* Thesis: King's College, London, 2007.

Ford, Peter S., "Israel's Attack on Osiraq." Thesis: Naval Postgraduate School, September 2004.

Harahan, Joseph P., *With Courage and Persistence: The United States, Russia, Belarus, Kazakhstan, and Ukraine and the Cooperative Threat Reduction Program.* Manuscript: Defense Threat Reduction Agency, 2010.

Jussel, Paul C., *Intimidating the World: The United States Atomic Army 1956-1960.* Dissertation: The Ohio State University, 2004.

Kluchko, Luke J., "Strategic Staffing to Meet CTR 2.0 Goals – Parental Guidance Suggested." Concept Paper: Harvard University, November 12, 2009.

Rogers, J. David, and Keith D. Koper, "Some Practical Applications of Seismic Forensics." Lecture: University of Missouri-Rolla, 2006.

Slantchev, Branislav, L., "National Security Strategy: Flexible Response, 1961-1968." Lecture: University of California San Diego, February 23, 2004.

ARTICLES AND WEB PAGES

Allison, Graham T., "Conceptual Models and the Cuban Missile Crises." *The American Political Science Review*, Vol. 63, No. 3, September 1969.

Allison, Graham T., and Morton H. Halperin, "Bureaucratic Politics: A Paradigm and Some Policy Implications." *World Politics*, Vol. 24, Spring 1972.

Arms Control Association, "Arms Control and the 1992 Election." *Arms Control Today*, 1992. Retrieved November 15, 2011, from http://www.armscontrol.org/1992election.

Art, Robert J., "Bureaucratic Politics and American Foreign Policy: A Critique." *Policy Sciences*, Vol. 4, December 1973.

Ambinder, Marc, "The Real Intelligence Wars: Oversight and Access." *The Atlantic*, November 18, 2009.
----, "Why Clinton's Losing the Nuclear Biscuit Was Really, Really Bad." *The Atlantic*, October 22, 2010.

Arkin, William, "The Buildup That Wasn't." *Bulletin of the Atomic Scientists*, January/February 1989.
----, "Those Loveable Little Bombs." *Bulletin of the Atomic Scientists*, July/August 1993.

Associated Press, "Army Review Finds That Use of Troops in Alabama Town Broke the Law." October 20, 2009.
----, "Layoffs at nuke lab stir fears of a brain drain: Lawmakers fear loss of nation's top nuclear minds will benefit hostile rivals." June 3, 2008.

Atomic Archive, "Information on Nuclear Smuggling Incidents." Retrieved June 15, 2010, from http://www.atomicarchive. com/Almanac/Smuggling.shtml.

Augustson, Ronald H. and John R. Phillips as told to Debra A. Daugherty, "Russian-American MPC&A: Nuclear Materials Protection, Control, and Accounting in the Russian Federation." *Los Alamos Science*, No. 24, 1996.

Axelrod, Jonathan N., "Allison Abandons Government Post." *The Harvard Crimson*, February 18, 1994.

Ball, Desmond J., "The Blind Men and the Elephant: A Critique of Bureaucratic Politics Theory." *Australian Outlook*, Vol. 28, No. 1, April 1974.

BBC News, "EU allies unite against Iraq war." January 22, 2003. Retrieved November 15, 2009, from http://news.bbc. co.uk/2/hi/europe/2683409.stm.

Bendor, Jonathan and Thomas H. Hammond, "Rethinking Allison's Models." *American Political Science Review*, Vol. 86, No. 2, June 1992.

Benjamin, Robert, "Yeltsin announces readiness to sign second arms-reduction pact with Bush." *The Baltimore Sun*, December 19, 1992.

Bernstein, Paul I., John P. Caves, Jr. and John F. Reichart, *The Future Nuclear Landscape*. Center for the Study of Weapons of Mass Destruction, Occasional Paper 5, Washington D.C.: National Defense University Press, April 2007.

Blechman, Barry and Leo Mackay, *Weapons of Mass Destruction: A New Paradigm for a New Century*. The Henry Stimson Center, Occasional Paper No. 40, October 2000.

Blitzer, Wolf, "Search for the 'Smoking Gun'." CNN, January 10, 2003. Retrieved November 15, 2009, from http://articles.cnn.com/2003-01-10/us/wbr.smoking.gun_1_smoking-gun-nuclear-weapons-hans-blix?_s=PM:U.S.

Boese, Wade, "State Department Reorganization Advances." *Arms Control Today*, Vol. 35, September 2005.

Boureston, Jack, "Assessing Al-Qaeda's WMD Capabilities." *Strategic Insight*, September 2, 2002.

Bowen, Wyn Q., "Libya and Nuclear Proliferation: Stepping back from the brink." The International Institute for Strategic Studies, Adelphi Paper 380, Routledge, May 2006.

Broad, William J., and David E. Sanger, "Iran has capacity for nuclear arms, report says." *The New York Times*, June 5, 2009.

Brodie, Bernard, "The Anatomy of Deterrence." *World Politics*, Vol. 11, No. 2, January 1959.

Brown, Cameron, "Israel and the WMD Threat." *Middle East Review of International Affairs Journal*, Vol. 8, No. 3, September 2004.

Bunn, Matthew, *Securing the Bomb 2006.* Cambridge, Massachusetts and Washington, D.C.: Project on Managing the Atom, Harvard University, and Nuclear Threat Initiative, May 2006.
----, *Securing the Bomb 2007.* Cambridge, Massachusetts and Washington, D.C.: Project on Managing the Atom, Harvard University, and Nuclear Threat Initiative, September 2007.
----, *Securing the Bomb 2008.* Cambridge, Massachusetts and Washington, D.C.: Project on Managing the Atom, Harvard University, and Nuclear Threat Initiative, November 18, 2008.

Burns, Robert, "GPALS: Bush's Missile Defense Proposal." *The Associated Press*, April 29, 1991.

Burr, William, ed., "The Creation of SIOP-62: More Evidence on the Origins of Overkill." National Security Archives. Retrieved April 9, 2009, from http://www.gwu.edu/~nsarchiv/NSAEBB/NSAEBB130/index.htm.
----, "The Nixon Administration, the SIOP, and the Search for Limited Nuclear Options 1969-1974." National Security Archive. Retrieved April 10, 2009, from http://www.gwu.edu/~nsarchiv/NSAEBB/NSAEBB173/index.htm.

Carus, W. Seth, *Defining "Weapons of Mass Destruction."* Center for the Study of Weapons of Mass Destruction, Occasional Paper 4, Washington D.C.: National Defense University Press, January 2006.

Center for Nonproliferation Studies, "Congressional Record Weekly Update March 31-April 4, 2003." Monterey Institute of International Studies. Retrieved July 15, 2010, from http://cns.miis.edu/archive/cr/03_04_07.htm.

Cerniello, Craig, "Gore-Chernomyrdin Expands Cooperative Measures." *Arms Control Today*, Vol. 27, March 1997.
----, "NMD Debate in Congress Heats Up As Lott, Lugar Introduce New Bills." *Arms Control Today*, Vol. 26, January/February 1997.

Cirincione, Joseph, "Rush to Failure." *Bulletin of the Atomic Scientists*, May 1998.

Clary, Christopher, "Dr. Khan's Nuclear Walmart." *Disarmament Diplomacy*, Issue No. 76, March/April 2004.

Clausen, Peter, "Star warriors try again." *Bulletin of the Atomic Scientists,* June 1981.

Clays, Michelle M., "The Interagency Process and America's Second Front in the Global War on Terrorism." Air University Report, April 2003.

Clifford, J. Garry, "Bureaucratic Politics." *The Journal of American History*, Vol. 77, No. 1, June 1990.

CNN.com, "Bush lifts sanctions against India, Pakistan." September 21, 2001. Retrieved November 15, 2010, from http://archives.cnn.com/2001/U.S./09/22/gen.america.under.attack/.
----, "Bush signs Homeland Security bill: Ridge nominated to head department." November 26, 2002. Retrieved November 15, 2010, from http://archives.cnn.com/2002/ALLPOLITICS/11/25/homeland.security/index.html.
----, "President Bush's Speech." June 6, 2002. Retrieved November 15, 2009, from http://transcripts.cnn.com/TRANSCRIPTS/0206/06/se.12.html.

----, CNN, "Senate backs missile defense system: 97-3 vote marks big shift for Democrats." March 17, 1999. Retrieved November 15, 2011, from http://www.cnn.com/ALLPOLITICS/stories/1999/03/17/missile.defense/.

----, "U.S. Imposes Sanctions on India." May 13, 1998. Retrieved October 12, 2009, from http://www.cnn.com/WORLD/asiapcf/9805/13/india.us/index.html.

Cox, Gary W., "Agenda Setting in the U.S. House: A Majority-Party Monopoly?." *Legislative Studies Quarterly*, Vol. 26, No. 2, May 2001.

----, "On the Effects of Legislative Rules." *Legislative Studies Quarterly*, Vol. 25, No. 2, May 2000.

Cumings, Bruce, "Korea: Forgotten Nuclear Threats." *Le Monde Diplomatique*, December 2004.

Dahl, Kenneth R., "New Security for New Threats: The Case for Reforming the Interagency Process." Brookings Institution Report, July 2007.

Daly, Sara, John Parachini, and William Rosenau, "Aum Shinrikyo, Al Qaeda, and the Kinshasa Reactor: Implications of Three Case Studies for Combating Nuclear Terrorism." *Project Air Force*, RAND Documented Briefing, 2005.

Dareini, Ali Akbar, "Iran: New Strides in Uranium Enrichment." *Associated Press*, August 29, 2008.

Daughtry, Emily Ewell, and Fred L. Wehling, Cooperative Efforts to Secure Fissile Material in the NIS." *Nonproliferation Review*, Spring 2000.

Davis, Jay, "The Attribution of WMD Events." *Journal of Homeland Security*, April 2003.

Diamond, Howard, "Cox Panel Charges China with Extensive
    Nuclear Espionage." *Arms Control Today*, Vol. 29, April/
    May 1999.

Dunn, David H., "A Doctrine Worthy of the Name? George
    W Bush and the limits of Pre-Emption, Pre-Eminence and
    Unilateralism." *Diplomacy and Statecraft*, Vol. 17, No. 1,
    March 2006.
----, "Poland: America's New Model Ally?" *Defense Studies*,
    Vol. 2, Issue 2, Summer 2002.
----, "Quacking Like a Duck? Bush II and Presidential Power
    in the Second Term." *International Affairs*, Vol. 82, No. 1,
    January 2006.
----, "Real Men want to go to Tehran: Bush, Pre-emption and the
    Iranian Nuclear Challenge." *International Affairs*, Vol. 83,
    No. 1, January 2007.

Dunn, Lewis A., *Can al Qaeda Be Deterred from Using Nuclear
    Weapons?* Center for the Study of Weapons of Mass
    Destruction, Occasional Paper 3, Washington D.C.: National
    Defense University Press, July 2005.

Eisenstadt, Michael, *Iraq and After: Taking the Right Lessons
    for Combating Weapons of Mass Destruction.* Center for the
    Study of Weapons of Mass Destruction, Occasional Paper 2,
    Washington D.C.: National Defense University Press, May
    2005.

Elazar, Daniel J., "Harmonizing Government Organization with
    the Political Tradition." *Publius*, Vol. 8, No. 2, Spring 1978.

Epstein, William, "Indefinite Extension-With Increased
    Accountability." *Bulletin of the Atomic Scientists,* July/
    August 1995.

Embassy of India, "India Conducts Nuclear Tests." Press Release, May 11, 1998.

Erlanger, Steven, "Clinton Seeks Power to Lift India-Pakistan Sanctions." *The New York Times*, July 14, 1998.

Fairhall, James, "The case for the $435 hammer – investigation of the Pentagon's procurement." *Washington Monthly*, January 1987.

Farr, Warner D., "The Third Temple's Holy of Holies: Israel's Nuclear Weapons." Counterproliferation Paper No. 2, U.S. Air Force Counterproliferation Center, Air War College, September 1999.

Federation of American Scientists, "DPRK: Nuclear Weapons Program." Retrieved June 9, 2009, from http://www.fas.org/nuke/guide/dprk/nuke/index.html.
----, *Osiraq/Tammuz I 33°12"30"N 44°31"30"E.* Retrieved April 8, 2009, from http://www.fas.org/nuke/guide/iraq/facility/osiraq.htm.
----, "The Former Soviet Union: Russia, Ukraine, Kazakhstan, and Belarus." Retrieved April 15, 2010, from http://www.fas.org/irp/threat/prolif96/fsu.html.
----, "The Pressler Amendment and Pakistan's Nuclear Weapons Program." Retrieved November 15, 2009, from http://www.fas.org/news/pakistan/1992/920731.htm.

Felton, John, "The Nunn-Lugar Vision, 1992-2002." Nuclear Threat Initiative. Retrieved November 15, 2009, from http://www.nti.org/e_research/nunn-lugar_history.pdf.

Ford, Christopher, "Some Thoughts on How Not to do WMD Intelligence: Lessons of Politicization After Iraq." New Paradigms Forum, January 4, 2010. Retrieved November

15, 2010, from http://www.newparadigmsforum.com/
NPFtestsite/?m=20100104.

Frederick, Lorinda A., "Deterrence and Space-Based Missile
Defense." *Air and Space Power Journal*, Fall 2009 – Vol.
XXIII, No. 3 (AFRP 10-1).

Gard, Robert G., Jr., "National Missile Defense in Europe:
Premature and Unwise." Center for Arms Control and
Nonproliferation, July 2007. Retrieved November 15,
2010, from http://armscontrolcenter.org/assets/pdfs/europe-
an_missile_defense_premature.pdf.

Garamone, Jim, "Wolfowitz Says Dirty Bomb Plot Highlights
WMD Dangers." *American Forces Press Service*, June 11,
2002.
----, "Mullen Urges New Methods of Deterrence." *American
Forces Press Service*, November 12, 2010.

Garwin, Richard L., "When Could Iran Deliver a Nuclear
Weapon?" *Bulletin of the Atomic Scientists*, January
17, 2008. Retrieved November 15, 2009, from
http://www.thebulletin.org/web-edition/features/
when-could-iran-deliver-a-nuclear-weapon.

Gjelten, Tom, "Intelligence Estimate on Iran Cuts Both Ways."
National Public Radio, January 17, 2008. Retrieved
November 15, 2009, from http://www.npr.org/templates/
story/story.php?storyId=18128448&ps=rs.
----, "Iran NIE Reopens Intelligence Debate." NPR, January 17,
2008. Retrieved November 15, 2009, from http://www.npr.
org/templates/story/story.php?storyId=18177103.

GlobalSecurity.org, "North Korea: Missiles: Taep"o-dong 2
(TD-2), NKSL-X-2." Retrieved April 8, 2009, from http://

www.globalsecurity.org/wmd/world/dprk/td-2.htm.
----, "Nuclear Posture Review [Excerpts]." January 8, 2002.
Retrieved November 15, 2009, from http://www.globalsecu-
rity.org/wmd/library/policy/dod/npr.htm.
----, "World Wide Military Expenditures." Retrieved April 15,
2010, from http://www.globalsecurity.org/military/world/
spending.htm.

Goodman, Michael S., and Wyn Bowen, "Behind Iran's nuclear weapons 'halt'." *Bulletin of the Atomic Scientists*,
February 19, 2008.   Retrieved November 15, 2009,
from   http://www.thebulletin.org/web-edition/features/
behind-irans-nuclear-weapons-halt.

Goodpaster, Andrew, *Dealing with Weapons of Mass Destruction:
Framing a Strategy*. The Eisenhower Institute, Washington,
D.C., 2003. Retrieved April 8, 2009, from http://www.ei-
senhowerinstitute.org/publications/opinions__editorials/
Goodpaster_dealing.dot.

Gorman, Martin J., and Alexander Krongard, "A Goldwater-
Nichols Act for the U.S. Government: Institutionalizing the
Interagency Process." *Joint Forces Quarterly*, Issue 39,
August 2005.

Government of Canada, "2008 Hokkaido Toyako Summit."
April, 27, 2009. Retrieved November 15, 2009, from http://
www.canadainternational.gc.ca/g8/summit-sommet/2008/
index.aspx?menu_id=9&menu=L.
----, *Global Partnership Against the Spread of Weapons and
Materials of Mass Destruction*. G8 Senior Officials Group
Annual Report, November 24, 2008. Retrieved November
15, 2009, from http://www.canadainternational.gc.ca/g8/
summit-sommet/2003/mass-destruction-massive.aspx.

Grant, Rebecca, "Osirak and Beyond." *Air Force Magazine*, Vol. 85, No. 8, August 2002.

Gusterson, Hugh, "U.S. Nuclear Double Standards." *Bulletin of the Atomic Scientists*, February 20, 2008. Retrieved November 15, 2009, from http://www.thebulletin.org/web-edition/columnists/hugh-gusterson/us-nuclear-double-standards.

Habiger, Eugene, "Alaska Missile Interceptor Site Has No Credibility." Carnegie Endowment for International Peace, *Proliferation Issue Brief*, Vol. 7, No. 14, September 29, 2004.

Hahn, Robert F. III, "The Congressional Defense Department: Competitive Strategy Making in the Post-Cold-War Era." *Airpower Journal*, Special Edition, Vol. VIV, 1995. Retrieved November 15, 2011, from http://www.airpower.au.af.mil/airchronicles/apj/apj95/spe-ed95.htm.

Halperin, Morton H., "Why Bureaucrats Play Games." *Foreign Policy*, No. 2, Spring 1971.
----, "The Decision to Deploy the ABM: Bureaucratic and Domestic Politics in the Johnson Administration." *World Politics*, Vol. 25, No. 1, October 1972.

Hammond, Thomas H., and Jack H. Knott, "Who Controls the Bureaucracy?: Presidential Power, Congressional Dominance, Legal Constraints, and Bureaucratic Autonomy in a Model of Multi-Institutional Policy-Making." *The Journal of Law, Economics, and Organization*, Vol. 12, No. 1, 1996.

Harrell, Eben, "Osama's Nuclear Strategy: What's Different." *Time*, April 7, 2010.

Hartung, William D., and Michelle Carrocca, "Star Wars II: Here We Go Again." *The Nation*, June 19, 2000.

Hawkins, William, "Chinese Realpolitik and the Proliferation Security Initiative." Association for Asian, Research February 18, 2005. Retrieved November 15, 2009, from http://www.asianresearch.org/articles/2505.html.

Hammock, Gordon R., "Iraq, Preemption, and the Views of Poland, the Czech Republic, and Hungary." *Air and Space Power Journal*, Fall 2003.

Harris, John F., "President Clinton Freezes Bin Laden Assets." *The Washington Post*, August 23, 1998.

Heller, Arnie, "Forensics Science Center Maximizes the Tiniest Clue: Livermore chemists are coaxing a wealth of information from increasingly small samples." *Science and Technology Review*, April 2002.
----, "Identifying the Source of Stolen Nuclear Materials: Livermore scientists are analyzing interdicted illicit nuclear and radioactive materials for clues to the materials" origins and routes." *Science and Technology Review*, January/ February 2007.

Hersman, Rebecca K. C., *Eliminating Adversary Weapons of Mass Destruction: What's at Stake?* Center for the Study of Weapons of Mass Destruction, Occasional Paper 1, Washington D.C.: National Defense University Press, December 2004.

Holmes, Sue Major, "Sandia Laboratories expects less than 100 layoffs for 2008." *Associated Press*, November 26, 2007.

Ikle, Fred Charles, "The Second Coming of the Nuclear Age."
    Foreign Affairs, Vol. 75, No. 1, Jan/Feb 1996.

Institute for Defense and Disarmament Studies, "Strategic
    Offensive Reduction Treaty: SORT." Retrieved November
    15, 2010, from http://www.idds.org/issNucTreatiesSORT.
    html.

International Atomic Energy Agency, "Communication dated 28
    September 2008 received from the Permanent Mission of the
    Islamic Republic of Iran to the Agency." *IAEA Information
    Circular 737,* October 1, 2008.
----, "Fact Sheet: IAEA Illicit Trafficking Database (ITDB)."
    December 31, 2007.
----, Illicit Trafficking of Radioactive Materials Database.
    Retrieved April 8, 2009, from www.iaea.org.
----, "Nuclear Trafficking Remains Global Priority." Retrieved
    April 8, 2009, from http://www.iaea.org/NewsCenter/
    News/2007/nucltrafficking.html.
----, Research Reactor Database. Retrieved April 8, 2009, from
    http://www.iaea.org/worldatom/rrdb/.
----, "Technical Guidance Reference Manual: Nuclear Forensics
    Support." *IAEA Nuclear Security Series No. 2,* Vienna,
    2006.
----, "The Implementation of United Nations Security Council
    Resolutions Relating to Iraq." *IAEA Director General
    Report, August 28, 1998.*

International Organization for Standardization, "About ISO."
    Retrieved October 27, 2010, from http://www.iso.org/iso/
    about.htm.

International Science and Technology Center, "ISTC Fact
    Sheet." Updated January 2009.

Isaacs, John, "Aiming at ABM." *Bulletin of the Atomic Scientists*, March 1998.

Jacobson, Ken, "Budget cuts lead to layoffs of physicists at National Labs." *Manufacturing and Technology News*, May 6, 2005

Jervis, Robert, "The Dustbin of History: Mutual Assured Destruction." *Foreign Policy*, November/December 2002.

Joseph, Jofi, "The Proliferation Security Initiative: Can Interdiction Stop Proliferation?" *Arms Control Today*, Vol. 34, June 2004.

Kaplan, Lawrence M. "Missile Defense: The First Sixty Years." Missile Defense Agency. Retrieved April 10, 2009, from http://www.mda.mil/mdaLink/pdf/first60.pdf.

Keefe, Courtney, "The Presidential Nuclear Initiatives (PNIs) on Tactical Nuclear Weapons at a Glance." Arms Control Association factsheet. Retrieved October 12, 2009, from http://www.armscontrol.org/factsheets/pniglance.

Kelly, Rich, "The Nunn-Lugar Act: A Wasteful and Dangerous Illusion." *Cato Foreign Policy Briefing no. 39*, March 18, 1996.

Kimball, Daryl G., and Stephen W. Young, "National Missile Defenses and Arms Control after Clinton's NMD decision." *Disarmament Forum*, Vol. 1, 2001.

Krasner, Stephen D., "Are Bureaucracies Important? (Or Allison Wonderland)." *Foreign Policy*, Vol. 7, Summer 1972.

Korb, Lawrence J., "Republicans, missile defense, and the Reagan legacy." *Bulletin of the Atomic Scientists,* 25 April 2008. Retrieved May 2, 2009, from http://www.thebulletin.org/web-edition/features/republicans-missile-defense-and-the-reagan-legacy.

Landay, Jonathan S., "U.S. Downsizes Its Nuclear-Weapon Ambitions." *The Christian Science Monitor,* December 24, 1997.

Larsen, Jeffery A., "National Security and Neo-Arms Control in the Bush Administration." *Disarmament Diplomacy,* Issue No. 80, Autumn 2005.

Laskow, Sarah, "Is Congress Failing on Homeland Security Oversight?" The Center for Public Integrity, July 15, 2009. Retrieved November 15, 2009, from http://www.publicintegrity.org/articles/entry/1549/.

Lee, Rensselaer, "Nuclear Smuggling: Patterns and Responses." *Parameters,* Spring 2003.

Leggitt, J., K. Inn, S. Goldberg, R. Essex, S. LaMont and S. Chase, "Nuclear forensics-metrological basis for legal defensibility." *Journal of Radioanalytical and Nuclear Chemistry,* Vol. 282, No. 3, 2009.

Lewis, George N., and Theodore A. Postol, "The European Missile Defense Folly." *Bulletin of the Atomic Scientists,* May/June 2008.

Lippman, Thomas W., "Clinton, Yeltsin Agree on Arms Cuts and NATO." *The Washington Post,* March 22, 1997.

Loeb, Hamilton, "U.S. Sanctions on India and Pakistan Following Nuclear Tests Likely to Have Broad Impact on U.S. Industry." FindLaw. Retrieved October 12, 2009, from http://library.findlaw.com/1998/Jun/1/127104.html.

Lopez, Edward J., "Term Limits: Causes and consequences." *Public Choice*, Vol. 114, 2003.

Loukianova, Anya, and Leonard Spector, "New WMD Director Has the Right Stuff, but Will He Have the Right Staff?" CNS Feature Stories, updated February 18, 2009. Retrieved October 12, 2009, from http://cns.miis.edu/stories/090213_wmd_coordinator.htm#fnB2.

Lundin, Martin, "When Does Cooperation Improve Public Policy Implementation?" *Policy Studies Journal*, November 1, 2007.

Matland, Richard E., "Synthesizing the Implementation Literature: The Ambiguity-Conflict Model of Policy Implementation." *Journal of Public Administration Research and Theory*, Vol. 5, No. 2, 1995.

Matthews, William, "U.S. Plans to Shrink Nuclear Weapons Complex." *DefenseNews*, July 17, 2008.

May, Michael, Jay Davis, and Raymond Jeanloz, "Preparing for the Worst." *Nature*, Vol. 443, October 26, 2006.

Mayer, K., M. Wallenius and T. Fanghanel, "Nuclear forensic science-From cradle to maturity." *Journal of Alloys and Compounds* 444-445, 2007.

McCartney, James, "Bush Arms-control Advisor Resigns." *The Philadelphia Inquirer*, April 27, 1990.

McColl, Angus, "Is Counterproliferation Compatible with Nonproliferation?" *Airpower Journal,* Vol. XI, No. 1, Spring 1997.

McManus, Doyle, "Arms Reduction Treaty Unlikely to Be Finished by End of Bush's Term: Defense: Nuclear weapons agreement is slowed by Russian requests for changes." *Los Angeles Times,* November 27, 1992.

Moore, Thomas, "White House Steps Back from National Missile Defense – Again." Heritage Foundation Executive Memorandum, April 8, 1999.

Moseley, Ray, "Bush Will Honor Arms Treaty Provisions." *Chicago Tribune,* March 28, 1989.

Murray, Mark, "FEMA Administrator Wins Management Kudos." *National Journal,* January 16, 2001.

National Defense University, *Interagency Management of Complex Crises Operations Handbook.* January 2003.

Natural Resources Defense Council, "Chinese Nuclear Forces, 2006." *Bulletin of the Atomic Scientists,* May/June 2006.
----, "Pakistan's Nuclear Forces, 2007." *Bulletin of the Atomic Scientists,* May/June 2007.
----, "Table of U.S. Nuclear Warheads 1945-2002." Retrieved April 9, 2009, from http://www.nrdc.org/nuclear/nudb/datab9.asp.
----, "Table of USSR/Russian Nuclear Warheads 1949-2002." Retrieved April 9, 2009, from http://www.nrdc.org/nuclear/nudb/datab10.asp.

Newmann, William, "Change in National Security Processes." *Presidential Studies Quarterly,* Vol. 31. No. 1, March 2001.

News Review, "Duma seemingly unswayed by Perry START II appeal." *Disarmament Diplomacy,* Issue No. 10, November 1996.

Nicholson-Crotty, Jill, and Susan M. Miller, "Bureaucratic Effectiveness and Influence in the Legislature." *Journal of Public Administration and Research Theory,* August 22, 2011. Retrieved December 10, 2011, from http://jpart. oxfordjournals.org/content/early/2011/08/20/jopart.mur054. full.pdf+html.

Nicholson-Crotty, Sean, "Bureaucratic Competition in the Policy Process." *Policy Studies Journal,* Vol. 33, No. 3, 2005.

Nitze, Paul A., "SDI and the ABM treaty - Strategic Defense Initiative; Anti-Ballistic Missile – transcript" Department of State Bulletin, August 1985. Retrieved April 10, 2009, from http://findarticles.com/p/articles/mi_m1079/is_v85/ ai_3875083.

Norris, Robert S. and Hans M. Kristensen, "New Estimates of the U.S. Nuclear Weapons Stockpile, 2007 and 2012." Natural Resources Defense Council, May 2, 2007. Retrieved October 12, 2009, from http://www.nrdc.org/nuclear/stock-pile_2007-2012.asp.
----, "Nuclear Cruise Missiles." *Bulletin of the Atomic Scientists,* November/December June 2007.
----, "Russian Nuclear Forces, 2008." *Bulletin of the Atomic Scientists,* May/June 2008.

Norris, Robert S., Thomas B. Cochran and William M. Arkin, "History of the Nuclear Stockpile." *Bulletin of the Atomic Scientists,* August 1985.

Nuclear Threat Initiative, "China's Attitude Toward Nuclear Deterrence." Retrieved April 8, 2009, from http://www.nti.org/db/china/deterpos.htm.

----, "China Opposition to U.S. Missile Defense Programs." Retrieved November 15, 2009, from http://www.nti.org/db/china/mdpos.htm.

----, "Clinton Lost Nuclear Launch Codes, Retired General Says." *Global Security Newswire*, October 21, 2010.

----, "Interactive Threat Reduction Budget Database: Second Line of Defense 1998-2008." July 15, 2010.

----, "North Korea Profile: Missiles." Retrieved June 9, 2009, from http://www.nti.org/e_research/profiles/NK/Missile/66_1279.html.

----, "Resources on Nuclear Trafficking." Retrieved June 28, 2009, from http://www.nti.org/e_research/e3_special_nuc-trafficking.html.

----, "The Nunn-Lugar Cooperative Threat Reduction (CTR) Program." Retrieved April 15, 2010, from http://www.nti.org/db/nisprofs/russia/forasst/nunn_lug/overview.htm.

Nuclear Suppliers Group, "History." Retrieved April 10, 2009, from http://www.nsg-online.org/history.htm.

Nuclear Weapon Archive.org, "Complete List of All U.S. Nuclear Weapons." Retrieved June 8, 2009, from http://nuclearweaponarchive.org/Usa/Weapons/Allbombs.html.

----, "The World's Largest Nuclear Weapon." Retrieved April 28, 2009, from http://nuclearweaponarchive.org/Russia/TsarBomba.html.

O'Harrow, Robert Jr., "Radiation Detection Plan Falls Short, Audit Shows: Concerns About Costs and Effectiveness Could Curtail Program." *The Washington Post*, September 4, 2008.

Orlov, Vladimir, and William C. Potter, "The Mystery of the Sunken Gyros." *Bulletin of the Atomic Scientists*, November/December 1998.

Ostrom, Vincent, "The Third Century: Some Anticipated Consequences of Governmental Reorganization." *Publius*, Vol. 8, No. 2, Spring 1978.

O'Toole, Laurence J. Jr. and Robert S. Montjoy, "Interorganizational Policy Implementation: A Theoretical Perspective." *Public Administration Review*, Vol. 44, No. 6, Nov-Dec, 1984.

Oxford, Vayl, "Needed: A Comprehensive Nuclear Forensics and Attribution Act." *Domestic Preparedness*, June 30, 2010.

Page, Scott E., "Path Dependence." *Quarterly Journal of Political Science*, Vol. 1, 2006.

Palla, Stephanie, "Review Set for Major U.S. Radiation Detection Program." *Global Security Newswire,* March 31, 2010.

Parrish, Scott, "Illicit Nuclear Trafficking in the NIS," NTI Issue Brief, March 2002. Retrieved April 8, 2009, from http://www.nti.org/e_research/e3_8a.html.

Perkovich, George, "Bush's Nuclear Revolution." *Foreign Affairs,* March/April 2003.

Pettigrew, Richard A., "Improving Government Competence." *Publius*, Vol. 8, No. 2, Spring 1978.

Phillips, Matthew, "Uncertain Justice for Nuclear Terror: Deterrence of Anonymous Attacks Through Attribution." *Orbis*, Vol. 51, Issue 3, Summer 2007.

Pierson, Paul, "Increasing Returns, Path Dependence, and the Study of Politics." *The American Political Science Review*, Vol. 94, No. 2, June 2000.

Poneman, Daniel, "History of the Agreed Framework." The Forum for International Policy, 2006. Retrieved October 12, 2009, from http://hnn.us/articles/31633.html.

Port of Los Angeles, "2006 Container Statistics." Retrieved June 15, 2010, from http://www.portoflosangeles.org/Stats/stats_2006.htm.

Postman, Max, "History, Design, and Prospects for Improving Pakistan's Nuclear Personnel Reliability Program (PRP)." The Center for Arms Control and Nonproliferation, March 5, 2008. Retrieved June 10, 2009, from http://www.armscontrolcenter.org/policy/nuclearweapons/articles/pakistan_nuclear_prp/.

Potter, William C. and Elena Sokova, "Illicit Nuclear Trafficking in the NIS: What's New? What's True?" *Nonproliferation Review*, Summer 2002.

Powell, Colin L., "U.S. Forces: Challenges Ahead." *Foreign Affairs*, Winter 1992/93. Retrieved November 15, 2009, from http://www.cfr.org/publication/7508/us_forces.html.

Prosser, Andrew, and Herbert Scoville, Jr., "The Proliferation Security Initiative in Perspective." Center for Defense Information, June 16, 2004. Retrieved November 15, 2009, from http://www.cdi.org/pdfs/psi.pdf.

Raach, George T., and Ilana Kaas, "National Power and the Interagency Process." *Joint Forces Quarterly*, Summer 1995.

Rak, Claire E., "The Role of Preventive Strikes in Counterproliferation Strategy." *Strategic Insight*, Vol. II, Issue 10, October 2003.

Record, Jeffrey, "Nuclear Deterrence, Preventive War, and Counterproliferation." *Policy Analysis*, No. 519, July 2004.

Rediff.com, "Clinton lifts sanctions, India welcomes move." October 28, 1999. Retrieved October 12, 2009, from http://www.rediff.com/business/1999/oct/28bomb.htm.

Rennie, Gabriele, "Tracing the Steps in Nuclear Material Trafficking: Forensic scientists are combining an array of technologies to track illicit nuclear materials to their sources." *Science and Technology Review*, March 2005.

Rice, Condoleezza, "Life After the Cold War." *Foreign Affairs* January/February 2000.

Rosati, Jerel A., "Developing a Systematic Decision-Making Framework: Bureaucratic Politics in Perspective." *World Politics*, Vol. 1, No. 2, January 1981.

Rosenberg, David Alan, "U.S. Nuclear Stockpile, 1945 to 1950." *Bulletin of the Atomic Scientists,* May 1982.

Rust, Dean, "Reorganization Run Amok: State Department's WMD Effort Weakened." *Arms Control Today*, Vol. 36, June 2006.

Sagan, Scott D., "Why Do States Build Nuclear Weapons?: Three Models in Search of a Bomb." *International Security*, Vol. 21, No. 3, Winter, 1996-1997.

Sanger, David E., "Pre-emptive Caution." *The New York Times*, October 15th, 2007.

Saunders, Philip C., *China's Global Activism: Strategy, Drivers, and Tools*. Institute for National Strategic Studies, Occasional Paper 4, Washington D.C.: National Defense University Press, June 2006.

Schneider, Barry R., "Seeking a Port in the WMD Storm." U.S. Air Force Counterproliferation Center, *Counterproliferation Paper No. 29*, May 2005.

Shapiro, Adam, "Nuclear-Weapon-Free Zones: The Solution to Nuclear Disarmament?" UN *Chronicle*, August 12, 2004.

Sharples, Tiffany, "A Brief History of: FEMA." *Time*, August 28, 2008.

Singh, Jaswant, "Against Nuclear Apartheid." *Foreign Affairs*, September/October 1998.

Sipress, Alan, "U.S. Seeks to Lift Sanctions on India: Aim is to Bolster Military Relations." *The Washington Post*, August 12, 2001.

Smith, Thomas B., "The Policy Implementation Process." *Policy Sciences*, June 1973.

Sonicbomb.com, "Atomic Test Archive." Retrieved April 9, 2009, from http://sonicbomb.com/modules.php?name=Content&pa=showpage&pid=39.

The Nuclear Weapons Archive, *Iraq's Nuclear Weapons Program*. Retrieved April 8, 2009, from http://nuclearweaponarchive.org/Iraq/IraqAtoZ.html.

The Russia Journal, "Powell sees Bush-Putin summit successful, November 2, 2003." November 11, 2001.

Tiron, Roxana, "Missile defense shift redirects billions in government contracts." *The Hill*, September 19, 2009.

Toth, Robert C., "Bush May Delay Resumption of Strategic Arms Talks." *Los Angeles Times*, December 15, 1988.

Uchida, Ted T., "Reforming the Interagency Process." Air University Report, May 2005.

United Nations, "Security Council Decides All States Shall Act to Prevent Proliferation of Mass Destruction Weapons." Press Release (SC/8076), April 28, 2004.

USA.gov, "Federal Executive Branch." Retrieved November 15, 2009, from http://www.usa.gov/Agencies/Federal/Executive.shtml.

Valencia, Mark J., "Is the PSI Really the Cornerstone of a New International Norm?" *Naval War College Review*, Vol. 59, No. 4, Autumn 2006.

Vandenbrouke, Lucien S., "Israeli Strike Against OSIRAQ," *Air University Review,* Vol. XXXV, No. 6, September-October 1984.

VOA News.com, "Bush-Putin Summit May Not Result in Formal Arms Agreement." November 12, 2001. Retrieved

November 15, 2009, from http://www1.voanews.com/english/news/a-13-a-2001-11-12-19-Bush-Putin-66967847.html?moddate=2001-11-12+%3B+http%3A%2F%2Fwww.russiajournal.com%2Fnode%2F7675.

Wallenius, M., K. Mayer, I. Ray, "Nuclear forensic investigations: Two case studies." *Forensic Science International* 156, 2006.

Wallenius, Maria, et al., "Nuclear forensic investigations with a focus on plutonium." *Journal of Alloys and Compounds* 444-445, 2007.

Warfare.RU, "SS-18 Satan." Retrieved April 15, 2010, from http://warfare.ru/?catid=265&linkid=1702.
----, "SS-19 Stiletto." Retrieved April 15, 2010, from http://warfare.ru/?lang=&catid=265&linkid=2310&linkname=SS-19-STILETTO-/-%28UR-100N,-UR-100NU%29.

Watson, Jack, "Making the Government Work Better." *Publius*, Vol. 8, No. 2, Spring 1978.

Weinberger, Caspar W., "Government Reorganization and Public Purpose." *Publius*, Vol. 8, No. 2, Spring 1978.

Weitz, Richard, "Global Initiative to Combat Nuclear Terrorism: Steady, but Slow Progress." *WMD Insights*, August 2008.

Wilson-Roberts, Guy, "'New' deterrence, post-Anti-Ballistic Missile Treaty: Guy Wilson-Roberts reviews the United States decision to withdraw from the Anti-Ballistic Missile Treaty." *New Zealand International Review*, May-June, 2002.

Wolf, Jim, "U.S. missile-defense salvage operations under way." *Reuters,* June 9, 2009.

Wolfensberger, Donald R., "Reorganizing Congress and the Executive In Response to Focusing Events: Lessons of the Past, Portents for the Future." Woodrow Wilson International Center for Scholars Paper, January 2004.

World Nuclear Association, "World Nuclear Power Reactors and Uranium Requirements." Retrieved June 15, 2010, from http://www.world-nuclear.org/info/reactors.html.

Yaphe, Judith S. and Charles D. Lutes, *Reassessing the Implications of a Nuclear-Armed Iran.* McNair Paper 69, Washington D.C.: National Defense University Press, 2005.

Yusufzai, Rahimullah, "Conversations with Terror." *TIME,* January 11, 1999.

Zaitseva, Lyudmila, "Illicit Trafficking in the Southern Tier and Turkey since 1999: A Shift from Europe?" *Nonproliferation Review,* Winter 2002.

Zangger Committee.org, "History." Retrieved April 9, 2009, from http://www.zanggercommittee.org/Zangger/History/default.htm.

Zenko, Micah and Matthew Bunn, "Interdicting Nuclear Smuggling: Second Line of Defense Program." Nuclear Threat Initiative, November 20, 2007. Retrieved July 15, 2010, from http://www.nti.org/e_research/cnwm/interdicting/second.asp#_ftnref13.